Getting Down to *e-business* with AS/400

Getting Down to

e-business

with AS/400

Bob Cancilla

First Edition
Second Printing—May 2000

ISBN: 1-58347-010-7

Midrange Computing
5650 El Camino Real, Suite 225
Carlsbad, CA 92008
www.midrangecomputing.com

V4R4

ACKNOWLEDGMENTS

It is the interaction with my many electronic friends and associates that has made this book possible. Specifically, I'd like to thank the folks at I/Net Inc., the developers of Commerce Server/400, Webulator/400, and Merchant/400. Special thanks go to John Dorn of I/Net, Inc., who has never refused to answer my stupid questions—sometimes over and over again in different ways until the message sunk in.

Thanks also go out to Nadir Amra, George Silber, and Mike Schroeder of IBM's AS/400 Net.Data development team in Rochester. I would also like to thank the many developers, system architects, managers, and others within the IBM AS/400 organization for all of their support and assistance.

Much of the research for this book comes from the folks on I/Net and Ignite/400's mailing lists, who have worked together to share the knowledge that we have acquired. Not to be left out are all of the people with whom I have "spoken" on the `comp.sys.ibm.as400.misc` USENET newsgroup and the folks who frequent IBM's Net.Data Forum on the Web. Many thanks to the *new and improved* IBM, which lets its developers communicate freely with the people who use its products.

CONTENTS

PREFACE

This book is the result of four and a half years of research and development activity that resulted in providing my organization, a major insurance company, with an e-business Internet presence to enhance its competitive advantage.

When I was assigned the task of evaluating Internet services and applications to determine how my company might benefit from an Internet presence, I was given no specific guidelines. Although we are and have been a large AS/400 shop for years, I was not restricted to the AS/400. I found that it required all of my 30 years experience in systems development and management to digest the technology and resources that the Internet had to offer. The result of this research effort was the development and implementation of an electronic business Web site, a public information Web site, e-business, and Internet-based 5250 terminal emulation.

The greatest obstacle I found in researching the technology was the vast amount of information I had to digest. It seemed that every time I found the answer to a question, I found ten new questions and new sources of reference material to be assimilated.

There is no shortage of Internet reference materials. IBM has introduced dozens of new manuals pertaining to Internet products and services; bookstores are packed with Internet-related references at prices ranging from $30 to $100; and the Internet devotes an immense amount of space to itself—thousands of standards and research documents that describe existing and emerging computer and networking technologies can be found at "official" Web sites on the Internet. Product vendors have also contributed extensive documentation about each of their products, and IBM has a vast sea of documentation on the Internet.

I hope this book will be a single source of reference for the issues you need to address to successfully create an electronic presence on the Internet.

I will provide the concepts, specific knowledge, and techniques required to build e-business Web sites. This is not a reference manual, but rather a guide. I have included references to many Web sites that will provide specific detailed reference material. Whenever possible, I will provide a reference to a Request For Comments (RFC), which is as close as the Internet community comes to a standards document. (RFCs can be found at *www.internic.net* under the resources link.)

When I started working with the AS/400 and the Internet, I was using a V3R1 and V3R2 CISC based system. Now, at the end of 1999, V4R4 is the current release and IBM's next release is well on its way to the market place. V4R1 (the "e-machines" release) and every release since has introduced revolutionary improvements in Internet technology.

I will introduce many technical topics in this book, but the information provided is no substitute for the many excellent specialized books available from your local or online bookstore. I recommend that you use the limited bibliography included in this book to begin to build a library of reference books essential to defining a corporate Internet presence.

There are four major Internet development paths that you can take when implementing your Internet presence with an AS/400. These include the handcrafted approach I describe in this book as well as IBM's WebSphere Application Server using JAVA Servlets and Enterprise Java Beans, Lotus Domino with its Lotus Notes based integrated development environment, and 5250-to-HTML or 5250-to-JAVA conversion technologies from IBM and third party vendors. I will not be covering Lotus Domino or WebSphere in this book in depth. I strongly recommend Jelan Heidelberg's book, *Lotus Domino for AS/400: Bringing the Best Together for Business*. This book does an excellent job of providing a high level view of Lotus Domino and IBM's strategic positioning of Domino on the AS/400.

WebSphere, which is introduced but not covered in depth in this book, may best be investigated at IBM's AS/400 Web site at *www.as400.ibm.com/websphere*. This web page will give you an introduction to this exciting new technology that can tap into high performance and advanced technology with the AS/400. WebSphere is an extremely important technology.

I will give you some pointers on hardware and software selection and configuration issues. The Internet, its tools, and facilities are evolving. Internet tools and facilities for the AS/400 are evolving at a pace that is almost impossible to keep up with. This book is based on practical experience with a live Web site. (I apologize for not being able to include examples from that Web site. One of the drawbacks of e-business is that developers can't show and brag about their work because it is highly proprietary and unique to their companies.)

No one can claim to be an Internet expert. Some of us have had a little more experience, but this does not entitle us to the title "expert." Don't ever forget that the original purpose of the Internet was the free exchange of ideas. The real heart and soul of the Internet is people exchanging ideas, knowledge, and experience. If you are new to the Internet and its technologies, people will help you learn.

Obviously, the opinions and recommendations expressed in this book are my own; there are many other approaches and many other opinions. The approach used to implement the various technologies described in the book worked for me. They should work for you.

FOREWORD

You're having a long lunch with a few close friends (and business rivals). "Well," one says, "I'm all set. I have that new intranet freshly running TCP/IP, the HTTP server is up and running with HTML files, and the CGI programs are humming smoothly."

"Oh yeah?" says another, "My mobile workers are FTPing new product files, and I'm saving money using the Internet for their networking with SSL connections to the home server. Each is using POP3 e-mail clients with SMTP connection to their customer accounts. Management has never been easier with internal DNS support, and I can bring clients online anywhere with the DHCP server. The NAT service made bridging from my intranet to the Internet easy."

You're not sure what the heck they're talking about, but you have the uneasy feeling that you should. You know that internal networking, telecommuting and remote employees, the Internet, and business-oriented Web sites are the future of business, but you're not sure you have the knowledge or the computer system, take advantage of this booming trend. Moreover, you're not alone.

Internet-originated technologies and standards have swiftly become the basis for wiring businesses and people together. The Internet has developed into the data equivalent of the telephone system, and as more and more people and businesses get connected, its value has increased exponentially. We are moving rapidly toward ubiquitous data network access. Even if that takes five years, the implications for the way you do business will be so profound it will seem to be overnight. That's where this book, *Getting Down to e-Business with AS/400*, comes in.

Most businesses are struggling to figure out how to use this new networking technology. Step one in that quest is to create an infrastructure that moves data quickly and securely over a data network that connects employees, business value chain partners, and customers.

Step two is to decide what content should be delivered on that network. What information should be made available and what programs need to be run? As familiarity with the capabilities of the technology develops and the value of "anytime, anywhere access" for everyone who is a part of your business—from employees to customers—becomes apparent, the potential of actually changing business processes and practices to take advantage of this unique capability becomes clear.

There is definitely a progressive process of learning and adaptation that IBM describes as "start simple, grow fast." The full implications of universal data access are too overwhelming to contemplate. You can quickly become paralyzed into inaction through the combination of uncertainties and unknowns. And the implications on the business can be profound. Studies done on the successful entrepreneurs of the Internet have shown that the most common success factor is a willingness and ability to adapt quickly. No one really knows where this technology will take us, or how fast we will get there. There are many ideas, good ones too, but there also are too many unknowns.

Start simple, and grow fast. The "start simple" is probably easy enough to figure out, but "grow fast" to what? A vision of how to become an e-business, even if indistinct in its particulars, is necessary to make choices about the areas of your business that need to be changed.

Vision comes from first understanding the technology enabling you to envision how it can be used with its current capabilities, and more importantly, to project where it will likely go in the future. You must appreciate its current capabilities and how it can be applied in new ways. It is, after all, the technology that will enable change.

Sound vision requires a deep understanding of the business. With a technology as potentially disruptive as the Internet, you must be sure you really know what business you are in, because it may need to be defined differently than it is today. You must look for ways to use the technology in the business to not just cut costs (start simple), but to be more competitive and make your company the one that everyone wants to do business with (grow fast). So what content do you to put on your infrastructure of Internet technologies that will make the difference in how effectively you take advantage of networking technology? You will find help on planning and building the content that is so important as you start to grow fast in the following pages.

Vision regarding how technology can make your business more competitive requires you to think about ways to change the processes within your business to take advantage of what can be done with universal access. Does the telephone network—with its audio and fax information exchange—play a role in how your business operates? Wait until you're online. Soon e-mail and electronically submitted business forms will vastly change the face of communication and order processing.

The contents of this book go a long way toward helping you to understand these technologies and how to use them. It is an excellent starting point for using the built-in Internet technology in AS/400 to get that fast start.

You have made a good start in becoming an e-business. You've probably already made use of the capabilities built into your AS/400 to create the infrastructure you need. Now, you will be planning the content to put on it, and thinking about how to adapt your business to become more competitive by using networking technologies.

Getting Down to e-Business with AS/400 will help you get started, and then grow fast as you see opportunities open up.

—Dick Kiscaden
AS/400 e-business Solutions Manager

INTRODUCTION

This book is intended for everyone involved in implementing an Internet presence through an e-business site. What am I talking about when I refer to e-business site? I'm talking about developing interactive Web-based applications that are unique to your company, its customers, and its vendors.

Information systems (IS) managers and executives will find that the first two parts of the book introduce the technologies involved in providing an Internet presence. In these parts of the book, basic concepts are discussed. Understanding these technologies and issues is essential to effective decision making. A major tendency of technicians venturing into the Internet is to want to learn about and try out every possible new technology. An effective Internet implementation is cost-effective and uses only the technology necessary to meet an organization's mission.

AS/400 Webmasters will find the book a good basic overview to Web site development and administration. The references will allow them to develop the detailed technical knowledge necessary to become proficient and effective.

Web site developers will find that the latter portions of the book contain everything they need to get started developing Web sites. References are provided for those who want a more comprehensive understanding of the technologies.

Network administrators, security administrators, and systems programmers new to the Internet will find the book useful as a starting point.

e-BUSINESS: WHAT IS IT?

e-Business is quite simply the process of providing interactive systems via the Internet. It allows your company to interact in real time with its customers, vendors, and others to perform critical business tasks more efficiently and more effectively.

Internet e-business maximizes efficiency and improves the service level provided by your organization by automating labor-intensive and time-consuming activities.

I have been building interactive computer systems for more than 25 years, and I have never worked with a systems development environment like the Internet and e-business before. Many of us have long felt that computer systems developers should be part of a corporation's business team. This goal has seldom been realized with traditional systems, but is becoming a reality with the demands of e-business and Internet-based commerce.

e-Business is causing modern corporations to re-invent themselves. Companies that don't re-invent themselves to take advantage of this new technology soon find themselves becoming its victims.

The "Webmaster" (i.e. the person coordinating the design and implementation of an organization's Internet-based systems) should first and foremost be a business person. Web-based systems are not about technology, but about business.

To understand the impact that Internet-based systems have on today's business enterprise, I strongly suggest reading *Unleashing the Killer App* by Larry Downes and Chunka Mui (ISBN 0-87584-801-X). This book should be mandatory for everyone working in a modern corporation, from the CEO to the application programmer. I also suggest visiting `www.killer-apps.com`.

TRADITIONAL WEB SITES

You've seen them. Flashy informational Web sites that talk about companies and their products. These sites are often developed by ad agencies to promote the company and its products. Some are successful, most are not. Recent research and articles in *The Wall Street Journal* indicate that this costly type of static Web site is not cost-justified. You build and publish these sites because your competitors do. And with some very specific exceptions—such as sites provided by software companies, which provide in-depth product descriptions, demos, technical support, and free trial downloads—most commercial sites tend to be necessary evils that look nice but produce little. If you want to develop a corporate presence, read the entire first part of this book and then Chapters 21 and 23 on Web Site Design and HTML.

Given the right resources and development products, you can easily create, maintain, and publish an informational Web site. The keys are to determine the audience and message, and then to keep people coming back.

CATALOG AND ONLINE SALES (E-COMMERCE)

Internet-based systems that result in the sale of a product are called e-commerce systems. Amazon.com is perhaps the most amazing success story on the Internet. The online bookstore has grown from nothing to become a corporate giant. Many catalog sales software products are available. If you think your company can benefit from direct sales on the Internet, consider buying a package instead of building. Contact your IBM sales representative, who can provide you with a list of excellent AS/400-based catalog and "market basket" applications that simply require providing the product data and graphics.

E-BUSINESS SITES

My first site was for a commercial insurance company. We started by providing our independent insurance agents with access to specific Web-based reports and inquiries regarding the status of their policies, the claims on their policies, and their billings.

All of these Web-based inquiries were previously handled by the agent or insured calling a person at the company who would have to look up information, print reports, and fax the information back to the requestor. Today, the agent or insured can access up-to-the-minute information whenever its needed.

"So?" you say, "we do that now. We have dial-up lines where our customers can dial into our AS/400 and access the data." Well, we did too—but we had to provide software, support the software, help configure the clients' personal computers, and pay for the telephone lines. The customers had to install dedicated software on their personal computers and dial specific telephone numbers. Due to the effort in setting up access, it was limited to only the company's largest customers. Now, agents and insureds provide their own software and communications by simply subscribing to a $15 to $19 per month Internet service provider (ISP). Now data-access services are available to all of the company's agents and policyholders.

The company saves the cost of supporting remote dial-up access and software. The client has hassle-free access to the company via a local telephone call to an ISP. The client also has the ability to choose his own hardware and software. The company need not be concerned about the computing environment the client uses.

e-Business can simply be the delivery of information from your database to the client, or it can be much more. In my insurance company application, agents and policyholders have prepared dozens of paper forms and sent them by mail or fax to the company. Both parties incurred the cost of preparing, transmitting, and processing the forms. e-Business provides a means of automating and streamlining these processes.

This book shows you how to develop this type of site. It shows how to retrieve and display business data directly to your customers, vendors, and employees; how to develop electronic forms and process the data they collect; and how you can take advantage of data captured on your customer's or vendor's computers and exchange and utilize this data at your site (a really exciting and cost-effective variation on the Electronic Data Interchange (EDI) theme).

Automatic processing of insurance applications, loan applications, leases, orders, and more has long been the goal of many major financial institutions. Today this can be done electronically via the Web, without paper. Human intervention can be limited to filling out an electronic form once.

PART I

THE INTERNET AND ITS COMPONENTS

It is not possible to detail all of the technologies involved in creating an e-commerce Web site in a single book. This book examines the information that you need to develop e-commerce Web sites with the AS/400. I hope to touch on most of the relevant issues and provide pointers to information sources where you can find more information. In this first part of the book, I introduce the technologies involved in setting up your hardware, software, languages, and environments.

I have more than 25 years experience designing and managing computer systems on virtually every computer platform. Putting together an e-commerce Web site has drawn upon every bit of knowledge that I have acquired over the years. I have been forced to learn almost as much in the past two and a half years as I learned over the previous 25—mostly because no single source of information is available to tell you everything you need to know. Building a Web site is easy. Learning what you need to know is not. You will not learn everything you need to know from this book, but I will give you a sound foundation upon which to build your knowledge base and identify resources that you can use to find additional information.

The old KISS (keep it simple, stupid) method works quite well in Web site development. Be practical and keep your primary mission in mind. Let others do the cute stuff. Effective Web sites convey a clear, concise message and enable the visitor to find information, buy products, or perform a business function quickly and easily.

My job was to design and develop a Web site that both communicated information about my company and attracted customers. The e-business site was designed to provide customers with critical information that would improve the business relationship between them and the company, saving time and money, and to enable the company to prosper. I have seen a very simple pilot project evolve into a large-scale strategic system. IBM and other vendors offer comprehensive sets of tools to assist you in building e-business Web sites ranging from very simple informational sites to extremely sophisticated e-commerce sites.

You must have a fundamental understanding of what happens on your browser, your server, and the Internet before you can begin to develop Web applications. When I started developing Web sites, I had been an Internet user for several years and thought I knew something about the Internet. I quickly proved to myself that I did not know much.

Supporting Internet products is a dilemma for vendors. A Web server, for example, is dependent upon many technologies, such as HTTP, hypertext markup language (HTML), computer languages, browser limitations and capabilities, Multipurpose Internet Mail Extensions (MIME), TCP/IP, operating systems, and more. What should the vendor be responsible for in terms of support to its customers? What should the customer be expected to know?

When there are problems with a specific software product that affects your entire system, the software vendor's responsibilities might be considered limited to a fraction of what you need to know. Unfortunately, many vendors take the attitude that if it is beyond their products' functionality, then you're on your own. IBM provides a wealth of information on its Web sites, in manuals, and within Redbooks. To effectively use IBM's materials, you need to know where to begin looking. I will cover many support-related topics, including HTML, Net.Data, IBM's HTTP Server, Lotus Domino, WebSphere, Basic SMTP and the POP3 servers, FTP, and more.

This first section is designed to provide some fundamental Internet concepts. A thorough conceptual understanding is necessary to make effective decisions about your e-commerce presence. The material presented in the following pages is essential, basic material for developers, managers, or anyone else participating in the design, development, and implementation of a Web site.

1 WHY AN AS/400?

Open standards and protocols are the basis of the Internet. As you start to formulate your decision-making process, you should remember that operating systems are irrelevant to the Internet. Communications protocols and standards and conformance to these standards are the important factors. The initial premise of the Internet and the single factor that has made it successful are the open standards and protocols. Any machine that runs software that is compliant with these standards and protocols will communicate with any other machine on the Internet.

Some will say you should choose a UNIX-based solution because it was the original platform of the Internet. They will point to the vast array of free public domain software. Others will advocate Microsoft's Windows/NT because of the low cost of PC-based servers and the vast array of tools to automate the development process.

With UNIX's history and Microsoft's tool set, why choose an AS/400? The answer is in four words.

Security, integrity, reliability, and economy.

If you have an existing AS/400 environment that provides primary support for your business, then why not stick with a sure thing? You do not have to introduce new technology or hire new people with specialized skills. You have direct access to your data, and can even distribute your present applications via the Internet.

Most likely, your AS/400 is the workhorse that serves your company by supporting your primary line-of-business applications. You probably have thousands of programs and most of your business data on this machine. You most likely have a staff of experienced RPG or COBOL programmers. What you probably don't have is a staff with UNIX, C/C++, or Java expertise, or any of the other skills required by a new technology.

You are probably comfortable with AS/400 operations and security, and also with IBM's support of both hardware and software. (Ask yourself who will service the server when it fails? How long does it take to get technical assistance from Microsoft when a software problem occurs?)

And what about a UNIX environment? Which flavor of UNIX should you run? Who is going to support it? What hardware are you going to choose? How much hardware is enough? How is a UNIX computer going to access the data that resides on your AS/400? Who is going to support the free software you can acquire (most of which is delivered "as is")? How much does "free" cost?

If you can deliver interactive Web-based applications on the Internet from your existing AS/400 at a cost equal to or lower than that of buying a new UNIX or NT system, why introduce foreign technology into your environment?

Each new technology introduces cost and risk. To succeed, you will have to acquire the knowledge necessary to support the technology (i.e. hire new people, train existing people, or use contractors). Each new technology also introduces a new point of failure into your environment. Once your public Web site is installed and functional, your Internet connection, e-mail, and Web server had better be operational during stated business hours—one complaint from a large customer to the president of your company can cause you extreme discomfort.

The AS/400 allows you to minimize your exposure to new technology and leverage existing skills. (Your staff may have to learn some new technology, but the learning curve is small compared to the alternative of mastering an entirely new system.)

The AS/400, used as a Web server, can do virtually everything any other server can do from delivering streaming audio or video, to animation, to complete multimedia. It can also access business data and conduct business transactions in real time.

Perhaps the most important feature of the AS/400 is security. AS/400 provides state-of-the-art security. There are hundreds of documented cases of hackers attacking UNIX and PC servers. THE NEW YORK TIMES (a UNIX site) was completely taken over and its Web pages replaced by hackers, and NASA and several major universities (PC server sites) have been hacked.

V4R4 of OS/400 provides all the software as part of the base operating system that you need to develop a sophisticated Internet presence. IBM and other vendors offer optional add-on software to enhance an Internet presence. This book focuses on exploiting the base operating system features that are included and shipped with every AS/400.

COST

Many will tell you the NT path is the most cost effective because you can use inexpensive personal computers running Microsoft's Windows NT operating system. This statement is both true and false. These environments require many machines, each running one component of the total system. UNIX system vendors also advocate multiple machines with each one running a component of the environment. UNIX and Windows vendors also recommend that you run one server per machine. This includes your firewall, Web server, database server, SNA server (to retrieve data from your AS/400), mail server(s), and FTP server. Then, they recommend you replicate these machines using various replication software with mirror images on a second set of machines, which adds system administration complexity.

After you have purchased the necessary equipment, you need to build the development environment. It is not unusual for a Windows NT based environment to spend $500,000 for computers, software, and networking equipment. A recent magazine article spoke of a shop that spent several million dollars to implement their Windows NT based environment.

A single AS/400 has all the software you need already built-in and is the most reliable computer sold. Companies that require 100% system availability can implement a large multi-processor AS/400 and use logical partitioning (at V4R4) to provide a completely replicated environment. V4R4 even includes automatic load balancing to route requests to the backup environment. If you prefer, you can use two separate AS/400s to provide this backup and replication. The second machine may be physically located anywhere in the world!

UNIX and Windows NT shops typically require expertise you probably don't have available in-house to design and implement a reliable, high performance Internet-based environment. If you use the AS/400, you will need to learn about new technology, but your existing staff is more than capable of supporting your AS/400 in an Internet environment with a minimal amount of assistance.

UNIX SYSTEM SUPPORT

The AS/400 is capable of running or supporting other operating systems via C/C++ and POSIX-compliant application programming interfaces (APIs). This Open Systems architecture was specifically designed to allow vendors to port UNIX applications directly to the AS/400. Novell, OS/2, and Windows NT operating systems can be ported to the Integrated Netfinity Server (INS). IBM's version of the UNIX KORN shell (Qshell (QSH)) provides the AS/400 with a UNIX personality, complete with a UNIX-like command line and the ability to directly execute UNIX commands.

TCP/IP with the Sockets programming interface, integrated file server (IFS) and QOPENSYS file systems, and Sun Microsystems Inc.'s Network File System (NFS) are all supported. (NFS allows users to attach directories from one system's IFS, QOPENSYS, or QSYS file system to another machine. Once attached, the files on the remote machine act as if they reside on the local machine.)

TCP/IP runs as a native facility on the AS/400.E-mail support is provided through simple mail transfer protocol (SMTP) and POP3 mail protocols. File transfer protocol (FTP), Telnet, domain name server (DNS) services, and several other UNIX services are all directly supported.

With release V4R2, the AS/400 system supports *threads*, which are tasks that can be created and run concurrently within a job. They communicate via a signaling mechanism called a *semaphore*. With threading, a job can run multiple independent processes, check for completion of any of the threads, and react accordingly, thus enabling the AS/400 to do anything that a machine running Windows NT, UNIX, or OS/2 can do. V4R3 and V4R4 have enhanced performance and functionality of all of these services and introduced advanced technologies such as the Internet standard LDAP (Lightweight Directory Access Protocol), NAT (network address translation), IP Filtering, VPN (Virtual Private Network), Load balancing, and more.

FUTURE OF THE AS/400

With the growth in popularity of Windows NT and UNIX, many people ask if the AS/400 has a future. Is the AS/400 an obsolete technology that will cease as a viable platform?

Once you understand that the AS/400 is not just a computer or an operating system, but a concept, you will see that it will grow and expand to fit whatever role is given it, now and in the future.[1]

As an old mainframe bigot, I laughed at the System 3, System 36, and System 38 computers (the ancestors of the AS/400). These were toy computers that served small companies. I felt the same when I saw the introduction of the AS/400 back in 1988.

Then I watched the AS/400 grow from a small single-processor machine to the current high-end 12-processor "e" model that can store more than 4 terabytes (TB) of data, with a processing power that overlaps some of the current line of IBM S390 mainframes.

I watched the AS/400 switch from a complex instruction set computer (CISC) to a reduced instruction set computer (RISC) architecture, an incredibly complex shift in operating system design that required the rewriting of virtually all of the operating system's internal code.

I watched the AS/400 shift from 48-bit to 64-bit architecture.

I've watched the AS/400 grow and expand until many of us old mainframe bigots have had to eat our words. I don't laugh anymore!

The bottom line is that I do not worry about the future of the AS/400. This rather incredible machine seems to become whatever the market says that it must become. It does whatever the market needs it to do. It has grown in power and capacity to the point where it is larger than the largest mainframes ever envisioned only a few years ago.

---

1 The book *Inside the AS/400* by Frank Soltis, the AS/400's chief architect, clearly explains the idea of the AS/400 as a concept, not a computer.

The Client/Server Paradigm

The Internet is physically built on the client/server paradigm. A request from a desktop browser to a Web server may be routed between many Internet routers—either locally or worldwide—until it reaches its destination. From the TCP/IP protocol level, all the way down to the physical hardware level, client/server conversations occur between each device and program through which an Internet request flows.

In the world of AS/400 computing, most of the complexities of client/server technology are masked by the operating system (OS/400) and necessary software packages. AS/400 commands simply configure links between machines to provide the needed services.

An AS/400-based browser is a powerful client that can process HTML text, graphic images, audio, and even full-motion video. It runs both JavaScript (Netscape's scripting language) and Java, Sun Microsystem's full-blown programming language and runtime environment.

An AS/400 Web server responds to requests from a browser and delivers content from a database server (which may be an S390 mainframe, RS6000, brand-x UNIX machine, or any other machine connected to the AS/400 via DRDA or DDM).

CLIENT/SERVER DEFINITIONS

We most often tend to think of a client as a personal computer or UNIX workstation, and of a server as being a larger machine like an AS/400, Novell, Windows NT, or UNIX file server. The terms client and server refer to the activities each machine performs, not to the machine itself.

To understand the implications of client/server in developing Internet-based applications we must look at client/server in its most primitive terms.

Server A server is any program that receives requests via a communications protocol and returns a response to the client that initiated the request.

Client A client is any program that initiates a request via a communications protocol to a server and receives a response that satisfies the request.

By viewing the client/server paradigm at the program level, we can infer that client programs can run on the same or different physical machines as server programs.

TCP/IP is an example of client/server technology. It is implemented by several distinct layers of software and hardware. TCP/IP is request/response driven. A request is generated by a client (generally a browser running on a client machine). The request is received and forwarded to a server by a network of routers and serviced by a server (in our case, server software running on an AS/400). Finally, the response from the server is returned to the client.

Servers are generally passive and initiated at machine startup. They wait for requests to be received before they do anything. Upon receipt of a request, the server performs whatever processing is necessary to satisfy the request. Once the request processing is complete, the server returns to a passive mode and waits to receive another request.

Servers are generally more complex than clients, because they must process many requests from many clients concurrently. To do this a server is divided into *master* and *slave* processes. All AS/400 Internet servers (Web servers, SMTP mail servers, POP3 servers, FTP servers, etc.) operate using the master/slave server paradigm.

When a master server process starts, it attaches to a TCP/IP socket (a socket is the combination of a port and an IP address), opens the connection, and waits for requests. When a request is received by the server, it starts a slave process (on pre-V4R2 AS/400s, the process is called a *job*; V4R2 and subsequent releases may use either jobs or threads). The slave performs all processing required to satisfy the request. The slave process terminates or becomes inactive when it completes, then notifies the master process that it is again available.

The master server process manages the dispatching and completion of multiple slave processes. Various types of requests may last for differing durations and may therefore complete their processing in a random order, so a signaling mechanism exists between slave and master server processes.

Servers also must provide authorization checking to determine that the resources requested by a client are authorized to be available to that client. On AS/400 servers, user profiles and standard AS/400 security enforce authorization.

A server handles all forms of errors without terminating. If a server receives an authorization failure, an input/output (I/O) error, an Object Not Found error, or invalid input from the client, it must be able to process the error and be ready to accept the next request seamlessly.

The client/server paradigm is at work anytime a browser-based client submits a request for information to an AS/400 Web server, which then retrieves data from another computer. A common gateway interface (CGI) program, invoked by the Web server, becomes the client requesting data from a database server (DRDA or DDM via SNA or TCP/IP). When data is returned to the CGI program, it formats the output and returns the data to the Web browser client that initiated the request.

A server can become a client in a multitier client/server environment. Consider an AS/400 running a real-time stock trading Web application. A client (browser) requests a purchase of 10,000 shares of IBM stock at market price. The Web server, via a CGI program, records the transaction request on the AS/400. A TCP/IP sockets connection is established by the server with a computer at the New York Stock Exchange and a trade requested. When the NYSE's computers process the transaction, a confirmation is sent back to the local AS/400, which must return the purchase confirmation to the browser that initiated the transaction. When the AS/400 communicates with the NYSE's computer, it acts as a client and the NYSE computer is the server.

Although a stock purchase is a rather complex transaction involving at least two acknowledged transactions by two servers, it is typical of the type of e-commerce processing that occurs.

THE INTERNET

Perhaps the most historically significant event that occurred in the ongoing history of the Internet was the Telecommunications Act of 1996. This act, among other things, allows cable companies to provide telecommunications links and cable television services to their customers. With the advent of WebTV, virtually every household in the United States can afford Inter- net access, with limited access at $8.95 per month and unlimited access for as low as $12.95.

This has not been lost on the entertainment industry, which is working with large cable and telecommunications providers to develop the technology to route high-resolution, full-motion video with high-quality audio over the Internet, using fiber optic connectivity or high-speed coaxial cable. Within the next few years, the Internet will be a commercial Mecca of high-quality multimedia.

As individual households move to the Internet, the opportunities for Internet commerce increase. Business that are not connected and providing electronic commerce applications for their customers, they are handing their competitors an advantage. It's my opinion that within the next three to five years, companies that fail to connect and do business on the Internet will cease to exist.

WHAT IS THE INTERNET?

Originally, the Internet consisted of the ARPANET, financed by the Advanced Research Projects Agency of the United States Department of Defense. The first node was implemented at UCLA around Labor Day, 1969. On October 1, 1969, Stanford Research Institute came online with the second node. The network was a research tool used by universities and research institutions to develop the communications technology that we use today. It was heavily funded by the United States government and was restricted to noncommercial use.

TCP/IP became the official protocol of the ARPANET and all follow-on networks on January 1, 1983. In 1986, the National Science Foundation (NSF) established the NSFNET to connect five super-computing centers (JVNC at Princeton, PSC at Pittsburgh, SDSC at UCSD, NCSA at UIUC, and the Theory Center at Cornell). This network was connected with a backbone speed of 56 kilobits per second (Kbps).

In 1989, the first gateways between private electronic mail carriers, and the Internet were established. CompuServe connected through Ohio State University, and MCI connected through the Corporation for the National Research Initiative. In 1990, the ARPANET ceased to exist.

The Internet as we know it today was born in 1991. NSF lifted its restrictions on the commercial use of the NSFNET backbone. NSF also outsourced the backbone to a newly formed company called Advanced Networks and Services (ANS), a partnership between MERIT, IBM, and MCI. ANS was authorized to begin charging for access, and thus the commercial Internet was born.

In 1991, the NSFNET backbone was upgraded by ANS to T3 (44.736Mbps) and traffic passed 1 trillion bytes and 10 billion packets per month. On April 30, 1995, NSF stopped funding the NSFNET backbone and the Internet was on its own: a government funded and controlled experiment had given way to a self-sufficient, profit-making, commercial enterprise.[1]

Today there are more than 63 million users of the Internet with more than 36,739,000 hosts[2] in 110 countries. There is no longer a central backbone, but rather more than 30

1 The United States Government is a major user of the Internet and its technology. The government still contributes substantial funding for research and development and subsidizes educational institutions' access to the Internet.

2 Source: Network Wizards. Data is available at www.nw.com/

U.S. backbone providers, all interconnected, with additional international backbone providers connected to create the Internet. Average connection speeds are based on multiple OC3 circuits (155Mbs).

The Federal Networking Council (FNC) on October 24, 1995 unanimously passed a resolution defining the term Internet. This resolution can be found at *www.fnc.gov/internet_res.html*.

It states: "The Federal Networking Council (FNC) agrees that the following language reflects our definition of the term 'Internet'.

'Internet' refers to the global information system that—

(i) is logically linked together by a globally unique address space based on the Internet Protocol (IP) or its subsequent extensions/follow-ons;

(ii) is able to support communications using the Transmission Control Protocol/Internet protocol (TCP/IP) suite or its subsequent extensions/follow-ons, and/or other IP-compatible protocols; and

(iii) provides, uses or makes accessible, either publicly or privately, high level services layered on the communications and related infrastructure described herein.

The Federal Networking Council (FNC) was chartered by the National Science and Technology Council's Committee on Computing, Information, and Communications (CCIC) to act as a forum for networking collaborations among federal agencies to meet their research, education, and operational mission goals and to bridge the gap between the advanced networking technologies being developed by research FNC agencies and the ultimate acquisition of a mature version of these technologies from the commercial sector[3]." Although the FNC is not the governing body for the Internet, it does govern the federal government's involvement in the Internet.

WHO CONTROLS THE INTERNET?

Possibly the most remarkable factor about the Internet is that it is made possible through the cooperation of a loosely controlled group of diverse organizations.

3 From the FNC's Web page at www.fnc.gov

Research and development was managed by the Internet Architecture Board (IAB). In 1991, the IAB became an independent entity and is today the governing body of the Internet. It consists of the Internet Research Task Force (IRTF) and the Internet Engineering Task Force (IETF). The IAB board consists of international representatives from academia, industry, government, and the military.

Technology research is conducted by the IRTF, which consists of temporary workgroups each headed by a workgroup manager. The workgroups consist of volunteers from various universities and governments, and from the computer and communications industries.

The IETF has more than 20 specific workgroups, each with a manager and volunteer members. The IETF concentrates on short-term problem resolution, and is responsible for publishing engineering standards.

The Internet Society (ISOC) hosts the IAB. The Internet Society is an international organization dedicated to promoting access and use of the Internet. It is located at *www.isoc.org*.

The IAB created an entity called the Internet Network Information Center (InterNIC), which is operated under contract by AT&T. InterNIC is responsible for network administration, the assignment of IP addresses and domain names, and the maintenance of a database of IAB documents. In April 1998, the InterNIC was reorganized. The InterNIC can be reached at *www.internic.net*.

Domain name services (DNS) are now operated by Network Solutions, Inc. They manage the root domain name servers and the assignment of domain names on a for-profit basis.

The Internet Assigned Numbers Authority (IANA) is operated by The University of Southern California's (USC's) research company, Information Systems Institute Inc. (ISI). IANA is responsible for the developmental and administrative policies governing the assignment of names and numbers throughout the Internet. The IANA is chartered by the Internet Society (ISOC) and the Federal Network Council (FNC) to act as the clearinghouse to assign and coordinate the use of numerous IP parameters, such as Internet addresses, domain names, autonomous system numbers (used in some routing protocols), protocol numbers, port numbers, management information base object identifiers (including private enterprise numbers), and many others. The IANA Web site is *www.isi.edu/div7/iana/*.

INTERNET STANDARDS

The IAB and its research (IRTF) and engineering (IETF) groups are responsible for creating and publishing RFC research and standards documents. RFCs are numbered (e.g. RFC1000 – Request for Comments Reference Guide), and are available from the InterNIC via FTP, e-mail, and the Web at `www.internic.net` (select the References option). The IAB is the controlling authority for TCP/IP, which is fully defined via a series of RFCs.

The World Wide Web was developed in 1990 by Tim Berners-Lee at CERN, the European Laboratory for Particle Physics near Geneva, Switzerland. The World Wide Web and its technologies are governed by the W3 Consortium, which can be reached at *`www.w3.org`*. At this location you will find the standards documents defining HTTP and HTML. You will also find the work papers of the groups working on enhanced standards for HTTP and HTML. A topic to follow is the work being done with extensible markup language (XML), which will provide integration between databases, text, and graphics.

INTERNET GROWTH AND CAPACITY

The Internet is growing at exponential rates. In September 1997, studies indicated there were 64 million end users with Internet access. According to a study released December 18, 1997, Frank Gens, senior vice president of Internet Research, predicted that the number of Internet users would reach 100 million by the end of 1998 and more than 1 billion by 2005, with estimated e-commerce revenues of $20 billion.[4]

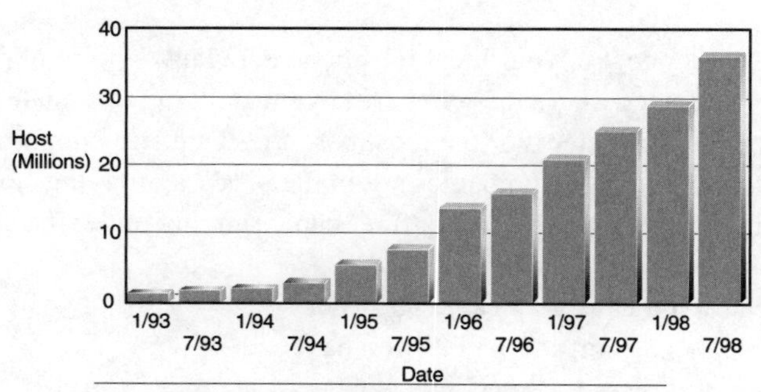

Figure 3.1: Internet growth in hosts 1993 to 1998.[5]

Mr. Gens missed his projection. Evan I. Schwartz in the September 1998 issue of his *Webonomics* newsletter reported that the Internet reached $22 billion in sales during 1997 and would reach $74 billion during 1998, with projected sales of $1.3 trillion by 2002. As Figure 3.1 indicates, growth rate for hosts on the Internet is increasing.

4 Source: C/Net news.com www.news.com.

5 Source www.nw.com.

CONNECTING TO THE INTERNET

To connect your network (maybe a single AS/400) to the Internet you need to contract with an ISP and provide a router and communications link (usually a T1 digital circuit) to the ISP's location in your geographical area. You pay for the link. Your ISP will sell a specific amount of bandwidth on the Internet (my company uses ½ T1 (750kbs)), for which they will charge a monthly fee. This is generally accomplished by setting limits on the ISP's router to which you are connected.

The ISP is a retailer of Internet bandwidth. There may be one or many layers between your ISP and its backbone provider, but bandwidth is a purchased commodity. The ISP buys bandwidth from a larger organization, and sells it to individual companies.

Let's look at the infrastructure a little more closely. The following description is applicable to all but the biggest corporations, which may bypass local telephone companies and ISPs. Extremely large organizations may become backbone providers themselves. These companies may buy direct DS3, OC3, or even faster fiber-optic access to Internet access points and bypass intermediaries. Companies like IBM use their own backbone networks and only leave the network when necessary to interconnect with others outside their network.

You connect to your local telephone company's point of presence (POP), which is the wire center where the wires from your building terminate at the telephone company's switching center. For the most part, these are still copper wires, although some telecommunication companies are in the process of laying fiber optic cables in many major cities. (My company has a fiber cable running under the street in front of the building.)

Once you have a T1 cable into your telephone company's POP, you have many choices for selecting a connection between the POP and your ISP's location. We chose an MFS fiber-optic connection from the POP to our ISP because it provided the lowest cost.

Figure 3.2 depicts a conceptual view of the Internet's architecture and organization. End users (individuals as

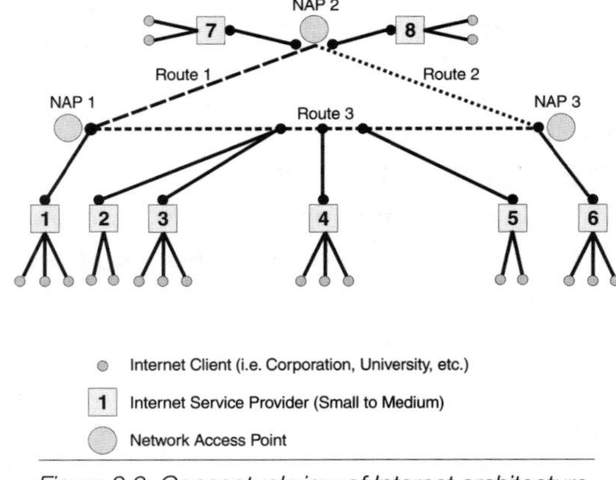

Figure 3.2: Conceptual view of Internet architecture.

well as content providers) contract with an ISP via local leased lines. You can select a large national or international ISP such as IBM Global Network, MCI, AT&T, Netcom, WorldCom, etc. You may also connect to small local ISPs that connect to one of the larger national companies. The primary difference is that the large ISPs own their own high-speed point-to-point lines, while smaller ISPs must purchase bandwidth and connectivity from a larger company. In both cases, you connect to a router at your ISP's local facility. The ISP connects to its backbone network via high-capacity routers.

NETWORK ACCESS POINTS (NAPS)

The major national and international Internet network operators interconnect with each other at Network Access Points (NAPs). These carriers exchange traffic under peering agreements that allow networks to route traffic across each other's networks without charge.

Each access point is connected by several of the 30-plus backbone providers at speeds ranging from DS3 (45 Mbps) to OC3 (155 Mbps). Major access points such as the west coast NAP in Palo Alto, MAE-LA in Los Angeles, Boston, New York, Chicago, Dallas, and others connect to virtually all of the backbone providers.

Figure 3.2 shows three NAPs, which interconnect several carriers. A NAP provides no routing, but interconnects networks via a high-speed local area network to which each network attaches a switch. Each "route" shown in the figure represents one or many high-speed DS3 or OC3 point-to-point long distance circuits owned by each of the large ISPs. Individual ISPs connect to a particular carrier's high-speed point-to-point circuits via access points provided by the carrier. The ISP in turn connects to its clients via leased lines, with speed capabilities usually ranging from T1 to T3. Many ISPs also support arrays of dial-up circuits at their access points to support dial-up Internet access.

METROPOLITAN AREA EXCHANGES (MAES)

For several years, an ISP in Los Angeles had to connect to the PacBell NAP in Palo Alto. A user in Los Angeles who wanted to access a host computer located in Los Angeles would first connect to his ISP, then be routed to the Palo Alto NAP, and finally be routed back to Los Angeles. Although the speed of the communications lines was not a problem, the traffic on the internal network and routers at the NAP was. The NAP itself became a bottleneck. The problem was far worse in states with small commercial populations, like Utah, where all network traffic used to be routed from Utah to the NAP in Palo Alto. This meant that a user at home in Salt Lake City trying to access a host at Brigham Young

University in Salt Lake City would be routed to Palo Alto and then back to Salt Lake City.

To address this issue, metropolitan area exchanges (MAEs) were established to route traffic within their service area. (Regional NAPs such as MPIX in Arizona were patterned after the MAEs on a smaller scale.) Now, if a user in Los Angeles wants to access a local Los Angeles host, he is routed directly by the MAE to that host without having to go through a NAP. Only when you want to make an out-of-area (U.S. or worldwide) connection are you routed out of the MAE or Regional NAP. When selecting an ISP, it is necessary to know where the majority of users are located and how the ISP connects to the backbone.

FUTURE OF THE INTERNET

Because of its phenomenal growth, the media is predicting a collapse, based on major incidents like America Online's recent capacity problems. There have been growing pains. We see occasional outages and recently lost Europe for nearly four hours. Telecommunications companies are constantly improving the capacity and reliability of the Internet. Once you have a general understanding of the economic and physical structure of the Internet and its backbones, you can clearly see that it will grow to accommodate its users.

ADDITIONAL READING

For a closer look at the history, organization, and structure of the Internet, the following references provide excellent and valuable information.

A word of caution. Each of the listed Web sites has links to literally hundreds of other technical sites. Some particularly fascinating sites are operated by universities and organizations doing the research to develop the next generation of Internet hardware and software. If you get hooked on the research and dragged into the Web, you may never come back!

HISTORY OF THE INTERNET

Brief History of the Internet and Related Networks, by Vinton Cerf
`www.simmons.edu/~pomerant/techcomp/cerf.html`

ARPANET
`www.yahoo.com/Computers_and_Internet/Internet/History/ARPANET/`

Brief History of the Internet from the Internet Society
www.isoc.org/Internet-history/

BBN Timeline
www.bbn.com/customer_connection/timeline.htm

Definition of Internet (FNC)
www.fnc.gov/Internet_res.html

History of the Internet and Web
www.dsu.edu/~anderbea/history/

Also go to YAHOO at *www.yahoo.com* and click on Computers and Internet, Internet, History for a comprehensive list of Web sites pertaining to the history of the Web.

OFFICIAL INFORMATION AND STANDARDS SITES

InterNIC database of RFCs
www.internic.net (click on Database and Directories)

Internet Assigned Number Authority (IANA)
www.isi.edu/div7/iana/ (This site contains the only complete list if MIME content types in addition to a vast list of resources controlled by IANA.)

World Wide Web Consortium
www.w3.org (The standards organization for the World Wide Web, HTTP, and HTML.)

INTERNET EXCHANGE POINTS, BACKBONE PROVIDERS, AND ISPS

The following sites provide lists of the current Internet exchange points (NAPs, MAEs, and Regional NAPs), with links to those ISPs and backbone providers servicing the access point. This is an excellent starting point in your search for an ISP. Find the access points closest to you and then locate the ISPs connecting to that access point. Look at the list of backbone providers connecting to the access point to determine if you want your data routed through the access point. Many of the links include throughput, outage, and congestion statistics.

Exchange Point Information Page by Bill Manning, ISI
www.isi.edu/div7/ra/NAPs/. Bill Manning is a senior staff member of ISI and project manager for the Routing Arbiter project, which is intended to develop a new routing

protocol for high-speed, high-capacity routers on the Internet and other communications networks. The fact that ISI controls IANA (which assigns the numbers for all of the high-speed routers on the Internet) and because of Mr. Manning's expertise, this is perhaps the most comprehensive and accurate list of exchange points in existence. The site also includes links to each of the exchange point's Web sites, which often provide performance and reliability statistics, lists of backbone providers, and ISPs that interconnect via each access point.

MAPNET

www.caida.org/Tools/Mapnet/Backbones/ This site contains the single most valuable Internet mapping tool available. The page contains a Java applet that allows you to select the entire world or the locality in which you are interested and allows you to examine the exchange points and backbone providers that service the connection.

Randy Benn's Information for Internet Service Providers

www.clark.net/pub/rbenn/isp.html This site is designed to be an information collection point for ISPs, but provides end users with a tremendous amount of information concerning the physical side of the Internet. This site even contains some pricing information.

Russ Haynal's ISP Page

navigators.com/isp.html This site contains links to all major backbone providers with direct links to network maps on the providers' sites. A great wealth of information.

Network Wizards Internet Domain Survey

www.nw.com/zone/WWW/top.html Network Wizards is owned and operated by Mark K. Lottor. Mark worked at the DDN Network Information Center (before it became the current InterNIC) at SRI International as a systems programmer and assistant computer facility manager for seven years, and has over ten years of TCP/IP experience. He was a member of the Internet Engineering Task Force for more than four years, mostly involved with the DNS working group, and has authored four RFC documents. Mark also produces the twice-yearly Internet domain survey, which counts the number of hosts on the Internet.

BROWSERS, IP ADDRESSES, URLs, AND DOMAINS

The browser is an incredibly powerful and well designed piece of client software. To surf the Web, a user need only type the address of the Web site he wants to access and press the Enter key. Once there, the user can click on *links* to other pages or Web sites and navigate between pages with the Back button, Forward button, and Home button. To understand what a browser can—and cannot—do, you need to learn how it communicates with a server via IP addresses, URLs, and domain names.

IP ADDRESSES

Each server accessible to the Internet has an IP address, a 32-bit binary address that enables a message to be routed around the world in a fraction of a second[1].

Although the rumors of imminent Internet collapse are untrue, it is true that we are running out of addresses. Unless your network is extremely large (approaching 65,536 computers), you will probably obtain one or more *Class C address blocks* from your ISP.

---

1 The current implementation of IP addressing is called IPv4. The IAB is working on a new version of IP addressing officially designated as IPv6 but referred to as IPng (IP the next generation). See the reference material at the end of the chapter for more information.

Internet addresses are controlled by the IANA, which is operated by the ISI. The InterNIC administers and assigns numbers for IANA.

Because there are very few Class A and Class B numbers available, the InterNIC assigns contiguous blocks of Class C numbers to ISPs, which then assign one or more blocks of Class C numbers to their clients. (Because an IP address identifies a communications link, not a specific computer, if you change your ISP, your IP address numbers will change too.) Generally, an entire Class C block of 254 numbers is assigned. For very small accounts with a limited number of computers that need an Internet connection, the ISP may assign less than an entire Class C block. It is possible that you will be assigned one or two numbers.

There are three classes of IP addresses:

Table 4.1: Classes of IP Addresses

Class	Lowest Address	Highest Address
A	0.1.0.0	126.0.0.0
B	128.0.0.0	191.255.0.0
C	192.0.1.0	223.255.255.0

Some computers and all routers have multiple IP addresses. When a computer has multiple IP addresses, it is said to be *multihomed*.

The IP address 128.10.2.30 is in *dotted decimal notation*. The physical binary representation for this address is:

10000000 00001010 00000010 00011110

Referring to Table 4.1, you see that this is a Class B address. Notice that the first bit of the address contains a 1 and the second bit contains a 0. Due to the address structure, computers and routers throughout the Internet determine the class by looking at the first three bits of the address.

Figure 4.1 shows the bit structure of an IP address. All IP addresses contain two parts, a network ID and a host or link ID. Routers operate on the network ID portion of the address and ignore the host ID unless the host is attached to the router's network.

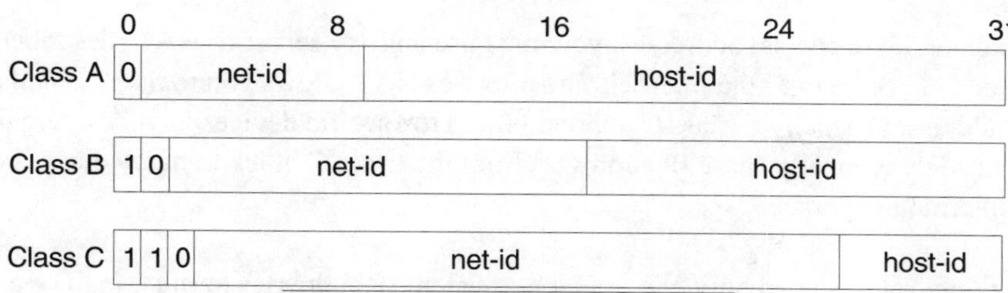

Figure 4.1: Bit structure of an IP address.

SPECIAL IP ADDRESSES

You can assign whatever numbering scheme you like to an intranet and use a software device called a network address translator (NAT) or proxy server to translate internal addresses to an external address. NATs and proxy servers allow you to define any internal numbering scheme using Class A or Class B naming with numbers that you do not own. As long as the internal numbers cannot be accessed via the Internet, it's completely permissible to use them within an intranet. NAT allows a small number of addresses (i.e. the 254 possible addresses available in a Class C address block) to support hundreds or even thousands of devices that occasionally connect to the Internet.

In a large organization with many locations or local area networks (LAN) connected via a wide area network (WAN), configure the internal network as a Class A network using the 10.x.x.x numbering scheme. (Class A addresses allow you to grow to more than 16 million devices.) A small shop with very few computers or other IP devices can use a Class B addressing scheme.

For intranets, the IETF has reserved IP addresses that will not be routed across the Internet[2]. Internet routers are programmed to ignore these addresses when they are used by companies to define their internal network addresses. These non-Internet routable addresses are shown if Table 4.2.

Table 4.2: Non-Internet Routable IP Addresses

Class	Range
Class A	10.0.0.0 – 10.255.255.255
Class B	172.16.0.0 – 172.31.255.255
Class C	192.168.0.0 – 192.168.0.0

2 In March of 1994, the IETF published RFC 1597 and subsequently revised it with RFC 1918 in February 1996 providing a mechanism to prolong the life of the current IPv4 address naming convention until the new IPng or IP6 naming convention can be finalized and implemented.

When using these special addresses, you must use a proxy server or NAT (described in Chapter 5) to connect to the Internet. The proxy or NAT allows you to map a small block of IP addresses (usually a Class C address block) to specific devices in your internal network or to dynamically share IP addresses from the Class C block to many devices on your internal network.

Most organizations need only one or two permanent IP addresses to run e-mail or a Web server. The majority of Internet access by other devices is limited, usually from end users who access the Internet from time to time. Thus, a Class C address block can support hundreds of personal computers that use the Internet via browsers.

LOCALHOST

A special IP address is assigned to each computer internally. Whether an AS/400 or a PC, every computer refers to itself by the IP address 127.0.0.1. If you use the PING utility, and type PING 127.0.0.1 on the command line, your AS/400 will respond with its name and address. All TCP/IP devices respond internally to 127.0.0.1. This special address cannot be routed across the Internet. Routers are programmed to ignore it.

URLS (UNIFORM RESOURCE LOCATORS)

Figure 4.2 is an example of a home page, displayed in Microsoft Internet Explorer Version 3.02 for Windows/95.

Notice the field following the word **ADDRESS** *http://www.ignite400.org.* This is Ignite/400™'s uniform resource locator (URL), sometimes called the uniform resource indicator (URI). In its simplest form it consists of the following parts:

```
http://domain.com:80/subdirectories
1          2         3        4
```

1. *http://* is the protocol being used. Other protocols include HTTPS, FTP, Gopher, Telnet, and others. We are primarily concerned with hypertext transport protocol (HTTP) and HTTP with secure sockets (HTTPS).

2. *domain.com* is the name of the site that you wish to access.

3. *:80* is the default port. You may specify any port that has been configured to run the site's Web server, but 80 is the default. (I run my test server on 8081. IBM's AS/400 Division runs some of its servers on 8081, which you can see when browsing through the *www.AS400.IBM.com* site.) Each Web server is also assigned a port number.

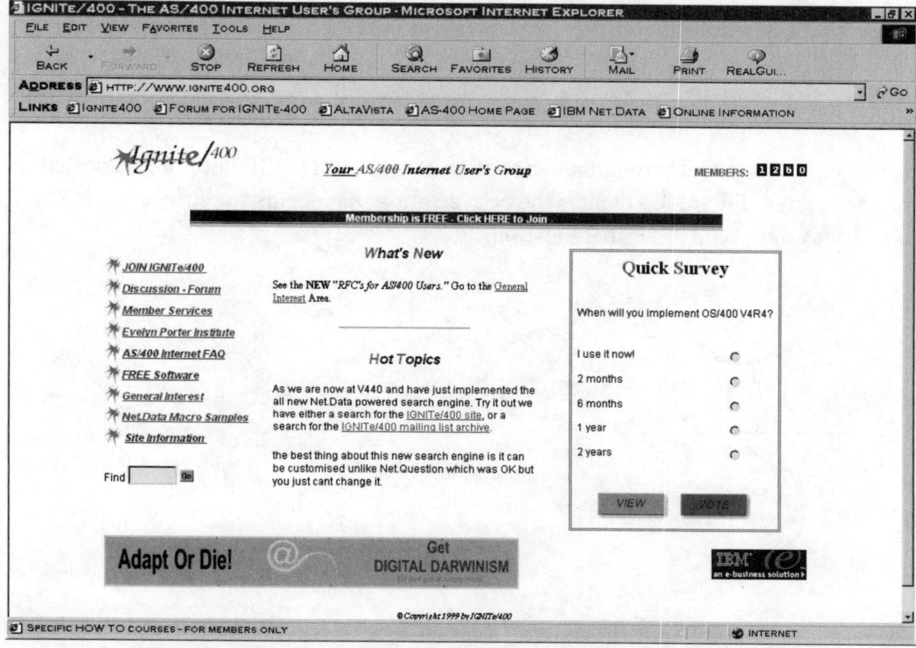

Figure 4.2: Sample Web page displayed in Microsoft Internet Explorer Version 3.02 for Windows/95.

Where the IP address is similar to a street address, the port number is like a room or suite number inside the building. Different types of servers are associated with different port numbers (commonly known ports). Most Web servers are configured to port 80, which is the default port. As long as your Web server is configured to run on the default HTTP port, you need not type the port number in the URL.

4. */subdirectory* is the location of a subdirectory at the Web site you wish to access. The example contains a page by the name of INDEX.HTML or INDEX.HTM depending upon server configuration. The page name may be anything that the Webmaster defines as the default. The industry standard is INDEX.HTML. You will sometimes see DEFAULT.HTM or HOME.HTML, which is usually set by a webmaster to indicate the home or initial page on the site.

When the user types the URL and presses Enter, the browser formats an HTTP header and sends it on its way to the Internet.

The first step in the process is locating the server. This is done by the domain name server (DNS), which translates English-language style names into numerical IP addresses. In the example above, the server *pages.prodigy.net* is 198.83.19.165. `www.as400.IBM.com`is 208.222.150.11. You can type the numerical address in the browser's address field and it will find the site without doing a DNS lookup.

The transmission is sent through a series of routers using TCP/IP until the requested server is located. Figure 4.3 depicts the conversation that occurs to retrieve the HTML page that resides at the requested location.

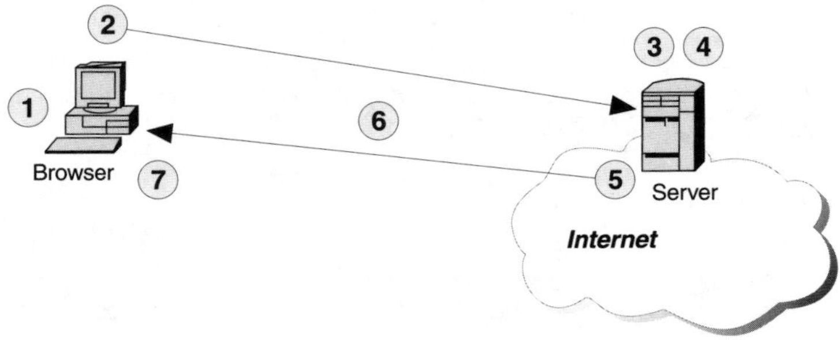

Figure 4.3: The conversation that occurs to retrieve the HTML page that resides at the requested location.

BROWSER/SERVER CONVERSATION

1. The user types the desired URL on the browser (or clicks a hyperlink on the current page) and presses Enter.

2. The browser sends an HTTP request header to the Internet. The DNS server locates the address of the server and returns the IP address to the browser. The browser then sends the request header to the server at its IP address.

3. The server decodes and validates the request.

4. The server locates the desired resource on the server.

5. The server generates the correct response headers and returns the requested resource to the browser.

6. The response headers are transmitted to the browser.

7. The browser interprets the request headers and file type returned, then performs all processing necessary to display the response to the user.

Let's build on this example a little bit. Let's assume that our previous example returns an HTML page. Embedded in the page are "<IMG SRC="xxx.gif"> *tags*, which instruct the browser to request a graphics file from the server. (Conversations between a browser are non-persistent and stateless. The server knows of the existence of the browser client only for the duration of steps 3 to 6 above. When the browser contacts the server again, a completely new transaction is started.)

The browser parses the HTML and identifies resources such as GIF, JPEG, AVI, WAV, AUD, etc., files. The entire process (steps 1 through 7) is repeated until all resources described in the page are retrieved by the browser, decoded or otherwise processed, and displayed.

Netscape, Microsoft Internet Explorer running under Windows 95/98, and some other browsers are capable of *multitasking*. They send multiple requests to the server and receive multiple responses at the same time—which explains why you see more than one image on a page fade into view at the same time.

HTTP REQUEST RESPONSE HEADERS

The browser and server communicate via HTTP request and response headers. To see how this works, bring up the Windows 95/98 Telnet utility (select start, run, type ***Telnet***, click OK). Click ***Connect*** on the Telnet menu bar. Click on ***Remote System*** on the Connect drop down menu. In the ***Connect*** dialog box type:

```
Hostname: www.inetmi.com
Port: 80
Termtype: vt100
```

Then click the ***Connect*** button.

When the Telnet program indicates that it has connected to the server, type the following HTTP request header: `GET / HTTP/1.0`. Press Enter twice. Note that HTTP request headers are always terminated with a CRLF (carriage return/line feed).

The server responds with the HTTP response headers and the default home page HTML. Here is what the transaction looks like (you might want to turn on Telnet logging to store the results in a text file). This request asks the server to send the default home page associated with port 80[3]:

```
GET / HTTP/1.0                         <-- browser's HTTP 1.0 request header

HTTP/1.0 200 OK                        <-- Server's status response header
Date: Sun, 12 Oct 1997 18:49:47 GMT    <-- Date and time response generated
                                            by server
Server: CommerceServer400/1.0          <-- Server identification header
Content-Length: 356                    <-- Content length header in bytes
Content-Type: text/html                <-- Content type header
Last-Modified: Mon, 14 Jul 1997        <-- Date document last modified
                   15:03:44 GMT

<HTML><HEAD><TITLE>I/NET, Inc.         <-actual HTML content
   Corporate Homepage</TITLE></HEAD>

actual html text goes here
```

Figure 4.4: HTTP browser/server conversation via Telnet.

HTML TAGS, GRAPHICS, AND TEXT

When a browser processes the HTML tags embedded in an HTML document, it applies text formatting such as font, size, color, and location; positions tables, frames, and other layout elements; draws predefined form elements such as text boxes, radio buttons, check boxes, drop down list boxes, etc.; and requests, retrieves, and displays various types of image files (GIF, JPG, etc.). It may also be able to receive and process audio and video files, depending on the browser or add-ins installed with it.

Browsers also adjust the HTML image they build to fit the physical and user-defined constraints of the user's environment. Users may choose to set their screen resolution at 640 *x* 480 pixels, 800 *x* 600, or 1024 *x* 728, even though most people prefer the preset 640 x 480 resolution most displays are shipped with, because it generally uses larger text fonts and is easiest to read.

---

3 The most authoritative source for information on HTTP is W3.ORG, which is the de facto standards organization for HTTP. HTTP 1.0 may be found in RFC 1945 at www.w3org/Protocols/rfc1945/rfc1945.

IBM's new V4R3 HTTP server will support HTTP 1.1.

Graphics will resize depending upon the methods used to define them. The right and bottom page margins will adjust to accommodate the graphic. Print fonts and settings may differ from the display settings.

Most modern browsers (Netscape 2.0 and above, Microsoft Internet Explorer 3.0 and above) can process the JavaScript scripting language and support the Java runtime environment. (Microsoft proprietary features such as ActiveX, Visual Basic, Visual C, and Visual J++ should be avoided, because they will run only on Windows, Windows 95/98, or Windows NT clients.)

As a Web designer, remember that browsers display text in the fonts that exist on the user's machine. You might like the looks of a font that exists on the computer you are using to build your site, but if the user doesn't have that font, your beautiful page may look like the worst nightmare an artist could imagine.

Test your Web pages on different browsers and computers, at different resolutions. You cannot predict or control how your users will configure their computers. If you plan to use tables, frames, or Java applets, post a notice on your home page that Netscape 2.0 or above or Microsoft Internet Explorer 3.0 or above, a current version of the IBM browser, or a current version of the Mosaic browser is required.

I generated my first HTML page using Microsoft Publisher 97. It looked great on my browser, which was set to 1024 *x* 728 resolution, but when I viewed it on the browser installed on a machine in the conference room where I was going to demo this wonderful first example of the site, it was hideous.

SPECIFIC BROWSER LIMITATIONS

Be sure you have several browsers on the PC you will be developing from and that you have access to others so you can see what users will most likely see. Plan for the following browser limitations:

- Java applets are not supported by Netscape browsers prior to release 3.0. In fact, not all Netscape 3.0 browsers support Java. Apparently, browsers shipped by some ISPs like PACBELL ship a version of Netscape 3.0 that does not include Java support.

- Microsoft browsers do not support Java prior to release 3.02. The HTML `<applet...> </applet>` tags allow you to embed alternative HTML code that will be displayed by browsers that are not Java capable.

- IBM's Navio browser (shipped with IBM's Network Station) is a part of Netscape 3.0 for UNIX and does not support Java unless you have at least 32 megabytes of memory.

- JavaScript is not supported by all browsers. At present, three versions of JavaScript are supported by various browsers. Version 1.0 was supported beginning with Netscape 2.0 and all subsequent Netscape browsers. Microsoft Internet Explorer supports JScript, which is a reverse-engineered version of JavaScript beginning with release 3.0. There are some nice features in releases 1.1 and 1.2 such as the image object, marquee, and layers that are supported only in Netscape Communicator 4.0 and to some degree in Microsoft Internet Explorer 4.0.

- Both Microsoft Internet Explorer and Netscape browsers have the ability to turn Java support off. You must provide alternative HTML for those users or you will be supporting less than 75 percent of the user base.

- Frames are not supported by all browsers.

- HTML tables were supported beginning with Netscape 2.0 and Microsoft Internet Explorer 3.0. I use tables extensively in my Web pages and post a notice to users that I require a minimum of Netscape 2.0 and above or Microsoft Internet Explorer 3.0 and above to view them properly.

BROWSER CACHE

Most browsers include a two-level cache. HTML pages, images, and multimedia files used in Web pages are stored in the browser's cache. The two levels of cache are *memory* and *DASD* on your hard disk. To recap, the conversation between a browser and the server occurs in four parts:

- The browser sends a request header.
- The server sends a response header.
- The browser acknowledges the request and authorizes the data transfer.
- The server sends the data.

Part of the response header is the modification date of the object requested. The browser checks to see if a current version of the object (e.g. an HTML file, graphic file, etc.) exists.

If the browser has the object stored in cache and the modification date is acceptable, then the cached version is used. If the object does not exist in the cache, or if the object has expired, the browser asks the server to transmit the object.

Each browser has user-defined rules concerning caching. Web site designer or administrators can assume that a substantial number of objects will be cached after the initial access to your Web pages.

Caching is extremely important to you to maximize performance. Here are some general guidelines to consider:

- Keep images that are used on multiple Web pages (like your logo) in the same subdirectory on your server. For an object to be located in cache, its URL must be identical. `Http://www.myserver.com/logo.gif` is not the same as `http://www.myserver.com/products/logo.gif`

  This is true even though LOGO.GIF is a copy of the same file. Some Web site designers keep all of their shared images in a separate /images directory off the root directory of the server so a URL reference to the LOGO.GIF stored in `/images` would be:

  `http://www.myserver.com/images/logo.gif.`

- A neat trick that produces a nice looking list with fancy bullets is to refer to the same bullet image file (i.e. bullet.gif) repeatedly on a page. One copy of the image is loaded and all other references use the cached copy.

TESTING YOUR WEB PAGE

Here are some testing tips:

- Test with your screen resolution set to 640 *x* 480. I had a nice invoice display that looked great on my browser at 800 *x* 600 dpi. I got a call from my client who told me that the display looked terrible. All of the spaces between fields in the table were gone, and various character fields (like user name, description, etc.) had wrapped onto multiple lines—you get the idea.

- Get a CompuServe account and use the Mosaic browser that comes bundled into its Windows software. This is by far the worst case you will ever run into. If your pages work with CompuServe, they should work anywhere! I also keep a copy of Netscape 2.0 around to ensure compatibility.

- Have as many people test your site, especially things like forms and JavaScript form validation. You will be amazed at what they can do and what you didn't plan for.

- America Online ships a homegrown browser on the diskettes and CD-ROMs that it ships to new users. The default browser must be upgraded to Microsoft Internet Explorer, which is provided by AOL via download, free of charge. You can also run Netscape Navigator on AOL.

- Put a link on your Web site to both Netscape and Microsoft. Both companies are currently giving their browsers away. Users can download and install them free of charge.

You must try to support as many browsers as you can, but the Internet, HTML, Java, JavaScript, and other tools are being enhanced constantly. You will not be able to be all things to all people. I try to accommodate 95 percent of the browsers in existence, which probably represents 98 percent of my prospective clientele.

FIREWALLS, PROXY SERVERS, AND NATs

There are risks associated with connecting your computers to the Internet. You must develop a comprehensive security policy that defines the type of access users are allowed for outbound access to the Internet, and what services you are willing to provide for inbound access to your network from the Internet. Three of the biggest threats to your network are Telnet, FTP, and e-mail communications.

More and more users can access their office desktop computer from a computer at home, or a laptop computer in the field. While the benefits of this remote access are enormous in time and cost savings, the risks are equally huge. In V4R4, IBM has implemented secure virtual private networking (VPN) support. IBM's VPN implementation is fully compliant with the Internet protocols and VPN standards and is compatible with many VPN clients. This means that an authorized user using a secure VPN configuration, may remotely access the same servers and facilities within the private network that they could access if they were plugged directly into a LAN. VPN provides full encryption and security.

Once word of advice. For a relatively modest fee, a unique service is provided by IBM, which employs a group of "ethical hackers" who will attack your system and report any security holes and breaches found. This service typically costs a few hundred dollars and is well worth it.

Their report must still be evaluated in terms of cost versus risk and determination of acceptable risk. A bank dealing in Internet-based financial transactions, needs more security than an insurance company providing claims information. An electronic store that asks users to submit credit card information over the Internet had better be able to ensure the user that the transaction is secure.

You must weigh the risks of all exposures and make some cost-versus-risk decisions about the level of security you want and need. Remember, in most of the publicly advertised cases of hacking, the least secure route into the network was not the Internet, but the modems attached to the network. Most PCs lack sophisticated security software, and remote-access software like PCAnywhere exposes your network more than an Internet connection.

TELNET, FTP, AND E-MAIL RISKS

A user with a Telnet client can connect to your AS/400 and log on as an interactive terminal user, with both positive and negative consequences. It is desirable to provide remote Internet-based connectivity to your system for employees and designated clients, because it eliminates the cost and complexity of maintaining dial-up access to your AS/400 via asynchronous modems and communications ports.

On the other hand, Telnet is one of the least secure Internet services because it transmits all screens as plain ASCII text across the Internet. Although AS/400 security ensures that a valid user ID and password is entered, it is possible for hackers to ferret them out by decoding the UUencoded user IDs and passwords "hidden" in the file's header.

The AS/400 (V4R4 and above) addresses this issue by offering Telnet over a secure sockets layer (SSL). This means that the entire conversation between Client Access Express or Client Access/400 TN5250 Client and the AS/400 Telnet server is encrypted. SSL for Telnet is part of V4R4 support and may be obtained as a PTF for V4R3.

FTP, by default, requires a valid user ID and password on the AS/400. FTP, like Telnet, uses simple UUencoding to provide some protection for user IDs and passwords. You can support anonymous FTP, but you must purchase or write a user exit program to do so. A risk associated with anonymous FTP is that of a malicious user uploading hundreds of huge files designed to fill your direct access storage device (DASD) and crash your server.

E-mail is a major exposure to your systems, and several types of attacks can be accomplished via e-mail. The greatest risk is from PC users who access their mail via a POP3 or other PC client that allows files to be attached to an e-mail note. Computer viruses are often transmitted in this manner, and although the AS/400 is extremely resistant to viruses, it can pass them on to your clients. Another risk is e-mail with a program attached to it that could contain a virus. Users should be advised never to execute a program attached to a piece of e-mail, even if they know the sender of the message. There are some ugly viruses transmitted in this manner: one of them, upon execution, sends a piece of e-mail containing the virus to everyone in the victim's address book before wiping out the boot sector of the user's hard disk.

Programs should be downloaded to floppy disks, when possible, then run on a standalone (non-networked) machine to test them for infection. (Some word processing programs like WordPerfect and Microsoft Word contain macros that automatically identify some viruses.)

Another nasty e-mail trick is to bombard your server with thousands of messages and either crash your server or overload it to the point that it becomes unusable. All that is required is to send messages to an invalid user ID at your domain name, such as *junkmail@mycompany.com.*

FIREWALLS

Most security exposures can be managed effectively with firewalls and proper AS/400 configuration. A firewall is a software product that provides access controls protecting private networks, servers, and other computers from the outside world when you have a live connection to the Internet. The firewall most often runs on a standalone processor. Many firewalls are available for UNIX and Windows NT, and IBM has a firewall for the AS/400, which runs on the Integrated Netfinity Server with its own network adapters.

The firewall allows or disallows access to selected ports on your computer, filters content, and looks up the IP address of anyone attempting to access your computer to verify that they are authorized. Some firewalls include features to scan mail for viruses, detect attacks on your computer by malicious hackers, and even counterattack the hacker.

Figures 5.1 and 5.2 illustrate two simple firewall-based configurations that provide a good deal of protection. Both configurations assume a single connection to the Internet from a central location. These configurations assume that your remote locations are connected via a WAN and do not have their own Internet connection. (If your remote locations have a direct Internet connection, identical firewalls and security policies are needed at each location. Failure to heed this warning may introduce a security exposure into your network.)

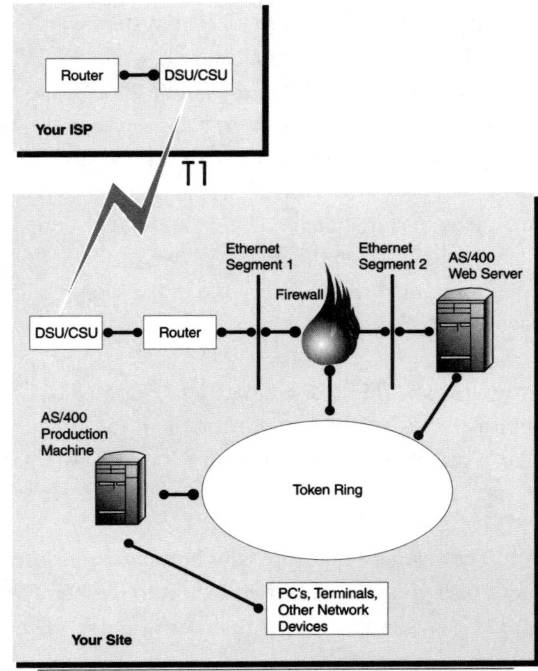

Figure 5.1: Network Configuration A: AS/400 server protected by firewall.

In Configuration A, in Figure 5.1, two Ethernet segments are used to isolate the entire environment from the Internet. All Internet traffic is routed through the firewall. The firewall can filter every packet, and examine every inbound or outbound IP address and destination. It has rules that determine what actions can and cannot pass through it. In theory, you have provided a layer of protection for your AS/400 and everything on your secure network.

In reality, this may be overkill and cause downtime. Unless the firewall resides on an extremely robust computer, you risk losing all contact with the Internet if the firewall fails. You are probably spending over $1,000 per month for high-speed connectivity with the Internet. Are you willing to route all of your traffic through a PC? Do you feel comfortable basing the availability of your network on an Intel PC running Microsoft NT with a couple of $100 network interface cards? And what have you gained? You will most likely allow all inbound traffic to access your Web server, SMTP mail server, and FTP server. You will use IBM's user exit programs to protect FTP, and you may put a mail filter/virus scanner between you and the Internet. But what you will not do—cannot do—is disallow any traffic.

Because I have experienced the agony of a failed firewall taking my entire network offline, I recommend the configuration shown in Figure 5.2.

In Configuration B, the AS/400 that is acting as the Web server, FTP server, and mail server is not protected by the firewall. The risks are minimal because the AS/400 can protect itself with a little help from you. (If you plan to use FTP, you must write or buy the

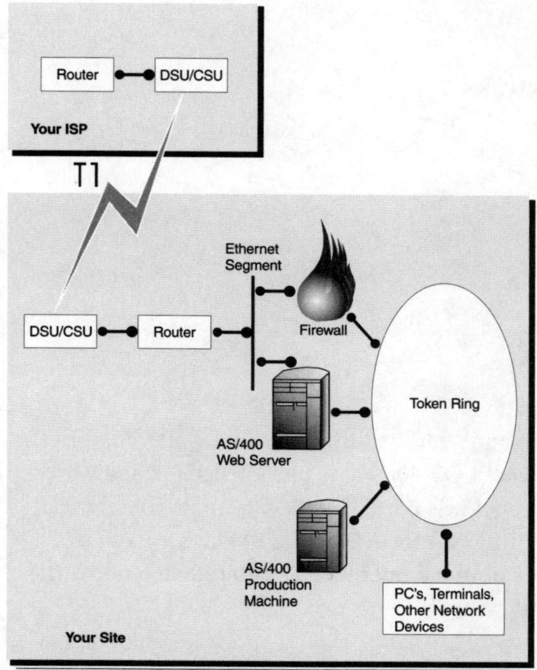

Figure 5.2: Network Configuration B: AS/400 server not protected by firewall.

FTP exit programs that are clearly illustrated with examples in the *Configuring TCP/IP* manual and a Redbook titled *Cool Title About the Internet.)*

If you plan to run AnyNet and connect via systems network architecture (SNA) over TCP/IP, you must take additional precautions. Terminal emulation products such as Netsoft, Client Access/400, and Reflection mean that you must write or buy OS/400 exit programs to protect against security risks like a PC user issuing Remote Command (RMTCMD) to your server. There are some excellent, albeit expensive, security products that provide protection from these exposures.

In Configuration B, the risk points for failure are the routers, channel service units/data service units (CSU /DSU), and the telephone lines. You can introduce redundancy, but most of the routers, CSU/DSUs, and telephone connections are reliable. Apply good operations disaster recovery planning to all of these devices, just as you would the AS/400, LANs, and WANs.

FIREWALL VENDORS

Although there are many vendors of firewalls, proxy servers, and NAT services, there is a short list of vendors providing excellent products for use on the AS/400.

New with V4R3 is a strong native implementation of IP packet filtering and NAT. Judicious use of these new facilities can eliminate the need for an external firewall. You can use IP Filtering and the NAT to limit access on an AS/400 configured as a network server to public services such as Web servers, e-mail, FTP, Telnet, etc. A firewall is still needed to control access to the private network.

IBM FIREWALL FOR THE AS/400

IBM's firewall provides the following services:

- IP packet filtering
- Proxy server
- SMTP store and forward server
- External DNS services
- SOCKS server
- NAT (with V4R3 of OS/400)

The IBM firewall integrates firewall protection very tightly with the AS/400. Significant violations of security policy and attacks cause OS/400 alerts to be generated and a break message to be sent to QSYSOPR. The firewall was ported by IBM from its commercially available UNIX firewall (IBM eNetwork Firewall for AIX). The SMTP server on the firewall isolates the AS/400 SMTP server from the Internet but, unfortunately, does not provide virus filters or protection for mail content.

The firewall software is stored on the AS/400 in a read-only area associated with the Integrated Netfinity Server and its software, making attacks against the firewall difficult. It can support both of the configurations depicted Figure 5.1 and 5.2. IBM recommends the approach in Figure 5.1, where all connectivity into your network is protected by the firewall. Considering the reliability of the IPCS card and the AS/400, this may be a good choice. Remember, when the firewall is offline, you are no longer connected to the Internet in this approach.

For more information visit `www.as400.ibm.com/firewall` See also *Firewall for AS/400 V4R1* (SC41-5424-00) and *Building a Firewall with the IBM Internet Connection Secured Network Gateway Redbook*, (GG24-3376).

FIREWALL-1 FROM THE QUALIX GROUP

This time-tested, reliable firewall has proven itself quite robust in the UNIX environment. A Windows NT version that provides all of the features the UNIX version provides has been available for some time . It does not incorporate SMTP, DNS, or a proxy server in the product, but does include a NAT facility. It is difficult to configure for a person new to TCP/IP and internetworking, because it uses commands and terminology common to those two concepts. For information, visit `www.qualix.com/html/firewall1.html`.

GUARDIAN FIREWALL BY LANOPTICS

Another option is the Guardian Firewall by LanOptics. It is oriented to people who are not intimately familiar with internetworking. It is easy to install and configure, and provides many needed features, including NAT. It incorporates dozens of screens that monitor activity on your network and access requests to your site from the Internet. For more information, visit `www2.aaafirewall.com`.

A WORD ABOUT USING PCS AS FIREWALLS

Although it is *possible* to run software other than a firewall on your Windows NT server, it is not a very good idea. Consider Figure 5.1, where all of your Internet traffic is routed through the firewall. This device had better be able to provide the throughput you require without becoming a bottleneck in your network.

Don't scrimp on the PC on which you run your firewall. All firewall vendors want to sell their software, so they provide minimum configuration information that is deceptively conservative. Although you can run on a 486/33mhz machine with 32 MB of memory and 300 megabytes of hard disk, *don't*. Buy at least a 133MHz Pentium processor, put as much memory on board as you can afford (not less than 64MB; I recommend 128MB), and get a 3GB to 5GB hard disk.

Also, remember that all network interface cards are not created equal. Look at the specifications for token ring and Ethernet cards carefully before choosing. Those that are more expensive include onboard memory buffering, high-speed caching, and onboard processor optimization. These cards will handle all of your Internet traffic, not just that of a client.

Implement an aggressive backup policy on your firewall. Learn how to restore NT and the firewall as quickly as possible and practice doing it. Write bulletproof instructions on how to recover from a failure and keep the instructions close to the firewall so that when it crashes, you will be able to recover and get back online.

One last point about firewalls and proxy servers. Just having one does not protect anything. A set of rules that allows access to the resources you want people to access must be carefully defined. You must also define rules that prevent unauthorized access. It may be a good idea to bring a consultant on site to help with firewall configuration.

ADDRESSING AND INTERNET ACCESS ISSUES

A major issue for many organizations is IP address assignment. When my company set up its LANs and WANs, we had no idea we would want to access the Internet. In fact, at that time, commercial organizations were prohibited from using the Internet.

As with many companies that built their internal networks without regard for Internet connectivity, we used Class A IP addresses assigned by the InterNIC to someone else.

There are two potential solutions to the IP address crisis:

- Proxy servers
- NATs

Both are software products that run on a networked computer with direct Internet access. Proxy servers may be bundled with firewalls, but are generally run on a standalone computer. (IBM bundles a proxy server with its IPCS-card supported firewall; current releases of the IBM Firewall include a NAT. As of V4R3, IBM's HTTP server now operates as a native proxy server.)

PROXY SERVERS

A proxy server provides security services to internal clients with outbound access to the Internet. Although some of the benefits of a proxy server are applicable to many Internet applications, the primary application of a proxy server is to provide clients in an internal network with Internet access. A proxy server provides three primary functions:

- IP address sharing
- Content filtering and access controls
- Performance enhancement through caching

A user must be defined to a proxy server as *authorized*. Browsers and other TCP/IP client software is configured to communicate requests to the proxy server. The server then passes the request on to the Internet on behalf of the client. The proxy server must be configured to check each request it receives and determine that the user is authorized to make the request.

The proxy server may be allocated a relatively small number of "legal" IP addresses (i.e. maybe 150 addresses from a Class C pool of 254 addresses). Each client in your network is assigned an internal IP address that is not legal for use on the Internet.

The proxy server issues requests to the Internet on behalf of its users, and temporarily assigns one of its legal IP addresses to the client originating the request. The length of time that a specific client controls the use of the IP address varies with the proxy server software and configurable options available in the software. Some proxy servers use a new IP address for every request from the client to the Internet. Others allocate a user an IP address for a specific duration (e.g. 10 minutes) and renew the use of the IP address as long as the client is active during that interval.

Because proxy servers "share" legal IP addresses with their clients, you can never use or depend upon the IP addresses of your clients to positively identify a user or create the illusion of a session in a stateless environment. America Online is an excellent example. Each request coming to a server from AOL may contain a new IP address. The benefit of this technique is that multiple users can share a very small pool of IP addresses for access to the Web or other Internet applications.

A proxy server allows its administrator to define and implement rules that prohibit users from accessing certain Web sites and IP addresses through *content filtering*. A great deal of planning and thought should go into creating rules that restrict access to various Web sites. It is impossible to find or restrict access to all objectionable content on the Web, and an administrator may find these rules keep users out of valid Internet locations. For example, by filtering URLs, as well as the textual content of Web pages, an administrator could define a rule that prohibits access to any page containing the word "sex." A medical or insurance-oriented company may need to access sites containing information about sex.

Implementing user limitations via a proxy server can be a major administrative task consuming many hours with a minimal return on the investment. A more sensible strategy is to work with your human resources professionals and develop an acceptable use policy for the Internet and its facilities. Treat users as adults, spell out the guidelines, and deal with those who break the rules. (Most proxy servers also allow an administrator to log all sites that a user accesses and produce reports that analyze a user's access to the Internet.)

PROXY SERVER CACHE

Proxy servers are used by major online services such as Prodigy and America Online, because of their cache facility and address sharing. The theory behind proxy server caching is that many users will access the same Web sites and want to view the same information. In theory, if multiple users want to access the same page on the Internet, subsequent users will retrieve the page from the proxy's cache. Also, in theory, it is quicker to serve a page from the proxy's cache than to retrieve it from the Internet. In practice, the benefits obtained from proxy caching are dubious.

The most definitive study on the performance benefits of proxy servers was done by the Network Research Group of the Computer Science Department of Virginia Tech. They published a paper titled "Caching Proxies: Limitations and Potentials." This paper concludes: "Our main findings are (1) that with our workloads a proxy has a 30–50% maximum possible hit rate no matter how it is designed; (2) that when a cache is full and a document is replaced, classic least-recently-used (LRU) is a poor policy, but simple variations can dramatically improve hit rate and reduce cache size; (3) that a proxy server really functions as a second-level cache, and its hit rate may tend to decline with time after initial loading, given a more or less constant set of users; and (4) that certain modifications of proxy-server configuration parameters for a cache may have little benefit[1]." Although a proxy server can be used to share a limited number of legal IP addresses for outbound use, it cannot support inbound mapping of addresses.

By design, proxy servers should not cache secure sockets layer (SSL) encrypted pages or pages requiring client authentication to access the site. If clients access secure authenticated sites, evaluate proxy utilization carefully.

If it is desirable to use proxy servers in your organization and you have many separate geographic locations, you may want to look at the IBM HTTP Server's Proxy function . The IBM HTTP Server when run as a proxy servers may be run on computers located throughout your organization, with users accessing the closest proxy server via a high-speed LAN instead of a slower WAN. IBM provides a mechanism to synchronize user information and cached pages via its lightweight directory access protocol (LDAP).

Another use of proxy servers is as a front-end for your Web servers, for reverse proxy access. This rather sophisticated use of proxy servers allows an external Internet user to access proxy server, which in turn accesses one or more mirrored Web servers behind the proxy. This scenario is beneficial if guaranteed access to your Web servers is critical. It requires mirrored or replicated physical AS/400s behind the proxy server.

When looking at proxy servers, examine the proxy server's policy towards refreshing page content. Some proxy servers refresh during non-peak times using a batch *look-up and refresh algorithm*. When users attempt to access news service pages or stock quota-

1 This paper is available at www.cs.vt.edu/~chitra/pubs.html.

tion pages, where it's essential that the page be updated constantly, a proxy server must be able to check for updated pages on every access to the proxy server and download only the most recently updated copy—an approach that seems to defeat the caching concept.

Additional cautions deal with proxy servers and streaming audio and video services. Many of these services will not work with some proxy servers. If you need access to streaming audio or video, Net Phone, or network conferencing software, be careful to select a proxy server that will not prohibit users from accessing such a service.

Proxy servers may be beneficial to Internet e-business, but be careful that the cost is not greater than the benefit, and be sure to factor into your evaluation the cost of proxy administration.

NETWORK ADDRESS TRANSLATORS

NAT software is built into many firewalls and the AS/400. The NAT deals effectively with the issue of internal-to-legal IP address translation and the sharing of IP addresses between a small pool of legal addresses with many of clients inside your network. NAT is very efficient and fast because it does not impose logical rules or restrictions on user access to network resources. It is a very low-level protocol-oriented function and simply uses a rule base to translate internal to external addresses and vice versa.

A significant benefit of NAT is the ability to map a legal Internet address to an internal client's internal address to allow access to the PC from the Internet. A user then can access critical documents or spreadsheets stored on the hard disk of a workstation from home via a dial-up Internet connection.

NATs are included with the Guardian firewall, Sun's Firewall-1, and many other standalone firewalls running on UNIX and NT platforms. With V4R3, IBM ported its NAT software to the AS/400 firewall.

ADDITIONAL READING

Building Internet Firewalls, D. Brent Chapman and Elizabeth D. Zwickey. O'Reilly & Associates Inc., ISBN 1-56592-124-0.

Firewalls and Internet Security: Repelling the Wily Hacker, William R. Cheswick and Steven M. Bellovin. Addison-Wesley, ISBN 0-201-63357-4.

Internetworking with TCP/IP—Volume I: Principles, Protocols, and Architecture, Douglas E. Comer. Prentice-Hall, Inc., ISBN 0-13-216987-8.

IBM SecureWay: AS/400 and the Internet, (G325-6321).

`Www.ibm.com/Security` (IBM's general-purpose site on security issues).

Domain Name Servers (DNS)

Domain name servers (DNS) translate numeric IP addresses into meaningful names. When a browser contacts its specified DNS server, the DNS looks up the English-language name and returns a numerical IP address that browser uses to access the server.

Let's look at the domain name portion of the URL `www.testcase.boulder.ibm.com`. The domain name is read from right to left, with major components separated by periods. In our example, *.com* tells us that this URL is a commercial United States domain. IBM is the name of the commercial domain. The name *ibm.com* is referred to as the domain name and is owned by the IBM Corporation. IBM has hundreds of machines and servers operating under the domain *ibm.com*. The name *boulder* is a subnet in the *ibm.com* network. A subnet identifies a group of machines, sometimes at a specific location. *testcase* is the name of a specific server in the *boulder* subnet of the *ibm.com* domain. *www* denotes a Web server running on *testcase*.

The *www* designation is actually (depending upon DNS entries) irrelevant unless the machine hosts multiple Web servers and Web sites. You can generally locate a URL named `www.testcase.boulder.ibm.com` by typing only `testcase.boulder.ibm.com`. The latter form assumes that the Web server is running on the default port 80 on the machine *testcase*.

You can look up the domain and find that it is owned by a company called International Business Machines Inc. by accessing the InterNIC[1] at `rs.internic.net` and using the WHOIS utility[2].

```
Record created on 19-Mar-86.
   Database last updated on 16-Nov-97 05:08:12 EDT.
   Domain servers in listed order:
   NS.WATSON.IBM.COM          198.81.209.2
   NS.AUSTIN.IBM.COM          192.35.232.34
   NS.ALMADEN.IBM.COM         198.4.83.35
   NS2.UK.IBM.COM             194.196.0.201

The InterNIC Registration Services Host contains ONLY Internet Informa-
tion (Networks, ASNs, Domains, and POCs).
Please use the whois server at nic.ddn.mil for MILNET Information.
```

Figure 6.1: WHOIS display for ibm.com.

Figure 6.1 shows the WHOIS display for `ibm.com` from `rs.internic.net`. When your browser wants to locate a computer in the IBM network, it is pointed to `ns.watson.ibm.com` at 198.81.209.2 This computer then very likely points to another DNS server that handles the `boulder.ibm.com` section of IBM's network. With the NSLOOKUP utility program[3], a user can interrogate the DNS servers directly.

In Figure 6.2, NSLOOKUP explains that the authoritative DNS server for `boulder.ibm.com` is called `ns.boulder.ibm.com`

---

1 The InterNIC is a cooperative activity between the National Science Foundation, AT&T, and Network Solutions Inc.

2 Network Toolbox is an excellent $19 toolkit that includes a WHOIS utility and other Internet utility functions. From the J. Rivers Corporation, it can be downloaded on a trial basis from \www.jriver.com.

3 IBM includes an NSLOOKUP command on V4R2 of OS/400. Another excellent tool is called Cyberkit, available free from www.tucows.com. This product includes an NSLOOKUP utility.

```
Answer Section:
   Name=boulder.ibm.com
   Type=NS, Class=1, TTL=43200, RDLENGTH=5
   Name Server=ns.boulder.ibm.com
   Name=boulder.ibm.com
   Type=NS, Class=1, TTL=43200, RDLENGTH=7
   Name Server=rock.boulder.ibm.com
   Name=boulder.ibm.com
   Type=SOA, Class=1, TTL=723, RDLENGTH=35
   Name Server=ns.boulder.ibm.com, Mailbox=postmaster.boulder.ibm.com
   Serial=98100811, Refresh=3600, Retry=600
   Expire=86400, Minimum=900
Authority Records Section:
   Name=boulder.ibm.com
   Type=NS, Class=1, TTL=43200, RDLENGTH=2
   Name Server=ns.boulder.ibm.com   < watson points to this server
   Name=boulder.ibm.com
   Type=NS, Class=1, TTL=43200, RDLENGTH=2
   Name Server=rock.boulder.ibm.com
Additional Records Section:
   Name=ns.boulder.ibm.com
   Type=A, Class=1, TTL=43200, RDLENGTH=4
   IP Address=198.17.57.70
   Name=rock.boulder.ibm.com
   Type=A, Class=1, TTL=43200, RDLENGTH=4
   IP Address=192.147.13.65
```

Figure 6.2: NSLOOKUP on boulder.ibm.com.

In Figure 6.3, we find that `testcase.boulder.ibm.com` is a host located at 198.17.57.67.

```
Header:
   ID=50847, QR=Response, Opcode=QUERY, RCODE=NO ERROR
   Authoritative Answer=Yes, Truncation=No
   Recursion Desired=Yes, Recursion Available=Yes
   QDCOUNT=1, ANCOUNT=1, NSCOUNT=2, ARCOUNT=2
Question:
   Name=testcase.boulder.ibm.com, QTYPE=ALL, QCLASS=1
Answer Section:
   Name=testcase.boulder.ibm.com
   Type=A, Class=1, TTL=900, RDLENGTH=4
   IP Address=198.17.57.67          < Address of testcase
```

Figure 6.3: NSLOOKUP on testcase.boulder.ibm.com.

Assuming that we had never looked up a host located at `boulder.ibm.com`, we could look up `ibm.com` at the InterNIC and find `ns.watson.ibm.com`, which would refer us to `ns.boulder.ibm.com`, where we would find *testcase*. We would have to query three DNS servers to locate *testcase*. Our local DNS server would cache the addresses of all of these severs so if, in the future, we wanted to find *testcase* again, we would find it in one lookup. If we wanted to go to another server on the subnet (for example, `support.boulder.ibm.com`), we could go to `ns.boulder.ibm.com` and bypass `ns.watson.ibm.com`.

Domain Name Structure

Domain names fall into two primary categories: organizational tree structure and geographic tree structure. The root of the tree is implied—the Internet itself. The *trunk* of the tree structure is formed by the organizational or geographic categories, and the *branches* are the specific companies and organizations using the domain. The United States has the largest population of domains and host computers, and uses an organizational tree structure to classify domains.Domains are managed by the InterNIC.

The organization structure is the rightmost designation of a URL (i.e. *.com* of `www.as400.ibm.com`). Table 6.1 shows the currently recognized organizational designations.

The geographic structure terminates in a country code. Organizations in the United States may elect to use the geographic structure, but most do not. An example of an organizational domain might be `cancilla.longbeach.ca.us`.

This means that an entity called Cancilla exists in Long Beach, California, in the United States of America. The obvious downside to this structure is the association of your organization with a specific geographic locality, which may present problems for an e-business that deals with international customers.

Table 6.1: Organizational Designations

Name	Meaning
COM	Commercial organizations
EDU	Educational institutions
GOV	Government institutions
ORG	Organization (i.e. non-profit)
MIL	Military groups or units
NET	Major network support centers and ISPs
INT	International organizations

OBTAINING A DOMAIN NAME

When an ISP is asked to register a domain name, the InterNIC's database is searched to determine that the name does not already exist. If the name does not exist, then it may be reserved for your organization for a fee of $70 for the first two years. You may renew the name every two years for an additional $70. A unique domain name may be registered via the facility provided at `www.internic.com` for a fee of $270. (Generally, an ISP registers the name.)

You may search the InterNIC's database of domain names, to ensure that the names you want to use are available. To look up a domain name, go to the InterNIC Web site and select Registration Services. Search the database using the Web-based version of WHOIS, a program for looking up names. You can also Telnet to `rs.internic.net` and log in as Anonymous with a password from your e-mail address. The InterNIC registration services and WHOIS facility have been extremely busy lately due to the increased activity on the Internet; you might have to try several times.

To purchase a domain name directly from the InterNIC, first determine that it is available. If it is, set it up on both a registered primary and secondary DNS server. (It is not possible to register a domain name if it does not exist on both a primary and secondary DNS server first.) Then fill out the InterNIC forms. The request is processed in 24 to 48 hours. This is a bit of a Catch-22 situation: If you don't have a domain name, you can't have a primary and secondary DNS. Generally, your ISP registers your domain for you.

When picking a domain name, get the principal people in your organization involved. In a company named World Wide Widgets, the technical people may want a name that is short, easy to type, and follows technical standards—like `wwwdgt.com`. Do not let these people prevail or you will eventually have to change your domain name when end users get involved. If you are known as the World Wide Widget company, consider `WorldWideWidgets.com`.

You may find that your preferred name has already been taken. The InterNIC will give you the information needed to contact the organization that has registered your preferred name to see if it can be relinquished. Domain names do not fall under the jurisdiction of patents and trademarks. Some unscrupulous folks have profited from the fact that they could register well-known names in the hopes that the companies would eventually want to use them. The company is then forced to buy its own name back from the InterNIC-registered owner to use their brand name as an Internet address.

PLANNING YOUR DOMAIN

Once you have acquired your domain name, you must plan how you name machines located at your site. We will illustrate a typical naming structure that is in general use throughout the Internet. The domain naming system and standards governing naming regulate only the primary domain and type (e.g. `ibm.com`). The guiding principles of subdividing a domain is to pass control to organizational units that are responsible for names within the unit. A guiding principle for names and numbers used throughout the internet is to allow subordinate organizations the ability to administer themselves and remain consistent and compatible with the parent.

A typical structure is *`<host>.<subnet>.<domain>.<type>`*. IBM's `testcase.boulder.ibm.com`conforms to this structure. We know that IBM owns the domain, `ibm.com`, which is registered with the InterNIC. We can infer that *boulder* is an organizational unit forming a subnet with administrative control over those computers. We know that Boulder, Colorado, is the location of IBM's data center providing computer services for its international support organization.

Because *testcase* is the last, or low-order name, we can infer that it is a host. Another familiar IBM URL is `www.as400.rochester.ibm.com` This is the address for IBM's AS/400 development laboratory in Rochester, Minnesota. Note that *rochester* implies a subnet in IBM's overall naming structure. In this case, *as400* may imply an additional subnet in the Rochester facility and the *www* further qualifies the host. This naming convention could also mean that there is a machine called `as400` at `rochester.ibm.com` that runs a Web server named *www*.

A point to remember is that domain naming components do not have to refer to a real computer. They can refer to a software server running on a physical computer. A single computer may run many Web servers in the same or different domains.

Multiple domains on the same computer are standard for ISPs who host Web sites for others. It is also common for large organizations where brand names are well known and the company name is not. Foodmaker Inc. owns the Jack in the Box restaurant chain and the Coco's restaurant chains. Most people would look for "Jack in the Box" or "Coco's" when trying to access information on these businesses. Foodmaker Inc. might run two Web servers on the same computer with the names `www.jackinthebox.com`and `www.cocos.com`.

Before deciding on a naming structure for an internal network, look at your organization's current and future needs to connect computers to the Internet. Let's examine some typical host services and possible domain name assignments for a fictitious company called Acme that owns the domain name `acme.com`.

Acme has two AS/400s at its central data center. One is configured as the primary Internet server, running a Web server, mail server, and FTP server. The second is the company's primary business machine and is not directly connected to the Internet. The Webmaster/Web site developer also has a Windows 95 PC that he needs to access when he works from home. Let's examine the names that ACME might use (there is no right or wrong way to set this up).

First of all, the Production machine is named PROD, the Internet machine is called GATEWAY, and the PC is called FRED. (My apologies to the legitimate owner of the IP address 206.101.40.xxx. I am using this Class C address block for illustration purposes only and it is not to be construed as a valid set of Internet IP addresses.)

Table 6.2: The Acme Company's Domain Name Structure

Machine	Domain Name	IP Address	Port	Service
GATEWAY	acme.com	206.101.40.1	80	Web server
GATEWAY	www.acme.com	206.101.40.1	80	Alias for Web server
GATEWAY	pop.acme.com	206.101.40.1	110	POP3 Mail Server
GATEWAY	smtp.acme.com	206.101.40.1	25	SMTP Mail Server
GATEWAY	ftp.acme.com	206.101.40.1	20/21	FTP server
GATEWAY	news.acme.com	206.101.40.1	109	USENET news server
GATEWAY	ns.acme.com	206.101.40.1	139	DNS server
FRED	fred.acme.com	206.101.40.10	80	Web server
FRED	fred.acme.com	206.101.40.10	20/21	FTP server

This configuration uses two IP addresses to uniquely identify the two machines. It sets the mail sever to `smtp.acme.com`, which allows mail to be sent from the mail-server machine. Incoming mail is retrieved from `pop.acme.com`, which allows users to use the e-mail address structure `user@acme.com`. It establishes the prefix www to the Web site name (`www.acme.com`). It also allows a user to access the Web server at `acme.com`[4].

If a network has multiple Internet connections, be careful with names. When there are multiple paths that a computer can take to get to the Internet, or you wish to receive mail on multiple machines that are connected to the Internet, the naming becomes much more complex. Unless you have a really good reason to support multiple connections, don't. If you have many computers that are widely distributed geographically, follow IBM's examples (fully documented in the *AS/400 TCP/IP Configuration and Operation* manual (GG24-3442-02)).

HOST NAME TABLES

In the early days of the Internet, the InterNIC maintained a simple file called HOSTS.TXT. All computers connected to the Internet copied this file to their local file systems. The HOSTS file had a couple of serious drawbacks: (1) it had to be administered centrally by the InterNIC, which became impossible, and (2) it had to be downloaded to each host on the Internet.

Almost all computers that support TCP/IP still have a HOSTS file. The AS/400 uses the HOSTS file when no DNS is configured. You can put the AS/400's name, along with any other names to identify to an AS/400, in the file. Note that this file is used exclusively by an AS/400. It cannot be used to resolve names for other computers on a LAN.

When you configure TCP/IP, provide the address of the primary and secondary DNS servers. The AS/400 can be instructed to look up names in the DNS servers or in your HOSTS names file and the DNS server.

When using a PC with Windows 95/98 or Windows NT you may have a file called HOSTS (no extension) in your Windows directory. If you do not have a file named HOSTS you will have a file called HOSTS.SAM, which looks like this:

The HOSTS.SAM file has one valid entry in it. This is the 127.0.0.1 entry for localhost. Localhost is a standard TCP/IP address and name for the computer where the hosts file

4 The www prefix is unnecessary. It was used in the early days of the Web to differentiate Web servers from other servers but has since become obsolete. People are still convinced it's necessary, however, so most will persist in typing www.acme.com to access acme.com.

resides—each computer is known by this same localhost address. You can enter additional IP addresses and domain name entries after the entry for localhost. The browser, and any other TCP/IP server that runs on the computer, will look in the HOSTS file before doing a remote DNS lookup. After you add your entries, save the file as HOSTS (no extension).

```
# Copyright (c) 1994 Microsoft Corp.
#
# This is a sample HOSTS file used by Microsoft TCP/IP for Chicago
#
# This file contains the mappings of IP addresses to host names. Each
# entry should be kept on an individual line. The IP address should
# be placed in the first column followed by the corresponding host name.
# The IP address and the host name should be separated by at least one
# space.
#
# Additionally, comments (such as these) may be inserted on individual
# lines or following the machine name denoted by a '#' symbol.
#
# For example:
#
#      102.54.94.97     rhino.acme.com          # source server
#       38.25.63.10     x.acme.com              # x client host
127.0.0.1       localhost
```

Figure 6.4: HOSTS.SAM file.

A HOSTS file also exists on the AS/400 or any other computer you intend to connect to a TCP/IP network. Access the HOSTS file on the AS/400 via the CFGTCP command and select the HOST Names options. Instruct the AS/400 to always look in the local HOSTS file before doing an external DNS lookup on a remote DNS server.

The table on the AS/400 is slightly different from the Windows 95/98 version. The AS/400 asks for an IP address and then allows a user to enter multiple names for the address. In Windows 95/98, each name–address combination must be listed on a separate line.

I have participated in a raging debate on the merits of using the HOSTS file. The argument against is that it is static and must be maintained by a system administrator. It is easy to forget that names exist in the table. This can become a problem if names are changed later. If you have a local DNS server, then don't use the AS/400 HOSTS tables. This is a point that we can all agree about. Every AS/400 since V4R2 has DNS server software built in.

I contend that names for the AS/400 can and should be defined in the HOSTS file if you do not have a local DNS. This allows server software to identify itself locally without having to do a remote DNS lookup at an ISP's site. Response times are improved greatly, and as long as you limit the names stored in the table to those by which the machine is known, the administrative effort will be minimal.

DOMAIN NAME SERVERS

Names are defined to a DNS using the BIND language. There are three data components to a DNS:

- A forward lookup file that maps domain names to IP addresses
- A reverse lookup file that maps IP addresses to domain names
- Cache storage for previously accessed domain names

To understand how the DNS works, remember that you had to define a primary and secondary DNS server IP address to your TCP/IP configuration when you set it up on the AS/400. You had to do the same thing (or at least your dialup ISP's installation software did) when you installed a browser on your personal computer.

Your Computer Must Know the IP Address of a DNS Server

Domain name lookups occur at sub-second speeds, even on slow-speed dial-up connections. In the WHOIS lookup we did on *ibm.com*, we found that the InterNIC listed four DNS servers for *ibm.com*. Each undoubtedly distributes its DNS responsibilities to lower levels of the organization. It is very likely that *boulder* and *rochester* have their own DNS server.

If the DNS server specified has never looked up an *ibm.com* name before, it must go to the InterNIC and find the address of IBM's primary DNS server, which should be able to return the address. The DNS server then caches the address for future reference.

Name and Address DNS records have expiration dates that inform remote DNS servers how long they can safely keep the names in cache. DNS gets complicated when names are changed. It can take two weeks or longer for a changed name to find its way around the Internet.

The DNS uses software distributed free for UNIX servers, bundled with Windows NT servers, and packaged as part of the IBM Firewall for the AS/400. (As of V4R2, there is a native (free) DNS server on the AS/400.) In all cases, the DNS uses a couple of files to accomplish *forward look-ups* (i.e. you know the domain name but not the IP address) or *backward look-ups* (i.e. you know the IP address but not the domain name). These are text files that contain several record types.

The type A record is a standard domain record consisting of a domain name and IP address. The server may also contain MX records that contain the name and addresses of mail servers for the domain. A mail server for the domain may be either the same or different from the computer that hosts the Web servers, FTP, Telnet, etc.

The NT server includes a DNS server. Implement a DNS server to identify client machines in a private network by name, both for internal use and possible external use. Otherwise, every TCP/IP device in a system will need its own HOSTS file, with the names of all other machines in the network. You and your ISP can configure the ISP's DNS server to point to your DNS server for local name lookups only. Major lookups, such as your Web server, mail server, etc., can be done in the ISP's DNS.

DNS configuration is critical and difficult. The documentation has a definite UNIX bias. To see a good explanation of a fairly complex DNS configuration and explanation of the BIND language see: *www.ludd.luth.se/~kavli/BIND-FAQ.html*. This site is UNIX oriented, but BIND is BIND regardless of platform.

DO YOU NEED A DNS SERVER?

If you are running a large TCP/IP network with multiple TCP/IP devices, the answer to the question is *definitely*! If, on the other hand, you are running a small network with few TCP/IP devices, the answer is *probably not*. Even if you are running a very large network, the question arises as to what *your* DNS should contain and what *your ISP's* DNS should contain. If your ISP does not provide DNS services, get a new ISP!

My personal recommendation is to use your ISP's DNS if possible. If you have a large number of TCP/IP machines, then put in your own servers (yes, plural, as in at least two). If you have your own DNS, I suggest you take responsibility only for your own names and use your ISP's DNS for external lookups. You may want to work with a consultant to set up a DNS.

DNS is so critical to the operation of an Internet connection that it is extremely rare to find shops that do not have two DNS servers. Generally, a computer running a DNS server is not used for any other processing. It is critical that no one has to wait for a response and to ensure that your users or your site do not go offline when a DNS server crashes (notice the word *when* not *if*).

IBM's integrated Firewall for the AS/400 includes a DNS Server that is suitable and secure enough to support external DNS on your AS/400.

The native DNS server for the AS/400 bundled with V4R2 is appropriate for managing internal names on your intranet, but it is not secure enough (V4R2 and V4R3) to run as an external DNS server. Go to IBM's INFOCENTER on their AS/400 Web site at: publib.boulder.ibm.com/html/as400/infocenter.htm and search for "ZONE TRANSFERS."

On October 31, 1997, Eugene Kashpureff (now living in a federal penitentiary) rerouted the InterNIC to his own computers, which he called AlterNIC. He accomplihed this with a DNS facility called Zone Transfer. What that means is a hacker can take over your DNS and route folks to strange places when they access a domain name that you control on your DNS Server. IBM has implemented adequate protection within the DNS Server, but you must implement this protection to be protected.

DHCP SERVERS

The number of TCP/IP-based devices in an organization is rapidly increasing. Personal computers, Network Stations, your AS/400s, and even printers now all have IP addresses. Managing the assignment of IP addresses can be an administrative nightmare requiring rigorous record keeping. If you inadvertently assign two devices the same address, one will fail. Finding the offender can be extremely difficult. Dynamic Host Configuration Protocol (DHCP) offers an automated solution to address management.

DHCP is a standardized protocol that dynamically assigns IP addresses, based on a set of rules, to devices in a TCP/IP network whenever a device inserts itself into (logs onto) the network.

By installing a DHCP server, you can automate this process. Client computers (or other networking devices) locate the DHCP server and negotiate an IP address assignment with it. The dynamically assigned IP address remains allocated to the device until it powers off and removes itself from the network[1].

1 A comprehensive explanation of both DNS and DHCP is available at the www.isotro.ca/ Web site. ISOTRO is a subsidiary of Bay Networks. RFC1154 is the specification for DHCP. You may want to also see RFC1533 and RFC1545, both of which are concerned with DHCP and BOOTP interoperability. BOOTP is defined via RFC951.

The bottom line is that as a TCP/IP network grows and a large number of clients (such as IBM's new Network Station, printers, or TCP/IP-based purchase) are added, you will need to control IP address assignment. Windows NT and the IBM Firewall include DHCP servers. A DHCP server is shipped with the AS/400 as of V4R2 as a no-charge component of TCP/IP utilities.

Once a DHCP server is installed, you can define rules so that certain devices will always be allocated IP addresses from a pre-defined block, permanently assign an IP address to a specific device, or dynamically assign addresses whenever a device inserts into the network after being powered up.

A properly implemented DHCP server can save countless hours of network problem analysis and resolution. While DHCP will handle most of IP address assignments, you will still have to manually assign addresses to Web servers, mail servers, and other servers that require a permanent static address.

Another service of DHCP is the ability to work with devices like the Network Station to load the operating system from the DHCP server to the device when the device is attached to the network and turned on. The device has client DHCP software built-in that locates a DHCP server, obtains an IP address, and then requests that the server send it a copy of its operating system image. BOOTP also handles sending devices a copy of their operating system, but lacks the sophistication necessary to handle address assignment.

Douglas Comer describes BOOTP and DHCP in detail in his book *Internetworking with TCP/IP—Volume I: Principles, Protocols, and Architectures* (Prentice-Hall, 1995).

5250 Terminal Emulation on the Web

Unless you are a new AS/400 installation, you probably have a substantial investment in 5250 terminal-based applications. The AS/400 offers several facilities to Web-enable these applications. You can also provide remote users with 5250 terminal emulation, including full printer support via a standard dial-up Internet connection. This chapter discusses several alternative methods of capitalizing on existing 5250-based applications via the Internet. A key benefit of providing Telnet access is the cost savings of Internet access over dedicated leased line connections or dial-up access where you pay long-distance telephone charges. You can connect via any $19-per-month Internet service provider.

Telnet

Telnet is a simple terminal emulation program provided and supported by most vendors of TCP/IP-based systems. It uses a character-based terminal display. As is the case with all Internet applications, a server is required. OS/400's TCP/IP implementation provides an excellent Telnet server that can be configured by selecting applications on the AS/400's TCP/IP configuration menu. Start the Telnet server with the STRTCPSVR command.

The Telnet protocol has two standards for passing control and functional options between clients. The first, basic standard must be supported by all clients and severs. The second, more advanced standard is reserved for more advanced systems. Although the AS/400 supports standard Telnet protocols[1] via clients such as the Windows 95 Telnet client (which emulates a VT100 terminal), best results can be obtained when a Telnet variant called TN5250 is used as a client. (Mainframe computers use a terminal emulator called TN3270. IBM created TN5250 or Telnet 5250 (a variant of TN3270) as an open standard.) The primary advantage of TN5250 is the fact that all of the keys on a 5250 terminal are supported via your keyboard.

Client Access/400 V3R1M2 and the new Client Access Express have a superb Telnet client. Not only can you assign specific terminal IDs to TCP/IP TN5250 devices, but you can create and name printer devices that can print via Host Print Transform (including AFP/DS files) to a PC-attached printer.

Telent (both clients and servers) implemented with V4R4 provide full SSL encryption. Prior to V4R4, SSL support for Telnet must be obtained with PTFs. Care must be taken to protect the transmitted data when running Telnet without SSL. The native Telnet clients and IBM's Telnet server do not encrypt data transmitted over the Internet. If you do not use SSL, it is possible (although not likely) for someone to "sniff" user IDs and passwords from a Telnet session and compromise a system. Carefully evaluate the security risk before turning Telnet (without SSL) loose in an organization. On the positive side, UNIX users have used Telnet (with its inherent security weaknesses) for years without significant impact on most commercial businesses. I would not send my bank account number or credit card number out onto the Internet via a non-secure Telnet session, but I would trust it with my user ID and password.

CLIENT ACCESS/400

IBM's Client Access/400 provides an exceptional Telnet client. Once CA/400 is installed on your client's PC, the client may access an AS/400 via any Internet provider, run a PC/5250 session, and connect with excellent performance and full terminal functionality. CA/400 provides many functions other than terminal emulation, including shared-folders-type connectivity and allowing a remote TCP/IP client to attach to the IFS directory. All

1 The Telnet protocol is defined in RFC 854. For more information, look at RFCs 854, 764, 856, 857, 858,859, 860, 861, 884, 1041, 1091, 1096, 1097, 1184, 1372, 1416, and 1572. TN3270 is defined in RFCs 1576, 1646, 1647, and 1041.

files to which the user is authorized appear in Windows 95/98's Network Neighborhood. With CA/400, file transfer, Open Database Connectivity (ODBC) support, and more are all supported on an Internet-attached PC. CA/400 has become an excellent TCP/IP client that elevates remote computing to a new level. CA/400 is extremely stable and very reliable.

CA/400 also allows users to run SNA over TCP/IP via the AnyNet/400 interface. AnyNet (which comes with OS/400 at no charge) must be configured and enabled. Then select AnyNet as the method of connecting to the AS/400 when the client is configured. AnyNet encapsulates SNA in TCP/IP packets and therefore provides all of the support of a local SNA device. This means that a PC can define virtual printers and print via the Internet.

Newer versions of Client Access/400 provide all features via TCP/IP connectivity. There is no need to run an SNA connection between a remote user and the AS/400. One hundred percent functionality can be obtained from Client Access/400 via TCP/IP. In V4R4, IBM announced Client Access Express, which is a variant of Client Access/400. It is a full TCP/IP version of CA/400 and does not include SNA connectivity. In case anyone had any doubts, SNA is now a relic of the past. TCP/IP is the communications protocol of today and the future. And because it offers SSL, which is the key to Internet security, it is IBM's preferred product.

I personally recommend that you use CA/400's TCP/IP connectivity exclusively. Most of the problems encountered with CA/400 in the past were in the SNA router product bundled with the client software. Additionally, the TCP/IP software occupies less disk space and runs much faster than the SNA support. When installing Client Access/400 choose advanced options and deselect SNA support. Or better yet, run Client Access Express (TCP/IP only).

Although other vendors provide good Telnet 5250 applications, none provides all of the features IBM provides via CA/400. CA/400 is invaluable in helping develop and administer Web sites. CA/400 is the only product I have found that gives complete access and control of the IFS root directories from Windows 95/98/NT. Using the Network Neighborhood, the AS/400 becomes an extension of the Windows 95/98/NT file system. This can be accomplished through any supported connection method (dial-up ASYNC, Internet-based TCP/IP, or SNA via local, dial-up, or AnyNet connectivity).

When Client Access Express is implemented, access to the AS/400 file systems is provided via IBM's superb new NetServer facility. It uses the Windows 95/98/NT client software to handle the client side connection and gives full file sharing and printer support via Windows client software. This important enhancement reduces the size and resources required on PCs and greatly improves performance and functionality. If you are not familiar with NetServer, visit IBM's Technical Studio and Information center on the Web and learn how to configure and run NetServer. NetServer is free; it's built-in; and it may prove to be a cost effective alternative to traditional LAN servers.

IBM WSG

The IBM Workstation Gateway (WSG) provides 5250-to-HTML translation, allowing a user to access 5250 applications via a Web browser. WSG supports HTML embedded in DDS display files. It does not map 5250 function keys to the browser. Printing is accomplished via the browser. It is free and included with V3R2, V3R6, and above as part of the TCP/IP package offering, but is not a particularly robust offering. IBM discontinued this product at V4R2 and now offers its Secureway and Host On Demand Java-based product.

SECUREWAY HOST ON DEMAND

A new entry into the AS/400 world is IBM's Secureway Host on Demand. This IBM product provides robust and high quality 5250 and 3270 terminal emulation and printer support through a Java client.

Java clients can be downloaded from a Web site or distributed via e-mail or other media and installed on the client workstation. The client will check for updates on the server and update itself as required.

Secureway Host on Demand allow you to configure sessions on one or many AS/400 hosts within a network and provide a single gateway to these hosts via a Web site. An administrator must enroll users and provide authorization to the machines that the users will need to access. Secureway implements SSL and digital certificates to encrypt and protect access to the servers that a user has access to.

Administration is simplified via Secureway's exploitation of the Lightweight Directory Access Protocol (LDAP), which is rapidly becoming an open systems standard for controlling user, security, and configuration information across heterogeneous platforms. Lotus Domino, Secureway Host on Demand, and the IBM HTTP Server all implement full LDAP support.

LDAP is completely user definable and can be configured to share information across many machines in a network. LDAP servers can be instructed to replicate their data and any changes made to their data or to look in other LDAP servers on the network.

The client looks very much like the Client Access Express client. If you have 3270 access requirements, Host On Demand can be configured to provide users with both 5250 and 3270 sessions. Terminal sessions can be configured to provide direct connections (not just passthru connections) to any authorized AS/400 in the network.

Host on Demand is the only Web-based terminal emulation product I have seen that provides full printer support. You can configure Host on Demand on a server machine and restrict remote access to this machine while allowing Host on Demand to provide secure access including secure printer access to the rest of the machines. This is an incredibly important feature. I strongly advocate use of a separate AS/400 to act as an Internet gateway and server machine. The production AS/400 is accessible to the Internet gateway machine, but this causes problems with routing print to a remote user. Now, with Host On Demand the problem is solved.

Host on Demand is also extensible. Because it is written in Java, its capabilities can be expanded or custom routines added to enhance the functionality, look, and feel of applications. The product is an extra cost product not bundled with OS/400, but well worth investigating for serious remote 5250 and printer access.

I/NET WEBULATOR/400

I/Net provides a robust 5250-to-HTML translation feature that includes SSL encryption and extensive security features. The major feature of I/Net's Webulator software is that 5250 screens can be turned into HTML webpages.

MOCHASOFT TN5250 JAVA APPLET

A company from Denmark called MochaSoft has produced one of the most cost-effective and spectacular Web-based TN5250 emulators I have ever seen.

The MochaSoft TN5250 Java applet is placed in an IFS directory on the AS/400 that runs the Web server. The Java applet loads and provides an almost perfect 5250 session. This is a complete terminal emulator with function keys. The applet can be configured to run as a pop-up that can be sized to nearly full screen, or as an embedded applet in your HTML page.

Mocha soft sells an unrestricted site license for $250. They can be reached at `www.mochasoft.de`. You can download a fully functional trial version. The product is well supported via e-mail.

The downside of this product is that it has no printer support and very limited per session configuration. A user may not customize their session and save it. It does not provide SSL encryption.

E-MAIL

Electronic mail is the lifeblood of e-commerce. An e-commerce site provides basic information for customers, vendors, and others who do business with a company. Although your Web site may answer many questions previously addressed by telephone, it can't take the place of direct communication between your staff and customer base. E-mail allows employees to control their time, while still providing excellent service to customers and business contacts. (Internet etiquette requires that e-mail messages be responded to within 24 hours. If it is not possible to answer a question in 24 hours, then reply with a message indicating when (e.g. two days, next Monday, etc.) a definitive answer can be expected.

TCP/IP for the AS/400 includes a SMTP server and a POP3 server. We will discuss these, as well as other mail handling services that are available for the AS/400 in the following sections.

To get started, decide which machine will be the primary mail server. Also determine if your ISP provides mail services, such as mail forwarding, and if you want to use their services.

Once you have decided which machine will be the primary mail server, get a domain name. Have the administrator of the DNS server (your ISP if you don't have an in-house DNS server) set up a mail exchanger (MX) record in the DNS that identifies the mail server's IP address.

There are no hard and fast rules about the machine that runs the mail server. All, some, or only one AS/400 can be mail servers. The suggestions given here are for a simple system; for complex needs—requiring multiple mail servers—you may want to get assistance from a consultant.

You can run IBM's built-in SMTP and POP3 servers as the basic e-mail handling software. I used this approach for more than three years before migrating to Lotus Domino.

In making the decision to run a mail server on a production AS/400, you must address and deal with the following risks:

- *Attack by denial of service.* This is the most common method by which someone can attack your site. It is simple. The attacker's mail software creates and sends thousands of mail items to the server, overfilling the DASD and shutting down the system. This technique is often compounded by sending mail to an invalid user address on your server (i.e. `Garbage@yourserver.com`). The system becomes overloaded attempting to handle the incoming mail, and because the user address is invalid, the machine must generate error responses to the sender. IBM provides some protection by allowing you to set resource limits for SMTP, which is the underlying mail handling protocol. SMTP then shuts down when the thresholds are met.

- *Mail attachment viruses.* A common practice by hackers is to send an e-mail message containing a binary-file attachment. When double-clicked, the binary file executes a program containing a virus. An extremely nefarious form of attack is a program that, when executed, sends a duplicate e-mail message (with an infected program attached) to everyone in the victim's address book, thus forwarding itself to dozens of unsuspecting victims. The program then destroys the contents of the client's hard disk, often by attacking the PC's boot sector. Some of these viruses are so virulent that they can even cause damage to a user's hard disk.

So, have I scared you away from using e-mail? Not to worry! It's fairly simple to protect an organization from e-mail attacks. First, every machine (including your personal computer at home) that can receive e-mail *must* have a good virus-checking software package installed and kept current. Additionally, a good firewall will have virus-checking software that scans the content of all e-mail received. otus Domino has a third party virus checker available that runs in the Domino enviornment. Firewalls can also detect the type of attacks described above and protect your AS/400 by temporarily blocking the receipt of incoming mail until the attack subsides.

My ISP provides mail protection on my company's behalf by running a mail-forwarding server. Mail is first routed to them and then forwarded to us. If we are attacked, the attack is first detected on the ISP's computer, which is equipped to deal with the attack.

SIMPLE MAIL TRANSPORT PROTOCOL (SMTP)

SMTP is the base transport mechanism upon which all e-mail is made possible. SMTP is an application protocol in the TCP/IP family of applications. Virtually all TCP/IP-capable machines can send and receive e-mail via SMTP.

SMTP is configured via the CFGTCP menu. Select TCP/IP Applications and then select SMTP. In all cases where an AS/400 is to send and receive e-mail via the Internet, SMTP must be configured and started. The AS/400 uses an IBM proprietary facility to handle exchanging mail between many different services including SNADS on the AS/400. This facility is called the Mail Server Framework (MSF), and must be enabled before mail can be processed on the AS/400.

Configuring the SMTP server is a prerequisite to processing mail, but far from the end of the line. Once SMTP is configured and started, the best you can hope for are primitive commands such as SNDDST to send mail. Mail can be retrieved via command also. To get the maximum benefit out of mail on the AS/400, also configure the POP3 server interface to SMTP.

A word of caution regarding SMTP. By definition, SMTP is an unsecured protocol. It does not require a user to log-in to your server to be able to send mail. Anyone that knows the domain name of the SMTP server can use it to send mail. Junk mailers use this technique to hide their true identities. Consider masking the SMTP port on your machine with a firewall, restricting the ability to send mail to specific users.

With release V4R4, IBM has enhanced SMTP to prevent unauthorized IP addresses from sending mail through a server. These enhancements are also available as SMTP enhancement PTFs for V4R3 and below. You must define the addresses that may send mail via your server. I recommend allowing outbound mail only from those users within a secure network. If you have users who need mail access, they can access the POP3 server to receive mail, but should use their dial-up ISP's SMTP server to send mail.

Junk mailers take advantage of the fact that you don't have to log in to an SMTP server to send mail. They purchase dial-up accounts with ISPs to gain Internet access. Then they point their mail-sending software at your SMTP server and send thousands of e-mail messages, which can be traced back to your machine. They steal bandwidth and computing power from you.

With the rapid growth of junk e-mail (SPAM), several Internet vigilante groups have formed to combat senders of junk mail. Two vigilante groups are the Mail Abuse Protection System Realtime Blackhole List (MAPS RBL), and the ORBS spammer database.

MAPS RBL, is an excellent service with a human touch. They take great care to work with sites originating junk-mail transmissions to ensure that the site is not an innocent victim. A site is added to the blacklist when all attempts to prevent mail originating from the site fail. Many large ISPs run mail server software that automatically checks the RBL before allowing a user to send mail via their server. The AS/400 SMTP server will provide access to blacklists in the next release of SMTP.

SMTP Store-and-Forward

Using store-and-forward SMTP technology helps protect theAS/400-based mail server from direct access to the Internet and, in some cases, limits denial-of-service attacks by hostile parties. Store-and-forward also ensures that when your machine is offline for backups, initial program loads (IPLs), or service, mail will be received, stored, and forwarded when the machine is back online.

Most ISPs will provide this service for you The MX domain record for your site will be pointed to the ISP's SMTP server, which is configured to attempt to forward all of your mail to your server if it is available. If the server is not available (i.e. offline) the forwarding server stores your mail for a predetermined and agreed upon period of time. The server constantly checks to see if your server is back online and forwards stored mail to you when you are back online.

Personally, I prefer to place the burden of keeping the server active 24 hours a day, 7 days a week, 365 days a year with the ISP, which should be equipped to provide uninterrupted server with online backup equipment that will immediately pick up your workload when a device fails or is taken offline.

Post Office Protocol VERSION 3 (POP3)

POP3, a server component of client/server e-mail, is in common use today. It requires an intelligent client, such as a personal computer, when implemented on the AS/400. POP3 requires that SMTP be configured and installed. POP3 logically sits on top of SMTP and acts as an incoming mail repository.

The term "post office protocol" is descriptive of the way POP3 operates. The post office receives mail and stores it in a "mailbox." The client goes to the post office, uses a secure mechanism to open the mailbox, and removes the mail. The POP client will periodically log in to the POP server and check to see if there is any mail. The client downloads the mail to the PC and notifies the user that mail has arrived.

All POP3 clients require the following information (the terminology used is from Netscape Communicator, but the concepts are identical):

- Mail Server User Name: The AS/400 user ID (some clients call this the *account name*).
- E-mail Address: The SMTP name and domain name (e.g. `johns@acme.com`).
- Outgoing Mail (SMTP) Server: Most likely the standard domain name.
- Incoming Mail (POP) Server: Again, most likely the standard domain name.

In most clients, there are some options that govern the operation of the client and the server:

- Leave Mail On Server: This downloads a copy of the messages to your PC and leaves the messages on the server for the duration that you have defined in the CFGTCP command for the POP server. The server deletes mail according to your specifications. This option is not normally set unless you use multiple PCs to check your mail. For example, I set this option to "YES" on my home computer so that when I log into my POP server from home I can get and reply to mail, then leave the mail on the server in case I want to file a copy on my PC at the office. I set the option to "NO" on my PC at the office so mail will be deleted from the server.

- Your Real Name: Most clients store your full name so that all mail can carry your real name instead of an often cryptic e-mail address.

- Signature File: You can define a *signature file* containing your name, telephone numbers, mailing address, title, or whatever information you might like attached to messages.

E-MAIL SOFTWARE

There are many software-based POP3 clients available. Lotus Notes, Eudora, Microsoft's Outlook, are among the most popular.

LOTUS DOMINO

Perhaps one of the most significant parts of V4R2 (and later releases) is the implementation of Lotus Domino as a native OS/400 based application. Lotus Domino has previously run on the Netfinity Server (formerly the IPCS card) as an OS/2 application with access to OS/400 data and some services. Today it is a native OS/400 application. As such, it now has robust strength and breadth.

Lotus Domino is the evolution of Lotus Notes. The component that is now called Domino was once the Notes Server. There is still PC-based client software that bears the name "Lotus Notes." The change from Lotus Notes Server to Lotus Domino however, was much more than just a renaming for marketing purposes. Today, it is a robust, platform independent server married to a Web server that can provide virtually all of the services associated with Notes and Domino via HTML and the Web server.

Lotus Domino does everything a good e-mail server should do. It works with its own Notes client; it works with any POP3 mail client; it even provides full e-mail access via HTML on a secure Web site.

Lotus Domino is the only product currently available for the AS/400 that provides IMAP encryption and digital certificate security. This means that you can send an e-mail and be assured that it will not be intercepted and read by an unauthorized person. IMAP provides two specific types of security:

- It uses an encryption algorithm similar to that used by SSL.
- It uses digital certificates for authenticating that the address that you are sending mail to is who you believe it to be.

This second point is an extremely strong argument for using Lotus Domino. When someone tells me to contact Fred Smith at `freds@yourcompany.com`, how will I know that my message gets to the correct person at the correct company? The answer is that unless we are using IMAP and digital certificates, I can never be sure. With digital certificates, the user's identity is authenticated before the mail is sent.

Lotus Domino can communicate with third party clients as well as communicating with its own Notes client. It also provides robust mail handling facilities on the receiving end of the line. I have a marketing mailbox, a claims information mail box, and several other generic email addresses that are published on my Web sites. Lotus contains the built-in logic to assist in analyzing and properly routing mail sent to these generic accounts. Lotus Domino has workflow software built-in to the product, so I can route mail to an entire team of people and ensure that required responses are handled on-time and according to approved procedures.

OFFICEVISION/400 AND 5250 DEVICES

If you are an OfficeVision/400 or JustMail/400 user, you should be considering Lotus Domino, IBM's recommended upgrade path. IBM has announced that OV/400 will no longer be supporter after V4R5. Lotus Domino for the AS/400 has utilities that will help migrate OfficeVision/400 users to Lotus Domino. Lotus Domino may be configured to co-exist with and exchange mail and calendar information between the two products.

A major area of concern that I had when implementing Lotus Domino was how to support users who had old 5250 terminals. Today, most of these terminals have been replaced with IBM Network Stations or Personal Computers, but I still have over 100 terminals.

There is a product called EverGreen/400 by Inventive Designs. This product provides a 5250 interface to the Lotus Domino mail and calendar environment and is an excellent transition tool.

File Transfer Protocol (FTP) 10

FTP is a valuable means of transferring files between Internet-attached computers. FTP can replace costly leased-line transfers of large files between organizations or locations within the same organization, and is rapidly replacing leased-line or dial-up EDI. You may find that FTP is an efficient and effective means of transferring data around the world between remote offices. You can write batch initiated file transfer using the FTP CL commands provided with the FTP client,

Both client and server software is required, and OS/400 is shipped with both. Using the client software, users can logon to a remote site and send or receive files if the remote site is running FTP server software. By default, AS/400 security is honored for FTP, so users must logon to the system using a valid user profile and password. Once logged on, users can access any resources they are authorized to access.

An important security tip to consider when configuring FTP is to turn off Remote Command capabilities in the user profile (WRKUSRPRF command, F10 Additional Parameters). Used in this manner, FTP is extremely safe for authenticated users. A word of caution for sensitive file transfers, though: FTP does not support encrypted data transmission via standard Internet connections. However, in V4R4 you can use the new virtual private network (VPN) support to provide a secure encrypted link over which FTP may be used between partner sites. FTP does not support SSL in V4R4 or any other version. It probably never will as the protocol does not have provisions for it.

FTP can be used effectively in a Web site by linking to FTP-type URLs on the server. Use CGI scripts to calculate specific locations for upload documents such as an application for insurance (i.e. *Ftp://mydomain.com/uploads/newapps/*).

ANONYMOUS FTP

Anonymous FTP is quite prevalent on the Internet. Many users have visited sites and downloaded a file using anonymous FTP. Anonymous FTP sites are identified by the URL *FTP://ftp1.xxx.com/pub*. This type of URL tells the browser to use FTP as its transfer protocol, access the file transfer server located at *ftp1.xxx.com*, and go to the */pub* directory. FTP offers a effective method of delivering large files of information to customers.

Anonymous is so named because users are required to logon to the FTP server using the user profile name ANONYMOUS (most browser and FTP client software does this automatically). An anonymous FTP server generally wants users to enter their e-mail address in the password field that gives the server's operator an indication of who is using the server. Most anonymous FTP servers check for the "@" character to verify that an e-mail address has been entered. More sophisticated servers do a reverse lookup on the e-mail address to verify that it is valid. By default, the server operator generally provides public download directories and may provide a public upload directory.

IBM has not provided any direct support for anonymous FTP. It has provided user exits, where you can code your own support for FTP. Samples are provided at IBM's Technical Studio Web site: *www.as400.ibm.com/developer/ebiz/nc_faq_exitpgm.html*.

Those who allow anonymous users need to code an IBM FTP exit program, which limits access to specific directories and defaults the user to a specific directory when he/she logs in. The exit restricts access to all other directories, files, or programs on the system.

For those planning to use anonymous FTP, I suggest looking at Alliance FTP from *www.patownsend.com*. Pat Townsend has automated the whole process of providing security exits. We use it on the *www.ignite400.org* Web site. Install his product and then use 5250 screens to define FTP security rules.

FTP SERVER

The AS/400 includes an FTP server. Documentation on the server can be found in the *TCP/IP Configuration* manual and the ITSO redbook *Cool Title about the Internet*. By default, a user must log in with a valid AS/400 user ID and password, which provides access to the directory defined in the user profile (or QGPL, if no directory is specified). Anonymous FTP is not directly supported. (An exit program must be written to provide anonymous FTP.) Exit programs are discussed in the above-mentioned manuals. Because of the security risk of anonymous FTP, consult the sections in the manuals that cover user exits that enhance FTP security.

With V4R4, the FTP server is fully compatible with most common FTP clients and the UNIX FTP servers currently available. V4R4 also introduces the ability to set a user's initial directory to an IFS, QOPENSYS, QDLS, or QSYS library upon successful login to the server. This is set via new parameters in the user profile (WRKUSRPRF). There are new configuration parameters in the Configure TCP Applications commands for FTP. I suggest choosing *UNIX as your default configuration choice. This insures compatibility between the AS/400, PCs, and virtually any other computer attached to the Internet with which you will need to exchange data.

FTP CLIENTS

Clients connect to an FTP server and either transmit (upload) data to the server or receive (download) data from the server. Clients run on many platforms in various forms. The AS/400, Windows 95/98/NT come with a character-based FTP client. These are command oriented. There are also many GUI-based clients available for download on the Internet for Windows, UNIX, and the Macintosh. Many of the Windows clients include drag-and-drop support for the Windows file system. FTP upload and download capabilities for anonymous FTP are built-in to most browsers. One of the world's favorite PC-based FTP clients is a piece of freeware called WS_FTP, which can be downloaded from *www.tucows.com*. It has a five-cow rating!

AS/400 CLIENT

The AS/400 includes a 5250-based FTP client, which can be extremely useful in uploading and downloading files with AS/400 software vendors. This is especially true for those who have a T1 or fractional-T1 connection. IBM's FTP site *FTP://testcase.boulder.ibm.com* features an AS/400 subdirectory that AS/400 support personnel in Rochester can access. Problem documentation can be uploaded and IBM-provided information downloaded directly in *SAVF file format.

The AS/400 client connection and request commands can be embedded in a command language program (CLP) to automate repetitive access to a specific site and run via the AS/400 scheduler.

The AS/400 division began providing PTF downloads via FTP in September 1998. Those who have a high-speed Internet connection can download PTFs via the Internet instead of dialing in at 9600 bps on an ECS modem. IBM's Internet PTF (IPTF) facility is an example of an application built around Java and FTP. IBM's level two support representative also have the ability to use FTP to transfer large files and objects from a customer's system to their laboratory for detailed analysis. These facilities dramatically improve support by reducing delay. I have frequently sent files to IBM for analysis by first transferring them to our Internet connected machine and then on to IBM from there.

WORKSTATION CLIENTS

Windows 95/98/NT have a command line-based FTP client built in to the operating system. (Just type FTP from a command line.) In addition, there are many FTP client packages available for the Windows platform; you can find a couple of excellent free packages—as well as some inexpensive shareware packages—at `www.tucows.com`.

A word about accessing the AS/400. Prior to V4R4, to access the IFS directory, the first command that must be issued after logging in to the system is a CD /HOME command to change directories to a valid IFS directory. I use /HOME because IBM providesM it as a default directory in the IFS, but any valid directory works. Then use the CD command to change to any valid file system library or directory. This is not documented anywhere that I could find. I picked it up from other users in the `comp.sys.ibm.as400.misc` newsgroup.

Prior to V4R4, the server did not support the LIST command. In V4R4, IBM has implemented the LIST command in it's UNIX form "LS," which is the form used by common FTP clients. If you are at an earlier release level, you can use the DIR command to accomplish the same objective (listing the contents of a directory).

UTILIZING FTP IN YOUR WEB SITE

You can link to an FTP server directly from a Web page via a standard hyperlink. It would look like this:

```
<a href=ftp://ftp.somesite.com/directory><a>
```

When you click on this link, the browser will login (as Anonymous) and display a directory listing of the contents at this site. If you fully qualify a file name in the link, the browser logs in, initiates a GET request, and starts transferring the file.

I have found from personal experience using FTP to transfer files between machines in a private Intranet (WAN) that FTP is much faster than using SNADS. FTP is a very old Internet utility. Transferring files was one of the very first Internet applications used by the folks who developed the Internet. It remains a very important part of our toolset today.

AS/400 WEB SERVERS 11

The Web server is both a simple and complex piece of software. The server's job is to receive and process HTTP requests from a browser. To do this, the server must locate the file requested by the HTTP request header and transmit the requested file back to the client's browser. This is always true regardless of what additional processing must be accomplished to create and deliver the file.

In addition to transmitting files to the client, the server performs several other tasks including security authentication, encryption, and execution of CGI programs. The server also provides many features to define and configure the operating environment.

Most commercial servers are patterned after two basic servers—CERN and NCSA servers. Both were developed for the UNIX environment and are available for free download (UNIX versions) from the Internet. The major difference between the two server models lies in the configuration languages used. Both models produce the same functional results.

For complete information about the CERN HTTPd server visit *www.w3.org/Daemon*. For complete information about the NCSA HTTPd server visit *hoohoo.ncsa.uiuc.edu/*. These URLs point to the authoritative sources for the original free versions of these Web servers. The free versions are stabilized and no longer supported.

The W3C has become the organization that sets standards for both Web servers (HTTP) and for HTML, XML, and the languages and protocols that support the World Wide Web. You will find the W3C at *www.w3c.org*.

IBM has offered a free Web server since it first began shipping TCP/IP-based software in V3R1. The original IBM Web server was the HTTP Server, which was very basic but functional.

Since then, IBM has upgraded the HTTP Server. At V4R4, it is perhaps the world's finest Web server. As we will discuss throughout this chapter, the IBM HTTP Server has more features and functionality than any other Web server, even the very popular Apache Web server.

In V3R1 and V3R2, you had to configure the server by directly editing the configuration file, which was difficult. At V4R1, IBM introduced a set of tools via a pre-configured Web server instance called the ADMIN Server. In each subsequent release, the ADMIN server with its Web-based configuration forms have been enhanced greatly improving the ease with which one can configure a Web site.

As of V4R4, the IBM HTTP Server can be configured as the Web server for native Lotus Domino for the AS/400 improving on Domino's promise of being a truly integrated business solution for the AS/400. This means that the same Web server that runs your company's informational Web site, e-business Web site, and e-commerce Web site can now support integrated communications and document management facilities provided by Domino.

Perhaps the single most amazing fact about the IBM HTTP Server is the fact that is included with OS/400 as a no charge option.

THE V4R4 IBM HTTP SERVER

I personally did not use the IBM HTTP Server when I started working with the Internet and the AS/400 back in 1996. At that time, I chose to use the Commerce Server/400 from I/Net, Inc., which delivered a robust server that would run on any release of OS/400 from V3R1 and up. It included Secure Sockets Layer (SSL) encryption, which was not available on the IBM server at that time. IBM introduced SSL security with V4R1 (the e-Business release of OS/400). Security and encryption offerings continue to be enhanced in each subsequent release. In V4R1, SSL was an extra cost option. Since V4R3, it is included t no charge (more on this later).

I have just completed migrating eight Web servers to IBM's HTTP Server. Today, there simply is no better server available. There is no Web server that I have seen on the AS/400, or any other machine for that matter, that offers so many features and so much functionality.

Installing the Web server is easy and completely reliable. First install TCP/IP, then the option for the HTTP Server (product 5769-DG1). Once the install is completed, start TCP/IP and then the administration server (*ADMIN). You can then use a browser that supports JavaScript to configure a Web server instance.

IBM HTTP SERVER FEATURES

Everyone assumes that Web servers can serve HTML page, images, motion video, and audio, IBM's HTTP Server can do all that and much more.

The HTTP server is a set of related jobs consisting of a "daemon" and some request processor jobs. The daemon receives all incoming requests and routes them to a request processor job where the request is processed and the results returned to the end user. This set of jobs is a "server instance."

One or many "instances" of the HTTP Server can be run. You may want to run many instances with each server supporting a specific audience. At Republic Indemnity Company of America, we run one instance for independent agents, one for policy holders, one for a public general information site, and one for employees. There is no physical limit to the number of servers you can run on your AS/400. It is simply a function of available resources. Each Ethernet or token ring network adapter card can support up to 256 IP addresses, which is the only limit is the number of cards a specific machine can support.

VIRTUAL HOSTS

If you need to run many server instances, consider the virtual hosts feature of the IBM HTTP Server (introduced in V4R3). This facility provides two types of virtual hosting allowing support of many Web sites with a single server instance.

- ***IP-based Virtual Hosting:*** Using the IP-based virtual hosting method, each Web server can have its own unique domain name, IP address, root directory, and Web pages. It can support older browsers without problems. When configuring a browser, specify the IP address to which a configuration directive applies. The only drawback to this method is that this server instance "binds" to all IP addresses on your machine, which means that only one server instance can be run.

  Configuration may become a bit tedious and care must be taken to insure that a configuration entry has been associated with the proper IP address.

- ***Name-based Virtual Hosting:*** This is a very attractive form of virtual hosting where a single HTTP server instance can run many domain names on a single IP address. Each domain has its own set of configuration entries, directories, Web pages, etc. Unfortunately, older browsers (MS/IE 3.0, Netscape 2.x) cannot support this form of virtual hosting. You may have to restrict clients to more modern browsers.

  This form of virtual hosting was first introduced in the Apache Web server, which has developed a work-around to the problem of old browsers. If the browser does not support virtual name-based servers, it will always go to the very first Web server it finds associated with the IP address. A simple one-page Web site can be built that contains links to the other Web sites hosted by the server.

While there are certainly some advantages to running one server instance, I have not noticed any performance degradation by running many instances. Many instances offer simple, easy-to-maintain Web servers that are logically easy for support personnel to understand and operations people to manage.

PROXY SERVERS

The IBM HTTP Server can be a proxy server. Many large on-line service providers use Proxy servers. Users log in to the network and route requests to the Proxy server, which can then use one or several IP addresses to initiate requests on behalf of the user to other servers on the Internet. This allows the service provider to assign internal IP addresses to many users and share a small number of public IP addresses. The proxy server releases IP addresses when the request is completed.

An additional benefit of the proxy server is page caching. As users of a proxy server access Web pages, the page is stored in the proxy server's cache. When subsequent users request the same page, it is retrieved from the cache.

Proxy servers can provide some measure of security. A proxy server can be used to provide unrestricted Internet access for some users while limiting access for others to selected sites or an internal intranet.

EXTENDED LOGGING

The V4R4 HTTP Server produces complete robust access logs that provide statistics about the types of computers and browsers used by site visitors. It provides "referrer" statistics that detail where the user was when the site was accessed. This is invaluable for those who pay for advertising on various Web sites and want to measure the effectiveness of each ad. It also reports how the site is positioned on search engines and how many users find the site through a search engine.

If you want to see an example of the types of statistics produced, visit `www.ignite400.org/week_stats/`, which displays a full set of statistics for one week. The report is produced with the Webtrends log analyzer for the IGNITe/400 site, which is hosted on IBM's V4R4 HTTP Server.

PERSISTENT STATE CGI

This new facility (first introduced in V4R3) allows the creation of a session and retains program variables and data in memory between interactions with the browser client. The server generates a unique "handle," which becomes part of the URL, identifies the session to the server, and instructs it to reactivate the session. This means that variables, large tables, etc. can be retained in memory, greatly improving performance of mission critical e-business transactions.

DYNAMIC CACHING

Another major performance enhancement introduced in V4R4 is the ability to cache frequently used pages in memory without manual configuration. This can be done by simply enabling dynamic caching and setting the memory limits for the cache. The server then manages the cache attempting to keep the most frequently used pages in memory. Work by IBM's developers is ongoing in this area with support for Net.Data macros and CGI programs to be delivered via PTF in the near future.

SYSTEM MANAGEMENT

One of the most irritating issues for a Webmaster is to get a phone call from a customer saying that the Web site is down or they can't access it. V4R4 solves this problem by introducing SNMP support into the Web server. You can download custom management information blocks (MIBs) provided by IBM from the HTTP Server's Web site at *www.as400.ibm.com/http*. MIBs allow products such as Tivoli and HP OpenView to monitor and interpret alerts sent by the server.

AUTHENTICATION

The HTTP server was one of the first Web servers to support digital client certificate-based authentication. IBM's Digital Certificate Manager (shipped with all copies of OS/400 since V4R3) can generate client side certificates.

The server now supports IBM's implementation of LDAP, which is becoming a popular means of storing enterprise-wide user information. It also has robust support for AS/400 user profiles and validations lists. Both mechanisms provide group support.

IBM is a leader in digital certificate technology and is bringing break-through technology to the AS/400 as rapdily as it is evolving. Look for digital-id cards and card readers soon.

SECURITY

IBM has moved SSL V3 out of the HTTP Server and provides it as a standalone facility included with OS/400. The HTTP Server is a client application that uses SSL to encrypt pages and forms data exchanged between the server and a browser.

SEARCH ENGINE

V4R4 introduced a new HTTP server-based search engine that searches an entire Web site. Net Question was introduced as a site search engine in V4R1, but was replaced in V4R4 with the AS/400 Webserver Search Engine, which is an improvement over previous engines on the AS/400. It provides complete control and customization of both the search form and results pages and is amazingly fast. Information about the search engine may be found at: *www.as400.ibm.com/tstudio/http/services/searchinfo.htm#Intro*.

BASIC CONFIGURATION

The HTTP Server provides more control over how the server runs and attaches to IP addresses and domain names on a system. The settings discussed below are found in the "Configurations, Basic" section of your Configuration and Administration Web page.

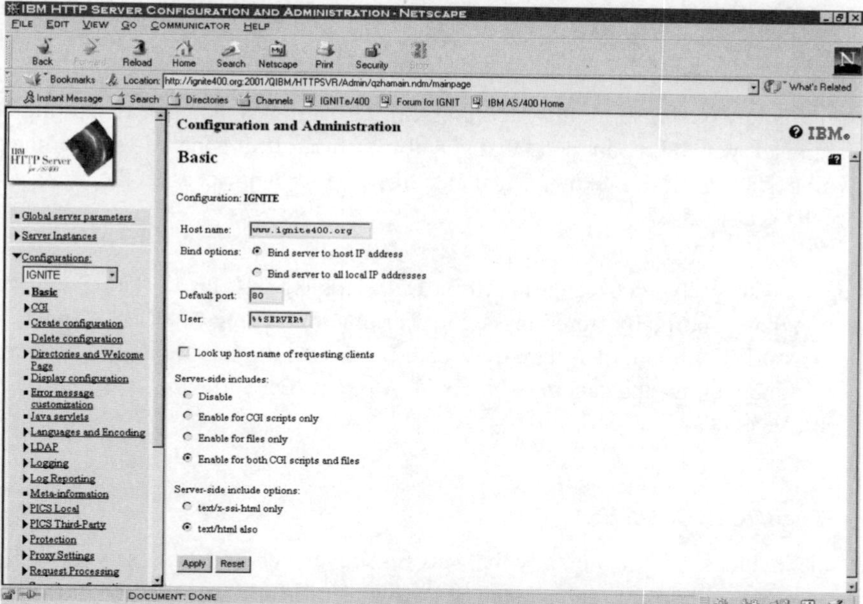

Figure 11.1: Basic Configuration

In this section you define how the server binds to IP addresses and what ports it will use. The first important directive is the "Bind options," which instructs the server to bind to one specific IP address or to all IP addresses on a machine.

If you choose "Bind server to all local IP addresses," you will be limited to one server instance on port 80 for your server. You can start additional instances, but each instance will require a unique port number. I have used this technique to implement development servers but do not recommend it. If you define a server to a port other than 80 (the HTTP default port), a user must type the port number to access the server. The URL they must type would look like: `www.mycompany.com:8081`.

"Bind server to host IP address" allows you to run one server instance per IP address, the most common configuration used by most Web masters. The server uses the "Host name" parameter to find its IP address at start up . You may type an IP address or a valid domain name in this field. If you provide a name, the server looks up the name in either the HOST names table for the AS/400 or in the DNS server and determines its IP address. Name resolution is controlled on the CFGTCP screen: Option 12. Change TCP/IP domain information. Using a domain name provides some degree of protection if you change ISPs and are assigned a new set of IP addresses.

Another important parameter in this section is the "Look up host name of requesting clients" parameter, which I recommend that you always turn off. It controls whether the server will perform a DNS lookup of the name of each user who accesses the server so it can store the access log.

Most log analyzer software packages perform DNS lookups and actually retrieve more information than is normally stored in the log. Turning this setting OFF (leave unchecked) saves a tremendous amount of system overhead. If it is ON, the server must connect to the DNS server and wait for the data to be returned. A typical DNS lookup takes between 15 and 38 milliseconds, which adds up.

SERVER SIDE INCLUDES

Server side includes (SSI) is a facility that was first developed on NCSA servers such as Netscape and Apache. IBM implemented SSI support in V4R3. This facility allows embedding of special SSI commands that the server processes as it loads the HTML page. SSI commands can execute programs or return information such as the date the HTML page was modified. Consult the HTTP Server for AS/400 Webmaster's Guide in the documentation link at *www.as400.IBM.com/http* for details or visit *www.ignite400.org* to see working examples with HTML source samples, including a hit counter, quick survey, and more.

SSI answers the question of how to retrieve dynamic data in an index page or welcome page by calling CGI programs or Net.Data macros. IBM has truly worked some magic in its implementation of SSI. Other servers require special names for pages containing SSI such as .SHTM or .SHT. IBM can parse any HTML page. Other servers issue a caution to limit the use of SSI because the server must parse the page looking for SSI tags. While I'm sure the HTTP server must do the same, the overhead is negligible making SSI a viable and valuable tool. Prior to switching to the IBM HTTP server I avoided SSI, now I use it extensively.

For example, my legal department requires me to post a copyright notice on every Web page along with the date the page was last updated. I use the following SSI tag to retrieve the date the HTML page was last updated:

```
<!—#ECHO var="LAST_MODIFIED"—>
```

As you can see, SSI is embedded within an HTML comment— "<!–#" indicates that this is an SSI command. ECHO is a specific SSI command that tells the server to find the variable named in the `var=` parameter (`var="LAST_MODIFIED"`), replace it with the value, and display it on the Web page. Note that the SSI command must be terminated with the "– >" end comment symbol.

URL STORAGE LOCATIONS

Before configuring a Web server, decide the structure of your Web site's resources and determine where the various types of objects used are to be stored.

IBM does not recommend one file system over another, but I do. There are some general guidelines about which file systems can store which types of objects. These guidelines apply to all AS/400 Web servers:

QSYS.LIB is the standard AS/400 library file system. It is the only file system at present that can store executable programs (both original program model [OPM] or integrated language environment [ILE]) written in any compiled language supported by the AS/400. It can also store database- and text-based objects. HTML pages can be stored in the QSYS file system, although it is not recommended.

Integrated File System (IFS) was new to the AS/400 as of V3R1. It uses a UNIX (or PC-like) directory structure and stores *stream files*. Files are physically stored in EBCIDIC, but are automatically translated to ASCII when served to an ASCII device such as a PC or browser. This is by far the best location to store HTML, text files, and binary objects such as image, video, and audio files. The stream file architecture is approximately four times as fast as QSYS or QDLS when serving these objects. Naming conventions for the IFS file system are compatible with Windows 95/98/NT and UNIX. Although the file system supports up to 256-byte file names with or without dotted file notation (i.e. extensions), I recommend limiting file names to 32 bytes, the UNIX limitation for compatibility with UNIX browsers.

While you cannot store executable AS/400 programs in the IFS, you can create a *symbolic link* to the program. A directory listing of the IFS would appear to have an object in it that is the program object for which you created the symbolic link. These symbolic links can be executed.

QDLS is the file system users have traditionally used for PC Support and for OfficeVision/400 objects. The file system is limited to the DOS naming convention of 8.3 or the equivalent (an 8-character file name and 3-character extension). QDLS is supported by, but not recommended for, use with servers. Limit use of QDLS for existing objects on the AS/400.

QOPENSYS is a 100 percent UNIX compatible file system and has all of the attributes and features of the IFS root directory file system except that file names are case sensitive. (ABC is not the same as AbC or abc.) All of the other file systems are case insensitive and internally translate names to upper case for comparison.

DYNAMIC INDEXING

Dynamic indexing displays a default page in a server directory. The page name is defined to the server and is, by Web conventions, usually named INDEX.HTML or INDEX.HTM, although some Webmasters like to use DEFAULT.HTM or HOME.HTM as their index page name. A server looks for the default file name in a directory specified in the browser's URL. If it does not find the default HTML page in the directory, the server displays a list of the files in the directory. The default page and appearance of directory listings can be customized with the "Directories and Welcome Page" options of the HTTP Server's Configuration and Administration Web page. Welcome Page is the term used to define the index page.

Consider the following URL: `www.mysite.com/customers/`.

Assume that the default index page name on the server is *index.htm*. It would be displayed automatically if found in the subdirectory */customers/*. If *index.htm* did not exist in the subdirectory, then a list of all files found in the subdirectory would be displayed. The HTTP Server has an option called "AlwaysWelcome." If turned on, the server will search for the index page name specified above.

The server will also display a directory listing of members in a physical file if the physical file contains multiple members. You may control whether the server will display a directory or not by setting the "DirAccess" directive to on or off.

The appearance of the directories can be customized with the "Directories and Welcome Page" settings in the Administration server. Select the fields to display (such as date last change, size, owner, HTML page titles, etc.). Icons can also be associated with types of files displayed in the directory listing. Specify the maximum length displayed so the server will truncate long names.

DIRECTORY ALIASES

An alias re-routes a browser's request from one location to another on the same server or on any other server. All of the AS/400 Web servers provide support for aliases in one way or another. The IBM HTTP server implements aliases via the MAP server directive.

A common use of the alias is to enhance system security by hiding the true physical location of a file or object from the user. Consider the following example.

The file *custinfo.htm* is stored in the physical IFS directory:

```
/webserv/mysite/private/customers/custinfo.htm
```

You have defined `/webserver/mysite/` as your server root document directory. This will never show on the client's browser as part of the URL, so you have some degree of protection and directory hiding built in to your server. To access the `custinfo.htm`, you would normally key the following URL:

```
www.mysite.com/private/customers/custinfo.htm
```

Let's assume that we create an alias called "customers" that is mapped to the directory:

```
customers = /webserv/mysite/private/customers
```

The URL to access the custinfo.htm page would be:

```
www.mysite.com/customers/custinfo.htm
```

You have hidden the intermediate directory *private*. Users do not know that it even exists. It also shortens the URL and makes it easier for users to type (if they have to type it).

In IBM HTTP server terminology, you would use a MAP directive in your configuration. It would look like:

```
MAP /customers/*  /webserver/mysite/private/customers/*
```

A word of caution. You may code multiple MAP directives, but the order in which you code them is very important and they must be coded from most specific to most generic.

USER DIRECTORIES

A user directory is common throughout the Internet. Large online services provide registered users with a "personal Web site" area on their servers, where members of the service can publish their own content. This facility exists on the AS/400.

You may have seen or even used "user directories" on your dial-up ISP's server and created a personal Web site. If I were to define a personal Web site on *www.ignite400.org*, it would be *www.ignite400.org~bobc*. Notice the tilde (~), which tells the server to look for a personal directory.

Any user who has a profile on the AS/400 can be set up with a Web-content area, which must be defined via the server and is not automatic. You must enable personal directories via the "User directories" option on the Web server Configuration and Administration page.

Beginning with V3R1, the user profile parameter *Home Directory* must be defined for user directories to work. The parameter is usually defined with the user's profile (use WRKUSRPRF) name of the user. Additionally, servers must be granted authority to access objects in the directory.

CGI SCRIPTS AND PROGRAMMING

All of the AS/400 servers support standard CGI protocol 1.1 (CGI/1.1). A script name, along with any input parameters passed in from the browser and any server environment variables set by the browser, is passed to the server via the URL. The program is located by the server, passed as input, and executed. The CGI program then produces output (usually a dynamically generated HTML file) that is returned to the browser.

CGI programming on the AS/400 supports:

- Integrated Language Environment (ILE) languages, RPG-IV, COBOL, C, C++, PL1.
- REXX/400 is directly supported via the Net.Data interface.
- Java is supported beginning with V3R7 PTFs for the beta version of the Java runtime environment on the AS/400. At V4R3, IBM introduced the WebSphere application server that provides Java servlet support. V4R4 provides Enterprise Java Bean (EJB) support.
- PERL 5 is supported.
- Java applets are supported (applets are just data files from the servers perspective).

The server can deliver many different types of graphic, audio, and video file formats, including Real Audio[1].

IMAGE MAPPING

The server provides the ability to create server-side image maps that store the coordinates of hotspots on a graphic image. You can build links that, when clicked, cause the browser to request a link to the URL named in the hotspot.

Server-side image maps are virtually obsolete. Today most browsers are capable of processing image maps via HTML tags, so mapping hotspots are done via HTML or tools like NetObjects Fusion, Macromedia Dreamweaver, Microsoft FrontPage, or Netscape Composer. These tools allow you to use the mouse and forms provided to define both the location of the hotspot on the image and the link to be executed when the user clicks on the link.

Browser-side image maps are more sophisticated than server-side image maps. They change the image when the mouse cursor passes over the hotspot. For more information on server-side image mapping, see the specific server documentation.

CONTENT TYPES

Within the HTTP header, content type is a field returned by the server telling the browser what type of file is being transmitted. The browser uses the content type field to determine how to process the filereceived. If the server sends the browser a GIF file, the content type tells the browser that it is sending a GIF file, and the browser knows that it must use its GIF viewer software to display the image.

Content types are defined by Internet standards and controlled by the IANA and MIME types. MIME and its content types are governed by RFC 2045, 2046, 2047, 2048, and 2049.

The IBM HTTP Server ships with a set of content types pre-defined to the server. You may need to extend this list as you introduce new file types or want the browser to handle certain types of files in a specific manner. On the IGNITe/400 Web site, I wanted to let a user view Net.Data macro source. I wanted to use the source file for the macro that I was executing. I used the content type for TEXT/HTML and associated it with the file exten-

1 See www.real.com for information about Real Audio and other streaming audio and video products.

sion .MAC and .HTI. When a user clicks on a link to a file with .MAC or .HTI, the server displays the file content as plain text.

You can configure content types on the HTTP Server via the MIME types configuration option on the Configuration and Administration page.

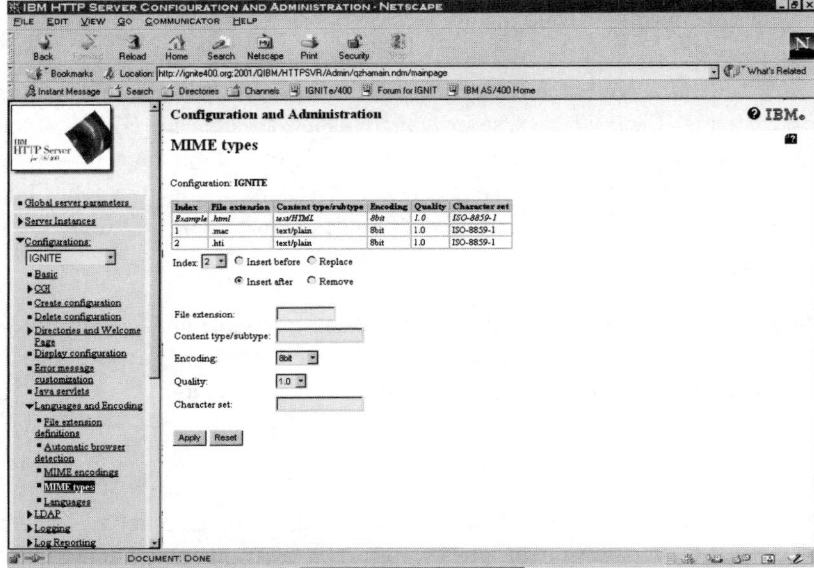

Figure 11.2: MIME types

All of the CERN- and NCSA-based servers for any platform (except Microsoft), and all browsers (except Microsoft) use the MIME content type to determine the type of file the server is sending. Microsoft ignores the Internet standards and makes its decisions based on the file extension. Although you will not deal with content types often, the key is understanding what they are and that browsers determine how to process files based on content type.

MIME content types are implemented as a type code followed by a subtype code. The basic type code is stringently controlled by IANA (Internet Assigned Numbers Authority) and the IETF. There are two subtypes:

- *Officially registered:* These are subtypes that have been submitted for recognition to the IANA via the procedure defined in the RFCs referenced above and have been approved.

- *Nonregistered:* Any user or vendor may implement a nonstandard, non-registered subtype. Nonregistered subtypes are prefixed with the characters ***x-***.

```
HTTP/1.0 200 OK
Date: Wed, 07 Jan 1998 06:32:23 GMT
Server: CommerceServer400/1.0
Content-Length: 5913
Content-Type: text/html        <-----content type
Last-Modified: Mon, 29 Dec 1997 10:10:16 GMT
```

Figure 11.4: HTTP response header.

Figure 11.4 is a typical response header returned by a server after an HTTP GET request from a browser. Note that the Content Type field is `text/html`, which tells the browser that it is about to receive an HTML file.

There are seven registered types—*text, image, audio, video, multipart, message, and application*—and many subtypes.

Some of the more common content types include those shown in Table 11.1.

Table 11.1: Common Content Types, ***part 1 of 2***

Content Type	File Extension	Remarks
application/msword		Microsoft Word files
application/octet-stream	.bin .savf .class .pcl .exe .dll	Executable program type files
application/pdf	.pdf	Adobe Acrobat files
application/postscript	.ps .eps .ai	Postscript files
application/rtf	.rtf	Revisable form text
application/x-tar	.tar	UNIX compressed file
application/zip	.zip	PC-type ZIP compressed file
audio/basic	.snd .au	Basic audio files
audio/x-pn-realaudio	.ram	Real Audio files
audio/x-wav	.wav	WAV files
image/bmp	.bmp	Bit-mapped image
image/gif	.gif	Compuserve image file

Table 11.1: Common Content Types, ***part 2 of 2***

Content Type	File Extension	Remarks
image/jpeg	.jpe .jpg .jpeg	JPEG image file
image/tiff	.tif .tiff	TIFF image file
multipart/alternative		
multipart/appledouble		
multipart/digest		
multipart/mixed		
multipart/parallel		
text/html	.ht3 .html3 .htm .html	HTML files
text/plain	.txt	Plain ASCII text file
text/tab-separated-values	.tsv	Tab-separated values
text/x-server-parsed-html	shtshtml	Supports server-side (NCSA servers)
video/mpeg	.mpe .mpg .mpeg	Movie files
video/quickfme	.mov .qt	Apple QuickTime movie files
video/x-msvideo	.avi	Movie files
video/x-sgi-movie	movie	Movie files

Items identified with "/x" are not registered.

AUTHENTICATION

Authentication is the server's form of restricting access to directories to authorized users. IBM introduced authentication in V4R1 with both its ICS and ICSS server. The following section will examine how authentication works.

Authentication is one of the most critical concepts to understand when building e-commerce Web sites. If all you are doing is putting up a public read-only Web site, you can skip over authentication. Those who want to be sure that only authorized people can access certain parts of their Web site, need authentication to build the gates and provide the keys to authorized users.

The HTTP server implements directory-based authentication. Limits can be defined for each directory or subdirectory (including QSYS libraries) to which access needs to be restricted.

The specifications for authentication (see the references to the CERN and NCSA sites earlier in the chapter and the World Wide Web Consortium at `www.w3c.org` provide for three types of security or authentication checking:

- IP address filtering
- Domain name filtering
- User and group authentication

In all three cases, you define rules pertaining to access privileges or restrictions for each directory or subdirectory in server configuration files .

IP ADDRESS FILTERING

A server allows rules to be defined that cause it to evaluate IP addresses using the dot notation (i.e. 111.111.111.111). Restrictions for complete addresses or generic portions of an address can be defined. You could allow all users from 38.0.0.0.0 to 38.255.255.255 (or in other words, any user in the Class A address group of 38) to access a Web site while all others were restricted.

In today's world of dial-up Internet access, the only valid use of this form of authentication is to protect an intranet where each address is known and controlled. This technique no longer works for restricting access to Internet users. Today, users access the Internet through proxy servers and network address translation software that allows literally millions of users to share a few hundred IP addresses. If a user accesses your site three times in a 10 period, there is no guarantee the same IP address will be used each time. This is especially true of those using large ISPs.

Be aware that this facility exists even if you never use it. Use IP address filtering with extreme caution or you will likely lock out someone (like your president who wants to access your site from home) who needs access.

DOMAIN NAME FILTERING

This authentication technique allows you to grant or deny access to resources stored in a directory or subdirectory based on the user's HOST domain name. Again, the specifications for this type of authentication are defined at the CERN, NCSA, and W3C Web sites. The bottom line again: Use with extreme caution!

Domain name filtering rules, like those for IP address authentication/filtering, were developed when the Internet was a much smaller place, and everyone had public domain names and addresses. Today, a user accessing a site via a service will be assigned a domain name, which can change during a session and will certainly change each time the user logs into the online service (for example, the first access may be via IP78.AOL.COM and the next access via IP104.AOL.COM).

You can define restriction that allow or disallow users with a domain name ending in .gov or .edu, or only to/from `ducks.com` or others on your list. This type of restriction or permission is cumbersome to maintain and will likely not work. You will find that access is restricted for users who should be allowed access and granted to those who shouldn't.

USER AND GROUP AUTHENTICATION

User- and group-level authentication are the best methods of limiting access to resources on your server. This method requires that individual users be defined to a user file of some type. A user may be assigned to a group. The server requires a user ID and a password. Access rules for each directory are defined on the server. You may use the following general rules:

- Allow any access. The directory is not protected by authentication. Anyone accessing the server can access objects in the directory.
- Allow any authorized user. This level of restriction allows any user who is defined to the server with a valid user ID and password to access the objects in the directory. When a user attempts to access a protected directory, the user is prompted for a user ID and password.
- Allow only named users. This type of restriction specifically limits access to users who have been explicitly granted access. All other users are rejected.
- Allow members of group. This is the type of authentication that I use throughout my site. It requires that a user be defined to the server's user file and be a member of a named group (i.e. customers, employees, etc.) or groups. A generic group called *employees* could be created to allow all employees to access certain directories. Additional groups, like *accounting*, *marketing, data processing,* etc., that differentiate between types of employees can also be created. An accountant who is a member of the employee and accounting groups may access any directories restricted to employee and those restricted to accounting. A user who belongs to employee and marketing could access the employee and marketing directories, but not the accounting directories.

Group authentication is a low-maintenance method of controlling access to your server's resources.

User and group authentication depend upon a close cooperation between the browser and the server. It is essential to understand how this works to implement server authentication successfully. We will examine a model based on a typical insurance company that wishes to grant limited access to the general public and specific access to restricted directories for employees, insurance agents, and policyholders.

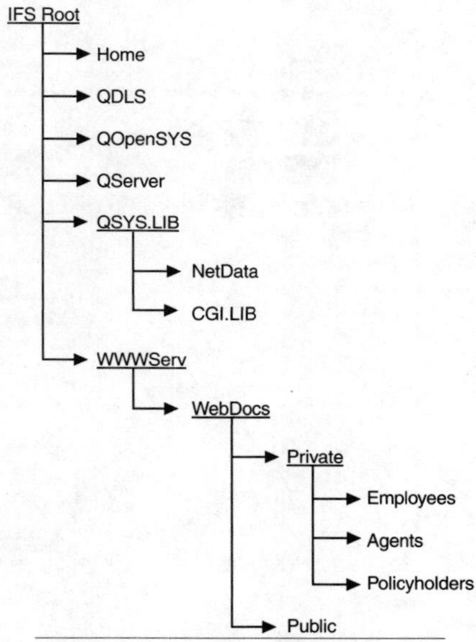

Figure 11.5: Sample directory structure.

The sample directory structure depicted in Figure 11.5 is typical of a directory structure that might be used on many servers. WWWServ is the name of an IFS root level directory containing all your Web servers, and WebDocs is the root directory for a specific server instance. WebDocs in this example is the default *document directory*. When configuring the server, tell it in what directory all documents (i.e. HTML files) will be stored.

In the example depicted in Figure 11.5, WebDocs may contain HTML or other resource objects that are open and available to the general public—no authentication is required. *Public* is also an unrestricted directory containing objects that may be accessed without authentication or restriction.

Private is a subdirectory that will generally not be seen by users of the system. On my system, it contains registration HTML forms that a user must complete to gain access to the system via a self-registration process. This directory is secured with a rule that only allows access to a user who is defined to the server's validation list.

Employees is restricted to members of the employees group.

Agents is restricted to members of the agents group.

Policyholders is restricted to members of the policyholders group.

Based on the above directory structure and authentication rules, Figure 11.6 illustrates an end user attempting to access an HTML page in the *Agents* directory.

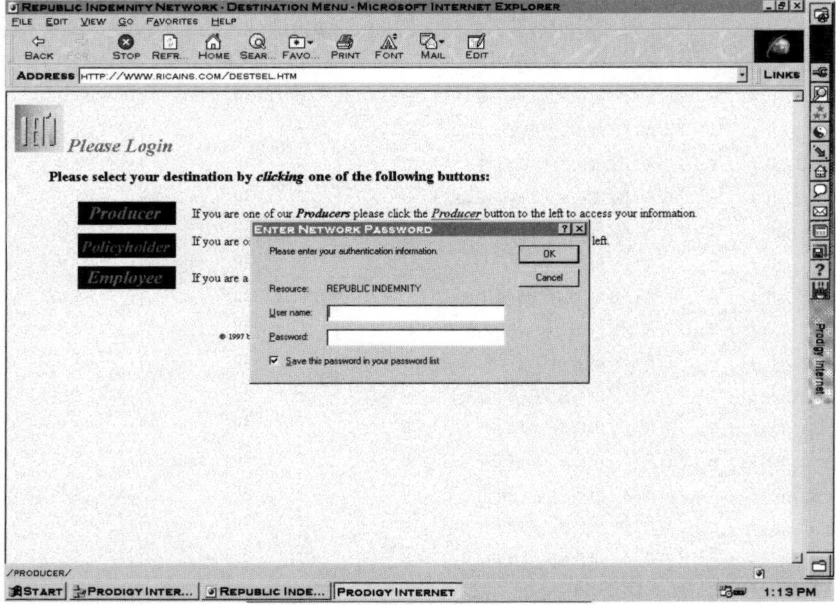

Figure 11.6: Authentication challenge.

This screen is taken from Republic Indemnity Company of America's Web site. In this example, a user clicked on the *Producer* button to access the producer (insurance agency) menu. Because this is a secured directory, the server responds with an HTTP return code indicating that access requires authentication.

In response to the return code, the browser displays the pop-up screen depicted in the example. Three important attributes are displayed on the screen:

- *Resource*, which is Microsoft's way of saying authorization realm
- *User name,* where the user must type a user ID
- *Password*, where the user must type a password

When the user clicks the OK button, the browser stores the user ID and password (in Netscape it is stored in memory until the browser is shut down; Microsoft stores the resource name, user name, and password on disk if the box labeled "Save The Password In Your Password List" is checked).

The browser then retransmits the request for the page along with the user name and password to the server. The server verifies the user ID and password. If the user ID and password are valid, the server checks to see if the user is a member of the agents group. If the user is a member of the required group, the user will be sent the requested resource (the `index.htm` HTML page in this case).

If you recall the discussion of browser/server communication, you will remember that the server has no concept of session. Each request to the server is new. The server has no memory of a user ever accessing it before. This is especially true in the case of authentication.

The first time a user accesses the secure resource after starting a browser, the pop-up screen is displayed as a result of the server sending back a request for authentication. The browser stores the *authentication realm*, user name, and password in its memory. When the user requests any additional pages from the server, it sends the user name and password. The server checks the user and group information on every request the browser makes.

Because the browser stores the user ID and password information in memory, it does not have to display the pop-up screen when the user visits the site again, even if the user has left the site, visited others, and then returned. When the user exits the browser program, authentication information is lost, and the user is required to complete the pop-up form the next time the browser is started and the site is accessed.

On the server side, each access to the site is new. The first access attempt will always fail because no user ID and password is transmitted. As long as the server receives a valid user ID and password with the HTTP header, it will grant access to the site.

The server, upon validating a request to access a restricted resource by the user, stores the user ID in an *environment variable* called REMOTE_USER. This field is available to CGI programs to perform further processing and build applications. This is the only reliable method of identifying a user who accesses a site repeatedly on the same or subsequent days. This will be discussed in detail in "Part III: Developing Your Web Site."

AUTHENTICATION OPTIONS

The HTTP server provides several authentication options from which to choose. Authentication is defined on the Configuration and Administration Web page by selecting "Protection."

You may choose to use a "Validation List" which is an AS/400 object that stores user-ids and passwords. Users defined to a validation list are not otherwise known to the AS/400. This means a user need not have an AS/400 user profile to be authenticated by the Web server.

The AS/400 also supports authentication using AS/400 user profiles. I recently implemented this method for our employees. All employees have an AS/400 user profile. Instructing the server to validate using AS/400 user profiles allowed an employee to have a single user id and password. If you choose to use AS/400 user profiles, be aware that it honors the security system values established, such as QMAXSGNACN and QMAXSIGN. This means that if a user being authenticated with AS/400 user profiles attempts to log on the number of times specified in QMAXSIGN and fails, the action specified in QMAXSGNACN (usually set to disable profile) is carried out. This means that a hacker could disable any user profiles they discover.

Passwords are encrypted when using validation lists or AS/400 user profiles. It is still possible to intercept and decode user ids and passwords unless SSL is used. The risk is relatively low, but you may want to use SSL to insure absolute security.

DIGITAL CERTIFICATES

A third method the HTTP Server can use for authentication is digital certificates. As of V4R2, IBM began shipping the Digital Certificate Manager, which allows the generation of personal digital certificates for users. A digital certificate is stored on the user's browser and associated with the URL and authentication domain. The public key portion of the digital certificate is stored in a validation list. The server can be configured to authenticate using digital certificates via the Digital Certificate Manager or a Certification Authority (CA) such as VeriSign, Inc.

You may want to allow access to anyone possessing a valid digital certificate or only those to whome you specifically want to grant access. You may require only valid signed digital certificates or give a user the option to log in with a user id and password in the event that the certificate is invalid, expired, or damaged. This setting is desirable for users who access Web sites from PCs at their office, but occasionally need to access the Web site from another PC at home or abroad. In all cases, SSL encryption must be enabled for digital certificates or the user id password fallback facility to work. Digital certificates enhance security and user authentication in serveral ways.

First a certificate on a Web server is required and should be issued by a recognized Certification Authority (CA). Your digital certificate is used to enable server encryption and prove to clients that you are who you say you are. Digital certificates even protect against a hacking technique called IP Spoofing where a server uses your IP address and pretends to be you. If you use SSL, clients can be guaranteed that you are who you say you are. The digital certificate is tamper proof and provides positive identification.

Just as the digital certificate identifies you, a personal digital certificate positively identifies your clients. Whether they use a certificate issued by you or by Verisign, Inc. you can be absolutely assured that the person is someone you know and trust.

Currently, most digital certificates are stored on the client's PC within the browser. You should insure that the client is aware of the physical security precautions that should be taken to protect this PC from unauthorized access.

You may also implement digital certificates via a credit card-like device that stores the certificate on the card. A special card reader reads the ard when prompted by the Web site. This is the most secure method of authentication, and I expect it to be common place with card readers being standard for PCs sold in the near future. This is emerging technology and moving very rapidly. Fortunately IBM is a leader in this movement and is bringing the technology to the AS/400 as it is developed.

SET SECURITY

The concept of digital certificates and SSL also introduces the concept of SET security technology, which IBM supports along with a digital wallet used with e-commerce purchasing. SET provides advantages over SSL by providing a completely secure link to a financial organization that processes a credit card transaction.

Using SSL technology, there is a secure encrypted link between the Web server and the credit card processing company. You do not control the link from the processing company to your bank. With SET technology, you know that you have reliable secure end-to-end protection.

LDAP

New with V4R4 is the implementation of LDAP, which provides an integrated cross-platform method of acquiring and validating user information. IBM has made a major commitment to LDAP, and it may emerge as the standard for storing user information on all forms of computer systems. A major advantage of LDAP is that user information may be stored on a single computer system somewhere in an organization. When you have many LDAP servers, you may want to store the personal information for employees on computers in each of the branch offices.

Depending on configuration, local LDAP servers can be instructed to interrogate remote LDAP servers. This means that an AS/400 LDAP server in Los Angeles could interrogate an LDAP server on a mainframe or NT server in Paris. LDAP introduces a security mechanism called the Access Control List (ACL), which grants access to certain LDAP user information while restricting other information. The contents of the directory server are dynamic and user defined. IBM supplies a sample LDAP schema representing the current AS/400 Directory system. The interesting fact about LDAP is that while certain common information (user id, etc.) must be present on all LDAP servers used, not all attributes are required.

AUTHENTICATION GROUPS

In addition to all of the options described above, users can be associated with authentication groups that are defined to a server group file stored in the IFS directory or with AS/400 groups if using the AS/400 user profile option. Groups can contain individuals or groups.

No other Web server that I have seen offers the power and options to configure the server to meet your specific requirements the way the IBM HTTP Server does. I recommend simplifying administration by keeping the configuration as simple as possible to support your requirements.

IBM also provides a full set of APIs so that you may automate the registration of users. Sample programs are available from the IGNITe/400 user group site at `www.ignite 400.org` in the FREE Software Sample code link courtesy of an IGNITe/400 member.

SSL and Encryption

IBM introduced SSL into its ICSS Web server at V4R2. Since V4R3, SSL and Encryption is packaged as a separate product and configured with the Digital Certificate Manager. You must install the optional Digital Certificate Manager Software and Encryption Libraries (avaliable on your OS/400 Installation CDs). SSL is now available to the IBM HTTP Server and Telnet servers. It may be extended to other servers in the future.

The encryption supported on these servers is based on a technique called *public key/private key encryption*. Using this method, a large binary number is created as a security key on the host server and on the client side. The public key is transmitted to the client via a secure handshaking protocol; the client then uses it to decrypt messages encrypted using the server's private key. Conversely, the client uses the server's public key to encrypt messages that it sends to the server; these messages are in turn decrypted using its private key. Private keys must be physically protected from disclosure, because they form the basis of the encryption methodology and protocol. Public keys can be freely exchanged. Encryption requres the pair of keys.

To enable encryption, an electronic certificate must be obtained from a third-party resource. A *digital certificate* is granted by the signing authority when it physically verifies that you are who you say you are. The digital certificate is a key element in forming public key/private key pairs and also provides proof that messages sent from your server are from your company and are authorized transmissions.

Prior to V4R2, we were limited on the AS/400 to *server certificates*. Since V4R2, however, AS/400 users can generate and use client certificates, which effectively eliminate the need for the authentication routine previously described. When a client accesses a server using SSL, it will be asked to send its certificate so the server can authenticate that it is communicating with a known, valid client. The server will send its certificate to authenticate to the client that information being exchanged is from the server and company that the client thinks it is doing business with.

Although the details of SSL are way beyond the scope of this book, it is becoming an important technology and is the only positive method of ensuring that you are communicating with a known party and that sensitive data is not being compromised. Your browser will have a symbol like a padlock on its status line at the bottom of the screen. If the padlock is closed, then you are communicating via a secure connection to the server. You further know that the URL used to access the server has been authenticated against the server's certificate. For example, if the padlock or other secure symbol is enabled, I feel confident to transmit my credit card information over the Internet. Without the symbol, I will not enter my credit card information.

The encryption algorithms used by IBM are licensed from RSA, Inc. U.S. companies may use 128-bit encryption, which is the strongest and most difficult to break. Most foreign countries allow 56-bit encryption, except France, which limits encryption keys to 48 bits. The U.S. algorithms, the strongest in the world, are regulated by federal law because they are used by the U.S. government, including the Department of Defense and the military. The government relaxed the regulations recently allowing international users to use

128-bit encryption for financial transactions. A definative document on SSL and export status is: the RSA Laboratories FAQ available at: *ftp://ftp.rsa.com/pub/labsfaq/labsfaq4.pdf*

For detailed information explaining these security concepts, please visit *www.rsa.com*. Netscape has also published a white paper on encryption and security, which is accessible at *www.inetmi.com/products/whitepg.html*. You may also want to look at the article "SSL Makes Headway as an Encryption Standard" by Stuart McClure of the Netscape Corporation located at *www.ne-dev.com/ned-01-1998/net-01-security.html*.

When running SSL and doing business with International users, the server will "step down" to the level supported by the clients. The 48-bit encryption used by France is deliberately weak to allow the French government to decrypt intercepted traffic. While 56-bit encryption can also be intercepted and decrypted, it requires a great deal more sophistication. Decrypting 128-bit encryption might be possible, but it would take the resources and expertise of an organization such as NSA (the National Security Agency).

Encryption, although great for security purposes and protecting sensitive information, has a cost. On U.S. systems employing encryption, every byte of data is encrypted using a 1024-byte security key. The algorithm is based on bit manipulation. Every byte of data transmitted from a server to a client must be encrypted, including large graphic files. This simply takes a lot of CPU time to accomplish.

Like the server that must encrypt an entire page (including graphics), the browser running on a much slower computer (the one on your desk) must decrypt the messages it receives from the server. It must also encrypt messages and data that it sends to the server. This is a costly, time-consuming process.

Those who plan to use encryption technology extensively and have a specific need for it, should plan to buy a large enough processor to handle the workload. Do not scrimp on the memory purchased. I run an S10 with 512MB of memory for my server, and I strictly limit the pages that use encryption. If I were to encrypt my entire Web site, I'm not sure the S10 would not be adequate for the job.

At present the AS/400 provides SSL support with the IBM HTTP Server, its Telnet servers (Client Access, Client Access Express, and Secureway Host on Demand), and all Lotus Domino servers and databases including e-mail. If you want secure encrypted e-mail transmissions, you must use Lotus Domino as the native AS/400 SMTP server and POP3 server do not.

It is possible for a hacker to intercept transmissions and obtain user ID and password when transmitting unencrypted data. Users of Telnet have been working for years without encryption and have remained relatively free from hacking. Although it is possible for someone to intercept communications with clients and pretend to be you asking them to buy merchandise and give you their credit card numbers, it is unlikely.

You must look at security from a risk-versus-cost basis. If you see a hacker behind every PC on the Internet, you will drive yourself crazy, spend a fortune, and alienate your users with horribly complex security schemes that ultimately won't stop an expert hacker with windows of opportunity to access or destroy a system.

Be prudent, but not fanatical, when implementing SSL and encryption. If you engage in International commerce or exchange sensitive messages with international users you should always use SSL encryption.

ADDITIONAL HTTP SERVER FEATURES

The V4R3 HTTP Server was developed in part via a new process of user-based analysis and design. IBM traveled the country conducting structured sessions with users contributing input in a formalized manner. Surveys were sent out to participants in the study, which were tabulated and used to assist in setting priorities for new features that have been implemented in the V4R3 and V4R4 versions of the server. Some of these features include:

ERROR CUSTOMIZATION

Have you wanted to display your own custom page when an error condition occurs: such as a user-authentication error, or file-not-found error instead of those maddening cryptic error messages you see on so many Web sites today? The HTTP server allows you to replace the default error message pages with your own HTML pages, which include any type of content you choose to provide.

AUTOMATIC BROWSER DETECTION

How about that customer who has the original copy of Netscape Navigator or worse an early version of a Mosaic browser? What do you do? You would like to support the user, but you would like to also use the advanced state-of-the-art features on your Web site only supported by current browsers. The IBM HTTP Server provides automatic browser detection and will route the user to an alternate location on the server or serve an alternate page compatible with the user's browser.

WEBSPHERE APPLICATION SERVER

The IBM HTTP Server supports IBM's WebSphere Application Server, which is shipped with AS/400 systems (V4R3 and above). This server was substantially enhanced at V4R4. WebSphere allows you to build interactive e-business sites using Java servlets (not applets) that integrate server-side processing with HTML pages.

The WebSphere application with the use of Java servlets and EJBs is IBM's clearly stated direction for the development of e-business applications. The WebSphere application server loads Java servlets upon startup and keeps the servlets resident until it is shut down. This offers a significant advantage over traditional CGI programs that must be loaded and initialized every time they are called.

WebSphere runs server-side Java on the AS/400. IBM has implemented the program template concept it uses with other languages in its native Java support, which means Java programs are translated to low-level machine code when first executed and run many times faster on subsequent execution. Java running on the AS/400 produces runtimes comparable to other compiled languages. Servlets can be threaded using the OS/400 native threading model.

The investment in Java- and WebSphere-based applications is well worth the effort, but may take time if you don't have experienced Java programmers on staff or are not willing to contract for these services. WebSphere is a direction that I am working towards while using other technologies to deliver immediate business results today. I have no doubt that this technology is the direction we should all be moving towards.

OTHER AS/400 WEB SERVERS

As of September 1999, Apache servers represented 55.5 percent of all Web servers, Microsoft IIS 22 percent and Netscape 7.5 percent according to the Netcraft Web survey at *www.netcraft.co.uk/*. Netcraft maintains an automated database of Web servers.

I/Net, Inc. sells three Web servers. They sell their own Commerce Server/400 and WebServer/400, which were very popular prior to V4R2. Commerce Server/400 provides secure SSL encryption back to V3R1.

I/Net also ported the Netscape Enterprise server to the AS/400 in 1998 and released it in January 1999. It is a good server based on the NCSA server model, but does not have the full set of features found in the IBM HTTP Server. It may be a good choice if you are currently running Netscape servers on other platforms and want compatibility.

IBM is porting the Apache Web server to the AS/400. Apache is a freeware open system that is the world's most popular server on platforms other than the AS/400.

Advanced BusinessLink sells Strategi, which is a customized Web server designed to leverage legacy applications providing 5250 to Web emulation and a custom proprietary API-based interface for developing Web-based applications using standard AS/400 programming languages such as RPG.

SUMMARY

The IBM HTTP Server is, in my opinion, the clear leader in AS/400-based Web servers. It provides more flexibility and functionality than any of the others available for the AS/400. It is developed and supported by IBM's AS/400 organization and does not have to meet cross-platform requirements imposed by the bodies that regulate Netscape, Apache, and other popular servers. At the moment, the IBM HTTP Server is the only server that supports the WebSphere application server.

I must also state, that the server is developed by a relatively small team of developers in Rochester, some of whom I have had the pleasure of meeting in person, and some electronically. This group of committed people takes great pride in its product. I am convinced that the people behind the IBM HTTP Server will do everything in their power to respond to user needs and continue to improve the world's finest Web server.

AS/400 E-BUSINESS PRODUCTS 12

The most popular Web-based applications on the Internet are e-commerce applications. These applications support the retail or commercial purchase of goods and services via the Web.

These applications generally provide a mechanism for assisting the online customer in locating the product the customer wants to buy, and then lets the customer place the item in an online "shopping basket." When customers have placed the products they want to buy into their shopping basket, they click a button and go to the "check-out" page. The check-out page brings up a secure HTML form asking for name, shipping address, contact information, and the user's credit card information.

There are several commercial services that provide merchant credit card support. You link to their servers and provide credit card information, your merchant account number, and the total of the purchase. The commercial service verifies the account and credit line, and sends back a confirmation number. The entire process emulates a store credit card terminal.

Two technologies handle secure credit card transactions, Secure Sockets Layer (SSL) encryption and the new Secure Electronic Transaction (SET) protocol. This is a new protocol developed by IBM and other major companies. It is very popular in Europe, but is not widely used in the United States. It requires the use of a SET wallet on your PC and a personal digital certificate. There are several vendors who have this support including IBM (see *www.software.ibm.com/commerce/payment/wallet.html*), and Microsoft (see the Microsoft update site if it was not installed with your copy of Microsoft Internet Explorer). Industry pundits project that within the next five years, banks will issue "SmartCards," which will replace your current credit cards. They will contain SET-compliant digital certificates and a microprocessor chip that can be run through a reader on your PC or store terminals.

SET technology is much more secure than traditional SSL encryption. It not only encrypts orders and personal information, it also insures that vendors are authorized to accept your credit card and provides a secure path from your computer through the merchants Web site and directly on to your bank. There is no risk of your credit card being intercepted and misused by an unscrupulous vendor. SET technology is being sponsored by VISA and Mastercard. They are working with many vendors including IBM to develop and deploy the technologies necessary to insure secure reliable electronic transactions via the Internet.

For additional reading about SET technology visit IBM's e-Commerce Web site at *www.software.ibm.com/commerce*, VISA International at *www.visa.com*, Mastercard International at *www.mastercard.com*, and the authoritative resource for SET technology *www.setco.org*.

SETCO is a company established by Mastercard, VISA, and others to establish and implement SET technology throughout the international financial community. SETCO manages the specification and performs compliance testing. Companies like IBM who produce SET compliant products like the IBM Payment Server are are issued authority to use the logo.

When looking at e-commerce software, you need to evaluate your specific needs. e-Commerce software runs the gamut from self-contained packages that have no interface; to existing databases; to software with extensive facilities to interface with existing order processing and inventory systems. There are also many PERL 5-based online storefront software that is available free for the download, but remember that you will need to do some modification to get this software to run on the AS/400.

IBM'S NET.COMMERCE

IBM has released Version 3.0 of its Net.Commerce product for the AS/400. Net.Commerce allows you to build an electronic mall with electronic stores. It features catalog sales and provides the tools to enable electronic credit card processing. The product can be customized to work with an order processing back-end system. Call IBM and ask for a demonstration of what it can do.

Version 3.0 is robust, has been tested with over 20,000 products in its database, provides support for sales tax and product surcharges, and is much easier to install and configure than previous releases and brings strong AS/400 integration to the product.

Version 3.0 adds a new very powerful facility called the "Product Advisor." This facility can be used to develop customized scripts that recommend additional products to a user based on his current selection. If the customer orders a golf club, for example, the system can prompt him to buy related products such as golf balls, shoes, hats, and shirts. Version 3.0 has also strengthened its secure purchasing options by introducing support for IBM's Payment Server, which supports SET and the interface to a large number of credit card clearing services. Net.Commerce 3.0 also provides euro support.

NET.COMMERCE 3.0 EXAMPLE

A good example of a commercial implementation of IBM's Net.Commerce 3.0 is The Box Office at `www.box-office.co.uk/`. The Box Office is part of the Earl's Court Olympia Group that operates the Earl's Court Exhibition Centre, Warwick Road, London.

This site was built by Bleddyn Williams of Morpheus Ltd., Ascot, UK. The site existed prior to the integration of Net.Commerce. It has been a very popular Web site, where people living in London, or planning to visit London, can find out what is going on at the Earl's Court Exhibition Centre. Each year, Earl's Court Olympia hosts more than 270 events and attracts more than 3 million visitors, making it one of London's most popular venues.

In March 1999, the Web site's home page was modified to include the Book Tickets Here link to a new Net.Commerce e-ticket Web site. In its first week of operation, with no advertising whatsoever, the site booked over 1,000 tickets based on the link you see in Figure 12.1.

Figure 12.1: The Box Office — Home Page.

Figure 12.2: The Box Office — What's On.

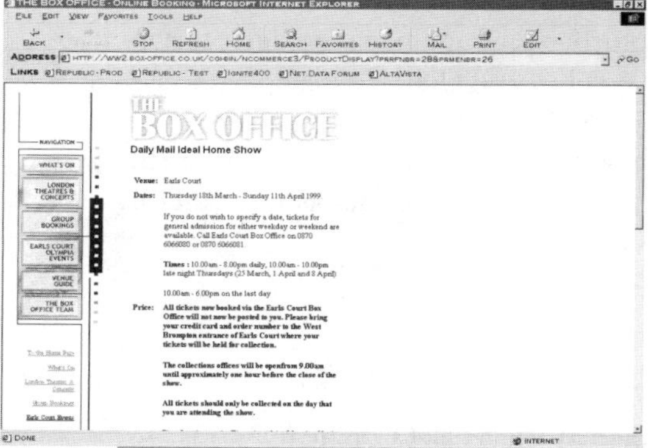

Figure 12.3: Show information — top.

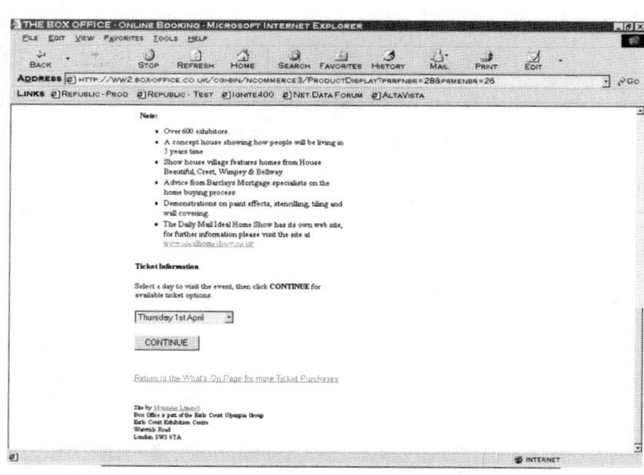

Figure 12.4: Show information — bottom.

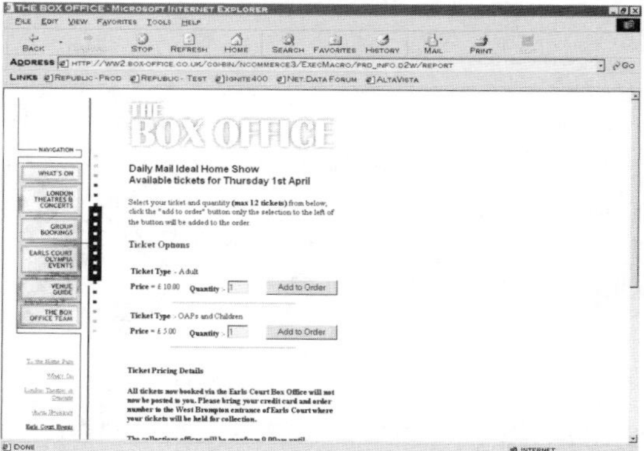

Figure 12.5: Purchase tickets.

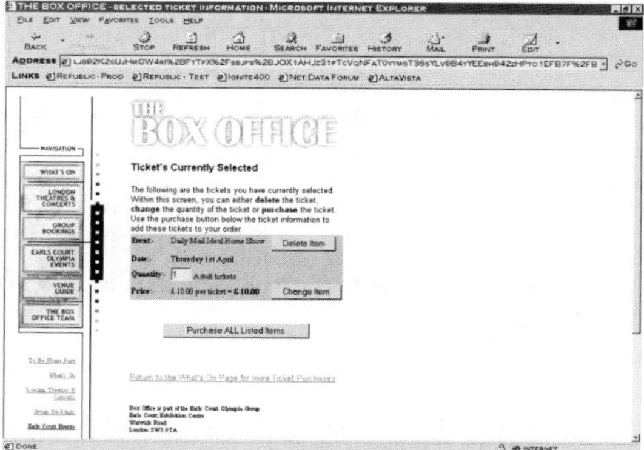

Figure 12.6: Purchase confirmation.

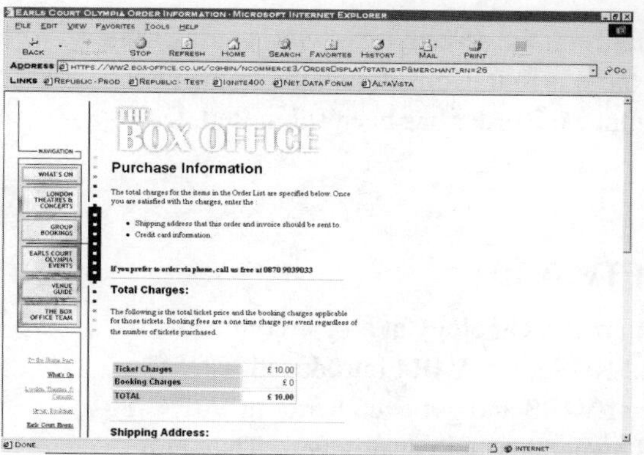

Figure 12.7: Purchase ticket screen — top portion.

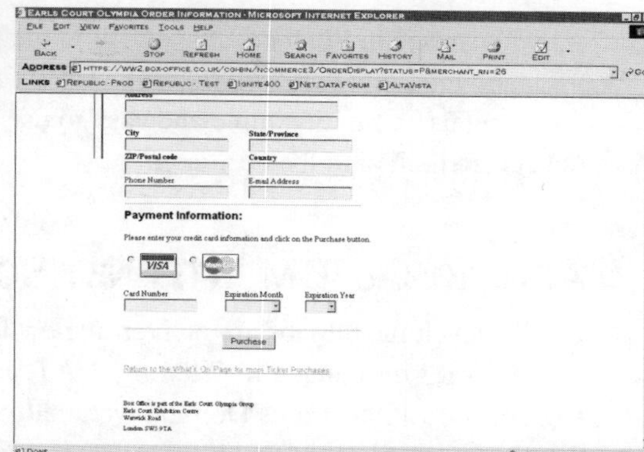

Figure 12. 8: Purchase ticket screen — bottom portion.

Net.Commerce hides the complexity of managing the e-commerce site, purchasing, security, and credit card transactions for The Box Office. Bleddyn has customized the site to meet the customers' specific requirements and integrate with existing ticketing systems. Bleddyn used Net.Data to implement the customization because Net.Data is fully supported without restriction under Net.Commerce 3.0.

When a user wants to purchase a ticket, he clicks the Book Tickets Here link on the home page shown in Figure 12.1.

The user receives a list of events that will be occurring, as shown in Figure 12.2. He simply clicks on the event he is interested in.

The next step is to give the customer a detailed description of the event, with times and pricing information, as shown in Figure 12.3.

In Figure 12.4, you see that the user may select a specific date for the show and continue to purchase tickets, or click the Return link and review another show.

Figure 12.5 shows the simple screen that allows the user to specify the quantity and type of tickets desired and purchasing button.

The user is given the opportunity to review his selection, continue shopping, change, or cancel his transaction, as shown in Figure 12.6. More important, he can click the Purchase All Listed Items link and buy his tickets.

Figure 12.7 shows the top part of the purchase screen, which gives the user the opportunity to review his charges and go back and make changes before proceeding.

As you can see in Figure 12.8, you fill in the fields on the screen, enter your credit card data, and click the Purchase button! That's all there is to it. Considering the tremendous response, users find it simple and easy to use. Once the order has been submitted, the tickets are mailed to the customer.

ADDITIONAL IBM INTERNET SOFTWARE

IBM's development labs are delivering new Internet technology at an incredible rate of speed. V4R3 introduced IP Filtering, NAT, and NetServer. V4R4 introduced VPN, LDAP, and LPAR. Lotus Domino went native at V4R3 and got even better in V4R4. Today, in the new IBM, developers take personal ownership in their products. They join user groups, mailing lists, and forums on the Internet to talk about their products and help folks get up and running. The result is robust products that meet the need of the marketplace.

The following is a brief introduction to some of these new offerings.

NETWORK ADDRESS TRANSLATION (NAT)

V4R3 introduced NAT, once a function reserved for standalone firewalls, to AS/400. It's built in and packaged with TCP/IP. IBM provides two forms of NAT, *hidden* and *mapped* addresses. You can map public IP addresses to internal addresses to facilitate connection by users on the Internet to your public addresses and users on your intranet to your private addresses.

I recently used this technology to configure 12 instances of an IBM HTTP Server on one machine so that users on the internal network could access the servers which were bound to addresses 10.10.10.1 through 10.10.10.12. I then mapped addresses from my public class C address block 156.96.80.1 through 156.96.80.12 to the servers with the NAT. When a request from the Internet is received on 156.96.80.5, it is translated by the NAT to 10.10.10.5 and passed on to the HTTP Server bound to that address. If users at 10.20.10.92 access the server at 10.10.10.5, they access the server directly bypassing the NAT.

A second scenario frequently found on many firewall implementations is the *hidden address translation* method. If you run a small office with an AS/400 connected to the Internet and several IP devices (PCs, Network Stations, Linux clients, etc.), you can use the NAT to allow all users to share a single public IP address. The internal devices are assigned non-Internet routable addresses 192... or 10... These addresses are then hidden behind a single public IP address. If a PC user wants to access the Internet, the PC address is translated to the shared public IP address and the packets sent on to the Internet. The NAT uses a technique where unique port numbers are assigned to the translated address so it can keep track of the device originating the traffic. When the return packets come back, they are routed to the originating devices. This technique offers exceptional security because the hidden device must initiate outbound traffic and cannot be located from the Internet.

You can use NAT to provide a safe and secure interface between an AS/400 that attaches to both your public and private networks. You may also use it to support some very sophisticated configurations isolating certain groups or individual users from certain computers in your network. With the help of IBM's NAT and IP filter developers, I worked out a configuration that supported a user with an AS/400, a low cost ADSL connection, and two IP addresses. We were able to develop a configuration using a single Ethernet adapter and the NAT to support e-mail, a Web server, and provide six personal computer users with Internet access. The only external technology was the DSL modem/router provided by his DSL provider.

IP FILTERING

Introduced in V4R3, IP Filtering provides a packet filtering mechanism that rivals any standalone firewall or router filter rules. IP Filtering blocks traffic not only at the IP address or port level, but by protocol (TCP or UDP), and blocks certain types of services and ICMP traffic. IP Filtering is robust, and efficient. It offers you the ability to restrict filtering to the initial packet from external sources or to filter every packet. It does *not* add significant overhead when used with a reasonable rule set.

The combination of NAT and IP Filtering provides as much protection as any firewall on the market. These two facilities make it possible for an AS/400 to protect itself without the need of an external firewall. I'm not saying you don't need a firewall, you just don't need one to protect your AS/400.

VIRTUAL PRIVATE NETWORKS (VPN)

VPN was introduced in V4R4 with many enhancements scheduled for the future. With this product, you can now take advantage of low-cost, Internet-based communication links to connect remote users and offices to your private internal LANs.

VPN provides secure (encrypted) connections between AS/400s and other clients (IBM publishes a list of tested clients in the INFOCENTER). This means that if you have employees working from home or a small branch office with a small number of people, a

Windows-based PC with a VPN client and dial-up Internet access is all you need to access your internal corporate network via your AS/400. See VPN in IBM's INFOCENTER on the Web (`www.as400.IBM.com`) for more information.

Lotus Domino

Lotus Domino went native in V4R3. V4R4 greatly enhances Lotus Domino and makes it *the* server of choice. My first experience with Lotus Domino was at V4R2 with Lotus Domino V4R6 running under OS/2 on an IPCS card. I didn't understand at that time why everyone thought this product was so important. It was a good groupware product with the ability to do some great things for remote employees with Notes software on their PCs, but beyond that, I couldn't see any great advantage in it.

Lotus Domino V5 (under V4R4) is much more powerful. It has two sides. One side is the Notes-based view of the product. Many people use this alone and build sophisticated systems using the Notes development client. The second side is Lotus Domino as a native OS/400-based product. This is where Lotus Domino shows its strengths and becomes a true industrial strength tool leveraging all of the best of the AS/400.

While the AS/400 includes an SMTP and POP3 server, they lack the security, encryption, and flexibility of the Lotus Domino mail servers. Domino (even without the Lotus Notes client) offers secure, reliable e-mail to any of the popular mail clients. You don't need to switch all your desktops to Lotus Notes in order to take advantage of the strong server side features.

As of V4R4, Lotus Domino can utilize the IBM HTTP Server with WebSphere and its Java Servlet and EJB (Enterprise Java Beans) support. It can also support and integrate with IBM's Net.Commerce e-Commerce flagship product, and you can integrate with Net.Data, RPG, Java, and other programs that run on the AS/400. You can use any Website development tool including the Lotus Notes client, but you aren't restricted to a single choice.

You can build integrated applications using many of the features built into Lotus Domino such as workflow, forms management, group based facilities, etc. IBM is working with Lotus to strengthen the Web-based interface and have shown remarkable improvements in V5 over previous releases. They are complying with open interface standards and RFCs to strengthen interfaces to external third party products.

I'm in the process of implementing several copies of Lotus Domino on AS/400s throughout my organization. One copy of Lotus Domino is on my gateway server. All Internet mail will be routed through this server. Domino will then handle the routing of the mail to machines in our branch offices where local users will pick up and send mail. We will also interconnect to our parent company.

One of the strengths of Lotus Domino is its built-in replication feature. It synchronizes its databases between parent, child, or peer level Domino servers throughout your organization. This means that users are always working on local current copies of data. If you have not adopted Lotus Domino for your company, I recommend you review it.

Another strength of Lotus Domino is Lightweight Directory Access Protocol (LDAP).

LDAP

If you use Web-based directory services to look up e-mail addresses, you have probably used LDAP. V4R3 introduced LDAP to the AS/400 and V4R4 introduced additional enhancements. I have been told that LDAP is a strategic direction for the AS/400. IBM is working to implement support for additional products and services. Today, the IBM HTTP Server supports LDAP as does Lotus Domino, and IBM's Secureway Host on Demand. In the near future, IBM will support virtually all applicable Internet servers on the AS/400 and will begin moving to provide object-level inclusion. Eventually, LDAP will be an alternative to the current user profile based method of user authentication for the AS/400.

What is LDAP and what does it do for you? It is an extensible *data store* (not a database) of information about people in your organization or with whom you do business. It is shipped with a standard set of attributes (all of the fields defined in the OS/400 System Directory). You can add additional information to the data store. If you want some company-specific fields (attributes, in LDAP terms), you simply use the Operations Navigator provided wizards to modify the LDAP schema.

Each attribute in the LDAP directory can be secured with an Access Control List restricting access to the attribute. You might store salary in the directory, or your president's direct dial telephone number and want access to those fields limited to a small group of people. LDAP is so flexible you can define rules that allow you to define global or specific access rules. Maybe only the top executives in the company can access your president's home telephone, but managers, directors, and officers can access any other employee's home phone. At the same time the general public or other employees cannot. This is all configurable.

LDAP allows you to establish relationships between other LDAP servers both within your organization and externally. You might define and maintain user information on an AS/400 in each branch or department of your company. If you were in the Los Angeles Information Systems Department, you might want to locate the Underwriting manager in San Francisco and obtain his e-mail address. You would search your local LDAP server, which would not find what you were looking for. It would then query other LDAP servers in your organization and find the correct person. LDAP uses sophisticated DNS-like logic to make searches across many LDAP servers very fast and efficient.

Take it for a test drive. LDAP like everything else we've talked about ships with OS/400!

NETSERVER

V4R3 introduced NetServer to the AS/400 and V4R4 enhanced it. NetServer is a file and print server. It allows Windows 95/98/NT PCs to access files stored in the IFS file system in the same manner that you would access files stored on a Novell, OS/2, or Windows NT file server. It also supports remote printing. This new facility is included with OS/400. PCs require no additional software to access NetServer files and printers. A Windows 95/98/NT PC uses its built-in Network Neighborhood software and internal TCP/IP protocols to access authorized resources. NetServer objects and printers are fully controlled via OS/400 security allowing you to grant and restrict access on a directory or object basis.

You may access NetServer locally over a LAN, remotely via VPN, or remotely via an Internet connection. I recommend VPN for providing remote access because VPN provides secure encrypted communications.

LOGICAL PARTITIONING (LPAR)

A key issue for large mission critical Internet shops is how to keep a system running 24 x 7 without taking a machine off-line for planned maintenance. In the past, you could buy an expensive special load balancing router and place that in front of a pair of AS/400s running a data replication product. A request would be received by the router and distributed to one of the two AS/400s based on a least-used algorithm to calculate the least-used machine. This same router could detect that one of its machines was off-line and would route all traffic to the surviving machine. This latter feature provided protection from system failures, and allowed system administrators to take the machine off-line for hardware and software upgrades.

As of V4R4 IBM has gone one step better on its high end multiple CPU based AS/400s. You can now logically partition your AS/400 running multiple copies or even different versions of OS/400 on each partition. V4R4 offers one partition per CPU at present. You can also use internal load balancing routing capabilities that are built in to the operating system and these new machines. This eliminates the costly front end load balancing router that was required in the past.

This feature allows you to take one partition off-line to apply service. IBM has had the ability to replace most parts of the AS/400 without powering down the machine for some time in their goal of non-stop computing. I have seen disks swapped out on machines with RAID5 arrays while the machine continued to process. The AS/400 may very well provide the best and easiest to support for non-stop operations available anywhere on any machine. See what it takes to accomplish this level of availability on other platforms for yourself and you will clearly see why the AS/400 is and should be the Internet platform of choice.

THIRD PARTY INTERNET SOFTWARE

When I started working with the Internet and the AS/400, I could count the number of vendors providing AS/400 Internet tools and software on one hand. Today there are dozens of vendors and hundreds of products with new products entering the market daily. Today you can buy utilities, add-in products, or complete integrated development environments.

IBM's Web site at `www.as400.ibm.com` offers a list of vendors providing Internet related products. The Web sites for all of the major AS/400 periodicals (including AS/400 Magazine at `www.as400magazine.com`) contain articles, reviews, and information about third party Internet products.

SECURITY AND THE INTERNET 13

Perhaps the greatest goal of this chapter is to put Internet security and security exposures on the Internet into perspective. There has been a great deal of media exposure about Web sites being hacked. This chapter will quantify Internet exposures and give AS/400 users a sense of comfort that owners of other platforms do not yet realize.

To understand how the AS/400 is the safest machine on the Internet, you must understand the various types of hacker attacks.

SNIFFING

The exposure that many people on the Internet are most concerned with is perhaps the least threatening exposure of all. This exposure involves a hacker using a *sniffer*, which is a hardware or software device that monitors traffic between your machine and other machines to obtain user IDs and passwords.

To sniff or monitor traffic between your machine and other machines on the Internet, the hacker must insert his monitoring device into your network, the network of your ISP, or the network of a major relay point on the Internet. He must gain access to a private network or router.

Contrary to popular belief, it is *not* possible to sniff out any data over the Internet. I cannot put sniffer software on my PC and target remote computers on the Internet. I must be able to insert the sniffer into a LAN over which traffic is routed.

If you take proper physical security precautions (i.e. routers and network hubs are locked in secure closets or computer rooms), this exposure is limited on site to your network management personnel. The next level of access is the telephone company or the data center of your ISP or a backbone provider. It is a federal offense in the United States to illegally access these facilities. Sniffing is a form of wire-tapping. When done on interstate telephone lines, it is a federal crime. I'm sure it has been done, but the risk is great, so the reward must be also.

One other possible access method is the router itself. Most routers offer some degree of exposure via their SMTP (system management) ports and their Telnet ports. Use of random password generation software will protect the routers adequately. You should consult your router manufacturer and ask your ISP how it protects its routers and physical data center. One incredibly stupid mistake that too many people make is to fail to change the default passwords on their routers. Check it! Change it! Anyone can gain access to your public router via Telnet!

Although sniffing is difficult, and the legal risks in the United States are so severe that it makes it an unlikely crime, there are significant risks when routing traffic internationally. Many countries do not have the strict regulations and enforcement practices that we have in the United States. Often, the major hubs in smaller countries are operated by universities and are open to curious or even malicious students. Companies with employees travelling in Asia, Russia, or the former Soviet Bloc countries should take protective measures to ensure the privacy of their transactions. Encryption is strongly recommended in these cases.

SPOOFING

Spoofing is a hacking technique where a hacker pretends to be your client or you. The objective is to trick a client into sending his credit card information or his user ID and passwords to the computer that is pretending to be you. This, like sniffing, requires access to a router that is upstream of you on the Internet (i.e. your ISP or at another major interconnect point through which your data must flow). Again, this requires a physical connection to your network or of your ISP. If a hacker could attach a device to your ISP's internal network, he could pretend to be you and your traffic would be routed to the hacker's computer. This is extremely unlikely to occur due the fact that the hacker must gain physical access to a major data center and, by doing so, violate several state and federal laws.

Spoofing is one of the least common types of attack today because it can easily be prevented bu using Secure Sockets Layer (SSL) protocol and a digital certificate. Your digital certificate is impossible to duplicate. A fictitious certificate alerts your client's browser of an invalid certificate. Spoofing was more common in the early days of the Internet when almost anyone had access to the Internet inter-connection facilities that were housed on university campuses and staffed by students. This is no longer the case, and security, in most ISP facilities, is extremely tight.

If you are using IBM's AS/400 DNS server with BIND version 4.9.3, it is possible to trick your DNS server into letting the hacker's router assume control of the domains that you have authorized on your DNS server. This hack is done by modifying the BIND source code on the hacker's computer and sending DNS service-level instructions to your server. Until IBM upgrades the DNS server, *do not* use it for external DNS services.

DENIAL OF SERVICE ATTACKS

A *denial of service attack* is intended to prevent you or your clients from accessing your computer system. It is not intended to gain access to your computer system. This type of attack is generally accomplished via programs that send very large numbers of e-mail messages to your SMTP server.

This type of attack is blocked by sophisticated mail software in place at your ISP's facility. This software monitors abnormal amounts of e-mail traffic, initiates analysis programs to verify that the site is under attack, and deletes messages sent from the attacker. Some products offer counter-attack software that sends the messages back to the sender. This is a very dangerous strategy, however, because most hackers use someone else's computer to send the messages to you. Standard procedure in case of an e-mail denial of service attack is to identify the messages constituting the attack and delete them. These types of attacks are extremely rare and relatively easy to protect against. You can normally identify the source of the attack and contact the sources's site administrator. Together you can devise methods of dealing with the offender.

FTP can also be the target of a denial of service attack. I do not have anonymous FTP enabled on my AS/400s, and I must know the user who sends files to my machine. Users of anonymous FTP should limit the size of files uploaded to their servers. You should also limit the number of concurrent users and the number of files that any given user can send in a single day. These are easy protections to take. FTP denial of service attacks attempt to fill your system's disk with junk files in hopes that your system will crash.

SERIOUS HACKERS

A serious hacker is an expert computer programmer. In the UNIX and Windows NT world, many computers have been hacked by these programming experts. These people are intimately familiar with the UNIX and Windows machine code. They also know of holes in the TCP/IP sockets protocol that allow them to write machine code into your computer's memory. These programs typically give the hacker access to a command line or the ability to pretend to be another user. These techniques are possible in the UNIX and Windows NT environments because the system memory architecture is an open architecture with well-defined interfaces between programs and shared memory modules, where control programs run in pre-specified locations. If you can gain access to a system management area of memory, you own the computer. UNIX is notorious for its lack of security mechanisms. Windows NT and PC/DOS are knock-offs of the UNIX operating system and are exposed to the same internal architectural design weaknesses. If you can gain access to Windows NT memory, you own the computer!

AS/400 STRENGTHS

An AS/400, running a security level of 40 or 50, is virtually an impenetrable fortress on the Internet compared to other computers. Due to its multi-level software design, users and programmers of the AS/400 are not even aware of the low-level code (the SLIC, or System Licensed Internal Code) that runs the computer. You cannot poke code into memory through a deliberate address pointer error and execute the code. If you attempt to modify an AS/400 program (assuming you can figure out how to get to it) and try to branch out of its assigned memory space, the system will abend the program with a protection exception. It is probably impossible for all but a handful of programmers working for IBM at IBM's Rochester Laboratory to be able to hack into an AS/400. I'm not sure if even they could do it.

At level 40 or 50 security (level 40 is an absolute must for machines connected to the Internet), you cannot access memory outside your *job*. Your job is the user profile associated with the server that lets you access the AS/400. Servers you can access are SMTP, POP3, HTTP, Telnet, FTP, DNS, and TFTP. These servers all implement user-profile level security. Many of these servers, like the HTTP Server, have their own user profiles. These user profiles should be set up with read-only or read and execute authorities. They should never have write authority or object management authority. All of the Web servers are designed to function with read and execute authority. They are all designed to use adopted authority for internal functions.

REAL SECURITY RISKS

The real security risks that exist today do not involve direct frontal attacks on AS/400s via the Internet. The most dangerous piece of equipment you own is a personal computer attached to your network with a modem and a direct dial telephone number attached to it. If the PC has a program such as PC/Anywhere installed on it, you have a huge security risk.

Think for a minute about dial-up PCs. They are generally attached to your telephone switch along with other direct-dial telephones in your company. If your area code and exchange were (213) 555-xxxx a hacker could run a simple program to dial all of the numbers in your 555 prefix and look for modems. It is entirely possible that many of your dial-up PCs, especially those with PC/Anywhere installed, will answer and instantly place the caller in session with the PC. Many PC products are notorious about failing to log off and drop a session when the telephone line disconnects. The next person to call the computer picks up the session exactly as it was before the telephone connection was broken. Test for this exposure. Does you network administrator have one or more PCs at the office that they dial into from home to fix problems? Imagine what fun a hacker could have if he could access that PC with your network administrator already logged in.

Often, PCs are left logged into the network. The biggest offenders in this security exposure are your own network management or computer operations people. They tend to use PCs with PC/Anywhere or similar software as remote consoles or service devices for remote AS/400s, PC servers, or network management equipment. These devices generally have sufficient authority to allow a hacker to set up his own user IDs and passwords with SECOFR authority and do with your system what he will.

While the world is looking for ways to block hackers on the Internet, we are leaving our back door wide open to the real hackers, who dial telephone numbers and access modems that are left unprotected. This is a far worse exposure than leaving an AS/400 directly connected to the Internet with minimal security protection.

Most well-documented cases of hacking are traced to personal computers with modems that were accessed by the hacker, not to a frontal attack via the Internet.

SECURE YOUR AS/400 WITH REASON

I strongly recommend running an Internet-connected AS/400 at security level 40. Run IBM's security audit programs to identify and remove standard user IDs and default passwords. Ensure that PUBLIC is *EXCLUDE on all objects on the AS/400 unless you specifically grant public access (you should have no need to do so). Make sure that all of your Internet servers use a bonafide user ID. This user ID should be given read and execute authority to those objects that are required to support the server, including your HTML pages and CGI programs. Grant write authority only to those libraries or directories where users must write data via FTP. Your Web server can be given write access to a limited number of directories where user data can be stored.

YOUR PEOPLE ARE A MAJOR SECURITY RISK

I can use firewalls, AS/400 security, run checks on my dial-up telephone lines, and be the most paranoid security administrator in the world. But no matter what I do as a security administrator, I cannot control the single greatest risk to computer security: my own employees. Unless you implement an automated system like Secure-ID, you are vulnerable to employees being talked into giving up their user IDs and passwords.

If a hacker can figure out your system administrator's user ID, he has improved his chances of hacking the SYSADMIN's password and accessing your system by 100 percent. If he can talk three of your clerical users into giving him their user IDs and passwords, he has enough information to establish a pattern and figure out what your rules for passwords are. The infamous hacker Mr. Mitnick gained access to most of the sites he hacked by conning targeted employees by telephone into giving up their user IDs and passwords. You must develop a very strong password protection policy and be sure that every employee with computer system access understands how important protecting his password is.

These folks are good. They often call and pretend to be IBM support and convince your system administrator to give them administrator access to the system. Don't think for a minute that you cannot be conned by a hacker who is a pro.

A WARNING ABOUT ANYNET AND SNA OVER TCP/IP

IBM's Client Access product, and several competitive products, support the use of SNA over TCP/IP with AnyNet. I would recommend approaching this combination of products with extreme caution. AnyNet enables the SBMRMTCMD that allows knowledgeable users to run commands from their AnyNet clients. They must still know a valid login to the AS/400 and know how to execute the command.

CONCLUSION

The AS/400, used with reasonable precautions, is the most secure server available for the Internet today. No other computer, including IBM's own mainframes, RS6000s, or personal computers, are as secure as an AS/400. Add SSL encryption and digital cryptography to the AS/400, and you have a rock-solid computing environment.

PART II

PLANNING YOUR INTERNET PROJECT

This section looks at the activities required to get your organization online with an electronic commerce Web site. We will explore the preliminary fact-finding activities prerequisite to the planning and design phases of your Internet project; the planning activities and deliverables; and the need to identify key people and the roles that they must play in a successful Internet implementation. The planning chapters also identify the elements of a requirements document and implementation plan.

Internet project planning can be broken down into six phases:

FACT-FINDING

Chapter 14 covers the preliminary fact-finding activities from which a plan can be developed. This includes identifying the participants in the project, business requirements, and goals.

REQUIREMENTS DEFINITION

Chapter 15 addresses defining the business requirements of an Internet project. You must identify why you need an Internet presence and what you hope it will do for your company.

PHYSICAL PLANNING

Chapter 16 addresses the physical planning necessary to acquire the necessary hardware, software, and communications facilities to host a Web site.

PLANNING YOUR SERVER CONFIGURATION

Server configuration is like database design. A well-designed configuration allows you to easily enhance and extend your Web site over time. Chapter 17 is a guide to planning your Web server configuration for electronic commerce.

PLANNING YOUR WEB APPLICATIONS

Chapter 18 provides a description of the tasks involved in developing an interactive electronic commerce Web site application.

PLANNING YOUR WEB SITE'S FUNCTIONALITY

Chapter 19 helps you decide what features your public Web site must contain, how it should look, and how it should work.

DEVELOPING YOUR PROJECT PLAN

Chapter 20 brings all of the elements discussed in this section of the book together and provides a sample project plan.

PLANNING ISSUES

Your planning issues should include:

- Knowing why you are going to do it
- Knowing what it is you are going to do
- Identifying your audience(s)
- Knowing what it is going to cost
- Knowing who is going to do it
- Building a consensus with all involved parties
- Developing an extensible architecture that supports future development

The general approach taken in this book is a *top-down planning* methodology that starts with business requirements and works down to technology and implementation. It should be pointed out that the planning process is an iterative process. Change is a constant in Internet systems development. A Web site is never complete. A successful Web site constantly changes to respond to your marketplace, new business requirements, and the needs of your audience.

Planning can be a formalize or informal activity. The importance of the following chapters is to identify the tasks necessary to make informed decisions and structure a project that meets the organization's objectives. Whether you implement a formal project plan with a large number of participants, or run a one- or two-person project informally, it is recommended that you follow the guidelines in this section.

Informal projects may not require written planning documents. If you do not prepare the planning documents suggested in this section, at least make some notes for yourself based on the following discussions.

Business Requirements: Fact Finding

Whether you have a large formalized development approach or are a one-person team, the initial step in beginning your Internet project is one of fact-finding. This can be done via informal discussion with members of your senior management team or via structured requirements planning sessions.

This chapter is written for the person or persons in an organization who will determine the feasibility and content of your presence on the Internet. This may be the the CIO or a member of the information systems organization.

The fact-finding phase determines why your organization should have an Internet presence, what that presence should consist of, who will be involved in the development process, and what results are expected from the successful implementation of your project.

Many AS/400 installations have limited resources. Often, one person is responsible for the planning, design, implementation, and administration of a Web site. Whether your project team consists of one person or many, the following issues should be reviewed and a strategic plan developed for your organization.

A good Internet strategic plan identifies long-term requirements for your organization. The plan will assist you in developing a Web server design and configuration that will grow with your expanding use of the Internet.

The fundamental concern is to identify all of your potential users or audiences. Identify the types of information and applications that these users will require. This understanding is critical to designing a directory structure, Web site navigation, and the physical resources required to support a growth-oriented Internet implementation.

During the fact-finding phase of your planning activities, an executive sponsor should be identified. A strong sponsor facilitates project development. Most often, the executive sponsor will be the vice president of marketing, but whomever the sponsor, the ability to build consensus and work with other senior staff members of the organization will greatly facilitate the success of the project.

WHY DOES YOUR ORGANIZATION NEED AN INTERNET PRESENCE?

There are many reasons for implementing a Web site or providing your organization with an Internet presence. Some of these reasons affect the strategic business goals of your organization and some are purely economic.

COMPETITIVENESS

A strong reason for developing an Internet presence is the fact that your competitors have one. An office supply company or bookstore that does not sell its products via the Internet may find that its customers are shopping online with its competitors.

As part of the fact-finding effort, identify which competitors have a presence on the Internet and what they are doing with it. Do they sell products, provide electronic information, supply online services, or something else?

If possible, determine how your customers react to your competitors' Web sites. Are they using competitors because of their Web sites? Are your competitors negatively affecting your sales?

IMPROVED COMMUNICATIONS

Are your customers, vendors, and others asking to exchange electronic mail with you? Many companies are finding that Internet-enabled electronic mail results in a substantial benefit to their organization. Electronic communications can save money, reduce response times, and optimize the efforts of those who deal with people outside the organization. How many of your external contacts have Internet access and can send and receive electronic mail? If possible, a formal or informal survey of your customers and suppliers will help guide your project efforts. It will also help your management team assess the benefits to be derived from connecting to the Internet.

REDUCED COMMUNICATIONS COSTS

Many companies provide employees, vendors, and customers with software and dial-up communications links to their computers. This generally involves providing the end-user with special communications software and paying for the telephone lines and communications costs.

The AS/400 provides several solutions to allow these people to use their browsers or standard terminal emulation software to connect via a $19.95-per-month Internet service provider, possibly saving thousands of dollars in communications and reducing support costs.

REDUCED MANUAL LABOR

Most organizations have forms that must be completed by their vendors, customers, and others with whom they do business. You may be able to implement these forms on your Web site and eliminate the human intervention necessary to enter data into your computer systems upon receiving the forms.

Ask yourself: Do your employees fill out and submit forms? Can these processes be automated via a Web site? Do you produce computer reports and fax or mail them to your customers or vendors when requested? Can you provide access to this information via your Web site? Would this improve service and reduce costs?

SELL YOUR PRODUCTS

Electronic commerce through a Web site is analogous to operating an electronic store on the World Wide Web. Most companies benefit from providing an electronic store on the Internet. Key questions to ask: Do you deal with the public? Do you deal with companies? Will you have to put a catalog on the Web? Do you take credit card orders?

IMPROVED SERVICE

An electronic Web site that automates aspects of customer service can make the difference between return customers and watching your customers migrate to the competition.

Key questions to ask: Who receives telephone calls from customers, vendors, investors, or others outside the organization? What type of information is requested? Can a Web site provide the information directly to the requestor? How can time and money be saved by providing this information? Will this saving result in a reduction in staff or support costs?

IDENTIFY YOUR AUDIENCE

Determining the audience of a Web site is perhaps the single most important task that you must perform. Ask yourself the following questions: Who is your customer? Do you deal with the public? Or do you deal with companies? Do you support employees who work in the field or at home? What services do they need that Internet connectivity can provide? Where are these people located? Do you do business internationally?

I recently visited two Web sites for convention centers operated by two different cities. One was oriented towards companies that might book trade shows into the convention center. It provided detailed maps of the facility, explained the resources (including electrical power) that were available, and provided critical details for prospective exhibitors. No information existed on this site about shows currently booked at the convention center; the targeted audience was the exhibitor, not attendees.

In contrast, another city provided a Web site built around a calendar of events booked into the convention center. It described each show in detail, with a section of the site allocated to each show, highlighted with graphics and lists of exhibitors. This site targeted the public and promoted attendance at the shows booked into the convention center. This Web site provided no information about the facility or its resources.

Both sites are successful in meeting the expectations of the organizations that built the sites; however,both might have benefited by targeting multiple audiences. The point here is not to demonstrate a right or wrong way of thinking about audience, but to illustrate that a Web site can have multiple audiences with different objectives.

ARE YOU A PUBLIC COMPANY?

Public companies often benefit by posting investor information on their Web site. Work with your investor relations person to determine the information investors ask for. Find out if your CEO will write and update an investors newsletter.

WHAT SERVICES DOES YOUR ORGANIZATION NEED?

To most people, the Internet means World Wide Web. In reality, there are many services available to companies that are connected to the Internet.

WORLD WIDE WEB ACCESS FOR YOUR USERS

Providing your users with the ability to access the Internet via a browser and other desktop tools is often a valuable objective of an Internet project. The Web has numerous services that are beneficial to many companies, including search services like Yahoo! and Excite, customized news services, a wealth of financial planning information, and government-related information ranging from technical safety to legislative analysis. In addition, many of your suppliers may have Web sites providing up-to-the-minute descriptions of their products, services, and prices. Consider who in your organization would benefit from having browser-based desktop access to the Internet. What Web sites provide information that would be beneficial to members of your organization?

FILE TRANSFER PROTOCOL (FTP)

If you are using conventional dial-up communications, explore using high-speed Internet communications to improve the speed and reliability of data exchange, while reducing cost.

Do you exchange data electronically with your suppliers or customers? Do the people that you exchange data with support FTP and have an Internet connection? If the answer to either question is yes, FTP should be included in your Internet plan.

ELECTRONIC DOCUMENT EXCHANGE AND E-MAIL

If your company routinely prints, faxes, and mails documents, you may find that employees may benefit from being able to attach word processing documents, spreadsheets, etc., to e-mail messages. The cost of facsimile transmission is an overlooked business cost. Exchanging documents via the Internet can greatly reduce communications costs.

USENET NEWSGROUPS

Almost every subject imaginable has a Usenet Newsgroup on the Internet. These newsgroups are bulletin board-like facilities where people post questions or comments and other members of the newsgroups reply or comment. Newsgroups can be an extremely valuable support mechanism for PC users and information systems professionals. Virtually every software company has a newsgroup where developers, support personnel, and other users help each other use computer products more effectively.

TELECONFERENCING

Many companies use free software provided by Netscape and Microsoft to conduct teleconferences via the Internet or via their own internal networks. This software provides the ability for as many as 20 users to conference and share facilities such as video (a $100 camera on each participating PC is required), audio (sound cards required), white boards, and other interactive facilities. These facilities can often be used in geographically dispersed companies to reduce travel costs and improve communications.

DETERMINE YOUR IMAGE

One of the most difficult and politically significant aspects of Web site development is deciding on the image that you want your Web site to project. Is your company formal and conservative or fun and humorous?

A good way to develop an image for your Web site is to collect company marketing material. This includes press releases, marketing brochures, and advertisements, including radio and television ads. Don't overlook the little things like letterhead, business cards, and newsletters.

Do you have a consistent, well-established image? Do you use your logo on all of your materials? What is the color scheme? Do you use cartoons or humor? Talk to your marketing people about your image. You need to know what type of image the company wants to project.

MANAGING YOUR PROJECT

Small projects with limited goals and objectives often will be the most successful method of getting an Internet project started and providing your organization with a direct tangible payback.

Consider the support you have for your Internet project. Who supports it? How much are they willing to spend? How long will it take to show results? The answers to these questions will determine how to approach your Internet project.

WILL THIS BE A LARGE FORMAL PROJECT?

If your organization has a formal project planning methodology in place, you may be required to use it to plan and manage your Internet project. If you use a formalized methodology, try to break the project into small, deliverable components that will minimize the number of people involved in the project and reduce the overall development time.

While most people in your organization have surfed the Net, few, if any, have a good concept of how to use the Internet to conduct business. Internet technology is new technology. You must develop one or two applications before you and your organization understand the implications of this technology and its benefits.

WILL THIS BE A SMALL TRIAL PROJECT?

Often, a small experimental project developed in the back room with a single sponsor produces the quickest and best results. Using this approach, try to find an executive who has the interest and desire to implement a pilot project. Keep the scope of the project limited. For example, in an insurance company, the project might be limited to providing insurance agents with basic application, policy, and claims information inquiry screens. In banking, you might display a customer's account balances and transactions.

In almost every industry, there is a single application that provides customers with information they want and need. Providing this information will be appreciated by your customers and keep your name in front of them every time they visit your Web site to view their information.

WHO IS YOUR SPONSOR?

Successful Internet projects require an executive sponsor. This should be someone in your organization who has the ability to get things done and has an interest in using the Internet as a means of communicating with the people with whom you do business. Often, your marketing vice president is a good candidate for sponsoring a Web site. Marketing is a traditional and viable use of a Web site.

DO YOU HAVE THE FUNDING?

A public Web site can be implemented on an Internet Service Provider's computer for as little as $50 per month. You can generally implement a public Web site and even use one of several services to implement secure credit card purchases via the Internet. A developer with a tool such as Microsoft Frontpage can develop a public Web site quickly and rapidly. Many companies have experimented with the Web by subscribing to a service such as America Online, CompuServe, Prodigy, etc., and using the personal Web page space provided by the service. Most online service providers provide limited space and access to personal Web pages as part of their basic monthly fee. These services may have restrictions regarding the use of their personal Web page hosting service for commercial use. If you wish to try this approach, the cost may be as little as $19 per month.

A private interactive Web site that uses your AS/400 and its data will typically cost $50,000 to $75,000 in start-up hardware, software, and communications costs. It will cost between $500 to $1,500 per month to operate. Additionally, it will require a substantial commitment in time by at least one senior-level information systems person.

WHO WILL PARTICIPATE IN THE PROJECT?

Over time, your Internet presence will involve virtually everyone in your organization in one way or another. Detailed roles must be defined and filled to develop a successful Internet presence. A single person or many people may perform the roles.

The following paragraphs identify and describe the roles involved in developing an Internet presence and managing an Internet project. A role is a *function*, not a position. Often, one person may perform many roles.

CORPORATE SPONSOR

The corporate sponsor sets the direction for the project. The sponsor is generally a senior executive of the organization who should be personally responsible for your Internet presence and, ideally, have decision-making authority. The sponsor will:

- Review and approve Web site content
- Be responsible for adding people to the project as warranted
- Build consensus with other members of your organization's management team
- Represent the organization's best interests in the project

PROJECT MANAGER

This role is one of planning, monitoring progress, and facilitation. The project manager develops and monitors the project plan and works closely with the corporate sponsor to ensure that required resources are made available to keep the project on schedule and within budget. The project manager's role is difficult because the resources working on the project rarely report to the project manager; the role of the project manager is, therefore, one of facilitator.

WEB CONTENT PROVIDER

Generally, a Web content provider is an end user with specialized knowledge, expertise, or information. Often specific individuals within the organization are asked to take responsibility for various parts of the Web site. Newsletter updates are such an area of responsibility. Content providers are generally brought into the project by the corporate sponsor. Some content providers' involvement is limited to a specific part of the Web site; others have ongoing responsibilities.

CORPORATE ATTORNEY

A Web site may be viewed by millions of people worldwide. It is extremely important that your Web site content be reviewed for statements that could be misinterpreted and result in potential litigation. Your organization may also have trademarks, service marks, and registered names that need to be properly protected. The same guidelines used for advertising and press releases should be used for Web content.

Rights to privacy and security are additional areas of legal concern when publishing information such as billing information, account balances, insurance claims data, and the like.

WEBMASTER

The role of Webmaster is somewhat ambiguous. In the context of this book, the Webmaster is the person responsible for implementing changes, monitoring access, and overseeing overall operations of the Web site. In some organizations, the Webmaster may have a more limited role, perhaps being responsible only for Web content or for site administration and change control.

WEB CONTENT DEVELOPER

The Web content developer is a combination of systems analyst, application designer, and high-level programmer. The Web content developer's responsibilities include:

- Determining the specific technical requirements for each application implemented on the Web site, including Web page design, navigation, data content, and forms design and validation.
- Visually developing Web pages using HTML and graphical Web page design tools
- Writing the specifications for CGI application programs that fulfill the business requirements of a Web-based application.
- Working with content providers and the corporate sponsor to test Web-based applications prior to implementation

GRAPHIC DESIGNER

A graphic designer may be asked to assist in the layout of HTML Web pages. Graphic designers specialize in the layout of text, color, and graphics to ensure proper visual impact. A good graphic designer is schooled in the marketing psychology of visual communication.

COMMERCIAL ARTIST

A commercial artist provides the artwork and advertising layouts that will be presented on your Web site. Web site art requires specialized skills; the artist needs to have experience with the tools and techniques specific to the limitations of Web sites and current technology, in addition to their skills as an artist.

APPLICATION PROGRAMMER

Interactive Web sites use CGI programs to retrieve, store, validate, and manipulate data displayed on a Web site or captured from Web site forms. The programmer must learn the specific techniques for writing programs that interface with your Web server. Often, the Web content developer develops HTML pages and the programmer writes programs that receive specific input data, perform specific processing, and return a result back to the HTML page.

On the AS/400, ILE/RPG skills will be adequate for most applications. C, C++, and Java skills are helpful.

AS/400 SYSTEMS PROGRAMMER

Regardless of your choice of Internet software, most Internet facilities are part of OS/400. The person in your organization responsible for installing software and configuring your AS/400 must become involved in your Internet project. This person may need to learn new skills and become acutely aware of the security implications of connecting an AS/400 to the Internet.

NETWORK SPECIALIST

The process of connecting your AS/400 to the Internet is one that requires knowledge of computer networking. A network specialist is involved in the connection of your AS/400 to the Internet. Responsibilities include:

- Implementing and configuring your firewall
- Designing internal and external routing
- Setting up and configuring your internal DNS and DHCP configurations
- Monitoring network traffic and network capacity
- Diagnosing communications problems

BUSINESS REQUIREMENTS: DEFINITION

After you've collected some general information about your organization and potential uses and users of the Internet, a requirements definition document should be written. It is a good idea to commit your requirements to paper even if your project is very informal. A requirements definition document crystallizes everyone's thinking about why your organization is creating an Internet presence and what applications and Internet services can be expected. A requirements document simply summarizes the information collected in Chapter 14.

The following is a requirements definition document prepared for a fictitious company called Acme Quality Fruits. The technical chapters in "Part III, Building Your Web Site" will use the requirements document as the basis for the illustrations and examples.

A BUSINESS EXAMPLE

Acme Quality Fruits (AQF) is a fictious midsize firm that buys and distributes unusual or exotic fruits via a network of distributors that sell to markets and restaurants. AQF buys its products from growers or grower representatives all over the world. AQF is headquartered in San Pedro, California, where it operates its offices and a warehouse and distribution facility. AQF employs approximately 100 people and has contract purchasing agents in 17 countries throughout the world.

The company uses an AS/400 with packaged software to handle the day-to-day operations of its business. The company uses a model 510 operating at about 70 percent capacity. The entire data processing department consists of a manager and two programmer/analysts.

The president of the company has been told that he should check out "this Internet thing" and "put up a Web site." He has asked his vice president of marketing and data processing manager to figure out what they need to do.

The VP of marketing and the DP manager read Chapter 1 of this book and collected a great deal of information about what they might do. The VP of marketing asked the DP manager to put together a requirements definition document. What follows details the document they produced.

COMPONENTS OF THE REQUIREMENTS DOCUMENT

The requirements definition document would normally be distributed to the decision makers in your organization and approved as the basis for your project. As illustrated in the sample document for Acme Quality Fruits Company, it consists of the following parts:

MISSION STATEMENT

The mission statement is a brief one-paragraph statement that summarizes the contents of the entire document. Most business readers are bombarded with reading material. The mission statement and the budget at the end of the document may be all your reader actually reads. Writing a short mission statement helps provide clarity and focus for the document.

AUDIENCE AND OBJECTIVES

This section should be kept short and to the point. It should identify each audience that the project will support. It should clearly identify Web Site objectives.

The document's purpose is to state what will be done in general terms. It should not provide detail. It should not attempt to be a design or technical document.

ACME QUALITY FRUIT COMPANY

INTERNET PROJECT - REQUIREMENTS DEFINITION

Mission Statement:

The Acme Quality Fruit Company shall use the Internet to provide the public with information about the products sold by the company. It shall provide distributors with World Wide Web-based tools to order, track orders, and review billing for products sold by the company. Electronic communications will be provided to support customer and public inquiry regarding the company's products and services. It will provide selected employees with access to the World Wide Web to support required research activities. It will provide remote employees and agents with Internet-based connectivity to computer systems that deal with purchasing and product sales.

Audience and Objectives:

1. General Public

   The company sells its products to distributors that in turn sell the products to high-end supermarkets throughout the United States. The company's Web site should acquaint the public with the company's products, provide information on how to use the products, and assist the consumer in locating the products.

2. Product Awareness

   This section of the Web site should list and describe the company's products and provide pictures of the products.

3. Product Utilization

   Many of the company's products are exotic fruits with which the public may not be familiar. The Web site should provide recipes and information on how to use its products.

4. Where to Buy

   A product locator system needs to be deployed to assist the consumer in locating the company's products at a retailer in their community.

5. Company and Investor Information

   The company is a public company. This section of the Web site should provide information of interest to investors, including financial information, and a newsletter describing the business activities of the company, which targets investors.

6. Distributor Support

   The company takes orders from distributors, but ships directly to specific stores on behalf of the distributor. This section of the Web site should be private and secure. A distributor should be able to log-in to the Web site, check product availability, order product, check the status of orders, track the shipment of orders, and review billing information. The distributor will also have access to information about when products are available throughout

7. Growers and Suppliers

   The system must improve communications between the company's buyers and the growers and suppliers of its products. Support will include providing the grower with the ability to submit an offer to sell, and describe the quality, quantity, and availability of their produce. The system must be able to accommodate and adjust for international differences, because the company does business with growers and their agents throughout the world.

8. Employees

   Many company employees must interact with suppliers, distributors, and government regulators worldwide. The company has a field sales force that visits and works with its distributors on a regular basis. It deploys a team of customer service representatives that assists retailers in marketing the company's products. Customer service representatives must be able to provide consumer information about their products.

   A. Consumer Relations

      Consumer Relations will receive e-mail inquiries about the company's products and uses. They may also receive inquiries about the safety of the company's products and the controls employed by foreign growers. Consumer Relations employees will need e-mail access and the ability to publish FAQs (frequently asked questions) about the company's products.

   B. Distributor Sales Representatives

      Distributor Sales Representatives in the past have placed all orders taken from the distributors. The sales representative needs access to product information and the ability to enter orders via the Web. If distributors use the Web as anticipated, the role of the field salesperson will change dramatically. Sales Representatives also need to be able to communicate with various individuals within the company via electronic communications.

   C. Buyers

      Buyers need the ability to acquire crop-availability information. Buyers often visit growers throughout the world and need the ability to purchase crops electronically. This can be supported via the Web site and via electronic communications.

   D. Headquarters Employees

      Headquarters includes legal and agricultural analysts who need to access the Internet via the World Wide Web to keep track of weather and crop conditions, as provided by various government agencies. These analysts must also monitor U.S. Department of Commerce trade agreements and regulations for importing fresh fruits from foreign countries. These people need both electronic communications and browser access to the World Wide Web. They may need FTP access in order to submit government mandated reports and filings.

E. Warehouse and Shipping

Warehouse and Shipping personnel interact with the company's business processing systems, keeping track of inventories and receiving and shipping its products to retailers via many independent shipping contractors. This information must be integrated with the Web site to facilitate order and shipment tracking. Electronic mail and communications will be required to facilitate order tracking.

Project Deliverables

The Vice President of Marketing will head the company's Internet project.

The Data Processing Manager shall be responsible for technology and development and provide the resources to implement the company's Internet technology.

The following facilities will be implemented at Acme Quality Fruits Company:

- A Web site providing public information about the company. To be implemented three months from project inception. Coordinated by the Vice President of Marketing.
- A private and secure Web site initially providing distributors with the ability to order products, tracks orders, and display billing information. To be implemented within six months of project inception. Coordinated by the Vice President of Marketing.
- Electronic mail communication between the company's employees and others with whom they do business. To be implemented within six months of project inception. To be coordinated by the Data Processing Manager.
- World Wide Web access to be available to designated employees. To be implemented within nine months of project inception. To be coordinated by the Data Processing Manager.
- Replace dial-up terminal access with Internet-based terminal emulation for employees and others. To be implemented within six months of project inception. To be coordinated by the Data Processing Manager.

Future Projects: After one year of operation, the effectiveness of the company's Web sites and Internet operations will be evaluated. This evaluation will determine the benefits derived from the previously stated requirements and specific objectives. If the company determines that the Internet project has been beneficial and cost effective, other projects will be identified and implemented based upon company requirements.

Project Budget: The cost for computer hardware and software necessary to implement the specific projects contained in this document shall not exceed $75,000. Monthly operating costs for the project shall not exceed $2,000 per month. The Data Processing Manager shall serve as general project manager. Regular status and budget reports shall be provided each month.

PROJECT DELIVERABLES

This section identifies specific tangible deliverables to be produced by the project. It provides a completion date and identifies the person(s) responsible for the deliverable. For the purposes of this book, I have expressed dates in terms of months from project inception. If I were going to submit this document to my management, I would put specific dates in the document.

PROJECT BUDGET

The sample document provides "not to exceed" amounts for both the total hardware and software acquisition costs and monthly recurring costs. This document by omission assumes that existing resources will be used to implement the project. Projects for other organizations may require specific costs, especially if all or part of the development project is to be contracted out.

PHYSICAL PLANNING

The requirements planning document prepared in Chapter 15 states what must be done, not how. It does not specify the technology to be deployed. The following pages address the fact-finding process preparatory to developing a physical requirements plan.

CURRENT SYSTEMS ASSESSMENT

The starting place for physical planning is to evaluate your existing systems and the budget that you will have available for your project. The following list of questions will get you started:

DATABASE ACCESS

- Where is the data required to support your Internet project requirements located?
- Is it centrally located on a single AS/400? Is it distributed across many AS/400s throughout your organization?
- If you have multiple locations, is the data physically distributed?

CURRENT CAPACITY

- What is the current utilization of your AS/400s?
- Can you afford to add significant workloads to your existing machine(s)?

USERS AND WORKSTATIONS

- Where are your users located?
- What type of workstations are they using?
- Do they have terminals, personal computers, or Network Stations?
- If they have personal computers, what is the breakdown of equipment and operating systems?
- Do you support DOS, Windows 3.x, Windows 95/98, Windows NT, or another OS?
- Do DOS and Windows 3.x users have adequate capacity on their machines to install browsers or other Internet software if access is required?
- If you have a mix of equipment, do you have a plan to replace terminals or older personal computers?
- What is the time frame for upgrading these desktops?
- Who specifically will require Internet browser access?
- What equipment do they have?

NETWORK AND CAPACITY

- What is the utilization of your internal network?
- Do you have adequate capacity between your locations to support the additional workload that providing your users with Internet access may require?
- What transport protocols are you currently supporting?
- Do you use token ring or Ethernet?
- What communications protocols are you currently supporting?
- Do you use TCP/IP, IPX, SNA, and NETBIOS?

E-MAIL

- Do you currently have e-mail software in place for internal users?
- Are you using OfficeVision/400?
- Are you using a third-party product?
- Does the product support Internet communications?

DIAL-UP COMMUNICATIONS

- Are you currently providing dial-up access to your network or your AS/400? Identify all users that are currently using dial-up modem-based communications. Identify the cost of providing this support.

INTERNET USAGE ANALYSIS

The requirements definition document should potentially identify users of your Web site and persons who will send you e-mail. Each audience should be evaluated to develop a preliminary estimate of the number of people who will access each of your Web sites, and the frequency of access.

You will also need some idea of the volume of e-mail traffic you will receive and send via the Internet.

Your marketing department may be able to provide some input regarding the number of users and frequency of access.

Referring back to Acme Quality Fruits Company's requirements document, we find that the company wants to put up a public Web site for consumers and a private Web site targeting the company's distributors.

The number of users who will visit your public Web site depends greatly upon the type and frequency of marketing material you distributed and upon the advertising policy of your marketing department. The visibility of your company also has a great deal to do with access to your public Web site. If you are a well-known company providing information of great interest to the public, you should plan to accommodate several thousand hits per day. You can estimate your bandwidth requirements by multiplying the estimated number of hits per day times 15kb per page. A company like Acme Quality Fruits Company is probably not well known and will be unlikely to generate more than 200 to 500 visitors per day.

Because we are now in the process of developing best-guess estimates of the utilization, e-mail may be the greatest unknown. As a rule of thumb, add 15 to 20 percent to your final estimate of Internet activity.

GEOGRAPHIC CONSIDERATIONS

- Do you support operations in multiple countries? International considerations can have a significant effect on your physical planning. You must determine the number and location of Web servers you must deploy throughout your organization.

INTERNATIONAL DATA CENTERS

- Do you have remote data centers, each center supporting one or more countries?
- Where is the data for each country's operations located?
- Does it make sense to provide local Web servers or a single centralized server for each country?
- What is your expertise in international data processing?
- Are you familiar with international character sets, currency conversion, etc.?
- Would your international audience be offended if you did not have a Web site home page in its native language?
- Can you create a single English-based home page and let international users choose their language from an option on the page?

INTERNATIONAL PRODUCTS OR SERVICES

- Is the Web site content for each international location specific to the location or is it generic to your entire organization? Many companies sell certain products or highly customized versions of their product in specific countries and not in others. If the product mix or other information provided via your Web site is highly customized for each country, you may want to consider implementing multiple Web servers. A Web server in this context is a *logical server.* You can support international multiple Web server environments on a single computer that lets the user think he is visiting a local Web site when in fact he is visiting a site on the other side of the world.

AVAILABILITY AND RELIABILITY

When initially implementing Internet services, it may be a good idea to put disaster recovery planning and redundancy planning on the back burner. You should however, at least think about these issues.

24-HOUR OPERATIONS

- Can you take your system offline for backup and system maintenance?
- When do you take your current system offline?

Although the AS/400 is certainly one of the most reliable computers available, it cannot run 24 hours per day, 7 days per week, 365 days per year without going offline for maintenance, product upgrades, or even backups. You must determine what is acceptable to your organization. If you must run 24 *x* 7 *x* 365, then you will need redundant mirrored machines and a *load-balancing router*. This is expensive but can be done. In fact IBM's Rochester Web site runs on a pair of AS/400s that are front-ended by a CISCO load-balancing router. The data on the machines are synchronized by the MIMIX data replication system.

DISASTER RECOVERY

Your Web site becomes an integral part of your corporate operations. Disaster recovery planning for the Web site can be deferred until you go public with your Web site and have a proven user base. Once the site becomes a mission-critical part of your total systems operations you will need to address disaster planning for the Web site.

Planning for disaster recovery depends heavily on your current disaster recovery plan. If you use a third-party service, such as IBM or someone else, can it provide a Web server and the necessary connectivity?

If you do your own disaster recovery, decide whether you will run a Web site on the same machine as your production work, or perhaps acquire a separate server machine for disaster recovery.

One important and often overlooked factor in Internet disaster recovery planning is connectivity to your ISP. Can your ISP provide services where your disaster recovery site will be located? You must assume that in case of a major natural disaster such as earthquake, flood, etc., that your ISP's local site will also be destroyed.

SPECIFIC INTERNET ACTIVITIES

The following activities are specific to establishing an Internet connection and selecting the equipment and communications technologies you will need to operate.

IDENTIFY, EVALUATE, AND SELECT AN ISP

Selecting your ISP is perhaps the most important single Internet specific activity you must perform. The task of selecting your ISP will influence most of the technical tasks associated with establishing your Internet connectivity.

Many other tasks are dependent upon selecting an ISP. Both pricing and services provided are significant issues and can vary dramatically between ISPs. An ISP comparison worksheet is provided below to assist in evaluating ISPs.

Where do you find ISPs? An excellent starting point is the Web. Try `navigators.com/isp.html`. This is Russ Haynal's ISP Page. Mr. Haynal lists all of the major ISPs and provides links to the ISP's home page, where you will find sales literature.

Internet Service Provider Selection Worksheet

ISP Name: ______________________________

Address:

____

____

____

Contact:

____

Telephone: ______________ Fax: ______________

E-mail: ______________________________

Don't neglect small ISPs. My company found a small, local ISP that connects via Worldcom's backbone at prices that were far below those of the large companies. Try your local newspaper or do a Web search on ISPs via one of the search engines on the Web.

Basic Bandwidth Charge

Port Speed MBPS	Month-Month Recurring	1 Year Recurring	3 Year Recurring	5 Year Recurring	Installation
ISDN					
½ T1 .75MB					
T1 1.54MB					
3 MBPS					
6 MBPS					
9 MBPS					
12 MBPS					
15 MBPS					
27 MBPS					
36 MBPS					
45 MBPS					

Enter the monthly recurring charges for each service in which you are interested in the
columns.

Do these fees include local telephone connectivity to the ISP's point of presence? YES NO

Do the ISP's fees include a router at your site? YES NO

Web Hosting

Does the ISP provide on-site Web hosting? YES NO

What server machine does it use? ____________________

What operating system does it use? ____________________

What server software does it use? ____________________

Does it support Microsoft Frontpage Extensions? YES NO

Does it provide CGI Programming support? YES NO

Does it provide Secure Sockets Layer (SSL)? YES NO

Does it provide Web statistics? YES NO

Do you have direct access to the servers log? YES NO

Web Hosting Charges

Item	Monthly	Installation
___ MB Disk Storage ___ E-mail boxes ___ Online Web Statistics ___ MB monthly traffic[1]		
Domain name charge		
Extra e-mail address		
Remote mail forwarding with up to _____ mailboxes		
Extra 500 MB traffic		
Extra 1000 MB traffic		
Totals		

Domain Name Services

Does the ISP charge for providing DNS? YES NO
(If yes, monthly fee ______ per change fee _______)
Does the ISP provide both primary and alternate DNS? YES NO
Does the ISP have a back up agreement with another ISP? YES NO
Does it provide DNS for both mail and other servers? YES NO
Will the ISP support you if you install a primary DNS? YES NO

Mail Services

Does the ISP provide e-mail store-and-forward services? YES NO
Monthly charge __________ Traffic charge _________
Can the ISP detect and handle denial of service attacks? YES NO
Does the ISP virus-scan forwarded mail traffic? YES NO

1 Monthly traffic is usually measured as total bytes received and transmitted by the server.

Security & Reliability

Is the ISP's facility physically secure?	YES	NO
Does the ISP have backup power sources?	YES	NO
Does the ISP have backup telecom links to its site?	YES	NO
Can the ISP support your disaster recovery plan?	YES	NO

Describe:____

____

Technical Support

Describe the ISP's technical support offerings:

Are there any charges for technical support? If so, itemize.

Other Issues

Will the ISP assist you in configuring your firewall?	YES	NO
Will the ISP provide a router on your site?	YES	NO
Will the ISP provide your IP address blocks?	YES	NO

Notes and Remarks: ____

____

____

TELEPHONE LINK TO ISP

Once you have selected an ISP, you must determine how to connect to the ISP's point of presence. Generally, a T1 leased line to your local telephone carrier is required. In some larger cities, there may be alternative services, but in most cities, you must use your local telephone company. Some ISPs provide this service bundled into their monthly charges.

The link from your local telephone company to your ISP's point of presence can generally be provided by several competing telephone companies. Shop around for the best deal.

Generally, you should consider a T1 leased line between your facility and your ISP even if you contract for less Internet bandwidth from the ISP. The ISP will restrict your bandwidth at its site. T1 service will vary by your distance from the local telephone company's local office and the distance to your ISP. In most metropolitan areas, the cost is under $1,000 per month. If you contract for bandwidth greater than T1, you will need a comparable link between your site and your ISP's site. Several companies are providing direct fiber optic connectivity in major cities between the end-user site (your building) and the ISP's. Costs for a T3 generally start at $15,000 per month, plus a substantial one-time connection fee.

INTERNET ROUTER

You will need a dedicated Internet router at your location. Some ISPs provide this router as part of their monthly service charge and will install and configure it for you. With other ISPs, you must buy the router and install it. In all cases, your ISP should help you configure it and be able to run connectivity tests between its location and yours. A typical router generally costs under $2,000. CISCO is by far the most popular vendor of Internet routers. Consult with your ISP for specific recommendations. Often, an ISP can sell you the router at a substantial discount.

ISOLATED ETHERNET SEGMENT

You will need to configure an isolated Ethernet segment between your Internet router and the devices that will connect directly to the Internet. This will generally be a firewall and a dedicated Web server. Your firewall will connect to both your private network and to the Internet segment. Costs will include adapters and an Ethernet hub, the type of which will depend upon your specific network. Costs can be as low as $200 for all the components.

FIREWALLS

If you wish to provide in- and outbound access to the Internet for devices other than your Web server, you will need a firewall. You have many choices. You can set up a third-party firewall on a Windows NT standalone platform, UNIX standalone platform, use the IBM IPCS-based firewall for the AS/400, or install a firewall on the new Integrated Netfinity Server for AS/400.

If you plan to provide any of your end users with Internet access to their desktop personal computers, you will need a firewall that supports NAT. Plan to spend between $5,000 and $7,500 for a firewall.

FIREWALL CONFIGURATION

You must formulate rules you will need to implement on your firewall. The following questions should be considered.

- Will any of your employees require access to your private network?

  If the answer to this question is yes, you will want a firewall that provides authenticated secure access to the internal network. This is usually accomplished by installing a piece of software, usually provided by the firewall vendor, on the remote client. It will handle the handshake with the firewall and the exchange and validation of a "challenge phrase." You will also need a firewall that supports NAT so external Class C addresses are translated by the firewall to internal addresses.

- Will your Web server and e-mail server be placed behind the firewall?

- Will you provide Telnet and FTP access to a machine behind the firewall?

- Will you provide AnyNet or Client Access/400 services (ODBC, File Transfer, network file access, Operations Navigator, print support, etc.) to a server located behind the firewall?

  If the answer to the last three questions is yes, you will need to specify rules for each IP address port combination to allow access for the services you provide.

PROXY SERVERS

Although much is said about the performance benefits of implementing a proxy server, the primary reason to implement a proxy server is to limit the outbound access of your users. Some companies allow users with Web browsers complete and unrestricted access to the Web. Others have strict rules that limit the sites a user can visit. If you wish to limit access to the Web, you need to implement a proxy server to restrict access to all but authorized Web sites. This requires the development of a list of "authorized" Web sites.

DOMAIN NAMES

A prerequisite to implementing your Web site is the selection of a domain name. You may find that a common reference to your company, or the abbreviation of your company's name, are not available. Going back to our sample case, Acme Quality Fruits Company, they might find that `acme.com` or even `aqf.com` are already allocated to someone else. It is strongly recommended that your marketing department participate in the selection of a domain name because domain names will be published in marketing and advertising materials.

Name recognition is more important than brevity. Names like *www.pepsi.com*, *www.coke.com*, or *www.disney.com* are instantly recognizable and are short and easy to type. Unfortunately, your company may not be able to get a short, easily recognizable name.

How many names do you need? I made the mistake early on of thinking that I needed multiple names for my public and private sites. We also made the mistake of letting technical people, instead of marketing people, choose the initial names. We now have four domain names. Here are my guidelines based on personal experience:

- Get one name for each recognizable company or brand name that your organization owns or controls. If, in our example, Acme Quality Fruits Company also sells apples under the brand name Worlds Best Apples, they may want a domain name for the company and one for the brand name.

- Use user-defined host names to identify different servers within your environment. To carry our example forward, let's assume that Acme Quality Fruits Company was able to acquire the domain name *aqfc.com*. The public Web site would be known as *www.aqfc.com*. Its private secure Web site might be known as *www.customerservice.aqfe.com* The term "customerservice" denotes a logical host.

- E-mail addresses should be kept simple and well known. I prefer *username@domain.com*. Some installations qualify the mail servers by type: *smtp.domain.com* and *pop3.domain.com*. Qualified names provide a measure of security by increasing the anonymity of the mail server. Mail would still be addressed to *user@domain.com*. The MX (mail) DNS entry would be *user@domain.com* and point to the IP address of your mail server. A hacker would have to figure out that to send mail you would need to specify *smtp.domain.com*. To receive mail, you would have to configure your mail client to get mail from *pop3.domain.com*.

- When naming internal hosts (i.e. personal computers, firewalls, proxy servers, and AS/400s), I recommend the following convention: *hostname.domainname.com* My personal computer is named *bobc.mydomain.com*.

INTERNATIONAL DOMAIN NAMES

If you decide to support multiple Web servers for some or all of your international operations, you may wish to acquire a country-specific domain name for each server. There is no limitation on where a domain can be used or who may obtain a domain typically associated with a foreign country.

If you had offices in Los Angeles and London, you might register the following domains: `mycompany.com` for the Los Angeles-based operation and `mycompany.ltd.uk` for the London-based operation.

Web sites for both domains would actually run on the same computer, which is physically located in Los Angeles. Your customers in the UK would think they were accessing a local UK-based Web site.

ORDER YOUR SERVER(S) AND SERVER SOFTWARE

This process requires some scientific guesswork. Typically, you will not have any idea what your Internet transaction volumes will be until you implement and go live with your Web site. Some of the factors to consider are:

- Do you deal with consumers? Even if you sell your consumer products through distribution channels, you may experience a high demand for product information. As a guideline, expect a hit rate equivalent to 10 to 30 percent of monthly units sold to a household. A retailer of consumer electronics that sells 100,000 products each month, and estimating that each product will represent one household, should anticipate between 10,000 and 30,000 visitors to the Web site per month. If the user can access specific product information within three links, anticipate between 30,000 and 90,000 hits per month (each page counts as a hit). This would average 3,000 to 9,000 hits per day. Most likely, this volume can be handled by a small server.

- Do you deal with commercial customers? If your products and services are used exclusively by commercial customers, your public Web site will most likely be visited by prospective customers, and your private site will be visited exclusively by current customers. A guideline of 200 to 300 users per day for your public site is probably overly optimistic. Anticipate that your private site will be accessed once per week by 70 percent of your active customer base. This level of usage would justify IBM's smallest server model machine.

- Estimating your e-mail volume is difficult. You might look at the number of customer service telephone calls and faxes you currently receive, make a giant leap, and guess that 30 to 50 percent might be transferred to e-mail.

SELECTING YOUR SERVER

At the time of this writing, IBM offers a low-end server AS/400 called the model 170. This machine uses the exact same processor as the high-end model 740 12-way machine. This machine, configured with adequate memory and DASD to support operations as an Internet server, retails for approximately $26,000.

You can acquire an entry level model 170e AS/400 for between $15,000 and $30,000. At those prices, I strongly recommend acquiring a dedicated AS/400 to act as your front-end Internet attached machine. I would attach it directly to a small Ethernet segment with your Internet router and possibly a firewall. I would also include a second Ethernet card or token ring card to attach it to your internal private network

A hacker would have an extremely hard time finding a way to route through your AS/400 into your private network. Using an SNA connection to your production AS/400 will allow your server to retrieve production data for Web server applications.

IBM offers a complete line of server model AS/400s ranging from the single-processor, low-cost model 150 all the way up to the high-end 12-processor model 740. Work with your authorized IBM reseller to determine the machine that is right for you.

If public access to your Web site is unknown, but thought to be low, or if you have a limited number of customers that you know will access your Web site, start with the model 170 and plan for upgrades as volume and capacity planning dictate. Unless you know that you will have a high volume of hits per day, start with a small server and plan to upgrade as workload increases.

If you look at the overall cost of system ownership, you will find the AS/400 to be as cost effective as any other system from a hardware and software standpoint. You will achieve dramatic savings in labor costs by using your existing AS/400 skills and not having to hire or contract for Windows/NT or UNIX expertise that you may not have on site today.

SELECTING YOUR SERVER SOFTWARE

You have three possible directions you can take for developing e-business applications via the Internet and the World Wide Web. The most advanced approach is to use the IBM

HTTP Server and WebSphere application server, invest in Java technology and build your systems around IBM's long term strategic direction which is WebSphere and Java.

The second solution is to base your solution around Lotus Domino and the IBM HTTP Server. This is perhaps the best short term solution. It leverages existing skills and provides the most robust, secure, and reliable Internet-based software available.

Some companies choose to use the Lotus Notes based development approach. I prefer to recommend using IBM's Net.Data e-Business development facility (also shipped at no additional charge with OS/400). Net.Data provides a very simple development language that integrates HTML and existing programming skills to rapidly develop and deploy e-Business Applications. Net.Data is an integral part of IBM's Net.Commerce product which I strongly recommend if you plan to sell merchandise or services via the Web.

If you have existing staff with traditional programming skills, Lotus Domino, the IBM HTTP Server, and Net.Data provide the minimum learning curve and maximum return on your investment.

E-MAIL

E-mail is an important part of your Internet presence. Users accessing your Web sites will want to communicate with a person to ask questions about information they see there. We discussed e-mail in detail in chapter 9, but here is an overview of what you should consider when you are assessing e-mail software and server requirements.

The AS/400 comes with good SMTP and POP servers. It also provides some internal software called mail server framework (MSF), which is designed to support virtually unlimited mail handling connections between the AS/400 and other mail handling facilities.

You will probably find that configuring a viable e-mail solution for your organization is one of the most difficult tasks in providing your company an Internet presence.

The following issues should be reviewedbefore deploying an e-mail solution.

- How many 5250 terminals do you have? Do you have a plan in place to replace these devices with personal computers or network computers? If you have 5250 terminals (real devices, not terminal emulation on a PC), you have two choices: You can use OfficeVision/400 (or its smaller, less costly version JustMail/400) or you can buy a product called Evergreen, which includes a 5250 POP3 client called POSTM@N. At present, these are the only software products that provide support for 5250-based e-mail access. (Note that OfficeVision/400 will be supported only through V4R5 because of Year 2000 readiness issues.)

- Personal computer users may be able to use the POP server and a PC-based POP client. If you have a Novell-based network, you can provide e-mail and Web browser support to your Windows 3.1 clients via Novell's Internet Gateway product.

- If you are a current OfficeVision/400 user using OV/400's calendar facility, and you want to provide support for both PC and 5250 users, consider Lotus Domino, which provides Lotus Notes client software and integrates the Domino server directly with the OfficeVision/400 mail repository and calendar facility. Remote users will require a Lotus Notes client on their remote machine.

- Do you have users that need to access e-mail from remote locations as well as their desktop? Do you have users that travel from office to office and need to access their mail from any terminal-type device in any office? If you do, implementing a solution for these users may require some extensive technical analysis and planning. It may also require the addition of third-party software such as POSTM@N or EverGreen/400 from Inventive Designs Inc.

I recommend that you acquire two copies of Lotus Domino. Install one copy on your main production machine for internal mail access and to exploit your database and the many fine groupware functions of Lotus Domino. Install the second copy on your Internet gateway machine. Domino can use this copy as a store and forward device. Mail from the Internet would be received by this Lotus Domino server and forwarded to your production machine.

Outbound mail would be forwarded from your internal production machine to the Internet gateway machine and then on to its final destination on the Internet. PC users can use Lotus Domino's secure POP server or Notes Client to remotely receive secure encrypted mail.

Web Server Configuration Planning

A Web server introduces new systems development issues into your environment. The new technologies and object types presented by the Web server introduce some administrative challenges to the information systems organization. Among these challenges are creating the development and production server environments.

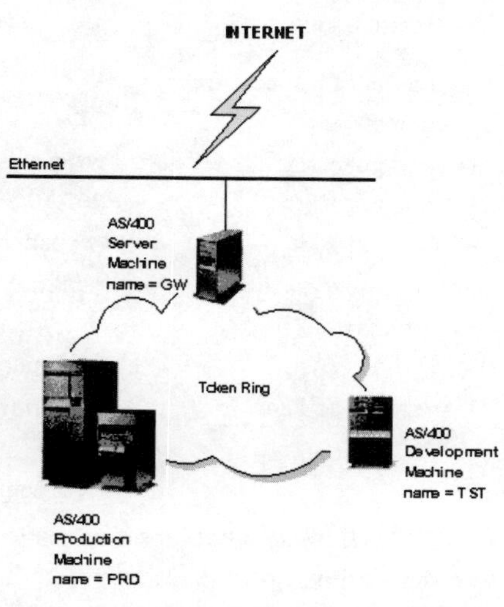

Figure 17.1: AS/400 e-commerce server configuration.

Production and Development Server Configurations

There are several methods of configuring a server to run multiple Web servers in support of a test and development environment.

The configuration depicted in Figure 17.1 is a typical e-business configuration for AS/400 shops. There is a Web server machine connected to an Ethernet segment and to an internal Token Ring network via SNA. The Token

Ring network connects the Web server and production machines that contains the organization's production databases and application programs (PRD). The server is also connected via SNA to a development machine containing the organization's development programs and databases (TST).

PRODUCTION AND DEVELOPMENT SERVER CONFIGURATIONS

Table 17.1 lists two methods of configuring production and development server environments on the same AS/400.

Table 17.1 Test and Production Environments

	1. Same Domain – two ports	2. Two separate domains
Production Public Server		
Server Instance	PROD	PROD
Server domain name	www.myserver.com:80	www.myserver.com:80
IP Address	207.101.193.1	10.10.10.1
IFS Root Directory	/webservers	/webservers
Production server root	/prdserver	/prdserver
Home page	index.htm	Index.htm
Public resources	/public	/public
Restricted resources	/private	/private
Development Public Server		
Server Instance	DEV	DEV
Server domain name	www.myserver.com:8081	dev.myserver.com:80
IP Address	207.101.193.1	10.10.10.1
IFS Root Directory	/webservers	/webservers
Production server root	/devserver	/devserver
Home page	index.htm	Index.htm
Public resources	/public	/public
Restricted resources	/private	/private

This table illustrates two approaches to creating test and production server environments. Another option, not illustrated above is to use the same HTTP server instance and create `/prod` and `/dev` subdirectories under the `/prdserver` directory. I do not recommend this approach because it might put your production server at risk.

If you are writing CGI programs or using SQL stored procedures on your remote machine, an error resulting in a message waiting on the QSYSOPR message queue will hang a server thread until the error is answered. Errors will occur during the development process. I would not want to risk hanging up my production server while a programmer was debugging programs. With the IBM HTTP Server at V4R3 and above, it is easier and safer to configure two server instances. I do not allow developers access to production resources.

There are some excellent new change control products from AS/400 change control vendors such as Aldon, Softlandings, and Silvon that address controlling the IFS type directories and all resources you will use with your Web sites. I recommend you consider a change control system when your development team grows beyond one person.

OPTION #1: PRODUCTION AND DEVELOPMENT – SAME DOMAIN, DIFFERENT PORTS

If you have a limited number of IP addresses, you might want to choose this option. To do so, set the BINDSPECIFIC server directive to OFF, and set the PORT for your production server to 80 and to a port of your choice (I used 8081 in the example).

If this server is using SSL, specify an alternate SSL port in your configuration for SSL. The default SSL port is 443, I suggest something like 8443.

Then create two server "instances." You might name them PROD and DEV as I have in the example in Table 17.1. PROD will run constantly and should be configured to autostart when TCP/IP is started. I generally set my development servers so they do not autostart, and I start them only as required.

OPTION #2: PRODUCTION AND DEVELOPMENT – DIFFERENT DOMAINS

In this scenario, each server is assigned its own IP address. If you are using IBM's network address translation (NAT) facility or a firewall-based NAT, you should have no shortage of IP addresses. The only limitation would be the public IP addresses assigned by your ISP. A good ISP will assign a minimum of 16 IP addresses; many provide a full Class C address block of 256 addresses.

In the example, I have assigned internal nonroutable Class A addresses 10.10.10.1 and 10.10.10.2 to the two servers. The IBM NAT maps these addresses to public addresses.

In this configuration, each server has BINDSPECIFIC set to ON and assigned to the default HTTP port 80.

OBJECTS AND NAMING CONVENTIONS

A proper Web server plan includes developing a set of naming standards as well as a clearly defined set of storage locations on your server. The objects you will be dealing with will depend on the development tools used in the development of your Web site. I suggest producing a document and making it available to all your developers. They must know where to put the objects they create. The following list is typical.

WEB RESOURCE ROOT DIRECTORY

You can place the Web resources anywhere you choose, but I always recommend creating an IFS root directory called something like `/webservers` under which all Web resources are stored. On machines prior to V4R4 you must use the CRTDIR CL command to create the root directory. V4R4 allows you to create directories in the IFS ROOT using Client Access or the Network Neighborhood via the AS/400's NetServer file server.

WEB SERVER ROOT DIRECTORY[1]

I create a root directory for each of my server instances under the `/webserver` directory. I use the server instance name as the name of the directory so there can be no confusion as to what it contains.

HTML PAGES

HTML pages are generally stored in the server root directory described above or in sub directories below the server root directory.

HTML FILE EXTENSION

You should choose a file extension for your HTML pages and use it consistently throughout your Web site. The IBM HTTP server can serve pages using .HTM or .HTML, (HTML is generally used on UNIX machines, while HTM is generally used on PC-based servers) but you can confuse developers and introduce errors into your site if you do not set a standard for consistent use.

---

1 The server root directory is where the server looks for your Web site's "home page" (usually named index.htm or index.html). It is generally subdivided into subdirectories created to support your applications.

INDEX NAME

You should decide on the Index page name that will be used in each server directory on the Web server. The most common name used is INDEX.HTM or INDEX.HTML. You can choose any name, such as HOME.HTM, DEFAULT.HTM, or WELCOME.HTM etc. I use INDEX.HTM to be consistent with other sites on the Web. You need to define this page to the server by setting it with the Welcome Page server directive.

PAGE NAMES

When developing standards for page names, the driving factor is your choice of file system. If you choose to use the IFS file system, names can be up to 256 characters long (32 for UNIX system compatibility).

Page names are generally visible to end users in the address field of their browser. I generally try to use names that are representative of the page's content. These names can get quite long, which means more typing for the developer but more meaning to the end user.

OTHER OBJECTS

You will be storing many other types of objects on your system, including image files (.jpg and .gif), audio files (.wav), and even video files. I use the same basic naming convention to name my graphic objects that I use for my HTML pages. Like HTML pages, any object stored in an IFS directory can have a name up to 256 characters in length. Some Webmasters prefer to store all of their images and support files in a single subdirectory. I personally like to put them in the same subdirectories with my HTML pages. I differentiate based on object extension (.gif, .jpg, .wav, etc.). This is a matter of personal preference.

CGI LIBRARIES

You can have one or many CGI libraries on your system. I use two. My production CGI library is named "CGI" and my development CGI library is called "CGIDEV." All of my Web servers share these QSYS libraries. You can choose to create many libraries for each application or purpose.

CGI PROGRAMS

CGI programs are application programs that will be called by a server. They may process input from an HTML form, or retrieve data from a database and create dynamic HTML pages as output. Regardless of the function, they must be stored in a library that is identified to your Web server as a CGI library.

NET.DATA LIBRARIES

Another tool in the Web site development arsenal is IBM's Net.Data macro language. We will discuss Net.Data in detail in Chapter 25, but for now, consider it a valuable macro language facility that is used to build interactive Web sites by combining HTML, AS/400 programs, SQL/400, REXX, and PERL 5 via a simple, but powerful macro language.

Net.Data requires that its initialization (INI) file, and either the DB2WWW program or a program that calls DB2WWW reside in a library that is accessible to your Web server. You may copy the DB2WWW program to your CGI library and create the INI file there, or create a separate library for these objects.

I recommend creating multiple separate Net.Data libraries that facilitate securing and restricting access to Net.Data macros. I create libraries for each server, plus one for public access and one for authenticated restricted access. Each library contains its own INI file, which points to IFS subdirectories containing the macros and macro include files used by a specific group of users. The program DB2WWW is shipped in the QHTTPSVR system library. You can copy it to your Net.Data library or write a simple CL/ILE program with one statement: CALL QHTTPSVR/DB2WWW and specify *CALLER in the activation group parameter. The use of this program insures that you are using the most current copy of the main Net.Data program (DB2WWW) when PTFs are installed on your system, and allows you to use multiple libraries and IFS macro directories within the same server instance.

NET.DATA MACROS AND INCLUDE FILES

Net.Data uses two object types: a macro file (identified by the extension .mac) and an include file (identified by the extension .hti). Macro and include files are text files that may be stored either as members of a source physical file in the QSYS library system, text files in the QDLS, or text files in the IFS directory system. I prefer to store them in the IFS directory structure and use a PC text editor to create and maintain them.

The planning issue is to determine where you will store your macros. If your developers have PCs with Windows 95/98/NT or UNIX workstations, the IFS is by far the best location. The files are stored as stream files and can be processed up to four times as fast as a member of a QSYS source physical file.

You will need to define the storage location for specific types of macros. I generally store my macros in subdirectories under each of my server document root directories. I name them `/macros` and `/includes`.

If I need to have unrestricted access to macros for some users and restricted access to others, I create two sets of the `/macro` and `/include` directories, one under the public directory, and one under the private directory. Then, I authenticate the macros stored in the private subdirectories. You might also want to create a subdirectory for each class or type of macro, for example one subdirectory for employee macros and another for customer macros.

The naming convention to be used for macros is the second standard. I use the same naming conventions for macros and include files that I use for HTML pages, using long meaningful names because the macro name appears in the address line of the browser.

PLANNING THE SERVER DIRECTORY STRUCTURE

The example in Figure 17.2 illustrates a typical Web site structure and the effect that index.htm files have on a Web server.

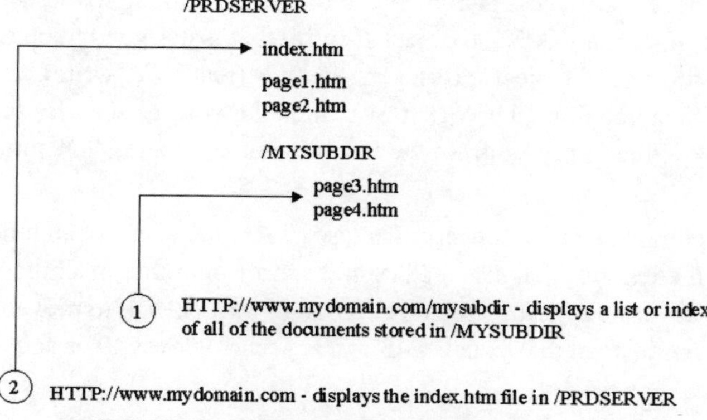

Figure 17.2: Web Server Directory Structure.

Figure 17.2 example 1, shows a URL that requests that the server display the default contents of the subdirectory named */MYSUBDIR*. Because there is no page named *index.html* (defined to the server as the default "Welcome Page") stored in the subdirectory, the server displays a list of the contents of the subdirectory. In this example, it lists *page3.htm* and *page4.htm*, and automatically builds hyperlinks to these pages, which will display if clicked. You can turn off this behavior in the Directories and Welcome Page settings, but if you do so it is for the entire server.

In example 2 of Figure 17.2, an HTML file named *index.htm* (our default page) exists and is displayed. The two files named *page1.htm* and *page2.htm* will be displayed only if the author of *index.htm* creates a manual hyperlink to the document, or the user knows that the file exists and types a URL such as *www.mydomain.com/page1.htm* There is no way for the user to learn that *page1.htm* or *page2.htm* exists.

If you create an HTML file and save it to */PRDSERVER* as *index.htm*, it will be presented with no additional parameters when you access your domain (for example, *www.yourdomain.com*). At this point, you should have created these directories using either the CRTDIR command or your PC's Network Neighborhood.

Directories and objects served by AS/400 Web servers must allow access by the server's user profile. AS/400 security limits access to these directories. The servers all have user profiles associated with them. The default user profile for the IBM HTTP servers it is QTMHHTTP. The server user profiles must have read (*R) and execute (X) (*USE in the QSYS library system) access to objects if they are to be served. Any object or directory that does not have read access is invisible to the server and the world. Note that the IFS uses a variant of standard AS/400 object security that is designed to be compatible with the UNIX environment. Objects are secured with R (read), W (write), and/or X (execute) authorities. When you issue the WRKAUT command, you see security settings like *R, *RX, or *RWX. Objects served from the IFS directories require *RX authority.

This is an important security concept. The use of AS/400 security and the server user profile is one of the features that sets the AS/400 apart from other machines and servers. Objects in your server directories should be *PUBLIC *EXCLUDE to prevent access to them. I strongly recommended that your server run at security level 40 or above.

You should always have a default home page in the default server document root directory. Now you must decide what additional subdirectories needed. Let's revisit our business requirements plan developed for the Acme Quality Fruits Company in Chapter 16. In the plan, we said we would host a site with access to:

- The public
- Employees
- Customers
- Vendors

The public will see general information pages with no security requirements. Using the IBM HTTP Server, I would recommend creating four separate server instances to handle our fictitious ompany's requirements. I would create a separate server for the public, employees, customers, and vendors.

You can investigate the virtual hosting options available with the HTTP Server. This example will illustrate creating four separate servers, each with their own IP address and domain name. There will be one server instance and one configuration file for each Web server.

This approach provides several advantages. It keeps each of the server configuration files simple and easy to maintain, simplifies authentication and security, and provides a degree of protection in the unlikely event that a problem should occur after making changes to one of the servers. The change would affect only the affected server. Additionally, while you would most likely provide links to each of the special purpose servers from your main public server, users could bookmark the direct access path to their particular server of interest and save time when visiting your site.

Let's examine the requirements for each server.

The public site can use Net.Data macros or CGI programs, but will not require authentication because it provides information about your products and services.

Because all your employees have access to your AS/400s and have user profiles, you can restrict access to this server via AS/400 system security. The only page that will be visible to the public is the initial index page, which will contain a link to the private employee pages. Different types of employees will need access to different sections of the Web site. This can be accomplished in several different ways.

The approach I prefer is to authenticate all users as employees, determine which department they work in by looking them up in the database, and displaying only links that they are authorized to use. An alternative approach would be to build authenticated subdirectories and use the HTTP Server's group authentication to restrict access.

Requirements dictate that customers and vendors need authenticated access to their respective Web sites. This can be implemented using validation lists that provide a means of storing user ids and passwords that are unknown to the AS/400.

A SERVER EXAMPLE

Figure 17.3 illustrates one possible directory structure that will support the requirements plan created for Acme. Obviously, there is no right or wrong way to structure the system. We will use this plan throughout the remainder of the book.

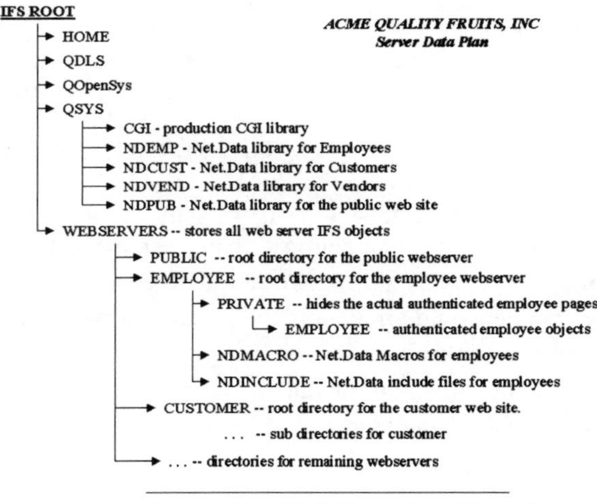

Figure 17.3: ACME Server Data Plan.

Figure 17.4 shows a sample configuration for our fictitious company and explains the major issues that may not be readily apparent.

To configure the server, start by clicking "Create configuration." When you get to the Create Configuration page, type a name for the configuration (usually the same as the name of the server), select the "Create empty configuration" option, and click the "Apply" button. You can base your new configuration on an existing configuration, but it is easier to use an empty configuration when first starting.

Be sure your new configuration appears in the drop down list box under the word "Configurations." Begin working your way down the list of options examining the setting in each box.

You can click "Display Configuration" any time to see what the programs have generated so far and review the configuration when you are done. The following sample configurations were copied from the display configuration Web page.

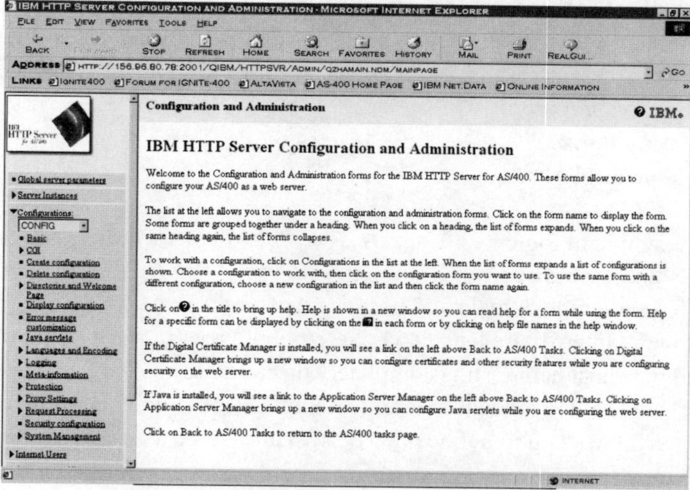

Figure 17.4: IBM HTTP Administration Server.

Figure 17.5 shows the first part of the server configuration for our fictitious company, Acme Quality Fruits. Item 1 indicates that we have set the welcome page to `index.htm`.

Item 2 illustrates a protection set-up which uses %%SYSTEM%% as the password file and instructs the server to validate users against AS/400 user profiles. The set of directives enclosed within the curly brace labeled "2" in Figure 17.5 is called a *protection setup*.

The directive "Protection emp" assigns the set up the name of "emp" so that it can be referred to by name.

The last line in Figure 17.5 is "Protect /employee/* emp." This line instructs the server to use this protection setup when accessing directories in URL's containing references to the subdirectory /employee. The /* means any files found within the subdirectory.

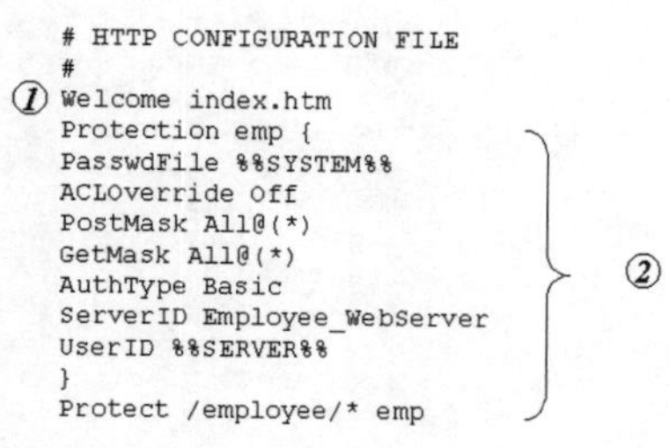

```
# HTTP CONFIGURATION FILE
#
(1) Welcome index.htm
Protection emp {
PasswdFile %%SYSTEM%%
ACLOverride Off
PostMask All@(*)
GetMask All@(*)
AuthType Basic
ServerID Employee_WebServer
UserID %%SERVER%%
}
Protect /employee/* emp
```
(2)

Figure 17.5: HTTP Server Configuration part 1.

If a user attempts to access the following URL: `employee.aqf.com/employee/sales.htm`, the server would authenticate the user by requiring a valid AS/400 user id and password. If the user failed to login properly a "401 Not Authorized" message would be displayed.

```
HostName employee.aqf.com     ◄──── ③
BindSpecific On  }
Port 80          } ④
UserID %%SERVER%%
DNS-Lookup Off
Imbeds On html
MaxContentLengthBuffer 100 K
AlwaysWelcome On
DirAccess On
AccessLog /webserver/logs/emptstacs 100000
AgentLog /webserver/logs/emptstagt 100000
RefererLog /webserver/logs/emptstrfr 100000
ErrorLog /webserver/logs/emptsterr 100000
CgiErrorLog /webserver/logs/emptstcgr 100000
Enable GET
Enable HEAD

Enable POST
```

Figure 17.5: HTTP Server configuration part 2.

Item 3 in the example in Figure 17.5 illustrates that we have assigned this Web server the domain and host name of `employee.aqf.com`. While many Web servers on the Internet are located via the symbol "www," this portion of the domain name is called the "host name." It is completely discretionary as long as it is defined to your DNS server. The domain name (in this example "`aqf.com`") is registered with the InterNIC, which allows you to define any "host" names to be associated with the domain that you want to define.

Notice that we have also turned DNS look ups off (DNS-LOOKUP Off), instructed the server to look for an `index.htm` page in each directory, and have allowed the server to produce a directory display if no `index.htm` page is found (DirAcess On).

```
Map /employee/cgi-dta/* /QSYS.LIB/NDEMP.LIB/NDEMP.PGM/*   )
Map /EMPLOYEE/CGI-DTA/* /QSYS.LIB/NDEMP.LIB/NDEMP.PGM/*   |
Map /employee/cgi-bin/* /QSYS.LIB/CGI.LIB/*               |
Map /EMPLOYEE/CGI-BIN/* /QSYS.LIB/CGI.LIB/*               |
Map /employee/* /private/employee/*                       } ⑤
Exec /QSYS.LIB/NDEMP.LIB/*                                |
Exec /QSYS.LIB/CGI.LIB/*                                  |
Pass /* /webservers/employee/*                            )

LogTime GMT                                     )
LogFormat Common                                |
UseACLs protectonly                             |
UseMetaFiles Off                                |
MinActiveThreads 10                             |
MaxActiveThreads 40                             |
PersistTimeout 4 seconds                        } ⑥
MaxPersistRequest 5                             |
InputTimeOut 2 minutes                          |
OutputTimeOut 20 minutes                        |
ScriptTimeOut 5 minutes                         |
ErrorPage notauthorized /emp_aut_fail.htm       )
```

Figure 17.6 HTTP Server Configuration part 3

This portion of the configuration also defines where the log files will be stored, and enables the GET, HEAD, and POST methods for the server.

Figure 17.6 illustrates the MAP, PASS, and EXEC directives that allow the server to serve Web pages, run CGI programs, etc. Without these directives (see item 3 in figure 17.5), the server can do no work. By design, the server is explicitly locked out of directories and libraries on the AS/400, the server must be explicitly instructed where to look for objects.

If you were serving only HTML pages, the only mandatory directive would be the PASS directive. Consider the directive:

```
Pass /*  /webservers/employee/*
```

This directive instructs the server to look for objects in "employee" subdirectory of the IFS root directory "webservers." If there were no protection directives, the server would serve anything in that subdirectory that its user id had read access for.

The EXEC directives enable the server to execute programs located in the libraries defined on the right hand side of the directive. Consider:

```
Exec /QSYS.LIB/CGI.LIB
```

This directive allows the server to execute programs it finds in the QSYS library named CGI. Note the format of the name and the extension *.LIB*. When working with the IFS, QSYS objects must conform to the rules of the IFS, which require fully qualified paths.

The MAP statements require a bit more explanation. Consider the following directive:

```
Map /employee/cgi-dta/*   /QSYS.LIB/NDEMP.LIB/NDEMP.PGM/*
```

This statement establishes an alias called `cgi-dta` for the path to the QSYS library NDEMP and calls the program NDEMP with any parameter string allowed. Lets look at a URL that uses this alias:

```
employee.aqf.com/cgi-dta/mymacro.mac/main?empno=123456
```

Users might think they are trying to access an object in the subdirectory `/cgi-dta` called *mymacro.mac*. In reality, `cgi-dta` instructs the server to substitute the fully qualified path */QSYS.LIB/NDEMP.LIB/* and call the program NDEMP.PGM passing it the remainder of the URL as parameters */mymacro.mac/main?empno=123456*.

NDEMP calls Net.Data program DB2WWW, which reads and processes *mymacro.mac* using the variable *empno=123456* as an input variable.

The upper case version of the same MAP statement is required if you want to allow users or developers to code links using either upper or lower case. MAP statements are case sensitive and will fail if case is not adhered to.

The directive:

```
Map  /employee/cgi-bin/*   /QSYS.LIB/CGI.LIB/*
```

does a couple of things. First remember that we showed how to code a Protect directive that associated the subdirectory /employee with the protection setup we named "emp."

```
Protect /employee/*  emp
```

The entire path segment */employee/cgi-bin/* is first authenticated by the server (the user must logon with a valid user id and password for processing to continue). Failure to do so will result in the server issuing the "401 Unauthorized" error message.

Consider the following URL:

employee.aqf.com/employee/cgi-bin/mypgm

If the user is properly authenticated (because of the subdirectory path */employee* is in the URL), then cgi-bin is translated into the path to the QSYS library CGI where the server will attempt to locate and run a program called *mypgm.*

The last MAP statement in this example hides the true location of HTML pages on the server:

```
Map  /employee/*   /private/employee/*
```

If you examine the Server Data Plan for our fictitious company, you will see that we created a subdirectory called "private" under the server root directory, which should never contain any objects. It is used for the sole purpose of hiding the subdirectory */employee* where actual objects are contained.

When a URL such as:

employee.aqf.com/employee/salary.htm

is processed, the alias */employee* is translated by the server into its full proper path name */private/employee/salary.htm*and the page is retrieved from the true directory. There is no way for the user to discover where the directory */employee* is actually pointing. Using aliases can help protect you from becoming a victim of hackers by making life as difficult for them as possible.

SUMMARY

Take the time to evaluate the configuration, naming, and organization of your Web site before beginning the development process. Analyze your site plan carefully and try to visualize the applications you will add to the site in the future. Do you clearly see where you will put the objects that will support these applications? Can you secure sensitive objects?

A well-designed Web site must accommodate change, which is a constant. Everything we build today will be changed tomorrow. If you find structural design errors in your pilot projects, take the time to rethink the structure of your site and correct the problems as soon as possible. Use naming conventions that are clear and self-documenting.

My experience is that standards documents rapidly become dated or lost. A good set of standards should be intuitive to the developers and users of your Web site. If you look at the directory structure of the site, the directory names should tell you what should be stored in the directory. A look at object names should make the naming conventions clear to a new developer.

APPLICATION PLANNING

An application is defined as a set of HTML pages, CGI programs, or Net.Data macros that provide specific business content. An application has a start and an end. The examples I will use in this chapter are based on the Acme Quality Fruits business requirements plan. The following application planning activities should always be completed. The degree of formalization of the design products is up to you and your organization.

DEFINE SECURITY APPLICATION

When building an e-commerce system, security is a significant issue. You must restrict access to Web pages and data to members of specific classes of your audience. You must also protect the privacy of your audience by ensuring that a person accessing your Web site only gains access to authorized data.

If you deal with individuals, you must ensure that the individuals gain access only to their data. If you are a bank, then each of your customers must be able to view only their own accounts.

Commercial account security is a more complicated issue. Customers and vendors are themselves companies consisting of many employees. Each company may wish to allow many employees to access some or all of their data.

One of your distributors may have many sales representatives. It would like each sales representative to view the orders they place with your company, but not the orders placed by other representatives.

Commercial users have employee turnover. When a sales representative leaves a company, the company needs to be assured that the employee can no longer access confidential data that may be available via your Web site. Your customer must be assured that their former employees cannot access your customer lists, orders, pricing, and other sensitive business data.

You will probably want to devise a security mechanism that incorporates both server-level security and supports your own security processing requirements.

There are three ways to deal with security administration. First, you may create applications that allow a security administrator at your location to maintain the security information necessary to access your site and their data. Second, you may develop a self-administration facility. And third, you may combine self-administration with internal administration.

Study your existing systems and data to determine how you identify members of your audience. The Web site may introduce new security requirements that your current systems do not support at present.

Almost all systems identify their customers by some form of customer number. The customer number is embedded in all customer-related data stored in your database. Unfortunately, a customer number is also published on virtually every document you print and send to your customers, thus providing a weak link in data confidentiality.

One method of providing a balance between internal administration and self-administration is to use an approach taken by many of the online service providers, such as Prodigy, CompuServe, and America Online when they register new users.

New users are provided with a temporary user ID and password. This takes them into a Web-based application that allows them to register to the service. Once they access the registration area, they are asked to provide a unique user ID and password. They are also asked to provide credit card or other billing information and an account is created for them. Some of these services consider that the person setting up the account is the "master" user. That user may set up additional family members or employees (if a commercial account). Once the account is set up, the master user may add or remove individuals from the account.

I took one such approach to creating a security mechanism for the Republic Indemnity Companies' Web site. We decided that we would generate a secret authentication code that selected employees would use and send to our insurance agencies and policyholders. Because the agencies and policyholders were companies that might wish to grant access to several employees, the authentication code was given to principles at the agency or insured company. These people were also given a special registration user ID and password that would allow them to access the registration procedures on the Web site.

On the home page of the Web site, there is a link called Registration. This is secured and restricted to a special user ID and password (the same user ID and password is used by all users). When a user clicks on Register, he is prompted for the registration user ID and password.

When the user logs in, he is taken to a page that asks for his customer number and authentication code. The authentication code is a 9-digit random number that is generated by a program on the AS/400 and stored in a file for each class of user. Two things happen when the user clicks Submit on the user authentication form. The authentication code for the particular class of user is checked to determine that the code exists. The customer number is then used to look at the customer file in the company's production database to ensure that the customer is an active customer in good standing. If these tests fail, the person attempting to register is given instructions to contact someone at the company. If the tests are passed, then a form is presented that asks the user to provide:

- A unique user ID
- A password
- His first and last names
- His e-mail address or the word *None*

When he clicks Submit, the server's user file is checked to determine that the user ID does not exist. If it does, he is told to pick another user ID. Passwords are checked to ensure that the password is different from the user ID. When the user clicks the Submit button and it is determined that the user ID is unique, a CGI program performs the following functions:

- Creates a Web-site user record that contains the user's user ID, customer number, name, e-mail address, and sets a "master user" flag to "Y"

- Adds the user to the Web server's user file

- Adds the user to the Web server's user group file for the group representing the class of user (i.e. insurance agent or policyholder)

The user is then allowed to log in to the private Web site. The user must log in with the user ID and password that he just created.

The user is then greeted with a personalized home page for his user class. This page is generated by a CGI program that looks up the user in the user file. It verifies that the user is currently a user in good standing. It also checks to determine if the user is a master user. If the user is a master user, a link to Security Administration is generated on the user's home page.

The Security Administration link displays all employees of the user's company that have been set up. It allows the master user to add new people to his account, each with his own user ID and password. It also allows the master user to delete users and to change user data, including passwords. A master user also may designate other employees of his organization as master users.

This process provides the customer with the ability to maintain control over who may access his data. This approach also places responsibility with the customer (rather than my own company) for removing terminated employees from the Web site.

Some companies may wish to provide even more information and controlling data for employees of the user. An office supply company may wish to allow a customer to define limits in terms of dollars as well as types of products that certain employees may purchase via the Web site.

The design and implementation of your security front-end will probably be the most difficult and important part of your Web site design and development. It is essential to the success of your Web site that the security implementation be carefully defined and developed before you begin to develop your line-of-business applications.

One last note on security applications. Security requirements will be different for each class of user. At Republic Indemnity, we originally contemplated self-registration for employees. Further analysis revealed the need to set up master users (managers and executives) who would in turn define other employees to the system and also be able to remove these employees. Each class of user will have different requirements.

DEFINE BUSINESS REQUIREMENTS

Review your prioritized business objectives. Identify the applications that will be required to meet these objectives. Identify and collect existing systems and system products that currently support these objectives.

I suggest that you organize the requirements by audience. Based upon our fictitious Acme Quality Fruits example, an application to do each of the following is needed to meet the company's objectives:

- Allow distributors to place orders via the Web site
- Allow distributors to display a list of all outstanding orders
- Display the detailed order with its status
- Display the billing status of each order

Working with your project team, you should be able to develop a comprehensive list. Each application should consist of no more than one or two screens. The application, when implemented, should provide value to both the company and its distributors. Each application should provide value on its own merits independent of related applications. For example, displaying a list of outstanding orders would provide value even if the details were not available.

When planning your applications, keep in mind that a Web site is dynamic. You can constantly add new functionality. It is better to define applications in as small a unit as possible. I personally define applications in terms of one or two HTML pages. It is easy to add small increments to a Web site, but often difficult to obtain the necessary approvals for large changes or the addition of many new applications.

DEFINE YOUR WEB SITE'S ORGANIZATION

Once you have identified the applications that you will build, look for the business objects and the relationships that exist between these objects.

It the example shown in Figure 18.1, Customer Order is an object that you will deal with. You know that your distributor is your audience. You need a Distributor home page that serves as a menu of functions and information that a distributor can access. This menu might contain links such as Place An Order or Display Outstanding Orders.

The Place An Order link transfers the user to a product catalog that allows him to select products he wants to order, specify the quantity, and complete the order by providing shipping instructions. The Place An Order function will need to integrate with your existing order processing system.

The Display Outstanding Orders link transfers the user to a list of outstanding orders for that customer. The list allows the user to select an order and display the details of that order.

The detailed order might display the payment status and shipping status. If the order is shipped via a shipper that supports shipment tracking through its own Web site, you might provide a link to the shipper's Web site that displays the location of the shipment in transit.

Write down a detailed specification of exactly what each application must do and what it must display. Draw a rough thumbnail sketch of your application, starting at the customer menu page and showing flow and links between Web pages.

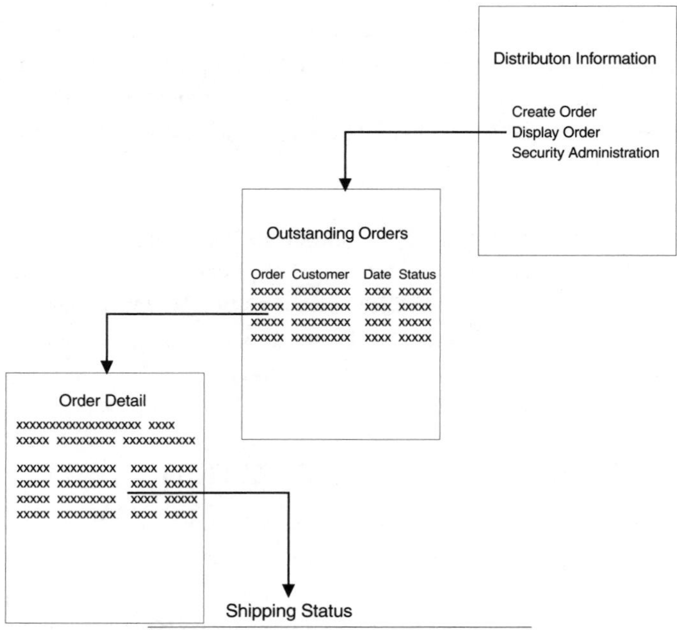

Figure 18.1: Application thumbnail sketch.

Figure 18.1 illustrates a typical application thumbnail sketch. It clearly illustrates what happens when a user clicks on a link called Display Orders on the Distributor Information Page. At the Display Orders link, a list of orders is displayed. When a user clicks on a particular order in the Order Detail link, the details of that order are displayed. From the Order Detail link, the diagram illustrates that the user may check shipping status by clicking on the shipping field of the order header. I often draw thumbnail sketches on a legal pad.

DEFINE DATA REQUIREMENTS

Once you've identified what to display or collect via HTML pages or forms, you must identify the data that supports your application. Often you must contact the person responsible for the existing application processing system within your information systems department to obtain the necessary information.

You must identify the files that contain data that supports your application. You must examine and define the relationships that exist between the files. In our example, there will be, at a minimum, a customer information file, an order header, and an order detail file. There may be additional files containing information about order items, sales person, shipping, billing, etc.

You must also identify fields that are the result of calculations. Often, calculated fields will not be stored, but are calculated as required. If this is the case, you must define the required calculations.

Be sure to obtain the file descriptions (run a DSPFFD LIBRARY/FILE *PRINT) for each file. Also run DSPFD for each file and logical file to obtain information about the index and key structure for each file.

DEFINE YOUR SCREEN LAYOUT

Using a product like Microsoft FrontPage 98, Netscape Composer, or Adobe PageMill, do a mock-up layout of what your screen will look like.

Validate your layout against the database to determine that you can support the information that you wish to display on the screen. Use the field lengths from the file description to ensure that the data will fit on your screen design.

At this point, you should be able to construct a demonstrable model of your application using the mock-up HTML pages you just created with your design tool. Obtain the required approvals from your user community or repeat the process until you do obtain the approvals.

DEFINE PROGRAMMING REQUIREMENTS

Determine how you are going to implement your screens. Are you going to use CGI programs in C++ or RPG? Are you going to use IBM's Net.Data? If you are planning to use Net.Data, do you need any other programs or will you use SQL to retrieve your data?

Define the exact processing flow and the parameters that must be passed between pages or programs. Here is an example of a minimal specification for the distributor information page for Acme Quality Fruits:

DISTRIBUTOR INFORMATION PAGE

The distributor information page is the first page accessed by a distributor after the distributor logs into the system from the system's home page. The distributor's user ID will be contained in an HTTP environment variable called REMOTE_USER. Use this field to look up the distributor in the Web site's distributor file. If you cannot locate the user ID, display an error screen.

Display the user's first and last name and company name (join to the production customer file) in the screen's header.

Assign the user's customer number to a variable. Create the two dynamic links:

- *`/distributor/order_form.html`* (a link to the order form)
- *`/cgi-dta/orderlist.mac/main?custno=123456`* (a link to a Net.Data macro that lists outstanding orders for the specified customer)

Check the Web site's distributor record to determine if the user is a master user. If the field is equal to "Y," then display the *`/cgi-dta/distsecadmin/main?custno=123456`* link to a Net.Data macro for security administration.

In this example, I have used the syntax to execute a Net.Data macro. The same basic construct of naming a CGI program or script and passing variables via the URL will work.

APPLICATION PLANNING SUMMARY

Planning your company's e-commerce Web site applications includes four important steps:

- Define application business requirements
- Sketch out a thumbnail screen flow with links
- Identify data requirements
- Specify program logic

PLANNING YOUR PUBLIC WEB SITE 19

One of the most significant projects you can complete is a public Web site. This site provides a marketing presence on the Internet for your organization. It tells people who you are, what you do, and how to contact you. It is the most important part of your Internet development activities, and one of the easiest. You must address 10 planning issues before you can develop an effective public Web site.

WHERE WILL YOUR PUBLIC SITE BE HOSTED?

Many ISPs provide Web site hosting in addition to simple Internet connectivity. FastLink Networks Inc. provides 20 megabytes of disk space and charges for access as part of its standard charges for connection bandwidth. FastLink guarantees that the site will be available 24 hours a day, 7 days a week.

The ISP provides hot backup machines that take over should the primary machine go offline. I cannot provide the same reliability with a single AS/400 (or any other computer for that matter). We therefore chose to host our public sites on the ISP's computer, with a link to our AS/400 that contains all of our private insurance agent, policyholder, and employee applications. The user can always get to the public site but may get a Server Not Available message if our AS/400 is offline for maintenance or backups.

WHAT IS THE PURPOSE OF YOUR WEB SITE?

Generally, the objective of your public Web site is to tell the world who you are, what you do, what you sell, and how prospective customers can contact you. If you are a public company, a public Web site is an excellent vehicle to provide current and prospective investors with information about your organization. Nonprofit organizations have used public Web sites to solicit donations and volunteers quite successfully.

A typical public Web site might include sections that addressed:

- Who we are…
- What we do…
- Company history…
- Press releases and media articles about the company…
- Products and services…
- Financial information…
- A letter from your president…

There are many forms and structures that a public Web site can take. Chapter 21, "Web Site Design" discusses Web site design and architecture in detail; Chapter 23 covers the HTML coding needed to develop the Web site.

WHAT IMAGE WILL YOU PRESENT?

The image you present via the Web site is as important as the words on your Web pages. An image is defined by the page layout, logos, colors, backgrounds, and other elements you use to create your Web site.

You must determine the image that is appropriate for your organization. A company selling baby products would use a very different color scheme and graphic design than an airline or an insurance company.

Collect samples of every marketing piece that you can find. Does your organization have a well-defined professionally planned image? If the answer is yes, you must follow that general appearance and image. Generally, a professional image will have a standard color scheme that is carried throughout your organization, from your signs to your letterhead and on all of your advertising copy and external documents and forms.

If you do not have a formal image, you must create one. Carefully study the materials that you have collected. Look for common themes, colors, your logo and slogans, and other design elements that identify your organization. A visitor to your Web site should be able to instantly identify your company from the visual impact it provides, without having to consciously read the text on your home page.

DESIGN YOUR PUBLIC WEB SITE LIKE A MAGAZINE

Borrow from the graphic arts and draw your reader into your Web site. Avoid too many graphics, but make use of headlines and graphic design techniques that make people want to read your content. Phrase your links in such a way that people want to click the link and see more information about your organization.

A cluttered, busy Web page (advocated by many Web site designers) drives people away from your Web site. Site designers who think that creating lengthy home pages with links to everything in the Web site is efficient are kidding themselves. I would rather design a simple Web site with a logo or significant graphic (not very big for performance purposes), a couple of lines of text succinctly describing the business, and one link to more detailed information, than a busy page that no one will read.

HIRE A CONSULTANT

Often a good method of building your public Web site is to hire a professional consultant. When hiring a consultant, look at his work. When you look at one of his sites, do you instantly know who the site belongs to? Do you know what the site owner does? Do you know why the site exists? Does it make you want to click its links for more information?

Beware of technicians. Many Web site development companies are run by technical people who lack any sense of marketing knowledge, graphic design, or presentation. Graphic design requires skill; sometimes specific techniques work for a Web site, sometimes they don't. If I had to work with a consultant, I'd rather work with professional public relations or advertising agency than with a Web development company.

USE A GOOD DEVELOPMENT TOOL

Microsoft FrontPage 98 is my favorite tool. It includes a set of wizards (pre-programmed design helpers) that prompt you step-by-step through the creation of a very professionally designed corporate presence Web site. FrontPage is easy to use, can be customized to fit your company, and lets you develop a public Web site in hours. There are several other excellent Web page development tools. I recently started working with MacroMedia's DreamWeaver product, and NetObject Fusion. IBM has integrated several of NetObject's products into their WebSphere Application Development Suite. An additional excellent tool is Homesite from Alliare.

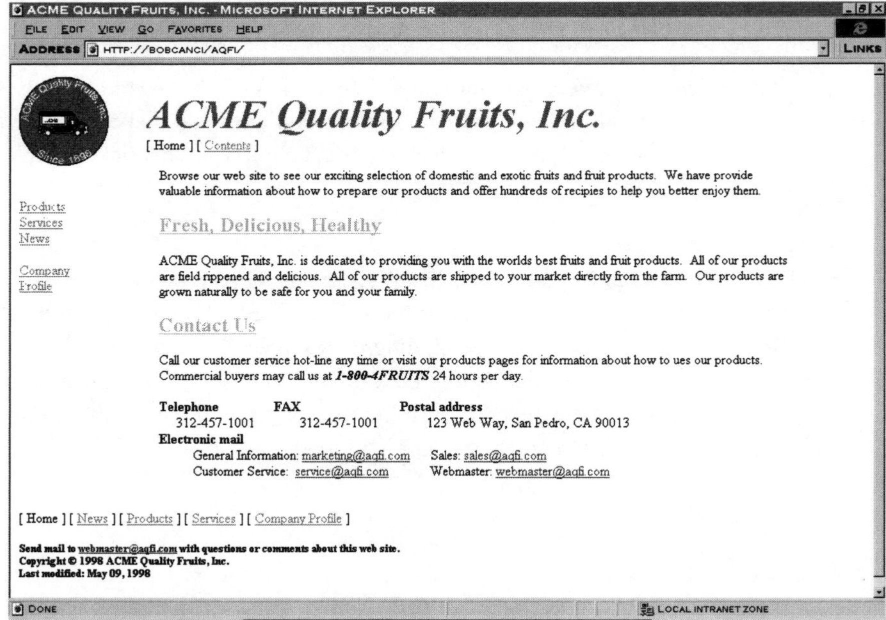

Figure 19.1: Acme Quality Fruits home page.

Figure 19.1 is the home page for our fictitious Acme Quality Fruits Inc. I developed a complete Web site for Acme in about two hours using Microsoft FrontPage/98 and its Corporate Presence Wizard (including time required to modify and customiz the site).

The Contents link at the top of the page displays a tree structure table of contents for the entire site. It is maintained automatically by the tool. The Products, Services, and News links in the left margin and at the bottom of the page were generated automatically. The link, Company Profile, was added to the left margin and also automatically added to the navigation bar at the bottom of the page.

Each subsequent page on the site has its links maintained automatically by the tool. All the designer has to do is focus on content.

PUBLISH THE SITE TO A TEST LOCATION ON YOUR SERVER

This can be accomplished by naming the default home page something other than index.htm. If I were to call it test.htm, you would only be able to find it if you knew it was there. It is important to publish a Web site to a real Web server for review and approval prior to implementing it. You should present the site to its approvers visually via a Web browser so that they can see what the world sees. Print-outs may not print backgrounds, may miss some content, and are misleading even if printed in color. By temporarily hiding the home page from the public, but letting your approvers know where it is, they can view it in the office (if they have the equipment) or at home at their leisure.

Web sites are interactive. Users need to experience the Web site to appreciate it or properly critique it. You will also discover the differences between the various browsers and configurations. You will see what happens when a user with a high-resolution monitor views the site and when a user with a 640 *x* 480 dpi monitor views the site.

FINALIZE CHANGES TO THE SITE

After your users review the site, changes to the Web site will need to be made. Make and publish the changes to the Web site. Ask your users to review the site again and approve the changes. This process may occur a few times before your approvers are satisfied with the result. Keep your ego out of the process; it is important that users see their ideas materialize on the Web site. Users need to take ownership of the Web site and this is one technique for them to do so.

OPEN THE SITE TO THE PUBLIC

Rename the home page to `index.htm` or to the name of the index page as defined to the server. The home page will then be visible to the world when users access your domain.

REGISTER YOUR SITE WITH SEARCH ENGINES

Visit each of the most popular search engines such as Yahoo, Lycos, Excite, AltaVista, Webcrawler, and others. Many search engines have links to the others or will find them if you search on Web search engines.

There are two types of search facilities on the Internet, directory servers and search engines or crawlers. Directory services like Yahoo search a local database that you update by providing information about your site. Generally, once you identify your URL, the search engine will visit your site daily, collect information, and index it for you.

A few Web crawlers are still around. These were popular in the early days of the Web but are no longer practical due to the number of Web sites. Crawlers automatically search for domains and index everything they find.

Other good sources of links are trade associations or periodicals that are specific to your industry. These Web sites generally like to link to others with related content.

DEVELOPING THE INTERNET PROJECT PLAN

Up to this point, we have the preliminary fact-finding necessary to develop an implementation plan. This chapter brings these issues together and presents a sample prototype for your project.

Figure 20.1 shows a timeline for a typical Internet project for a company without Internet connectivity. The project is scheduled to take between eight and nine months. This is a realistic time frame for your initial project.

We hope this book will help you build your Web site more quickly and efficiently. Even with the book, some activities simply take time. Selecting your ISP, having your telephone company install telephone lines, and ordering and receiving your equipment take time. There isn't much you can do about that.

A substantial amount of the time built into the estimates for this initial project accounts for the learning curve as you learn new tools, techniques, and establish your environment. Subsequent projects will capitalize on the skills acquired during this project, and on your established environment. You should discover that Internet applications can be developed three to five times faster than a traditional programming-based project. I can develop in one day a Web-based application using Net.Data that will take an RPG programmer three to five days to develop.

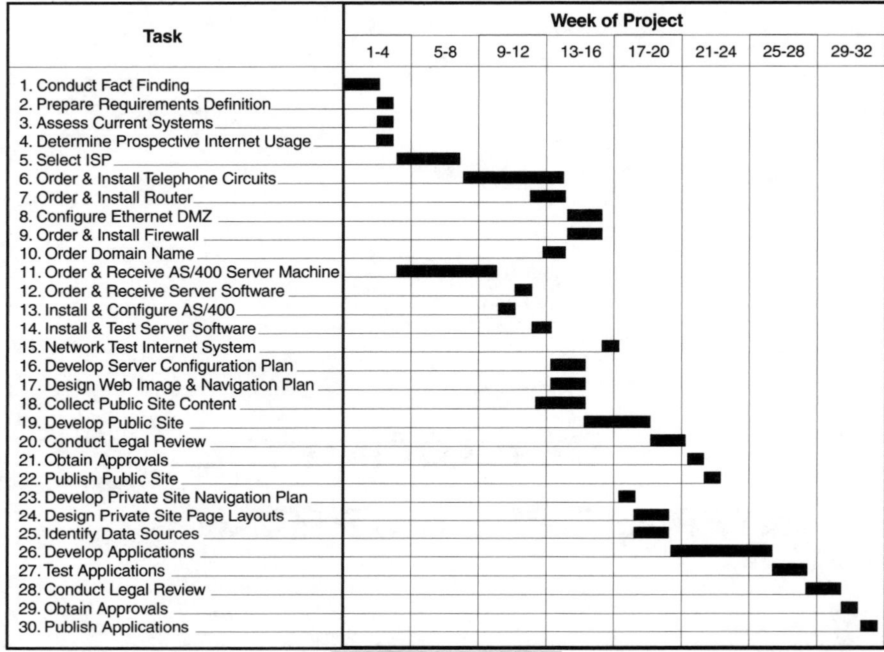

Figure 20.1: Project plan.

Table 20.1 represents a summary of a typical initial Internet project. The third column labeled "Response" refers to the person(s) responsible for each item. This table recaps the tasks and resources described in Chapters 14, 15, and 16.

Table 20.1: Web Site Development Tasks

ID	Task	Response	Duration in Weeks
1	Conduct fact finding	Project Manager	2
2	Prepare requirements definition	Project Manager	1
3	Assess current systems	Project Manager	1
4	Determine prospective Internet usage	Project Manager	1
5	Select ISP	Project Manager, AS/400 Systems Programmer, Network Specialist	4
6	Order & Install telephone circuits	Network Specialist	6
7	Order & install router	Network Specialist	2
8	Configure Ethernet DMZ	Network Specialist	2
9	Order & install firewall	Project Manager, Network Specialist	2
10	Order domain name	Webmaster	1
11	Order & receive AS/400 server	Project Manager	6
12	Order & receive server software	Project Manager, AS/400 Systems Programmer	1
13	Install & configure AS/400	AS/400 Systems Programmer	1
14	Install & test server software	Webmaster, Network Specialist, AS/400 Systems Programmer	1
15	Network test Internet system	Webmaster, Network Specialist, AS/400 Systems Programmer	1
16	Develop server configuration plan	Project Manager, Webmaster, Web Content Developer	2
17	Design Web image & navigation plan	Webmaster	2
18	Collect public site content	Project Manager	3
19	Develop public site	Webmaster, Graphic Designer, Commercial Artist, Web Content Developer	4

Table 20.1: Web Site Development Tasks, *continued*

ID	Task	Response	Duration in Weeks
20	Conduct legal review	Corporate Attorney	2
21	Obtain approvals	Project Manager, Corporate Sponsor	1
22	Publish public site	Webmaster	1
23	Develop private site navigation plan	Project Manager, Webmaster, Web Content Developer	1
24	Design private site page layouts	Webmaster, Web Content Developer	2
25	Identify data sources	Webmaster	2
26	Develop applications	Web Content Developer, Application Programmer	6
27	Test applications	Webmaster, Web Content Developer	2
28	Conduct legal review	Corporate Attorney	2
29	Obtain approvals	Project Manager, Corporate Sponsor	1
30	Publish private site	Webmaster	1

PART III

DEVELOPING AN E-BUSINESS WEB SITE

In this section, we explore the process of developing an electronic commerce Web site. The section begins by explaining the concepts and facilities of the common gateway interface (CGI). It is not intended to be a comprehensive HTML guide, nor is it designed to replace vendor manuals. Instead, it will explain the concepts necessary to develop interactive Web sites, providing practical examples and explanations of how to develop real-world applications.

I focus heavily on IBM's Net.Data product because, in my opinion, it is a tool that provides the leverage to make doing business on the Internet with an AS/400 not only desirable, but easy. Almost anyone can create dazzling interactive Web-based applications in hours instead of days, weeks, or months. When I say almost anyone, I include non-programmers. Although some programming language is helpful, it is not mandatory.

When you have finished reading this section, you should have an understanding of the concepts and facilities involved in developing interactive Web sites. Web site development and CGI programming is very different from traditional AS/400 programming. Therefore, you need to toroughly understand the concepts.

WEB SITE DESIGN

Chapter 21 details all the design elements and issues to consider when designing an effective, attractive, and functional business Web site. It covers the basics of color and font selection, layout, graphics, backgrounds, and text formatting.

THE CGI ENVIRONMENT

Chapter 22 starts out by explaining how the Web server environment is structured. It covers the relationship of objects used in Web site design, and also explains how data flows from the user to your CGI programs and Net.Data macros. The programming explanations are at a relatively high level, but theyshould still provide the necessary detail.

HTML AND WEB SITE DESIGN

Chapter 23 is a concepts and facilities chapter. You must understand HTML to design a Web page. Don't despair—HTML is easy to learn. This chapter provides the concepts behind designing pages and forms with HTML. It illustrates and explains the most common HTML tags.

CGI PROGRAMMING WITH AS/400 LANGUAGES

Chapter 24 explains the concepts behind writing CGI programs in languages such as RPG, COBOL, C, C++, PERL 5, REXX, CL, and Java.

NET.DATA, IBM'S HIDDEN TREASURE

Chapter 25 describes Net.Data, the amazing free product shipped with the AS/400 since V3R2. This incredible tool allows anyone to develop complex applications to run on your Web server. We cover it in depth and provide many illustrations of Net.Data macro programming.

21 WEB SITE DESIGN

This non-technical chapter addresses basic Web site design concepts, providing fundamental understanding of what it takes to develop an e-business Web site, while addressing application design issues. See Chapter 23 for the behind-the-scenes HTML programming that makes these design elements work.

BASIC DESIGN CONCEPTS

These fundamental design concepts that are described throughout this chapter:

- ***Keep it simple.*** The biggest mistake Web designers make is putting too much information on a single page.
- ***Think about response time and performance.*** Limit the size and number of graphics on each page.
- ***Test your site at 28.8kbs.*** I always test my site before publishing via a dial-up 28.8 kbs modem connection to test response time. Some technical tricks (described later) speed up performance.

- ***Avoid cute, technical gimmicks.*** Unless it contributes specifically to conveying your message, stick to basic text and graphics.

- ***Avoid too many hyperlinks too soon.*** Try to limit hyperlinks to five or six categories that draw the user into the site.

- ***Listen to user feedback.*** You will get plenty. I designed what I considered a great looking background (it did look great on my monitor), but was told that it made the text hard to read. I changed the background. Users may not know how to vocalize the exact problem, so listen carefully, because you may have to research what they are saying.

- ***Design at 640 x 480 dpi.*** Unfortunately, most users will view your Web site at this resolution. If you design at higher resolutions, you will present a garbled mess to low-resolution users. However, check your design at higher resolutions to make sure that it still looks good.

- ***Test your Web site with different browsers.*** There are major differences among browsers, and each can make your site look completely different. On my site, I draw a line in the cyber-sand and tell my users that I support Netscape 2.1 and Microsoft 3.02 and above. Other browsers may work, but I will not guarantee what the site looks like.

- ***Follow basic rules of graphic design.*** Draw your user into the Web site with headlines because they may not read your text.Use basic rules for headings (i.e. capitalize first letter and proper nouns only). People tend to read headings if they are easy to read.

- ***Limit your use of fonts.*** A list of universal system fonts supported by Microsoft Windows and Macintosh is outlined later in the chapter. Limit your font selection to these fonts.

- ***Avoid breaking up paragraphs with bold and italics.*** Anything that breaks the reading rhythm causes the user to stop reading your text.

- ***Avoid the use of horizontal rules.*** I have seen pages that place a horizontal rule (the <HR> HTML tag) all the way across the page after every paragraph on the page. The horizontal rule says STOP to the user...don't read further.

- ***No borders around tables.*** Although HTML provides the ability to put a border around the cells of a table, avoid this technique. It detracts from the appearance of the Web site.

- ***Avoid long pages.*** Before you design a page longer than the screen can display, be sure the viewer will want to see the content that must be scrolled into view. Use long pages for technical textual content, but never for a menu-type page. Navigation buttons, e-mail links, and other elements that are out of site will never be seen. Users will not scroll down unless they must. (I learned this one the hard way. I had some explanatory text that told the user how to do something located out of site on the opening screen. Because they didn't scroll, I kept getting questions about how to do what I told them.)

- ***Avoid long lines.*** Many studies conclude the optimum line length is eight to ten words per line. Readers develop a reading rhythm and have a visual limit to the amount of text they can view comfortably while scanning the page. Long or short lines disrupt this rhythm. This is especially true when dealing with a computer terminal and a screen that is 640 pixels wide. If you attempt to put more than eight to ten words on a line, it will be too small to read comfortably and impossible for readers with diminished vision. Remember, users can adjust the font size; there is nothing you can do about it. To illustrate, set your text size to "large" in Microsoft Internet Explorer and your screen resolution to 640 *x* 480.

- ***Be sure it prints.*** Those great looking pages you designed with white type on a dark blue background look great on your monitor, but what happens when they print? The white type prints on white paper and now the text is invisible because backgrounds do not print. Sorry folks, most people print your pages to read offline. This is especially true if they contain text and information that the reader wants to absorb.

- ***Be careful with color.*** There are a whopping 256 colors to work with. When you mix colors, a dithering pattern is introduced into your color. A light yellow background may have little spots of black or red introduced into whatever you are coloring. When colors like this are used in backgrounds, they have the effect of blurring the type, making the page hard to read. Another factor to consider: printers print in limited colors. Be sure that the great design you created in Corel Draw and printed and presented to management for approval works in a browser. Odds are, it won't!

- ***Don't try to port graphic designs intended for print media to the Web.*** I was working with an artist who prepared printed layouts of what she thought the Web site should look out. She prepared the output using Adobe PageMaker and printed the output on landscape 8 ½ *x* 11-inch paper. It looked great on paper. It was impossible to implement on the Web. Don't present concepts to management unless you know they will work.

BASIC BUSINESS-ORIENTED DESIGN ISSUES

In Chapter 14, I walked you through a business requirements study, identifing the mission and business requirements for the Web site. The design and layout of the Web site is where the plan becomes a reality. At all times, your business requirements must be in the forefront. A good graphic designer knows this rule, a graphic artist may not. It is the responsibility of the Webmaster to keep the graphic artists and designers focused on the company's target.

PURPOSE OF YOUR SITE

To understand exactly what the company is trying to achieve for each audience, work with the marketing department and read your business requirements document. You will need to understand a great deal about your audience. Following are some considerations:

- ***Age of your audience.*** Profile your audience by age group, then evaluate what appeals to each group. If you are dealing with an audience over 50 years old, keep in mind that theey may need extra help in terms of Web site legibility. You may want to increase the type size to ensure that it is easy to read. With younger people, you may want to use catchy headlines and graphics to keep their attention.

- ***Social and economic background of your audience***. Over 70 percent of the American population hates to read. Whereas less than 15 percent are such avid readers that they read the fine print on the cereal box just because it is there. Most people scan headlines and look at graphics. The headlines you use on your Web site are by far the most important part of the Web site. A general recommendation is to write the text in a word processor that includes a grammar checker with grade-level checking, setting it to sixth grade. Don't talk down to your audience, but keep the text simple.

- ***Cultural differences.*** Your Web site is international. If you are targeting an international audience, be extremely careful with your content. Words, phrases, and even graphics that are very appropriate for one audience can be extremely offensive in other countries. A large company selling cake mixes tried to sell its product in Japan and failed miserably after spending millions on its advertising campaign because it ignored the fact that many people in Japan do not have ovens or bake.

WHO ARE YOUR USERS?

There are also different ways in which people will navigate the Web site. A Web site is dynamic, allowing users to choose how they want to navigate it. Users determine what to read, where to go, and when to leave. Thus, you need to accommodate your diverse visitors.

- ***Web surfer***. Home pages designed for Web surfers should resemble magazine covers or book jackets. The objective is to provide something of interest that draws users into a Web site. All links on the home page must point inward towards the content. Do not put links to external sites on your home page.

- ***Novice and occasional users.*** These people depend upon clear and concise visual clues on how to navigate your site. According to Sun Microsystem's Jakob Nielsen, less than 10 percent of your users will ever scroll beyond the top of your Web pages and many do not even know how to operate the scroll bars. Instead, they use the Forward button, Back button, Stop button, and Home button on the browser. They like graphic buttons that clearly say "Push Me." They are confused by long complex text menus and may not be able to clearly recognize hyperlinks. (It's important to avoid changing the default hyperlink color if you intend to attract novice users. Most browsers display hyperlinks as underscored bold blue text. It may look ugly, but it is a clear visual signal that the user quickly learns to recognize.) The organization of your Web site is important to these users because they will get lost in a maze of pages. Provide visual clues showing where the user is and how to get back to a familiar point in your Web site.

- ***Expert and frequent users.*** These people want to access information quickly and easily; they don't want to wade through endless pages of gratuitous advertisements and other material to get to the information they need. In business terms, this customer is visiting your site to order products. Assume that you sell business supplies to regular customers. They want to find the product, place the order, and get out. If they can do this efficiently, your site will be successful. Otherwise, customers will take their business elsewhere.

ANATOMY OF A COMMERCIAL WEB SITE

A commercial Web site has many components and each should be clearly defined in the business requirements plan because each may have a different audience. This chapter will focus on the basic rule of journalism: who, what, where, when—and, because this is a commercial endeavor, how much. How many times have you visited a Web site to obtain product information and couldn't find out how to order the product or its cost? Why did they bother to put up the Web site?

WHO ARE YOU?

Who is publishing this Web site? It is imperative that you identify your company and provide background information. If you are a subsidiary of a large conglomerate, you need to identify your parent and provide a link to it. Provide a link on your home page labeled "Who we are," or "About XYZ Company." Then link to a simple page telling how long you have been in business, your size ($100 billion in assets), and more.

WHAT DO YOU DO?

Placing a statement or motto on the front page is a good strategy, such as "America's Supermarket," "Workers' Compensation Insurance Specialist," and the like. It is disappointing to see so many Web sites failing to outline the company's function.

HOW CAN I CONTACT YOU?

If you have stores, where are they located? If you do business electronically, by telephone, or by fax, how can you be reached? If you are a distributor, who sells your products? A page with a geographic locator is worth the investment, especially if you operate a store chain. Companies like Vicinity Corporation will assist in the implementation of geographic locators for a fee (see `www.vicinity.com`.)

WHAT ARE YOU SELLING?

It is generally not a good idea to put product information on your home page. A simple button labeled Products or Services can transfer customers to product information pages. The exception to this rule is when your company is associated with a product. If I were building a Web site for a car manufacturer like Rolls-Royce, you had better believe there would be a picture of a Rolls on the home page!

WHEN WAS THIS UPDATED?

In terms of a Web site, the issue here is when was the information updated? It is good a practice to put the date a page was last updated on each page of the Web site. (In Part III, we provide some techniques to automate this task.) There are two reasons to date Web site pages. Your corporate legal department will require that each page is copyrighted and dated. Also, your audience will know how current the information is. You may also put dates on links to other information that show recent updates. My insurance company site has a "What's New" link on its home page that is updated at least twice per month with news articles. The date of the most recent update is placed in the description of the link to tell people that it is fresh news and to let them know if they have read the news.

HOW MUCH DOES IT COST AND HOW DO I BUY IT?

Why would you create a Web site describing products without providing this information? Many companies fail to put this critical information on their sites. If they are hoping that customers call for pricing, the simple fact is that many customers want to know the ballpark price before they call. If your product is expensive, do you want people calling you who can't afford it? Many marketing people say, "Well, we offer quantity discounts and prices will vary by customer." Tell them that! Show the base pricing and tell them that quantity pricing can be negotiated. At least they know what the retail price is and they will be inspired to think that they can get a deal by calling you.

In the early days of the Internet, there was fear about releasing credit card numbers. Today, you can use SET or SSL technology to encrypt your customer's personal information, credit card numbers, or customer account numbers. Tell customers their information is secure (the browser will signal the customer with a closed padlock or other graphic symbol when using secure technology). Don't make them call or e-mail for more information. Put an order form on your site and let them buy it! (Do include an e-mail address for those who want more information on your site. They should be able to click the address that brings up their mail client pre-addressed. If you provide an e-mail link, be sure that someone responds within 24 hours.) You should note that SSL, while providing a secure link between the client's browser and the merchant's Web site, will not protect the credit card from unscrupulous merchants or operators of the merchant's Web site. Only SET technology provides secure end-to-end security by passing the credit card through the merchant's site directly to the credit card clearing company. The merchant does not see the credit card number when SET is used.

If you sell computer software, consider having the user download the product from the Web site immediately after placing the order because users don't want to wait. They want to take advantage of the convenience that the Internet offers.

WHAT'S NEW?

What is your company doing? How is it changing? How is it serving your customers? A link to articles written frequently telling customers how you are serving them is a great way to keep them interested and coming back to your Web site. In addition, date this link so customers don't waste time clicking the link only to find out that they have already read the news.

INVESTOR INFORMATION

If your company is public and want to attract investors, its Web site is one of the best possible sources of information for busy investors. Determine who buys your stock. Are the majority of your investors institutional investors or sophisticated investors? Do individuals buy large blocks of your stock? Provide something for everyone. Publish your annual and quarterly reports here. Talk to your investor relations representative. Find out what potential investors ask when they call for updates. Are you a retailer? You'd better publish store sales data. Be careful about what you publish, but publish what you legally can. If you experience problems, beat the analysts to the punch. Explain the problems and explain how you are resolving them.

YOUR PEOPLE

The Web is a personal medium. I recommend communicating in the first person. The content of your Web site should be written from you to the person who is reading it. Along those lines, people want to know that your company is not huge, nameless, and faceless. At a minimum, you need a letter from your president describing your company and its mission. I recommend a small picture accompany the letter. It is a good idea to identify other people in your organization that deal with your customers and put their pictures on the site. People like dealing with people.

YOUR CUSTOMERS

We are talking about building an electronic commerce Web site. You need to provide a clear and visible link on the home page to the private sections of your Web site that contain information and data for regular customers.

I recommend a home page for each type of customer that contains a menu of all of the products and services provided for the customer.

If you provide ordering, billing, shipping, or other types of information, it should be customized to each type of customer. I always look up and display customers' names when they login to my sites. It is a nice personal touch, and it communicates a sense of partnership.

SITE ORGANIZATION AND STRUCTURE

Most of your Web site is hidden from the user at any given time. Users may enter your Web site at many different places. Search engines may locate a page containing specific content that is logically quite far away from your home page. An effective Web site provides the user with a clear sense of organization.

Consider a book for a moment. It has a table of contents, chapter headings, section headings, and an index. The reader knows he should open the book to the front page and move forward through the book. He also knows how to find specific content by scanning the table of contents or searching the index. When scanning and searching, the reader uses headlines to locate the general area of a page or group of pages.

Well-designed brochures are based around headlines. Most people do not read the text of a brochure. People focus on the pictures and scan headlines. They may read one or two paragraphs that attract their attention.

Newsletters, like brochures, usually contain a table of contents on the front page telling the user what articles are inside. They also use headlines, pull-quotes, and graphics or photographs to draw a reader's attention to specific content.

Your Web site is visible one page at a time. And often, not even an entire page is visible. If you are selling products on the Web and have indexed your Web site properly, a search engine will often take the user to the page that describes the product found in the search engine.

When designing the structure and flow of the site, look at each page as if it were the entry point to your site. You must clearly identify whom the page belongs to and provide a method of linking to the starting point of your site.

Four structures can be supported by the Web and these structures can be intermingled to form complex structures. Each structure has a specific purpose.

SEQUENCE ORGANIZATION

Sequencing (shown in Figure 21.1) is a technique used for presenting long technical or educational documents on the Web. A good rule of thumb is to keep the length of a single Web "page" to two or three printed pages. Each Web page in a sequence should cover a specific subject. You must carefully evaluate the need for this organization structure because it can be extremely frustrating to your readers.

The best use of a sequence is when presenting or demonstrating a product. This technique is particularly useful for computer software products. You may walk the user through a screen-show presentation that shows step-by-step how the product works.

Figure 21.1: Sequence of pages in Web site.

When deciding to use this technique, the last page must take the user where the user wants to go. It is probably a good idea to have escape points on each page that take the user back to the point where he chose to enter the sequence. Remember that the user can always get out of a sequence by hitting the Home key on their browser or by typing a new URL.

When using a sequence, the use of Forward and Backward arrows or other visual indicators should be provided to help the user move through your sequence. Do not depend upon the browser's Back and Forward buttons to navigate through your sequence. The browser uses relative references, so you may be surprised where your user ends up.

GRID ORGANIZATION

A grid structure (Figure 21.2) is common to education. The horizontal path across a row represents specifically related topics. The vertical path also represents a series of related topics. This technique is useful for representing a combination of time and events. An example borrowed from the *Yale C/AIM Web Style Guide* is the example of part of a Web site dedicated to disease. Each column might represent a discussion of a disease. Tuberculosis might be the topic of column one. And row 1 might discuss a diagnostic technique such as medical imaging.

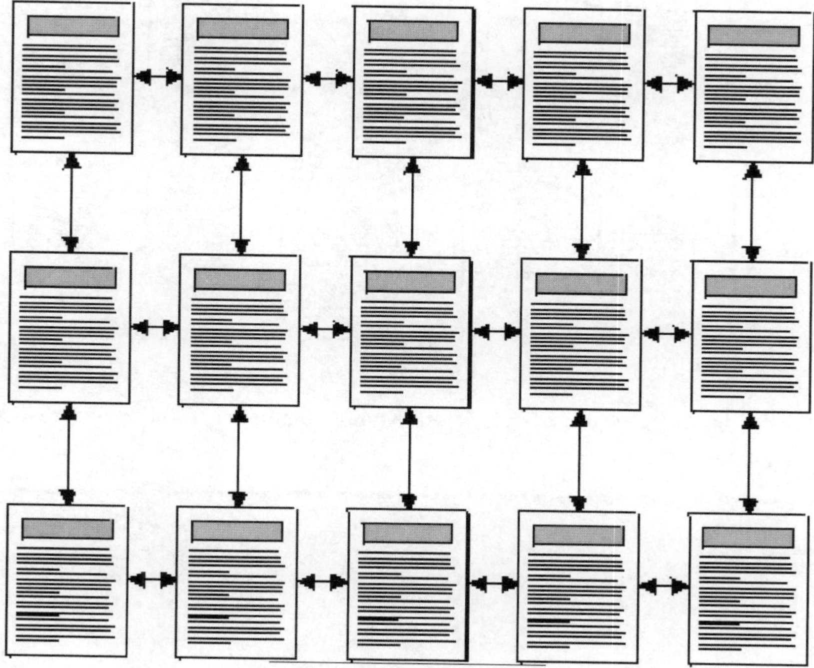

Figure 21.2: Grid organization.

Because grids are difficult for your reader to visualize, it is a good idea to put a diagram of the site on screen or one link away to show readers where they are in the grid.

HIERARCHICAL ORGANIZATION

The hierarchy (Figure 21.3) is the most familiar and comfortable organizational method for Web site visitors. It is important to keep the depth of the hierarchies relatively shallow, and I suggest not using more than three levels of nested menus.

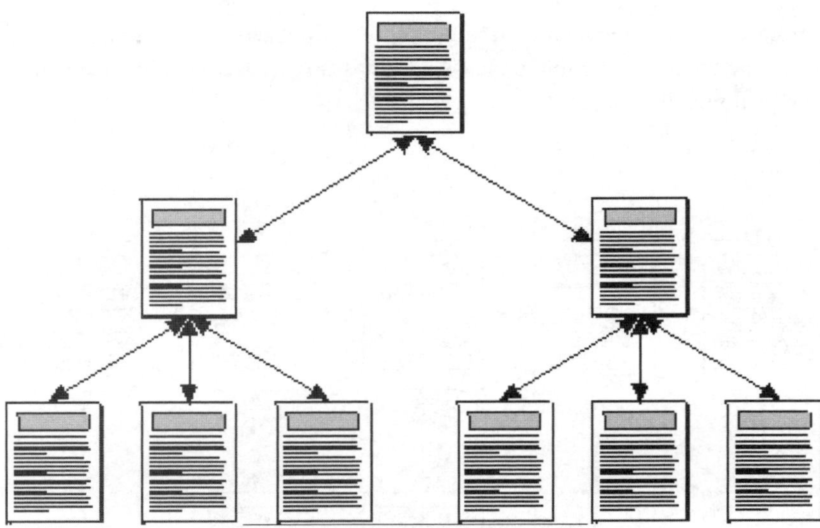

Figure 21.3: Hierarchical organization.

Table 21.1 illustrates the power of the hierarchy and the number of first pages that can be stored using three levels of menus.

Table 21.1: Hierarchy Menu Items

Number of Nested Columns	5	7	8	10
1	5	7	8	10
2	25	49	64	100
3	125	343	512	1000

As you can see, very large Web sites can be organized into a relatively flat structure. Here are some guidelines to follow when using hierarchies:

- Try to use no more than three levels of menus.
- Do not create a menu that has fewer than five links.
- Link back to the previous level of menu from each page below it.
- Link detail pages back to the previous menu.
- Link menus back to the previous menu

WEB ORGANIZATION

The Web (Figure 21.4) is a flexible and interesting navigational structure. It allows a user to get virtually anywhere within your Web site from any other place in the site.

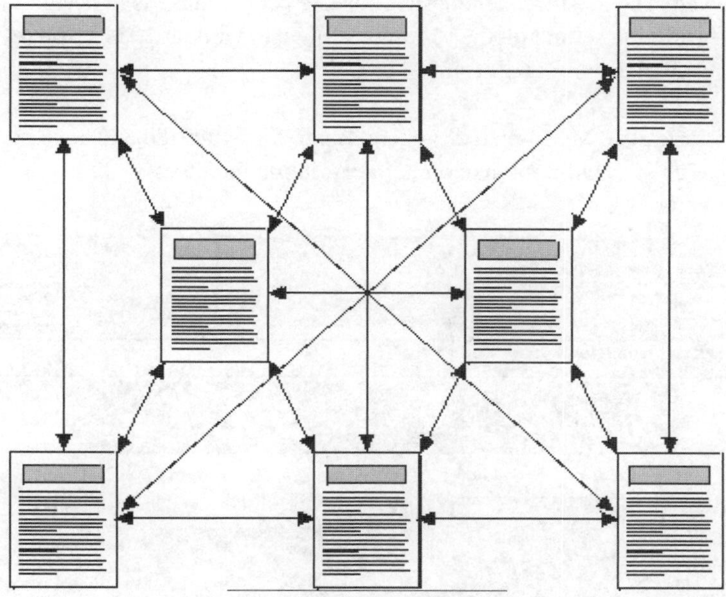

Figure 21.4: Web organization.

This structure can be confusing to many users who quickly lose their place. The structure works well for sites with a great deal of independent content. It demands a navigation bar or navigation margin clearly identifying the destinations that can be reached via each link on the page. A navigation bar at the top of the page is the preferred method to support this type of Web site structure. Each location is represented by a button or link at the top of every page. The bar is dynamic and drops the current page from the list.

WEB PAGE DESIGN

Web page design uses techniques developed in traditional print- or television-based graphic design. One must learn the limitations and capabilities of HTML and then work them. Many graphic designers have problems adjusting to the medium of the World Wide

Web. We will explore some popular Web sites in this section and discuss what works, what almost works, and what doesn't.

RESOLUTION

All Web pages should be designed to dynamically adjust to the browser on which they are being viewed. The most frequent design mistake people make is to design their pages using a high resolution setting on their browser. I love to work at 1024 *x* 768 on my PC, but I design my Web pages at 640 *x* 480.

The reverse is true also. Many Web designers design for 640 *x* 480 and have no concept of what their Web sites will look like on high-resolution monitors.

Figure 21.5: Disney home page at 640 dpi.[1]

The Web site depicted in Figure 21.5 is the Walt Disney Company home page located at `www.disney.com`. As you can imagine, Disney uses the finest commercial artists and graphic designers to design and implement its Web site. At 640 *x* 480 pixel resolution, it looks fantastic.

1 Used by permission. © Disney. All rights reserved.

Figure 21.6 shows Disney's home page again, only this time at 1024 *x* 728 resolution. Would you believe that it is the same Web site? How does it look now?

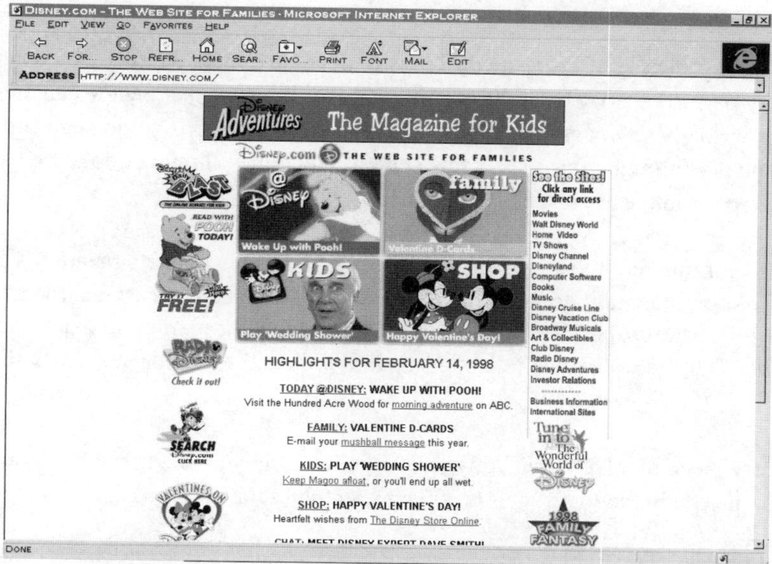

Figure 21.6: Disney home page at 1040 dpi.

This shows how radically different the same Web site can look by simply changing the browser resolution. Wait! The situation with your Web site could get worse! Users can hide the status line at the bottom of their Windows 95/98 PCs. They can turn off the button bar at the top of their browser. They can turn off the address line on the browser. And they can also display the browser as a segment of their PC screen that affects presentation.

Designers can optimize for a 640 *x* 480 screen but this leaves the high-resolution user with an inferior display. I design for 800 *x* 600 and test on 640 *x* 480. I use relative measurements when I define my tables and most other graphic HTML resources. My pages tend to fill large screens, but are tested to ensure that they still look good on a low-resolution screen.

Before we leave this example, notice the amount of information that is displayed on the 1024 *x* 768 version of the screen. Will the 640 *x* 480 user ever see this information? Also note that even at 1024 *x* 768, there is more information that cannot be displayed on the screen. This is important only if you want your users to see it. Studies indicate that less than 10 percent of Web page viewers ever scroll down beyond what they can see on the page.

OVERALL IMAGE

A fundamental principle of Web site design is to develop a look and feel that is consistent across every page on the Web site. It is important to remember that people can enter your Web site at virtually any page. They do not have to start with your home page and navigate sequentially through your site. A few general guidelines should be followed across every single page in the Web site.

Work with your marketing department to identify and define your organization's public image. If your organization does not have a formal public image (i.e. standards for advertising copy, letterheads, brochures, and such), work with your marketing department to develop one. The Web site must reflect a standard look and feel consistent with the organization.

Collect every piece of advertising copy, brochure, catalog, and letterhead that you can get your hands on. Study the logos, colors, slogans, graphics, and style.

Identify your organization on every page, because you never know where the user will enter the Web site. If you look at *www.republicindemnity.com*, you will see two distinct page styles. Both styles have the company's logo in the upper left corner of the page. Public pages have the company name at the top of every page. The copyright notices at the bottom of every page serve to protect and identify the company. The date last updated is both a legal requirement and serves to tell the user when the content was last changed. Adobe's Web site uses its logo and button bar on every page of its site, as do Microsoft and several other Web sites.

Always put a link back to your home page on every page that can be directly accessed. This is not quite as important on pages generated by CGI programs that can only be accessed from a specific link.

Consistency of style using two or three layout styles allows programmers and content developers to work within a pattern and eliminates the requirement for a graphic designer to review and modify each page. Programmers and end users can design pages if the layout is clearly defined and documented.

YOUR HOME PAGE

Your home page is the page that most people will see when they type your URL (i.e. `www.mycompany.com`) and access the default page (usually `index.htm` or `index.html`). Your home page is generally the page that you advertise. Your marketing literature, radio, television ads, and mailers should refer to your Web site address. It is also the page most likely to be found by a search engine.

A home page should be considered to serve the same purpose as a book jacket or magazine cover. It should draw people into your Web site. It must accomplish the following basic objectives:

- Tell the viewer who you are.
- Tell them what your organization does.
- Tell them where to find items of interest within your Web site (links to products, services, background information, news, etc.).
- The page must load in the length of time that you can hold your breath. If you follow this rule people will view your page. If you break the rule, most users will hit the stop button and go somewhere else. Use graphics, but limit their size.
- Make sure the entire screen is visible at 640 *x* 480 resolution. The user should not have to scroll to see anything on the page. If they have to scroll, they won't and will miss potential valuable information.
- Tell the user when the page was changed. A simple "date last updated" date at the bottom of the page will work well.

This is the time for your graphic artists to shine, but very carefully. Art and color bring users into the page. Unfortunately, you must be extremely careful to keep the load time for the page to a minimum. This means that those stunning photographic Rembrandts that you created for the Web site may not be appropriate. A good graphic artist can limit the number of colors and detail in a graphic to reduce file sizes and still produce a great looking page.

While I disagree with the length of Disney's page, look again at the 640 *x* 480 view of Disney's home page. They are dealing with all age groups from toddlers to grandparents. The page loads remarkably fast even though it is full of graphics. The graphics have been carefully designed and optimized for performance, each hyperlinking to additional content. The design is similar to many children's point-and-click toys that are on the market today. I would be extremely surprised if a five- to seven-year-old viewing this Web site did not click on at least one of the graphics to find even greater treasures inside the Web site. Mature users may quickly choose a destination from the list of links in the upper right screen.

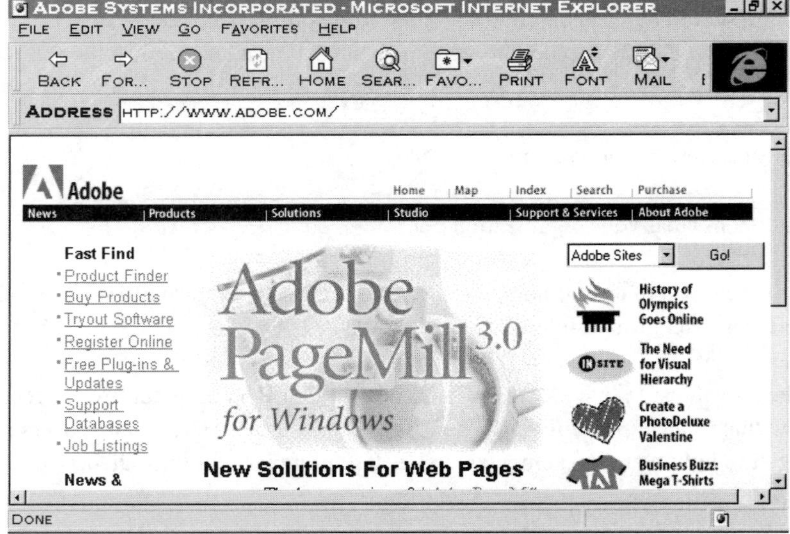

Figure 21.7: Adobe's home page[2].

Adobe has one of the better home pages on the Web, as shown in Figure 21.7. Notice the black menu bar at the top screen. This construct is used consistently on all of Adobe's Web pages. This page is designed using tables and columns. Adobe assumes that you know what they do and features one product in the center of the page when a new product release has been created or is about ready to be released to the public.

Adobe took the approach of putting more data on the page than can be seen on the screen, but they use a clever technique to lead the audience to the scroll bar. Notice that "News &" at the bottom of the screen is unfinished. This is a clear visual indication that there is more unseen content. Notice that you can see the very top of a line of text under "New

2 Used by permission. © Adobe. All rights reserved.

Solutions For Web Pages," another visual clue. One last visual clue is the fact that the bottom scroll-bar cuts off the blue T-shirt. All three clues clearly tell you that you need to scroll down to see more information.

Figure 21.8: FedEx home page[3].

The home page for FedEx (Figure 21.8) follows all the rules. This home page is one of the best on the Internet. Let's take this page apart and see what makes it work.

First, the page is simple and uncluttered. The Welcome message in several different languages coupled with a graphic of the world clearly states that the company does business worldwide. The text under "Welcome" tells you exactly what this company does and what you as a customer can expect from them. The four links on the page—Track, Ship, Find, and Start Now—are clear invitations to act.

The FedEx page incorporates several elements of graphic design that work well. Formal studies have been done to track a reader/viewer's eye movement when looking at an advertising piece. They show that the eye is attracted to the page starting at a point just be-

3 Used by permission. © Federal Express Corporation (FedEx). All rights reserved.

low the top left of the page. It moves to the upper left corner of the page, then to the right corner, then diagonally down to the bottom left, and finally over to the right corner.

This pattern of vision can be controlled by the graphic designer. In the case of this page, your eye is attracted to the FedEx logo. Your eye is then attracted to the graphic, which guides your eye to move in the direction that the little package is moving. You cannot help but follow the package that points to Track and Ship. The graphic designer then uses white space and follows the shape of the graphic to force your eye to move down to Find and Start Now. Your eye ends up resting on the Choose Country pull down and Go button. The text on the left side of the page will only be read by a small percentage of compulsive readers. It doesn't really matter because the graphics and headlines get the message across.

FedEx's overall advertising campaign helps make this Web page work for them. Everyone recognizes the FedEx logo. The logo alone tells you instantly where you are and whose site you are looking at. Most companies do not have this kind of international name or logo recognition. If you had any doubts about what this company does, the graphic makes it clear that they "send packages around the world." The headlines (links) are simple, clear action verbs that tell you to do something now! This page is most likely viewed for one to three seconds before the user clicks onto a link.

Remember, you want users to see your home page, then move into the Web site to get more information about your company and its products. The objective is not to have users sit around and admire your artwork.

FRAMES

Netscape introduced a design feature called *frames*, which has become the staple of technical-based Web site designers. Frames are functionally equivalent to PC windows. Each frame can be controlled separately from each other frame. You can change the content of one frame while retaining the content of another.

The Web page in Figure 21.9, shows a fictitious example of typical abuse of frames. It contains four separate frames. The top frame is static and contains the fictitious company's name. The frame to the left contains links to all major locations on the Web site. The bottom frame contains copyright information. Many companies use this section for a slogan. The right hand frame is reserved for content.

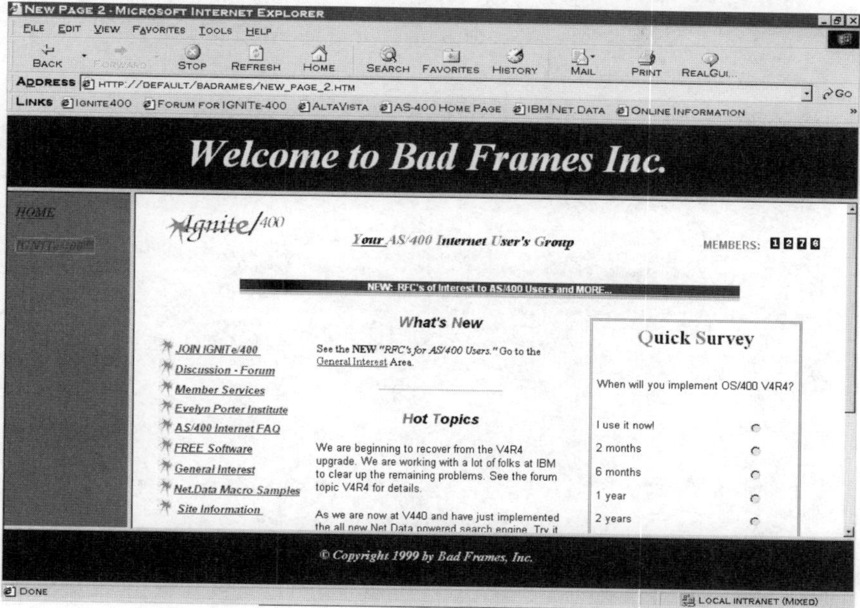

Figure 21.9: Typical abuse of frames.

The design uses up valuable screen space to support the top and side frames, thus limiting content to the small left-over space in the middle. It also hides the true URL or address of content on the site and prevents the user from bookmarking important pages that the user might want to return to. (The HTML source for a frame shows the URL for a specific page of content and views the page without the heading and menu frame.)

Frames handling introduces a level of complexity in Web site design. There is a different and perfectly valid position that recommends the use of frames. If you wnat no page on your Web site to be greater than 40k so that it can rapidly load even at slow modem speeds, frames are a good choice. In some cases, performance is the essential factor in designing a Web site, in which case, frames work well. If you determine that the audience for your site wants information, wants it rapidly, and is concerned with rapid access to content, you should select the frame model.

Figure 21.10 shows a different use of frames.

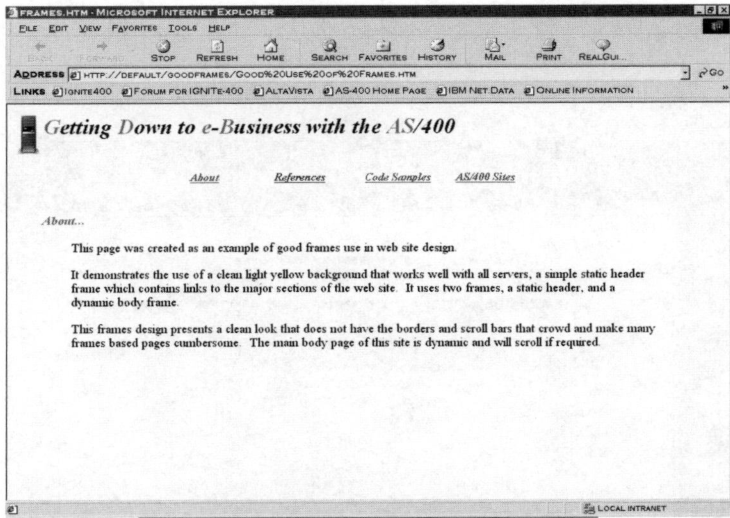

Figure 21.10: A different use of frames — frame 1.

In this approach, the masthead (top portion) is a frame that includes the four links. When you click one of the four links, the main screen changes, but the masthead remains constant. This conserves resources, improves performance, and locks the link controls on the page. Figure 21.11 is another frame example.

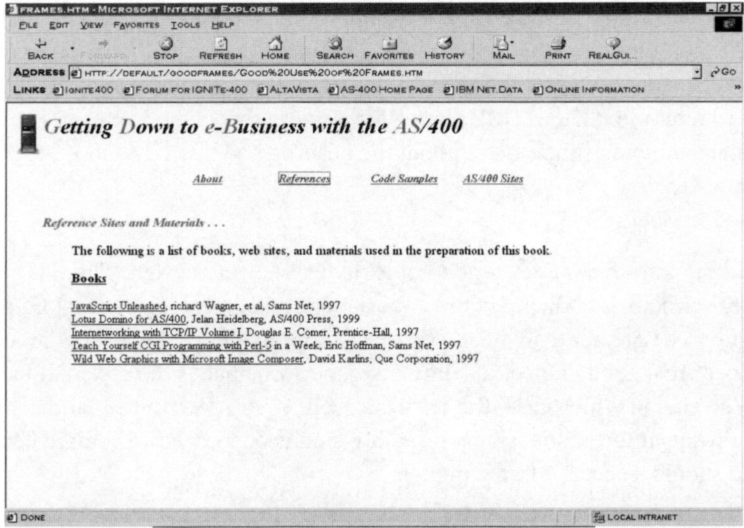

Figure 21.11: Different use of frames — frame 2.

Notice that the masthead at the top remains the same. Each of the four categories is but a click away. Users can always find what they is looking for and, because the bulk of the pages are static text, the site rapidly displays pages. The only graphics used in the site are the two GIF files in the masthead.

As is always the case in Web site design, frames are but another tool for the Web designer's tool chest. As with all tools, they should be used when needed to fulfill the business requirements of the Web site. Always remember that the audience and end user are the driving forces in Web site design.

UNDERSTAND HOW VIEWERS SEE YOUR WEB SITE

It is important to understand how your viewers see your Web site. Graphic design leads a viewer through masses of shape and color. We first perceive shape, then color. We then begin to pick out detail items, first from graphics and finally from text. Our eyes are drawn to headlines, which contrast with the rest of the page. Only as a final step do we see the detail text on a page.

Age, education, and reading style play a very important part in what users see. Many people resist reading. We are exposed to an incredible amount of text each day of our lives, and our brains have to work hard to read and comprehend it. Older readers have difficulty with small typefaces and may adjust their browsers to display text in a very large size, which alters the appearance of our graphic masterpieces. Care must be taken with the use of colors like red and green on the same page when the colors are of approximately the same shade and hue. A very large number of people are color blind and will not be able to differentiate between red and green. Depending upon the type of color blindness, other colors may be difficult or impossible to see. Try to visualize the text in terms of its gray-scale representation. Ensure that there is sufficient contrast in the text.

Figure 21.12 illustrates the result of studies that analyze how people see an 8½ *x* 11 inch piece of paper. Their eyes are first attracted to the circled number one. They then move up to item two, over to item three, down to four, and finally come to rest on item five. They see headlines that may fall between three and four, but are unlikely to stop and read the content.

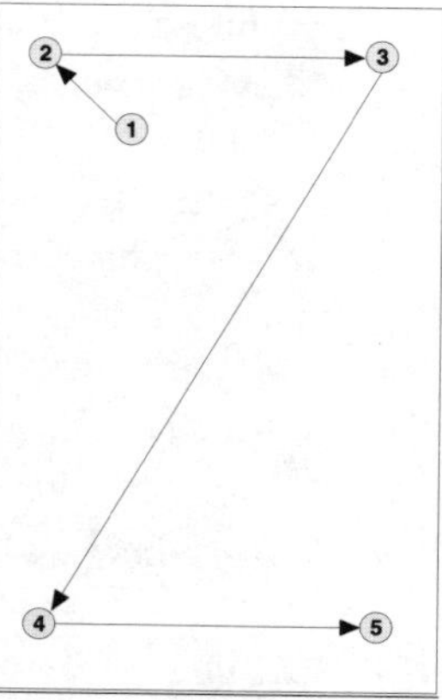

Figure 21.12: Eye movement over a typical Web page.

When designing Web pages, you do not have absolute control over locations 3 and 5, which may easily be out of view in a 640 *x* 480 pixel window. Even item 4 may be out of view.

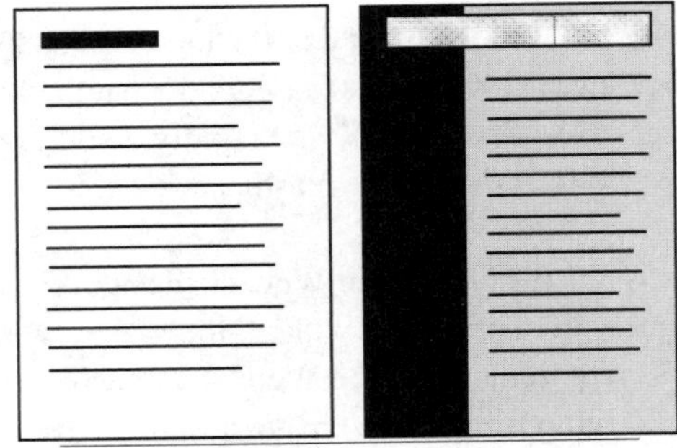

Figure 21.13: Contrasting two page layouts.

Figure 21.13 shows two pages that could contain exactly the same text content. The layout on the left is boring and unlikely to be read. The one on the right introduces shape and contrast, making the content much more readable.

The example shown in Figure 21.14 adds more graphic design elements. We have added graphics and titles to the margin and bold headlines in the body of the text. The eye now has a much more interesting series of patterns and shapes to view. This greatly improves the probability of some part of your message being seen by viewers.

There are several techniques to catch your reader's attention and cause their eye to move where you want it to go. Here are some examples:

Figure 21.14: Layout with graphic design elements.

- Use headlines. Headlines should be at least one type size larger than the text that follows. Try using a different color or make the headline bold. Headlines should follow standard rules for capitalization. Capitalize only the first word and proper nouns.

- Avoid the use of bold, italics, or underscores in the body of your text. This disrupts the reader and improves the probability that the reader will leave the paragraph.

- Use *subheads* to expand on headlines and bring the reader into the text.

- Use *sidebars* (a section of text in a box or with a different background color).

- Use *pull quotes*. A pull quote is a quotation pulled from a paragraph and displayed between two horizontal bars or in a box, usually with a larger typeface than the text of the paragraph and often in another color.

- On the Web site, you have less control over columns than you do on paper. A very effective technique is the use of the *scholars margin*. This is a small column on the left side of the page with a larger column to the right containing the bulk of the content.

- Use motion or the sense of motion to attract the viewer's eye. The FedEx site leaves the eye little choice but to follow the package around the world. It leads the eye into the text at the right of the graphic.

- The FedEx home page also illustrates the use of *white space* to cause the eye to follow the curve suggested by the headlines on the page. White space chases the eye to move away from it.

When designing and laying out Web sites, try sketching them on paper using shapes such as rectangles, circles, and ovals to get a feel for the concept of your page. Try drawing small thumbnail sketches of each page and then draw navigation arrows to begin to get the feel for the organization of your Web site.

Avoid graphic distractions. Horizontal rules across the page tell the user to stop at the rule. (We don't cross solid lines.) Bullets, icons, and other visual markers can be effective if used sparingly, but when they are overused, they distract. They also have the effect of drawing the eye to unimportant areas of the page.

Constantly evaluate your work in terms of the purpose of the Web site, what the page is trying to say, and what you want your user to do.

TYPOGRAPHY

This will undoubtedly be the most difficult area for graphic designers who begin to work with Web pages. Under no circumstance should a graphic designer be allowed to represent sample Web pages on paper because they will not work on the Web! If graphic designers work on the Web site, they must work with tools that incorporate the limitations of the medium.

Graphic designers spend time kerning to get spacing between letters to look just right. They use leading to make sure that letters do not touch each other between lines of text. None of these features exist in HTML.

TYPE AND LEGIBILITY

The human mind reads by recognizing the shape of words, not by parsing each letter and then assembling words. Avoid all uppercase words in headlines. They are much harder to read than mixed-case headlines. Uppercase tends to hide the characteristics of a word and creates a visual block or blob that must be parsed out letter by letter to be read.

Use the standard system or Times Roman font because it is a serif-based font. Serifs are those little decorative curls on letters. Serif fonts give the reader a better clue as to the meaning of the words. Sanserif fonts are harder to distinguish than serif fonts. Use sanserif fonts like Helvetica to accentuate your content.

TYPEFACES

Be extremely careful when choosing typefaces on your Web site. There is a very limited number of fonts delivered with the Windows, Macintosh, and UNIX operating systems. If you have word processing or graphics software installed on the computer with which you are developing your Web site, you may have hundreds of fonts installed by your graphics or page layout software. Most users will not have these fonts installed on their computers. Figure 21.15 shows the default fonts for Windows and the Macintosh.[4]

HTML allows you to specify the name of a font and size in either fixed or relative sizes. The base font size is approximately 12-point type on a 640 x 480 resolution display. Both Netscape and Microsoft browsers allow the user to increase or decrease the font size within the current resolution. Microsoft provides the user with six font size settings. These range from very large to very small. They can be selected from the View menu bar pull down of the browser.

Relative sizes of True Type font display

Windows95, 12 pt type	Macintosh, 12 pt type
Arial	Arial
Arial Black	**Arial Black**
Arial Rounded MT Bold	**Arial Rounded MT Bold**
Book Antiqua	Book Antiqua
Bookman Old Style	Bookman Old Style
Century Gothic	Century Gothic
Century Schoolbook	Century Schoolbook
Courier New	Courier New
Garamond	Garamond
MS LineDraw	**MS LineDraw**
Times New Roman	Times NEw Roman
Verdana	Verdana

Figure 21.15: Web type styles and sizes.

4 Font samples from the Yale C/AIM Web Style Guide at info.med.yale.edu/manual/.

A user can destroy a beautiful typographic layout and there is nothing you can do about it. I have found that it is relatively safe to design for the "normal" setting at a resolution of 640 *x* 480. The default typeface on most systems is a Times Roman font that is a compressed serif font. The font was designed for newspapers to deliberately compress the width of the typeface to allow as many characters per inch as possible. This works well when dealing in the relatively large typefaces used on low-resolution computer monitors.

If you want to put some controlled special fonts on your screen, you must create a GIF or JPEG graphic file and store the text as part of the graphic. All computers will reproduce the graphic faithfully. Do not overdo this technique or you will create pages that load too slowly.

When working with typefaces, minimize the number of typefaces used on the page. Two typefaces are more than enough when coupled with size and color to make your point. I have rarely found the need to use more than one typeface.

The objective of type is to convey information. People read headlines and captions under pictures or graphics. People only read text when they need to. You can often get your point across using headlines and graphics. When a user clicks on an FAQ list, or on a page that contains detailed information about your company, product, or service, they do so because they *want* to read it. Make it easy to read and to print.

Younger people, age 35 or less, generally read online. Older people (40 and up) are more likely to print your pages and read offline. You must consider that long passages of text may be printed, so make sure the user can print information clearly.

TYPE AND COLOR

One of the most challenging aspects of Web design is selecting text and background colors. The graphic artist that I worked with came up with a white text on dark green color scheme that looked great as a concept. The problem was that HTML backgrounds do not print. We ended up printing white text on white paper. Light colors like yellow may be barely visible on the printed page.

An excellent reference site on Web site design is *Web Page Design for Designers* by Joe Gillespie (`www.wpdfd.com/wpdhome.htm`). This site is an excellent source of Web design concepts and information. The one negative aspect of this site is the use of white text on a dark blue background. The text disappears when you print it. If you are going to use light colored text on a dark background, be sure to provide a printable version of your pages for black-and-white or color printers.

Another aspect of type and background color has to do with the color palette used by browsers. The browsers are limited to a 256-color palette. When you mix colors to create custom background colors, you are often *dithering* color patterns (look closely and you will see a color pattern or mesh) on a solid color to form the illusion of the background color. This can create a problem for typefaces typed over the background. Often it will cause the typeface to appear fuzzy, blurred, or to lack contrast with the background.

Test your choice of background and foreground text on different computers with different settings to be sure that your page is legible. Graphic artists often work with large monitors, high resolution, and 24-bit true color using products like Adobe Illustrator, Photoshop, Corel Draw, and other high-end graphics design tools. Work designed with these tools often looks terrible on the Web. Be careful and TEST! TEST! TEST!

BACKGROUNDS

Backgrounds bring an appealing look and feel to Web sites. Background can also create a mood. There are many excellent books on color psychology. Colors toward the red spectrum are considered warm while colors towards blue are considered cool. Graphics may also be used to create a unique background. A general rule is to design backgrounds with a left color bar and light text background on the right, or design a pattern for the entire page.

An effective background technique is to create a very light-faded image of your logo and let it repeat to form your background.

Browse the Web looking at site backgrounds that work and sites that don't work. The best sites use simple, unobtrusive backgrounds. (When I first started, my graphic artist wanted to use a half-toned photograph as the background on my home page. We tried everything to make this combination work. Finally, we gave up and settled for a clean two-color background.)

SOLID COLOR BACKGROUNDS

Use a simple color as the background. I do not recommend a plain white background; remember that colors on a PC monitor are in fact colored light. White is a very bright (absence of color) light. Other colors reduce the amount of light transmitted to your eye. If you choose to use a plain white background, be careful. You may find that the mood of your Web site is entirely too stark. You may also find that, although a white background offers the best possible legibility for text on the screen, the contrast makes it difficult to read.

I find myself gravitating towards shades of yellow for my backgrounds. Yellow is a warm neutral color that works well with many other colors and allows text in several colors to be quite legible. Avoid vivid colors for backgrounds unless you are trying to achieve a very specific effect. You will find that the background limits the choices of text and illustration colors and can have a positive or negative impact on the graphics you place on your site.

Remember that your eye plays tricks when processing visual images. Sometimes the tricks are not very pleasing. Most software tools have a custom color-mixing tool. The yellow that I have used in my site has a great deal of white in it (it has very little yellow) and is pushed towards the red side. The Republic Indemnity Web site uses a yellow that is pushed slightly towards the green side to create a cooler appearance.

This is marketing and advertising. Think carefully about what you are doing and how you present it. Something as simple as your background makes a huge difference as to how your viewers perceive the site.

Graphic Backgrounds

A Web page also may use a graphic as a background, which gives you, the designer, greater control over the look and feel of the page. There are many sources of background graphics available on the Web; you can download a background graphic that someone else has designed.

Browsers use a technique called *tiling* to efficiently handle backgrounds. A background is typically a small square pattern of color and texture ranging in size from 10 pixels by 10 pixels to 150 pixels by 150 pixels. File sizes should be 2k to 3k. The browser repeats the pattern horizontally and vertically, filling the screen with the pattern.

Striped bar patterns are accomplished by putting the color pattern (i.e. the green portion of the Republic Indemnity background) on the left side of the graphic and the plain color on the right. The color bar should be 1200 pixels wide so the browser cannot tile the graphic horizontally. The graphic can only be tiled vertically.

You can create elaborate patterns or use a single photographic or graphic art background if you carefully size them to your page. This technique is extremely difficult when you take into consideration the size variations of the screens that will be viewing the background. It is a technique that graphic designers love, but it is almost impossible to effectively implement.

If you search the www section of `www.yahoo.com`(or the search engine of your choice) for "backgrounds" you will find thousands of free background patterns and images that you can download and use.

With all these free backgrounds, why would you ever create your own? The answer is simple: fancy backgrounds are incredibly difficult to work with. You have a 256-color palette available to work with on the Web. Picking colors that work with your background is extremely difficult. Most often, text becomes fuzzy or disappears into the background. My advice is to keep the background simple. Use a very simple color or texture for your background. Make your designs work with the careful use of graphics and text layout.

(A technique supported by the Microsoft Internet Explorer is the use of *watermarks*, or a half-toned image on your background. Unfortunately, it only works on the Microsoft browser.)

GRAPHICS

Using graphics on your Web site brings it to life, but graphics are both a blessing and a curse. Graphic files can become extremely large. It is common to see them over 1MB in size, and even larger for high-resolution photographs. Large size graphics may look beautiful on the designer's monitor, but are unlikely to be seen by user—they will click the stop button before they finish downloading.

If a user is connected with a 28.8bps modem, a 1MB file can take 5 or 6 minutes to download and be processed and displayed. A typical user will wait no more than 30 seconds for a page to be displayed. Acceptable response times on the Web are usually 15 seconds or less. Use of large, high-resolution graphics chases people away from your Web site. Remember, if your competitor has a site with good response times and the products and services that your customer wants or needs, they will go there rather than wait for your beautiful art to appear!

This warning does not mean that you cannot use graphics or photographs on the Web. Instead, use practical, creative design techniques for effective graphics. Take advantage of the fact that the human mind will resolve images that lack resolution or large numbers of colors. Use simple color backgrounds with word art or simple geometric shapes to form your graphics.

The Internet supports two types of graphic files, the CompuServe *GIF file* format and the *JPEG file* format.

GIF files have color palette limitations. They are ideal for simple graphics, line art, and graphics with a small number of colors. They reproduce faithfully at multiple resolutions and compress to extremely small file sizes.

JPEG files are designed to reproduce large numbers of colors and shades faithfully on any monitor. JPEG files are the only file types appropriate for storing and displaying photographs. JPEG files can be compressed to a user-designated level of compression when you create the file. When you compress JPEG files, you begin to lose resolution and color. Increasing the amount of compression used results in greater loss in quality. You can find the right balance of compression and quality to create a relatively small file and still produce an acceptable image.

The *GIF89A* file format is a special file format to familiarize yourself with. GIF89A is a variant of the basic GIF file format that adds two major and important enhancements—animation and transparent backgrounds.

Animation is accomplished in the same manner that a cartoon filmstrip is created. Individual frames are created and displayed one after the other to create the illusion of motion. An animation contains many copies of the same image in slightly different positions; these files can quickly grow to extremely large sizes. I have used three animated GIF files in my Web site to add just a touch of motion to some of the pages. Use animation with caution. Be sure it adds to the graphic content and is not just a gimmick that someone decided would be cute on the site.

There are many graphics animation software packages available to help build these files. One of the best is a product called Webpainter from Totally Hip Products (`www.totallyhip.com`). What makes this product unique is the image compression methods it uses to compare each image in the animation and store only what is changed in each frame. Most other products store the image exactly as you create it for each frame. Webpainter will produce a file that is a fraction of the size of those produced by other sites. It is also very easy to use.

Transparent backgrounds can be invaluable and cost nothing. A GIF file is a rectangle. It usually has some content on a colored background. If you don't specify a colored background, it will default to white. This looks good when viewed on a white background, but if you use a nice blue background, you get a big ugly white rectangle behind your great graphic. Using transparency, you can draw a logo and make the background disappear. You can put a flag on a blue background and eliminate the ugly white rectangle around the flag. Transparent backgrounds give your Web site a more professional look.

There are excellent resources on the Web and in print that describe the GIF and JPEG file formats, including:

- The Yale C/AIM Web Style Guide: `info.med.yale.edu/caim/manual`
- Guide to Web Style: `www.sun.com/styleguide/`
- Developer Edge Online: `developer.netscape.com`
- Web Page Design for Designers: `www.wpdfd.com/wpdhome.htm`
- Web Reference: `www.webreference.com`

See also *Wild Web Graphics with Microsoft Image Composer* by David Karlins, published by QUE.

E-BUSINESS DESIGN

So far, we have addressed the design of standard text and graphic pages that present textual or graphic information. The fundamental principals of Web page graphic design apply to the design of commerce-based pages.

e-Business pages are generated by some form of CGI programming dynamically based on user input and requirements. The key to tying your commerce pages into your site is to use the same background you use everywhere else in the site. If you have a small, standardized masthead (top border), you may put the masthead on each commerce page. I tend to bring in the logo on a plain background.

The important design concept is to make sure that the pages look like they belong to the Web site. It is also important to allow commerce applications to use the full width of the screen.

The following are some design structures that should serve as nothing more than examples of what is possible. I have seen some sites that break graphic design rules and work quite well. (One general rule is to avoid the use of borders and colors in tables. Yet I saw a site designed by Sarah Poger of Sunguard Systems that uses a colored background table for each row of data. That design works incredibly well.)

With e-business data, you are presenting business data. It must be legible, readable, and attractive. But the primary objective is to convey content. Don't try to crowd too much data on a single screen.

Watch out for your browser. I illustrate some screens captured at 1024 *x* 768 resolution. They work at 640 *x* 480, where they were developed using a standard font or a font size of –1. I tested them with Microsoft Internet Explorer using the Normal font setting on the View, Fonts menu pull-down. But they don't look very good if the user selects Large or Very Large. You have to make some judgment calls in this area and pick a design style that works for most users.

The pages that are developed in support of electronic commerce are similar to traditional online computer system applications. The user is generally in control and may choose from menus of options that retrieve customized information for the user or allow the user to communicate (i.e. place an order, submit a form, etc.) with your organization.

We will explore some approaches to organizing the presentation of business data. I'm sure that you will find variations of these methods and completely different ways of presenting information that work for you. There is no right or wrong as long as the Web site works for the end user. As Web site designers, we must learn to put our (sometimes extremely large) egos away and be willing to discard great ideas and techniques in response to our user community.

TRADITIONAL TEXT MENU

Figure 21.16 shows the first page that one of Republic Indemnity's producers (insurance agents) see when they visit the company's private electronic commerce Web site.

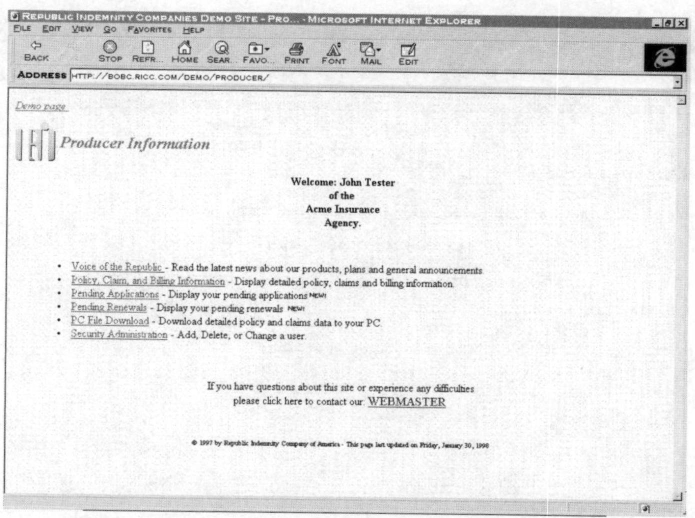

Figure 21.16: Republic Indemnity producers home page[5].

5 Used by permission of Republic Indemnity Company of America. All rights reserved.

This page is deceptively simple. It is generated by an IBM Net.Data macro when the user logs into the site and identifies himself to the server. It first determines that the user is a currently appointed agent. If the user is no longer valid, a polite message is displayed asking the user to contact his marketing representative.

The name of the user and the user's company is retrieved from the company's production database, which resides on the company's production machine. The database tables containing the names must be accessed to authenticate the user.

The link to Security Administration is a conditional link. Only those users who have been designated as User Managers see the Security Administration link. The ability to conditionally display links or data depending upon user information or other data is an important feature of CGI programming and electronic commerce.

LISTS

The list is an extremely useful electronic commerce design construct. I have used it extensively both to allow a user to select an object for viewing and to display data in a list format.

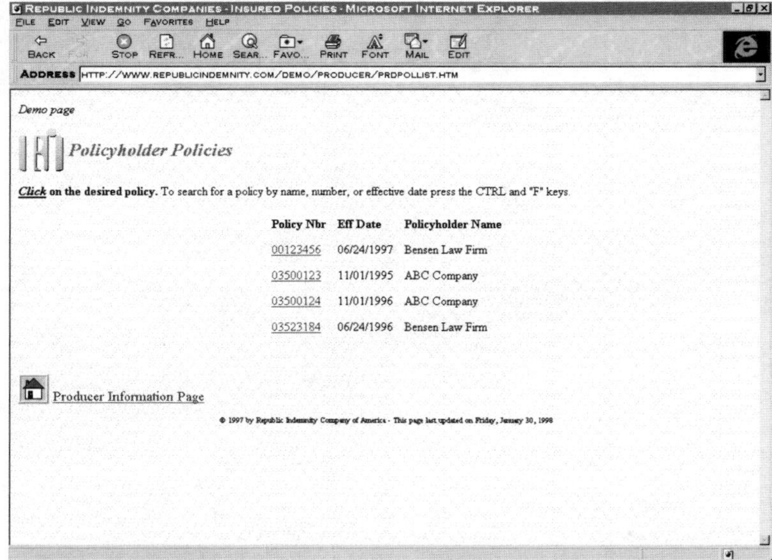

Figure 21.17: e-Business list.

Figure 21.17 shows a page captured from the Republic Indemnity Companies' demonstration site. It shows a very small list of policies that have been issued on behalf of an insurance agency. This list is produced as a result of a simple SQL statement. The policy number hyperlinks are a link to a Net.Data macro, which passes the policy number as a query string parameter when clicked.

The user is given an option before this screen is displayed to search by policyholder name or by policy number if known to reduce the size of the list. Although the demo screen shows four policies, live data could result in hundreds or even thousands of policies.

SUB-MENUS

Sub-menus are useful to establish an anchor point when selecting an object can result in multiple choices.

In Figure 21.18, the user may review basic information about the selected policy in the screen header (this also serves to help the user know where they are in the hierarchy). The user may choose to display claims information or invoices. This screen will be enhanced in the future to add additional navigation choices, all anchored on a single selected policy.

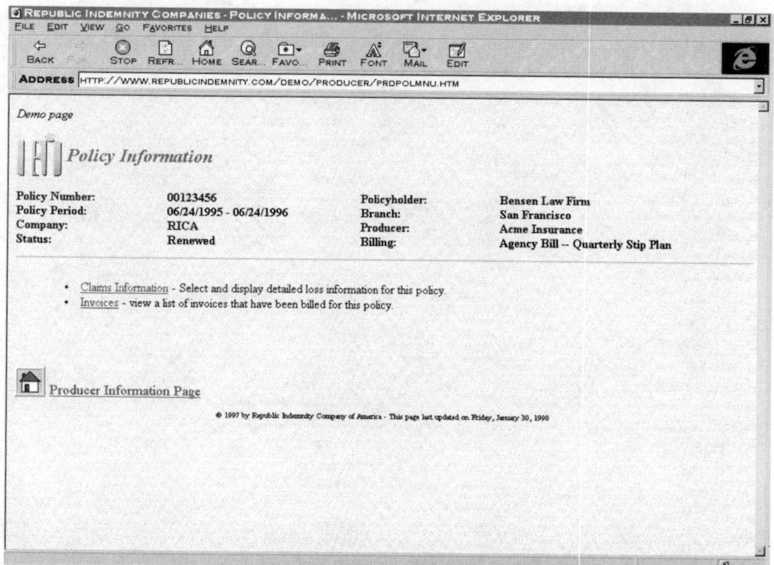

Figure 21.18: Sub-menu.

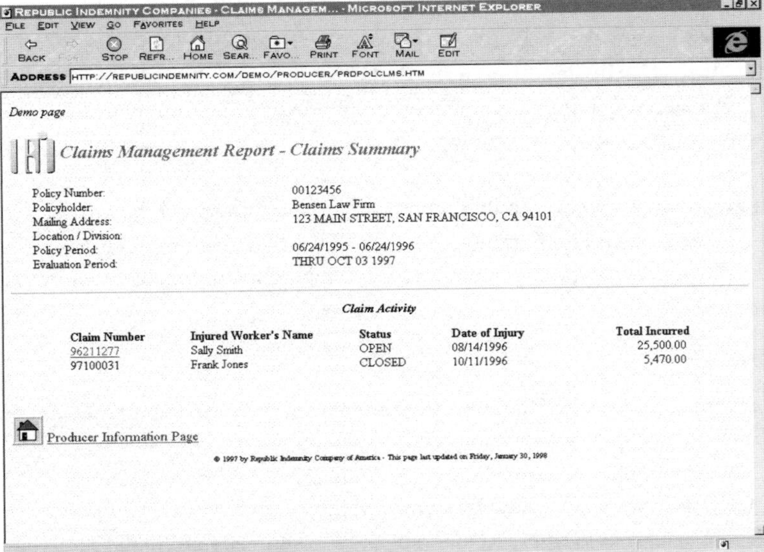

Figure 21.19: Claims sub-menu.

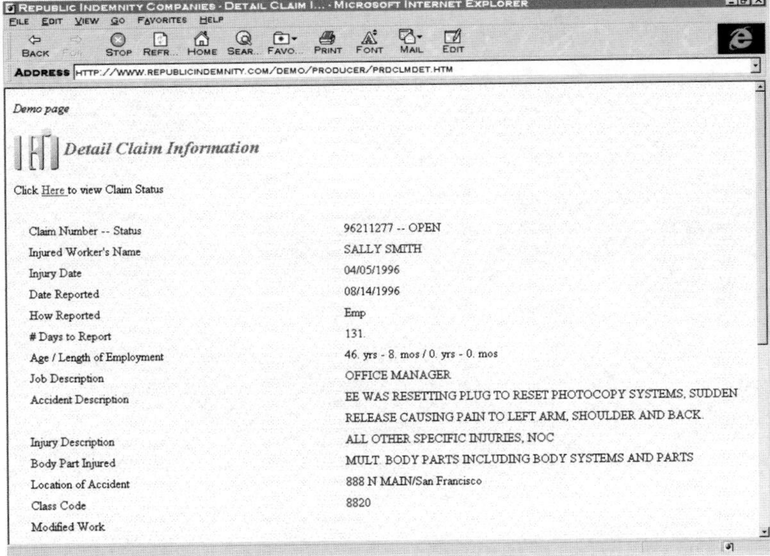

Figure 21.20: Detail information display.

Figure 21.19 uses another list to display claims information for the policy. A policy for a large account may have several hundred claims. Again, the claim number is used to link to a Net.Data macro that displays detailed claims information and pass the claims number to the macro as a query string parameter.

DETAIL INFORMATION DISPLAY

Figure 21.20 is a typical detail display. It uses a two-column table to display field labels on the left and values on the right. The data is retrieved from the database via SQL and a Net.Data macro.

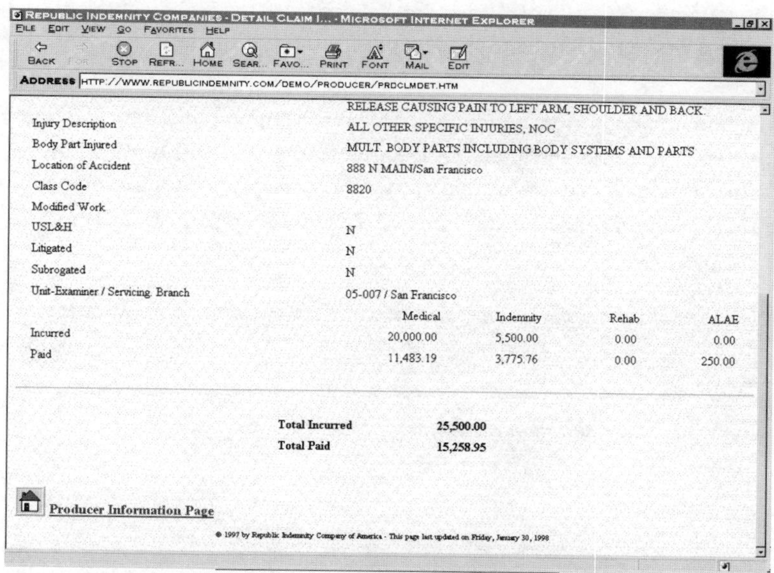

Figure 21.21: Detail page (continued).

Figure 21.21 shows the lower portion of the claims detail screen. The data source is the same SQL query, but the screen uses an additional HTML table to display the Incurred and Paid loss data. Another table is used to display the Total Incurred and Total Paid data.

A link back to the producer information page is provided on all pages and most pages are one click of the browser's Back button from the previous anchor point. (I may add a link from the claims data back to the policy information page, which serves as a sub-menu.)

These are certainly not the only ways to display detailed business data, but they have proven effective with the company's agents. The most important design factors are identifying the objects to be displayed. Once the objects are identified, identify the information that the audience needs for each object type. Create sub-menus to organize the information around the objects types.

FORMS

HTML forms are the glue that ties an electronic commerce application together. The design of forms is straightforward once you understand the components and elements that can be used to make up a form. A certain degree of complexity is added to the technical design process when integrating forms with CGI programs. The following paragraphs deal with the layout and design of forms. Part III provides the technical detail to work with forms and the programs to send data to and from the forms.

From a forms layout and design standpoint, a form is nothing more than text and graphic design elements. If you find and study Web-based forms, you will find that the most common format is a style that places one or two form elements on a line and continues downward for the length of the form. Figure 21.22 shows a typical HTML form.

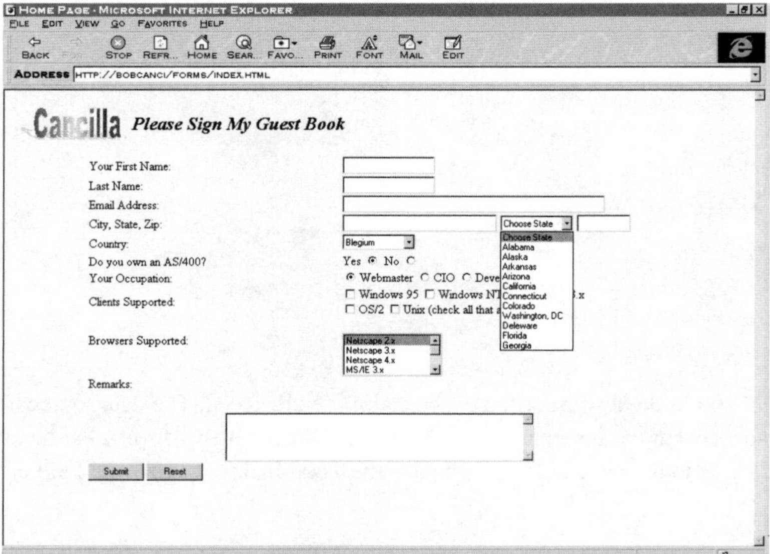

Figure 21.22: An HTML form.

Form elements such as text boxes or scrolling text boxes have a width attribute. The width must be consistent with the size of the database field that will store the text entered in the box. You must work with your CGI developer to be sure that you are aware of these widths. You must be careful to allow enough room on a line to allow low-resolution browsers to display as much of the form field as possible.

The form in Figure 21.22 was designed specifically as an illustration for this book. It consists of all possible form design elements. It was created using a two-column table. Label text such as Your First Name, Last Name, etc., is created as normal text. The form-input elements are special HTML objects. In products such as Microsoft FrontPage, the elements are selected from a tool bar and pasted into the form at the insertion point. The vertical size of the form element is not under your control. For some strange reason, the designers of HTML did not see fit to allow the user to control the vertical size, colors, font, or any other attribute of an HTML forms element. You have a great deal of control over the content of the element, but not of its appearance. All data typed into a form field is considered a string of characters by HTML. There is no concept of numeric data.

TEXT BOX

The text box (Your First Name, Last Name, E-mail Address, City, and Zip) are the basic building block of HTML forms. This simple input field is designed to capture whatever the user types and return that to a CGI program in a named variable.

You may specify the number of characters that may be typed into the field and the number of characters that will display (i.e. the width of the field) on the screen. You may also indicate that the field is a Password field. Password fields display an asterisk for every character typed by the user, thus hiding the real value typed into the field.

From a forms design standpoint, you control the width of the field. Note that you can have very long field values typed into a small field. The text will scroll to the left as you type. The user can use the cursor movement keys to position to text that has scrolled out of sight.

DROP-DOWN MENU

There are two types of drop-down menu objects. The first type allows you to select one item from a list and the second allows you to select many items from the list. They are presented differently on the screen. In both forms of the drop-down menu, you may display a descriptive value in the list and return a code to the program. In the example, we display the full state name (e.g. California). We return the value “CA” to the CGI program.

Single Selection Drop-Down Menu

Country and State are examples of a single-selection drop-down menu element. The example shows the display as it would look after the user left clicks on the arrow button at the right-hand side of the field. The user may then click on any value in the list. The list will close. The selected choice will display in the field (if you clicked on California, California would replace "Choose State" and the list would disappear).

Multiple-Selection Drop-Down Menu

The Browsers Supported field is an example of a multiple-selection drop-down menu. This field is sometimes called a *scrollable list*. Notice that while similar to the single-selection drop-down menu, this field has no selection box. When you click on an item in the list, it appears in reverse video. You may use typical Windows' conventions to select additional items from the list. You may press Control and click an item to add the second item to the your selections. You may also use the Shift and Click option to select all items from the first selected to the last selected.

Use of this field type assumes that users are familiar with Windows selection functions. Be careful with the use of this field. Many users do not know that they can perform the Shift Click and Control Click functions. If you are dealing with an audience that is not very computer literate, avoid this field type. You have very little control over the appearance of this field; you have some vertical sizing of the entire object, but not the text displaying in the box. Notice that the scroll bars that are generated allow the list to be much longer than the vertical space allocated on the screen. It also assumes that users are familiar with the scroll bars and know what they mean. You may be surprised to learn that contrary to popular opinion, many users do not know what the basic visual signals used in a Windows environment mean. There are people using the Web that would otherwise never touch a computer

RADIO BUTTONS

The fields labeled "Yes" and "No," which are the possible answers to the question "Do you own an AS/400?", are radio buttons. So are the buttons used to allow the user to select Webmaster, CIO, or Developer in response to "Your Occupation." The term was taken from the old-fashioned car radio. When you push a button on the radio, it releases the button that was previously pressed. Only one button in the group can be selected at a time. Radio buttons are an excellent choice when a user must select one and only one choice from a short list of choices. The drop-down menu is a better choice for longer lists.

CHECK BOXES

The square boxes followed by text to answer the question "Clients Supported" are examples of check boxes. Check boxes are perhaps a better alternative to the multiple-selection drop-down-menu if you have a relatively short list of choices. The user simply clicks on all of the square boxes that apply. A check mark appears in selected boxes in visual response to the user's choice. You may have to use additional cells or even a separate table to make the appearance of check-box choices attractive and readable. Watch the length of text that you wish to appear on a single line. If you design at high resolution, you may find that low resolution browsers leave a check box on the first line and wrap its label to the next line, creating total chaos and user confusion.

SCROLLING TEXT BOX

This box is very similar to the standard text box. It allows the user to enter text. The difference is the manner in which text is displayed to the user as it is entered. You may specify text wrapping at the width of the box and the user can type as much text as you allow them to type. You must specify a maximum length for the field, but it can be quite large. You may specify the visible width as well as the absolute length. Interestingly, the object tends to size itself based on the width and maximum size parameters that you provide. You will probably have to experiment to position the box effectively on the screen. (In my example, I had originally positioned the box at the left of the screen. I could not force the element to expand, so I finally chose to center the field on the page.)

BUTTONS

Buttons cause something to happen. An HTML form on its own is passive and does nothing but store data typed in its data entry elements. Nothing is transmitted to the server for processing until the user clicks the Submit button. Two buttons have default actions. They are Reset and Submit.

Reset

This button's function is obvious. It clears any typing or selections made by the user and resets the form to the condition it was first in when it was first displayed by the browser.

Submit

This button actually executes a link to a URL that contains the name of a CGI program on the remote server that will process the data entered by the user.

User-Defined Buttons

Some designer's like to use buttons to perform functions other than the two basic functions explained above. A button can be used to link to a URL on a server. It can also execute a JavaScript function that a programmer has provided to perform some advanced processing locally on the browser.

Personally, I have not used any but the default buttons. I use image maps or standard HTML links to link to another page. I also try to keep my forms extremely simple and minimize the functions provided by JavaScript.

IMAGE MAPS

Image maps are often used in conjunction with forms, and they may also be used as general navigation design tools. An image map allows the designer to select an area of a graphic image as a *hot spot*. When the user moves his mouse over the hot spot, he should see explanatory text telling him that clicking the spot will take him somewhere else. There are two methods of creating image maps.

Server-Side Image Maps

This is a horrendously tedious and difficult process where the designer must define the exact horizontal and vertical coordinates of a rectangle, circle, or polygon that becomes a hot spot in a graphic. Consider a map of the United States, where each state is a hot spot. When you click on the picture of a state, you will be taken to a page that has information about the state. To create server-side image maps, you must create entries in a file on your server. This technique is available on the IBM server (and most other servers for that matter), but is arcane and ridiculously cumbersome. I have never used them and have no plans to even try one.

This technique has no advantage whatsoever and in fact has a major performance disadvantage because it requires that a click on the image map must be returned to the server for interpretation. The technique was used back in the Dark Ages (about three to four years ago) when Mosaic was the browser of choice.

Browser-Side Image Maps

Almost all of the WYSIWYG HTML editors have a browser-side image map creation tool. You select a rectangle, circle, or polygon tool from a toolbox. You then use your mouse to place an outline around the area where you want your hot spot to appear. A form pops up to allow you to define the link. That's all there is to it. These hot spots also have the advantage of being processed by the browser on the client's computer and saving resources and time on the server.

CONCLUSION

I have presented many, but certainly not all, the design considerations that a designer should think about when designing a Web page. I recommend that you read many of the excellent books available on print media graphic design. The concepts associated with print media are valid, even though the Web is a different medium than print, television, or even other forms of computer graphic design.

Do not use graphic design tools or a word processor to design Web sites. These tools are designed for print media and produce less than disirous results on the Web. Although most word processors have the ability to publish your text documents automatically to the Web. They do generate HTML, but the result is not professional. Consider the section on fonts and colors in this chapter; PC software cannot make intelligent choices about font substitutions. Instead, use a tool specifically developed for Web site design.

If you plan to develop Web sites, you must learn HTML. I don't care how great your tools are, there is no tool on the market that generates perfect HTML. You will have to make some manual adjustments to the HTML generated by the tools.

Don't let your graphic artists present layouts on paper. The Web is the only method of evaluating designs. Buy your graphic artist a good Web site design product that includes a design tool and page editor. Work with your artist to help him understand that colors, fonts, and layout are different on the Web. Follow my suggestions, try your own techniques. Critically study dozens and dozens of Web sites. Write down what works and what doesn't and why. Consider, what was the designer's objective? Did he achieve his goal? Can you find everything you need easily? Did the page load fast enough or did you have to wait too long? What did you see when you first looked at the page? What did your eyes avoid? What is the primary focus on the page? What did you read? Did you read the headlines? Did you read the text?

Try this experiment. Look at a Web site. Browse wherever the site takes you. After you leave the Web site, write down a list of things that you saw on the site. Check the site again and see what you missed.

You may look at the strictures placed on you by HTML and browsers as serious limitations or simply a challenging opportunity to be creative with a different tool set. An artist who works with acrylics and an airbrush would probably find charcoal extremely limiting and frustrating. The charcoal artist would disagree entirely. The medium is different; the tools are different. Learn the medium; learn your tools!

THE CGI ENVIRONMENT 22

In Part I, we discussed browsers and their relationship to the server. We briefly introduced you to the HTTP GET command and showed you how a browser sends requests to a server. We showed you how a server interprets the request and sends a response to the browser. If this chapter gets a little technical, my apologies. I found it helpful to understand what happens under the covers when developing and testing CGI applications. I promise to lighten up in the remaining chapters. I can assure you that understanding the material presented in this chapter is worth the effort.

WEB SERVERS ARE STATELESS

Communication between a browser and a Web server is *stateless*. Each time a browser contacts the server a new transaction occurs. The server has no concept of logon and does not store variables between transactions. This is the single most important concept in Web site development. As Web site developers, we must create the illusion of a conversation in order to develop e-business applications. It is not difficult to comprehend, it is simply different.

INTERACTIVE PROGRAM FLOW

The AS/400 programmer who develops interactive online programs is used to a fully conversational programming environment. The programmer issues the op code to send a screen to the user and the program waits for a response. When the user presses the Enter key or some other Function key (command key), the program resumes processing at the line of code following the op code that transmitted the screen to the user.

In addition to the conversational nature of AS/400 online programming, all of the variables used by the program remain available to the programmer in the user's process access group (PAG).

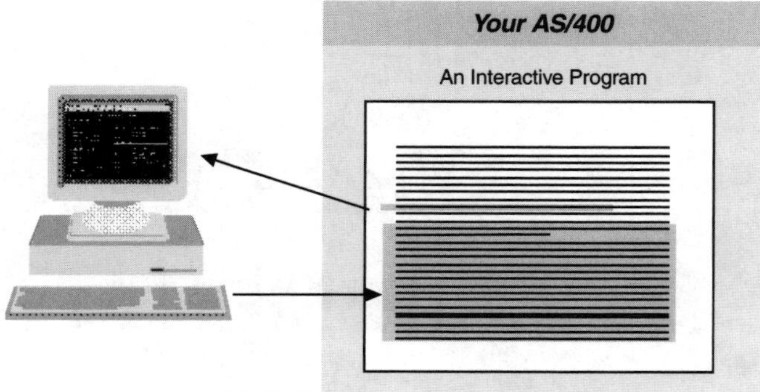

Figure 22.1: Interactive program.

Figure 22.1 depicts an AS/400 application program that sends a screen to a terminal via the WRITE opcode. The program remains in the system waiting for a response from the user. When a user presses a key on the terminal, control is returned to the program at the next line of code following the WRITE.

CGI FLOW

This is not the case when programming for the Web. A Web server has no concept of session, state, or conversation. Every contact between browser and server is a new transaction. The server has no concept of logon and does not store variables (i.e. PAG type data) between transactions. Figure 22.2 illustrates this step-by-step process.

The browser sends an HTTP GET request to the server for the URL *www.inetmi.com/cgi-bin/cgitest*.

- The server locates CGITEST in the directory associated with the alias CGI-BIN (this is a library in the QSYS file system). The server determines that CGITEST is a program and executes it by issuing a simple CALL.

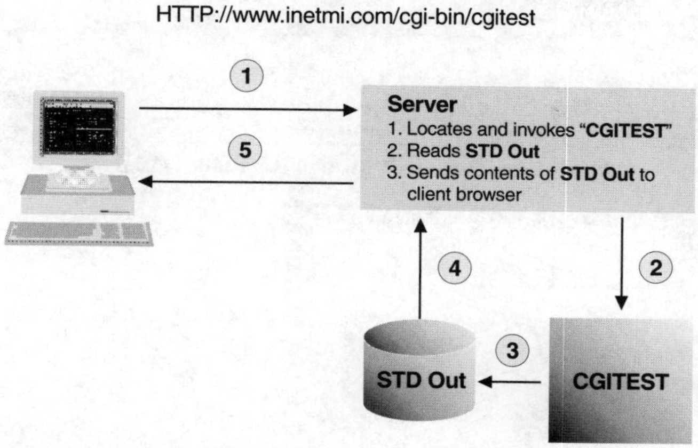

HTTP://www.inetmi.com/cgi-bin/cgitest

Server
1. Locates and invokes **"CGITEST"**
2. Reads **STD Out**
3. Sends contents of **STD Out** to client browser

STD Out

CGITEST

Figure 22.2: Diagram of typical CGI transaction.

- The program CGITEST does whatever it is supposed to do and writes all output to a special system file called STDOUT. The program then returns to the server.

- The server reads the content of STDOUT and transmits the content of STDOUT to the browser.

As you can see, the job that controls the process is that of the Web server running under the Web server's user ID (QTMHHTTP for IBM servers). Notice that the server calls the program, which executes and returns. Notice also that when the program completes, it is gone and forgotten by the server. The server returns to the state that it was in prior to the program call. It knows nothing about the program that it just called or the request that it just processed.

THE ILLUSION OF STATE

There are several methods for creating the illusion of a conversation. All of these methods involve using facilities built into the browser. To create the illusion of state, we must send data to the browser that identifies the user or the last function processed by the user. This data must be returned to the server the next time the browser requests execution of a CGI program.

HTTP METHODS

The HTTP protocol supports two *methods* for sending parameter type data (input fields) to the server from a browser.

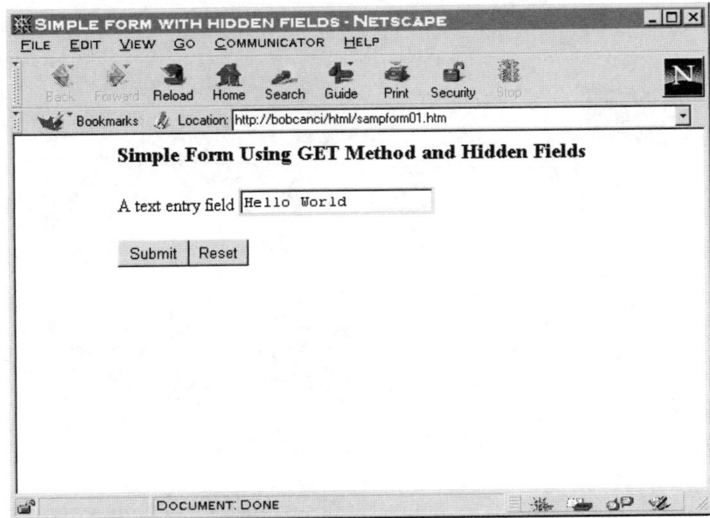

Figure 22.3: Illustration of a simple HTML form that uses the GET method to pass data to a server.

The GET method sends data to the server in the form of a URL query string. It is illustrated in Figure 22.3.

Figure 22.3 contains two hidden fields: `fname=Bob` and `lname=Cancilla`, plus the text-entry field containing the value "Hello World" that the user typed on the form. When the user clicks the Submit button, the following URL is sent to the server:

```
http://www.ricains.com/cgibin/cgitest?fname=Bob&lname=
        Cancilla&field1=Hello+World&B1=Submit
```

Notice the query string beginning with the question mark (?). It consists of a series of name value pairs separated by the ampersand (&).

- `fname=Bob` is the first *hidden field.* (Hidden fields create the illusion of state by passing hidden data into a form.) This value could be hard-coded into the form (as it is in this example) or set by a CGI program that created and sent the form to the browser (most often the case in real applications).

- `lname=Cancilla` is the second hidden field.

- `field1=Hello+World` is the content of the text-entry field typed by the user. Notice the plus sign (+) between `Hello` and `World`. This is a form of URL encoding, a technique implemented by all browsers and servers to handle the transmission of characters that might otherwise be ambiguous. We will address URL encoding in depth a little later.

- `B1=Submit` is the Submit button on the screen. B1 is the button, with a value of Submit.

The important concept here is that when using the GET method, input data is transmitted to the server via the URL's query string. The query string is passed to the program as an input parameter. It is up to the program to parse the string and deal with the values. There are server APIs that help with this task.

The POST method is the other method of passing data to a server from an HTML form. The POST method causes the server to write data to a special file on the AS/400 called STDIN. Unlike the GET method, data transmitted to the server is not visible to the user via the URL or address display on your browser.

The POST method is most often used with HTML forms. In the HTML for your form, you code:

```
<FORM METHOD="POST" ACTION="/your_cgi_program" NAME="FormName">
```

When the user clicks the Submit button on your HTML page, the browser sends the data to the server, which writes it to the STDIN file as `name=value` pairs. The data is URL encoded and separated by "&" symbols. If you are using a language like RPG, COBOL, C, C++, etc., as your CGI program, you must decode the data and parse the text string into fields locating the name then the value, and move the value to your defined fields. IBM's Net.Data language handles the POST method for you. It decodes the string and parses it into variables that you may use. Most CGI programmers write utility modules that handle parsing and decoding for them.

The GET method has a limitation on the amount of data that can be passed between the browser and the server. This limit is 4,096 bytes of data. The POST method can pass an unlimited amount of data as the server is writing it to the STDIN file. You should always use the POST method when sending user input captured via HTML forms to a server.

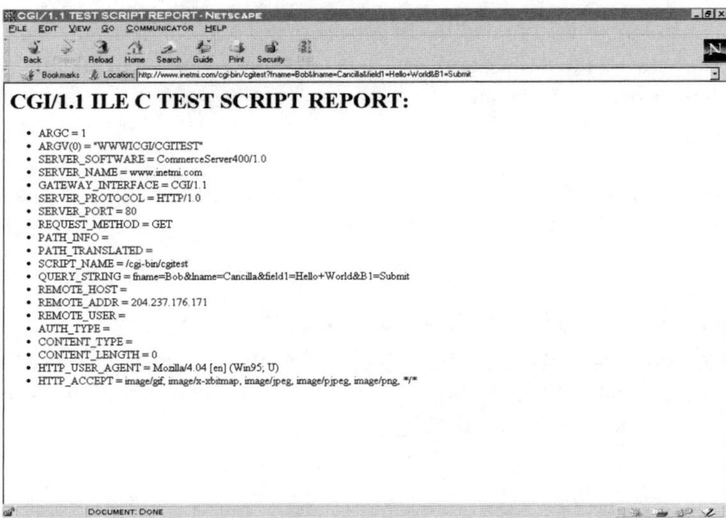

Figure 22.4: Program cgitest script report on Netscape.

Figure 22.4 shows the result of executing the test script CGI program.Notice the variable labeled QUERY STRING that contains the fields passed to the server by the browser. The GET method makes use of a data storage area provided by IBM since V3R1 called the *environment*. The environment is an area of memory created in memory and allocated to each job in the system.

If you have ever worked with a DOS, UNIX, or Windows PC, you will be familiar with the concept of the environment. In DOS, you type the command SET from the command line and all of the environment variables are displayed (see Figure 22.5).

Notice that the environment for Windows 95 is identical to that used for the AS/400 and UNIX computers. Variables are implemented as name value pairs separated by an equals (=) sign. This facility was implemented on the AS/400 in V3R1 to provide open systems compatibility. It also simplifies dealing with parameters, because all parameters are text strings.

The environment can accommodate up to 1,024 environment variables. One of the advantages of the environment is the fact that the system allocates and manages environment memory space. This is not a concern to those of us developing Web-based applications, but it is to the vendors who develop servers. The environment is available to programs invoked by a job. The environment of a job like the server daemon is passed to jobs invoked by the daemon.

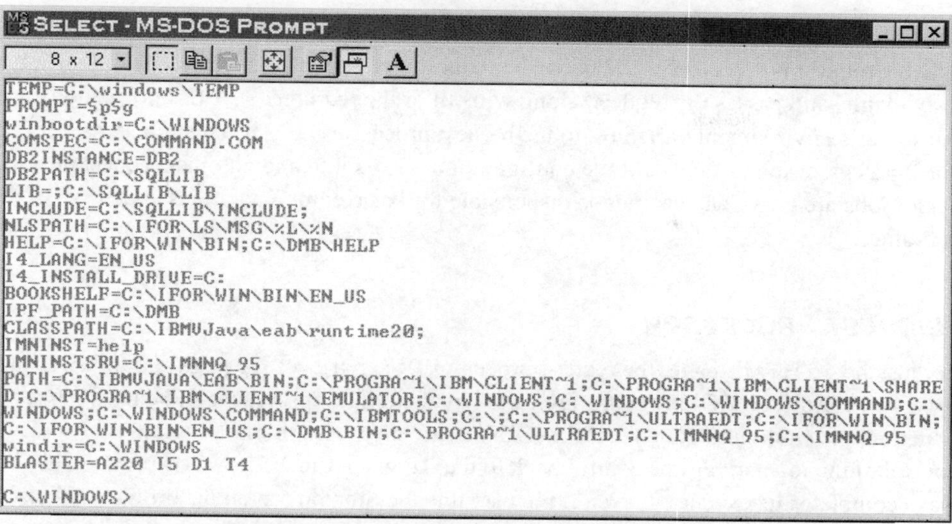

Figure 22.5: Sample of typing the SET command from a DOS command line in Windows 95.

SERVER STRUCTURE

Let's look at the structure of a Web server (Figure 22.6) to more clearly understand the concepts and terms just discussed. Figure 22.6 illustrates the five jobs that run in the QHTTPSVR sub-system on your machine if you are running the IBM HTTP Server under V4R4. If you do a WRKSBSJOB QHTTPSVR you will see five jobs with the name you gave your Web server. The first job shows that it is TYPE BATCH, it will generally be ACTIVE, and show PGM-QZHBHTTP. This is the server daemon job. The other four jobs will show TYPE BATCHI, will be ACTIVE and show PGM-QYUNLANG. Now, let's look at the function and behavior of each job type.

SERVER DAEMON

The server daemon is the main job of the server. When you start your server, you will start the daemon job and as many request processors as you have specified in your configuration. The daemon creates a TCP/IP socket using its IP ad-

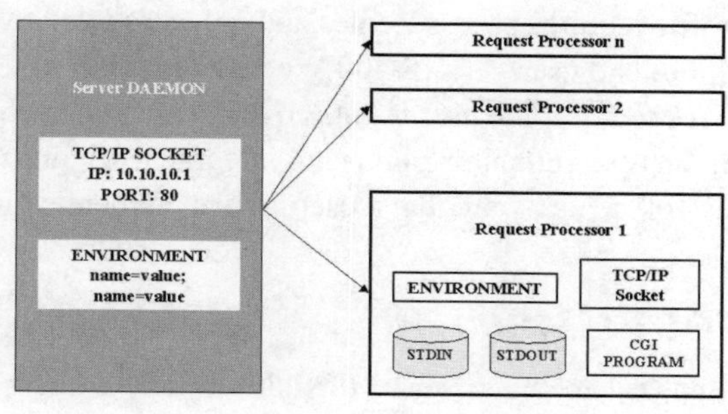

Figure 22.6: AS/400 server structure.

dress and assigned port number. It goes inactive and waits for a request to be received. When a request is received, it evaluates the request, determines if a request processor job is available, and passes the request, along with all of the required TCP/IP information and the server's environment variables, to the request processor job. The daemon starts a request processor job or threads if the configuration allows it to and all other request processor jobs are busy. The daemon is responsible for basic communications and error handling.

REQUEST PROCESSOR

For a standard HTML page, the request processor (RP) retrieves the page and transmits it back to the browser. CGI programs are called by the request processor and data is passed either via the environment or via the STDIN file to the program. The program runs under control of the job and returns control back to the RP when finished. A CGI program always completes its execution, even if the user hits the Stop button on his browser. Clicking stop on the browser causes the browser to send a header to the server, which causes the server to log an error message and discard the output that would have been sent to the user. This is an extremely important issue when processing database updates. The updates will be processed regardless of whether the user waits for a response or not.

When the RP finishes processing a request and sends the result back to the browser, the daemon is notified that it is available to process another request. Each RP processes a single request at a time.

A very active system processing thousands of requests per day will most likely run no more than 50 RPs. My server, which has relatively low activity, has never started more than four RPs (i.e. four users processing requests at the same time).

The server runs under a user profile created when the server is installed. The server's user profile requires access to files and objects served to the browser. The browser has no concept of end user. All AS/400 Web servers support user authentication. Authentication is a check to see if the user is authorized to access an object stored in a directory available to the server. Authentication is not integrated within AS/400 object-level security. The AS/400 is not aware that a user with an authentication user-id of BOBC has logged in.

POST METHOD

The POST method is more flexible and offers many advantages to the Web site developer over the GET method. If you look at the sample URL for the GET method that invokes the CGI program CGITEST (Figure 22.4), you will notice that all of the parameters are visible to the user in the URL. Another limitation is the size of the URL. On the AS/400, you are limited to 4,096 bytes of URL and QUERY STRING.

The POST method uses another built-in facility of the AS/400 server, the STDIN file. STDIN is a file-like device where input is written by the server when receiving a POST request. Data is sent to the server by the browser in a different format. When a form uses the POST request, the browser forms a request header and a body that contains the data to be written to the STDIN file of the server.

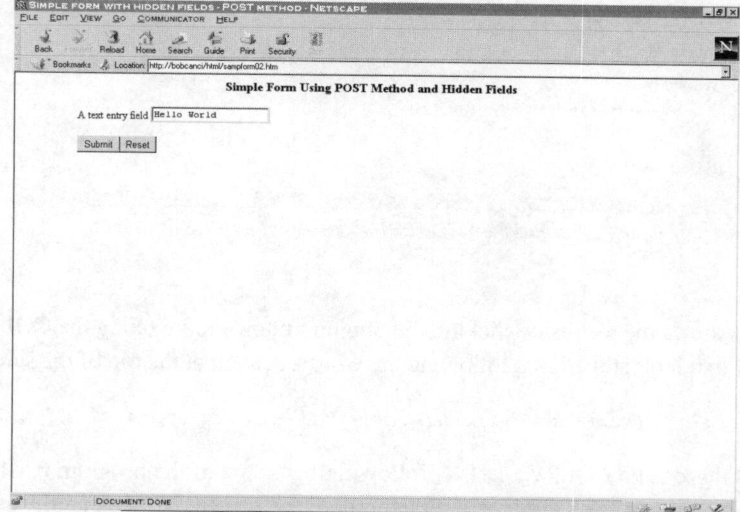

Figure 22.7: The POST method to enter data to a form.

Figure 22.7 illustrates a variation of the previous form used to illustrate the GET method. This form is identical in every respect. It has a single entry field on the screen, a Submit button, and two hidden fields. The only difference is that this form has been defined to use the HTTP POST method.

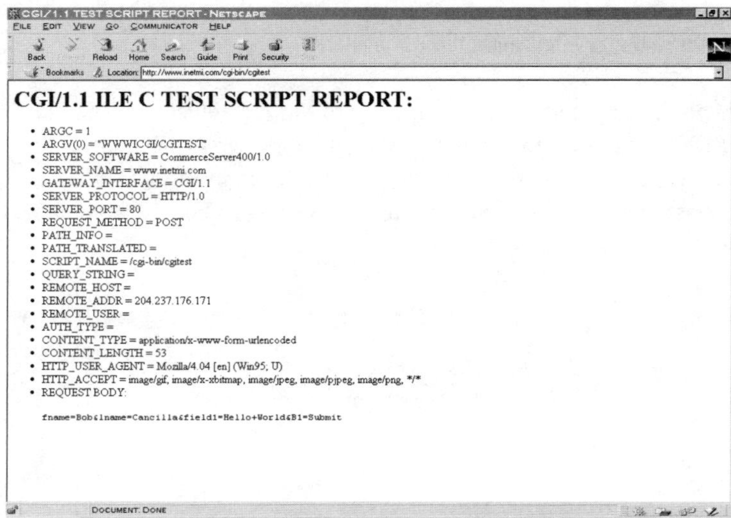

Figure 22.8: Program CGITEST script report for POST method.

Figure 22.8 shows the results of clicking the Submit button and invoking the CGI program CGITEST. First, look at the URL following the word Location at the top of the screen.

```
http://www.inetmi.com/cgi-bin/cgitest
```

Notice that there is no QUERY STRING following the name of the program (CGITEST). The environment variables are listed in the body of the screen. Notice that the environment variable QUERY_STRING is empty (null). At the bottom of the screen, following the label REQUEST BODY, are the hidden variables (fname and lname), the value of the text input field (field1), and the value of the button (B1). This test program reads and displays the content of the STDIN file.

The primary advantage of the POST method is that the parameters passed between the browser and the server are not displayed in the URL, and that there is no limitation on the amount of data passed to the server.

IDENTIFYING YOUR USERS

HIDDEN FIELDS

The two examples that were used to explain the GET and POST HTTP methods used hidden fields. Hidden fields are a way of creating the illusion of state by passing hidden data into the form that will be returned to the server.

HTML forms have the ability to send field values to a browser in the form of NAME=VALUE. You could send a form with a hidden field that contained CUSTOMER=123456. When the user clicks a button on the form, the hidden field is returned to the server.

COOKIES

Yes, the AS/400 does cookies. A *cookie* is data sent by the server to a browser and stored by the browser. This data is then sent back to the server on every subsequent interaction between the browser and the server. A cookie consists of sets of name value pairs, and can specify an expiration date.

Cookies are frequently used in shopping-cart applications where a user selects a product to order, continues to peruse a catalog and select items, and finally checks out and pays for the items selected.

SERVER AUTHENTICATION

Most e-business applications require that a user register with your site. A user ID and password are assigned to the user and stored in the server's user authentication file. When a user attempts to access a Web page in an authenticated directory, the user is challenged for his user ID and password. The user ID and password are stored in the browser and transmitted to the server each time the browser requests a page. Generally, a browser will require that a user login once during the life of the browser session (i.e. until the user stops the browser). The user ID/password login screen is generated and displayed by the browser. The server sends a three-digit code to the browser informing it that the page requires authentication. An authentication dialog works something like this:

- Browser requests a page
- Server returns an error code indicating that access is denied because this is an authenticated page
- Browser displays the pop-up screen for the user to enter his user ID and password

- Browser sends request for the page to the server again, this time with the user ID and password
- Server validates user ID and password and posts user ID and the encrypted form of the password to environment variables: REMOTE_USER and REMOTE_PASSWORD_MD5; if user ID and password are valid, then the page or object is transmitted to the browser
- If the user requests another object within an authenticated directory, the request is sent to the server; if the directory is the same as the previous request, the browser automatically sends the user ID and password

The user ID can be used to identify the user by CGI programs and is available via the environment variable REMOTE_USER to the CGI program. Because most of my applications run in an authenticated environment, I use this technique to obtain additional information about my users. In addition to the server's user file, I maintain an AS/400 database user file. This file contains the user ID, name, e-mail address, and various attributes that can be checked to determine what the user is authorized to access. I also store an ISO timestamp indicating when the user record was created, a timestamp representing the date the user last "logged in," and a count of the number of times the user visited the site.

DATABASE

Sometimes, hidden fields, cookies, and user authentication information are combined with a database lookup to obtain further information about the user. I always use a server user authentication file with a database user file to capture and retrieve information about each user authorized to access my systems. Many shopping-cart–based catalog systems make use of database files to store items selected by the user while he is shopping.

COMMON MISTAKES

Many Webmasters try to make use of the user's IP address or domain name to identify him. If your users subscribe to America Online, Prodigy, or just about any popular proxy-based online service, you will soon see the futility of this approach.

AOL and Prodigy (with millions of online customers) dynamically assign a new IP address and domain name each time their browser makes a request to your server. During the life of a logical session each access could have a different IP address and domain name. Depending upon either a domain name or an IP address is an extremely dangerous and unreliable method of identifying a user.

IBM AND PERSISTENT-STATE WEB SERVERS

IBM is working on technology to implement the illusion of a conversation in its Web servers and with its Net.Data product. Although this may ease the task of programming in a CGI environment for people new to the Internet, it will increase the cost of operating a Web server. Web servers are simple and efficient simply because they do not have to maintain a job or conversation between a user and the server.

I strongly suggest learning to handle stateless communications even if IBM succeeds in implementing persistent state communications.

CGI SCRIPTS

A CGI script is any program that runs on the server. It can be written in any language supported by the server. The program is identified in the URL. Let's revisit the sample CGITEST program that displays server environment variables.

In this example, we ask the server to run a program called `cgitest`, which is located in a subdirectory called CGI-BIN on a server with a domain name of `www.inetmi.com` CGI-BIN is an alias for a library in the QSYS file system. (On the AS/400, all executable programs must reside in the QSYS file system.) You cannot execute a program stored in any other file system (i.e. QDLS, the IFS, QOPENSYS, etc.).

CLIENT-SIDE CGI PROGRAMS

Most Web sites are a mixture of object types. They include HTML pages with text, graphics, links to other Web pages, and links to CGI programs.

Client-side CGI scripting languages run on the user's desktop. Client-side scripting languages have the advantage of consuming no resources on your server and letting the client computer do the work. Client-side and server-side languages are not interchangeable. Generally, client-side scripts are used to do basic editing and validation on the client. They can also be used to process and display business graphics, perform calculations, etc. What they cannot do is access data on the server.

Netscape's JavaScript and Sun Microsystem's Java (both applets and applications) run on the browser. Microsoft's Active-X and Visual Basic applications can be invoked and run on the desktop.

All other CGI scripts run on the server. When you invoke a CGI program via a URL, you ask the server to run a program and return the results of the program's execution to you.

There is one other form of client-side application, called an *add-in*, which can be run on the client machine. These programs must be installed and configured on the browser before they will work. If an add-in has not been installed, then attempting to download a data file designed for that add-in will result in an error. Add-in programs are invoked by the browser based on the content type (Netscape) or file extension (Microsoft).

With the exception of Adobe's Acrobat viewer, I personally prefer to avoid add-ins. Many users are afraid to download and install an add-in program regardless of how easy it is to do.

SERVER-SIDE CGI PROGRAMS

AS/400 Web servers can call programs written in any AS/400-supported language. They can call RPG, COBOL, PL1, C, C++, CL, and REXX programs. The IBM HTTP servers support only ILE programs.

A server-side program is invoked via a URL and used by passing it parameters. HTTP and HTML support two methods of sending parameters to a CGI program, the GET and POST methods.

Programs perform their processing and write output to a file called STDOUT. STDOUT is created by the server in QTEMP of the server's request processor job. This output must include the appropriate HTTP headers, all necessary HTML tags, and, of course, the variable data produced by the program.

All program output data is first written to the STDOUT file. The program then returns to the server that called it. Only then can the server begin to transmit the data to the browser.

DATA PASSED BETWEEN THE BROWSER AND YOUR CGI PROGRAM

All data is handled by browsers and servers as text string data. When a user enters a number such as 123.10 in a field on an HTML form, it is passed to your program as an alphanumeric text string. You must determine that it is a valid numeric and convert it to a numeric data type before attempting to perform calculations on it.

URI ENCODING

The terms URI (Uniform Resource Indicator) and URL (Uniform Resource Locator) are synonymous. The term URI is used by the NCSA in its standards and documentation for the NCSA server. URI encoding is a method of differentiating between special characters used in text and special characters used as control characters in a communication sequence between the browser and the server.[1]

URI encoding prefixes the hexadecimal equivalent of a character with a percent sign (%NN). A question mark, for example, encodes as %3F. The rules for URI encoding are:

- Data is transmitted in name/value pairs.
- Name/value pairs are separated from other name/value pairs by an ampersand (&).
- Name/value pairs separate name from value by using an equal sign (=). If a value is not specified, then name=0 is sent. The value of name= returned is assumed to be its default value (if a value is returned) or null (if no value is returned).
- Space characters are encoded with plus signs (+).
- All characters that may be used as control characters in HTTP or HTML must be encoded to prevent ambiguity. Browsers, servers, and CGI programs must know if a character is data or a control character.
- Characters are encoded by converting them to their hexadecimal values.
- Encoded characters are identified with a percent sign followed by two hexadecimal digits (%NN). All hexadecimal numbers are the hexadecimal equivalent of the ASCII character.

Table 22.1 lists URI encoded characters with their decimal and hexadecimal (ASCII) codes.

1 URI encoding is defined in RFI 1552 that describes MIME message header extensions.

Table 22.1: URI Encoded Characters (decimal & hex ASCII codes)

	Character	Decimal	Hexadecimal
Tab		09	09
Space		16	20
Double quote	“	18	22
Open parenthesis	(	40	28
Close parenthesis	)	41	29
Comma	,	44	2C
Period	.	46	2E
Semicolon	;	59	3B
Colon	:	58	3A
Greater than	>	60	3C
Less than	<	62	3E
At sign	@	64	40
Open bracket	[	101	5B
Back slash	\	102	5C
Close bracket	]	103	5D
Caret	^	104	5E
Apostrophe	‘	106	60
Open brace	{	113	7B
Bar	|	114	7C
Close brace	}	115	7D
Tilde	~	116	7E
Question mark	?		3F
Ampersand	&		26
Equal sign	=		3D
Number sign	#		23
Percent sign	%		25

ENVIRONMENT VARIABLES

The server posts certain standard variables to the environment for both the server and the browser. The following variables are generally available:

SERVER ENVIRONMENT VARIABLES

The following variables are posted by the Web server and are always available.

Table 22.2: Server Environment

VARIABLE	Description
GATEWAY_INTERFACE	The name and version of the protocol in use for calling scripts. The format is name/version. The current protocol is CGI/1.1.
SERVER_NAME	The TCP/IP host name of the AS/400 currently running the Web server. This is either obtained from the machine or configured using the Server Host Name configuration directive. This would be www.ricains.com on my server.
SERVER_PORT	The TCP/IP socket port on which the server runs. Default is port 80 for HTTP.
SERVER_SOFTWARE	Name and version of the software running as a Web server on this machine. It is in the form name/version.

BROWSER ENVIRONMENT VARIABLES

Table 22.3 identifies environment variables passed to the server by most browsers and posted to the environment by the server.

Table 22.3: Browser Environment Variables

VARIABLE	Description
AUTH_TYPE	At the present time this is always *BASIC. It is the protocol type used by the browser and server for authentication.
CONTENT_LENGTH	Length in bytes of the request body that follows the HTTP request header. In the case of the POST method, the length of the form data that is sent by the browser. If the variable is null or zero, then the browser only sends request headers.
CONTENT_TYPE	MIME content-type of the request body sent by the browser. This is usually HTML.
PATH_INFO	Remainder of the URL path following the script name. If /cgi-bin/cgitest/extra/path was sent, PATH_INFO would contain /extra/path.

Table 22.3: Browser Environment Variables

VARIABLE	Description
PATH_TRANSLATED	Similar to PATH_INFO, but the server attempts to resolve the path to its root directory.
QUERY_STRING	Everything following (but not including) the ? in a URL. In the URL /cgi-bin/cgitest?fname=Bob, QUERY_STRING would contain fname=Bob
REMOTE_ADDR	IP address of the browser. It is always available and is represented in dotted decimal notation.
REMOTE_HOST	Host name of the browser making the request. It is set via a reverse DNS lookup. If it cannot be determined, it is left null.
REMOTE_USER	Plain text user ID provided by user for authentication of access rights by the browser. It is only set when the server sends a challenge and the browser responds with a valid user ID.
REMOTE_PASSWORD_MD5	Password in MD5 encrypted form. It follows the same rules as REMOTE_USER. There is no way to see the password in plain text.
REQUEST_METHOD	HTTP request method made by the browser. Common request methods are GET, POST, PUT, DELETE.
SCRIPT_NAME	Name of the currently running script as it is known by browsers. The name is escaped and does not include any query strings or path info. http://www.inetmi.com/cgi-bin/cgitest?fname=bob would have a SCRIPT_NAME of /cgi-bin/cgitest
SERVER_PROTOCOL	HTTP version requested by the browser. It can be either HTTP/1.0 or HTTP/0.9. It can only be HTTP/0.0 if requested by the browser.

Any other request headers that are sent to the server by the browser are made available to scripts through environment variables. Each header has a prefix of HTTP_ added to the header name. Any dashes (-) appearing in the header are translated to underscores (_). If a header appears multiple times, it is translated to a comma-separated list of each of the header values created. A common example is the header User-Agent: Mozilla/4.04, which would be translated to HTTP_USER_AGENT with a value of Mozilla/4.04.

SUMMARY

Programming for the Web is different than programming interactive applications on the AS/400. There is no concept of state, login, or job. Each request from the browser is a new request. The server has no memory of previous requests from a client. Although a different style of applications development, difficulties in working with the stateless environment can easily be overcome with tools such as hidden fields, cookies, and server authentication.

When coupled with data stored in the database, and with the proper tools, programming for the Web is quick, easy, and fun. I haven't done any programming in over 20 years, yet I've developed all of the applications (with the exception of two RPG programs) for my company's Web site. Developing applications for the Web is not like anything you've ever done. Approach it with an open mind.

HTML and Web Site Design 23

In Chapter 21, we saw the elements that go into good Web site design. That was the fun part. Now we must learn how to write the code that produces those elements for our Web site.

No book dealing with Web site development would be complete without a chapter on HTML. HTML defines what your user sees. It doesn't matter whether you type it yourself, generate it with a tool, or embed it within a program, HTML is the language that makes things happen on the Web.

HTML changes constantly. The following pages address the essentials of HTML that you absolutely need to know in order to survive as a Web site developer.

Why learn HTML when you can download free HTML page builders or buy powerful Web site development tools that will do much of the work for you? Because even if you use a tool to generate HTML, you need to understand what the tool is doing. Even if you have a tool, you will find that you will frequently write your own HTML. Sometimes it is easier just to write a little HTML than it is to use the tool.

I personally use Microsoft FrontPage 98 for all of my plain HTML pages and to layout pages that I will embed within Net.Data macros or CGI programs. I find, however, that I still write about 50 percent of my HTML by hand. I also find that I often have to make minor changes to the generated HTML.

The only alternative to HTML is the Java programming language that can create its own screens. Guess what! You still need an HTML page to invoke a Java program in your browser.

At the end of this chapter, I have included links to excellent resources for learning about HTML. When I started, you could come up with about half a dozen reference sites. Today, there are several hundred. The sites include tutorials, lists of tags and parameters, and tips and techniques that explain how to accomplish specific tasks.

GETTING STARTED WITH HTML

The first thing you must do is determine where you are going to store your pages on your server and how you are going to get the pages to the server. I strongly recommend using the integrated file system (IFS) on the AS/400. IBM notes that the IFS is four times faster than the traditional QDLS library and file system. IFS files are stream files and are processed extremely quickly.

An additional advantage to storing your HTML files in IFS directories is the fact that you can use Client Access/400 to edit them in your favorite PC text editor. Windows 95/98 or Windows NT with Client Access/400 provides you access to any directory (that you are authorized to access). You may access files via the Network Neighborhood folder on your desktop or via the File Open dialog of any text editor.

Because an HTML page is simply an ASCII text file with an HTM or HTML extension, you can use Notepad, WordPad, Lotus WordPro, Microsoft Word, or any other word processor or text editor to create and maintain your HTML files. (If you use a word processor like WordPro or Word, be sure to specify ASCII Text when you save the file.)

Two other text editors, Editpad.exe and Ultra_Edit, may be found in the Windows 95/98 section of the *www.tucows.com* software repository. Ultra_Edit costs $30 but has the ability to display a page in hexadecimal. It can convert between ASCII and EBCIDIC, and has a compare utility to compare two versions of a file.

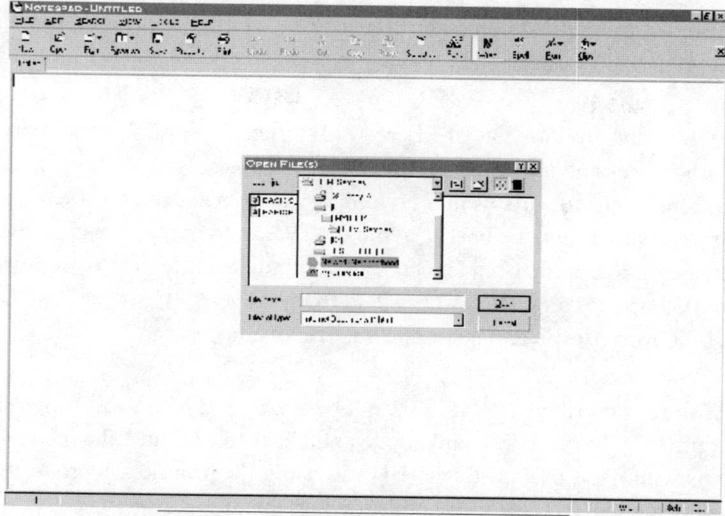

Figure 23.1: NotesPad with File Open Dialog.

When you create an HTML file, save it into whatever directory on your server you want. The AS/400 handles all ASCII to EBCIDIC conversions for you. As far as you are concerned, you are storing an ASCII text file on your computer. You also may create your files on a PC with a text editor and upload the files via FTP to the AS/400.

You may also store your HTML file in a source member on the AS/400 and edit it with SEU. All current servers will process server files from source physical file members.

HTML STANDARDS

The authority for HTML is the W3C World Wide Web Consortium located at `www.w3.org/MarkUp/`. HTML 4.0, the latest version, includes support for style sheets, internationalization, accessibility to Web pages for people with disabilities, frames, and richer tables and forms. Although HTML 4.0 has many exciting new features, it is not widely supported and may cause problems; I recommend avoiding its use for now.

While HTML is standardized, no one is required to follow the standards. Both Microsoft and Netscape have added proprietary extensions to HTML. Neither vendor offers a browser that is fully compliant with any of the standards. Some features are not supported by one, the other, or both. It is important to note that not all browsers support all HTML tags. Even the most recent browsers do not support all HTML 3.2 tags. (Contrary to popular belief, Netscape and Microsoft are not the only browser vendors in the market place.

Sun Microsystems sells a 100 percent Java-based browser, IBM has a couple, and the old Mosaic browser is still in use.)

Frames and tables are supported as of Microsoft Internet Explorer 3.x and Netscape Navigator 2.0. Both frames and tables are relatively safe to use on your Web site. However, browsers built by some ISPs may ship very old copies of Netscape browsers. When designing your Web site, it may be best to avoid the latest and greatest tags or risk losing a large percentage of your audience: The general computer user tends to use the browser that was installed on his computer and is afraid to upgrade to a newer release even when it is free (as both Microsoft's and Netscape's currently are).

All HTML features described are safe for both Netscape and Microsoft browsers. The tags are supported by Explorer 3.0 and above and Netscape 2.0 and above. You may still have problems with AOL users if the user is still using the proprietary browser that AOL shipped on its diskettes, CDs, or came preloaded on the user's system.

Netscape Communicator 4.05 and Microsoft Internet Explorer 4.02 support many new HTML functions and tags that are not addressed here. These pages are intended to get you writing some HTML that produces fairly sophisticated results. To explore more advanced HTML features, I strongly suggest you check out the reference material at the end of this chapter.

USING HTML SAMPLES

You may try all of the examples illustrated in this book by typing them in a text editor and saving them as files on your PC. Access them with your browser; your PC does not have to be connected to a network—just click OK if the browser cannot connect to the network. Assuming the files are stored in a subdirectory called /MYHTML on your C: drive, type the following on your command line or in the address field of your browser to view the sample pages you create: `c:\myhtml\example1.htm`

HTML BASICS

HTML uses *tags* or keywords that instruct the browser to do something with the following text. Tags begin with an < (greater than sign), contain a keyword like HTML, and end with a > (less than sign). *<HTML>* is an example of such a tag.

Most tags are paired. You code a starting tag to turn on a function like *<HTML>* and use a *terminator tag </HTML>* to turn off the function. A terminator tag always has a / preceding the name of the keyword. HTML keywords are not case sensitive. They may be typed in uppercase, lowercase, or mixed case.

Required Tags

There are two tags required in every document. They are the *<HTML>* tag and the *<BODY>* tag. Figure 23.2 shows a basic snippet of HTML code with these tags in place.

```
<HTML>
<BODY>
Hello World
</BODY>
</HTML>
```

Figure 23.2: Example1.htm.

The *<HTML>* tag tells the browser that the page contains HTML.

The *<BODY>* tag tells the browser that the text following it should be parsed, processed, and displayed to the user.

The *</BODY>* tag tells the browser that it has processed all of the text on the page.

The *</HTML>* tag tells the browser that it is done processing the file.

The code in Figure 23.2 is a complete HTML page that will display the text "Hello World" in the upper left corner of your browser. Try it!

Headers and Titles

Headers (identified by the *<HEAD>* tag) and titles (identified by the *<TITLE>* tag) are extremely important. They are not mandatory, but should be included in every Web page. We will revisit headers later in the section on *meta tags*, but for now let's look at the *<TITLE>* tag, shown in Figure 23.3.

```
<HTML>
<HEAD>
<TITLE>This is HTML Example 2</TITLE>
</HEAD>

<BODY>
Hello World
</BODY>
</HTML>
```

Figure 23.3: Example2.htm.

The *<TITLE>* tag allows you to apply a title that is displayed at the top of the page in the browser window bar. Title tags are also used by many search engines to display information about your Web site. It is good practice to provide a meaningful title. Do not use the brilliant and ever so witty title "Home Page." This is often generated by many HTML tools and never changed by the person using the tool. If you use the term "Home Page," at least use phrase "My Company's Home Page" (where the words "My Company" are replaced with the name of your company). The title is also displayed in the button bar at the bottom of the screen on a Windows 95/98 or Windows NT PC when the browser window is minimized.

If you look at the green banner across the very top of the browser screen in Figure 23.4, Example2.htm – Hello World, you will see the words "This is HTML Example2". Yes, that is there because of the *<TITLE> </TITLE>* tags.

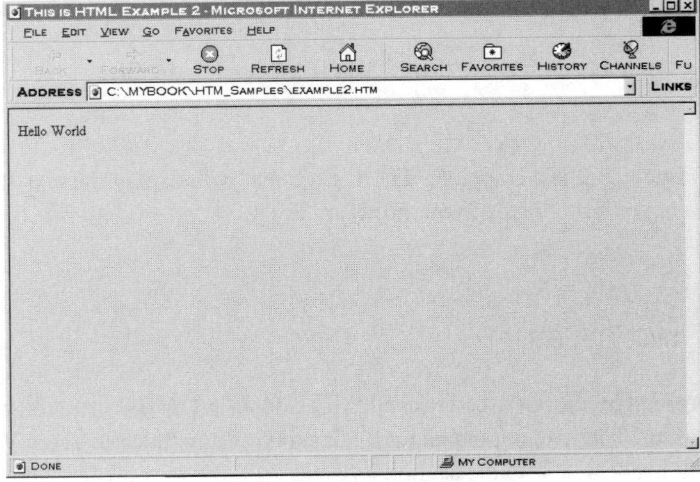

Figure 23.4: Example2.htm – Hello World.

PARAGRAPHS AND LINE BREAKS

When you type text, using a text editor, between the *<BODY>* and *</BODY>* tags, it is displayed in the browser. The browser (with one special exception) does not honor a carriage return line feed (Return Key). Type the HTML shown in Figure 23.5.

```
<HTML>
<HEAD>
<TITLE>Example 3 No Paragraphs or Line Breaks</TITLE>
</HEAD>
<BODY>
This is short line of text.
This line of text is terminated with a carriage return line feed
sequence (return key).

There appears to be a blank line between the last line and this
one.
</BODY>
```

Figure 23.5: Example3.htm.

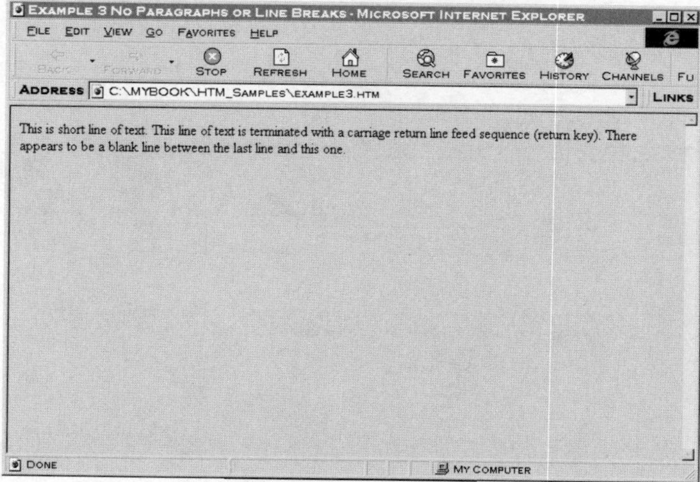

Figure 23.6: Example3.htm.

Figure 23.6 shows the results. As you can see, the browser ignores the carriage return line feed characters (CRLF) and displays the text as one long line. This is a very important fact to consider when dealing with text, especially text retrieved from a database file and displayed on the browser.

HTML uses two tags, the paragraph *<P>* and the line break *
* tags to implement line and paragraph spacing. Neither of these tags requires an end tag, although the *<P>* paragraph tag may be terminated with an end tag *</P>*. The *<P>* paragraph tag has one attribute, Align. You may code *<P align=xxx>* where xxx is left, right, or center.

Figure 23.7 illustrates the same text that was illustrated in Figure 23.6, but this time we inserted *<P>* paragraph and *
* line break tags. The resulting display is shown in Figure 23.8.

```
<HTML>
<HEAD>
<TITLE>Example 4 Paragraphs and Line Breaks</TITLE>
</HEAD>
<BODY>
This is short line of text.<br>
<p>This line of text is terminated with a carriage return line
feed sequence (return key).</p>

<p>There appears to be a blank line between the last line and
this one. </p>
</BODY>
</HTML>
```

Figure 23.7: Example4.htm.

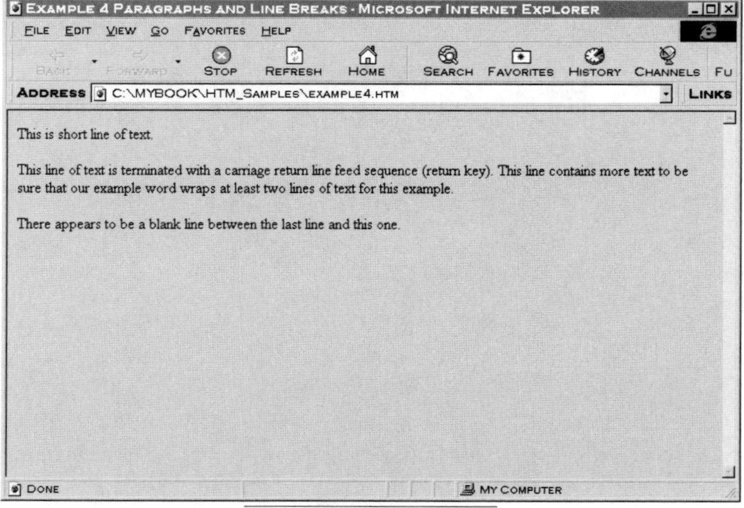

Figure 23.8: Example4.htm.

The *
* simply terminates the line and starts the next line on a new line. The *<P>* paragraph tag inserts a blank line before starting the text that follows it on a new line. Work with these tags to gain a good understanding of their uses.

There is one special tag pair, the *<PRE></PRE>*, or *preformatted text tag* set. These tags are the exception to the rule about carriage returns and line feeds. Everything typed after the beginning *<PRE>* tag and before the ending *</PRE>* tag is spaced exactly as typed. For text inside the preformatted text tag set, carriage returns are honored.

Create a test page using the *<PRE>* tag somewhere following the *<BODY>* tag. Type some text. Leave more than one space between words and press the return key several times to create blank lines. End the sample with a *</PRE>* tag. View the result in your browser. It should look exactly the way you typed it. That is the purpose of the preformatted text tags.

HEADINGS

HTML incorporates six paired heading tags that produce a heading in boldface type ranging in size from large to very small. The size ranges for the heading tags are shown in Figure 23.9. H1 is the largest and H6 is the smallest.

```
<html>
<head>
<title>Example 5 - Heading Tags</title>
</head>
<body>

<h1 align="center">Example 5 – Heading Tags</h1>

<H1>This is Heading 1</H1>
<H2>This is Heading 2</H2>
<H3>This is Heading 3</H3>
<H4>This is Heading 4</H4>
<H5>This is Heading 5</H6>
<H6>This is Heading 6</H6>
<p>This is as line of normal text</P>

</body>
</html>
```

Figure 23.9: Example5.htm.

I rarely use headings. You can accomplish exactly the same effect by using the bold tag and text alignment tags. The use of tags gives you greater control and flexibility over heading tags. Heading tags are convenient, however, when you are testing or throwing together a very quick page. Figure 23.10 shows the output from the code in Figure 23.9.

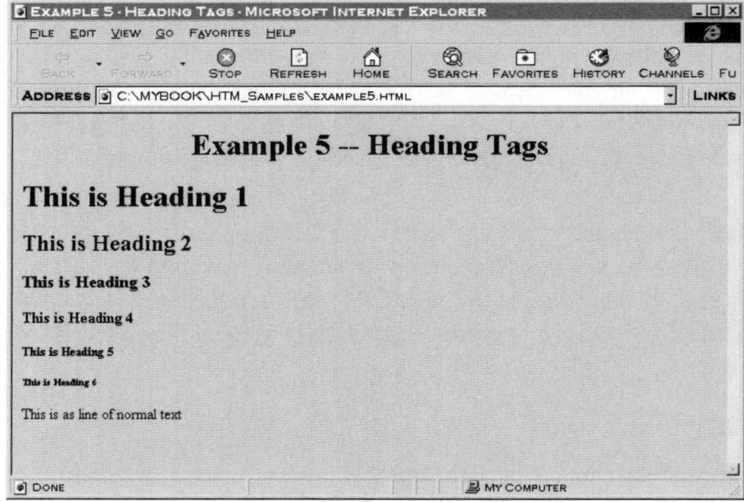

Figure 23.10: Example5.htm.

VIEWING WEB SOURCE

At this point, you know how to compose a very basic Web page. You can view HTML code for any Web page you see on the Web using your browser's View options.

To view the HTML source for a document, position your mouse over a blank area of the Web page and right click. A pop-up menu appears. Click on View Source or View Document Source. The HTML for the document appears either in a text editor or in a separate window (depending on how your browser is configured).

GRAPHICS AND BACKGROUNDS

You can right click on any image that you see displayed (including animation) and then click the Save Image As option to save the image to your PC's hard disk. If the image is not copyrighted, you may use it in your pages. That said, it must be emphasized that determining whether something is copyrighted is not easy. Just because it is not marked as copyrighted, does not mean that is not copyrighted. Many Web pages have copyright information not readily apparent on some remote page. Although it has been quite common practice to "borrow" images from other Web sites, you should be extremely cautious. The risk of copyright infringement is not trivial.

LINKING WEB PAGES

The single most important feature of HTML is its ability to link to locations within the same page or other pages. HTML can link to a page on the same computer or computers thousands of miles away.

LINKING TO ANOTHER WEB PAGE

Linking to another page is extremely easy. It is accomplished with the anchor tag. To link to a Web site on another server, enter the following:

```
<a href="http://www.ignite400.org">IGNITe400</a>
```

The *<a>* (anchor tag) indicates that this is a link. *Href="http://www.ignite400.org"* is the address of the Web site or page that you wish to link to. The > terminates the tag. The word "IGNITe400" is the text that will appear on your Web page. By default, it will appear in blue and be underscored. The mouse will change from a pointer to a hand when you pass the cursor over the text. *</a>* terminates the link.

Figure 23.11 shows an example that links to a page in the same subdirectory on the server that the current page resides in. There is also a link to an external Web site.

```
<HTML>
<HEAD>
<TITLE>Example 6 HTML Links</TITLE>
</HEAD>
<BODY>
<h1 align="center">Example 6: HTML Links</h1>
<p><a href="mypage.htm">Link to My Page</a>My Page</a> – a link
to a page in the same directory.</p>
<p><a href="www.ignite400.org">IGNITe<sup>sm</sup></a> – a link
to another Web site.</p>
</BODY>
</HTML>
```

Figure 23.11: Example6.htm.

It produces the output shown in Figure 23.12.

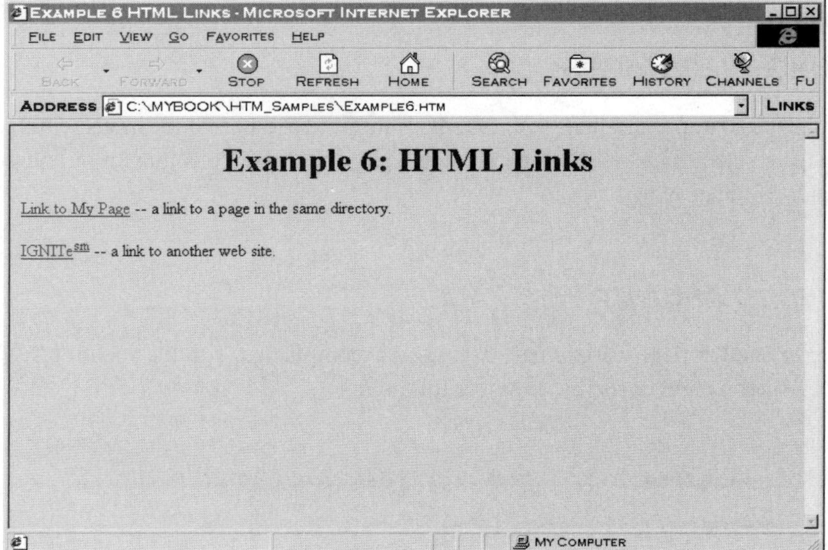

Figure 23.12: Example6.htm.

LINKING TO YOUR OWN WEB PAGE

The intra-document use of the *<a>* tag was originally used to provide a quick means of jumping around long scientific documents written by physicists. Often a table of contents would be created at the top of a very long document. You could then click on a link in the table of contents and jump to a point in the document many pages from the link.

These tags are rarely used today because most Web pages are one-to-one and half screens of text and graphics long. The tag is quite useful, however, for user manuals, contracts, and other wordy documents.

To use the intra-page form of the hypertext link, you must use two variations of the tag. The first form of the tag marks locations in your document that you want to link to. It is constructed as: *<a name="top">*. This is the anchor point that a reference tag will jump to.

The second tag will jump to the tag named by the *<a name=...>* tag. The form of the reference tag is *<a href="#top">*. The keyword HREF means jump or link to and the #

means that the following text ("top" in this case) is the name of the previously defined *<name=...>* tag.

```
<HTML>
<HEAD>
<TITLE>Example 7 HTML Links</TITLE>
</HEAD>
<BODY>

<a name="top">
<h1 align="center">Example 7: HTML Intrapage Links</h1>
<p><a href="#Par1">Paragraph 1</a><br>
   <a href="#Par2">Paragraph 2</a><br>
   <a href="#Par3">Paragraph 3</a><br>
   <a href="#Par4">Paragraph 4</a><br>
   <a href="#Par5">Paragraph 5</a></p>

<h2><a name="Par1">Paragraph 1</a></h2>
<p>This is the content of paragraph1. It consists of a quite a bit
more text than we will use in our example.
We are just using enough text to word wrap for a few lines. Please
note that we are also illustrating a good use of both the line break
"BR" and the paragraph "P" tags. I am repeating this paragraph over
and over again changing only the heading so that you can see how the
Intrapage Links work.<br>
<a href="#top">Jump to Top of Page</a>

<h2><a name="Par2">Paragraph 2</a></h2>
<p>This is the content of paragraph1. It consists of a quite a bit
more text than we will use in our example.
We are just using enough text to word wrap for a few lines. Please
note that we are also illustrating a good use of both the line break
"BR" and the paragraph "P" tags. I am repeating this paragraph over
and over again changing only the heading so that you can see how the
Intrapage Links work.<br>
<a href="#top">Jump to Top of Page</a>

<h2><a name="Par3">Paragraph 3</a></h2>
<p>This is the content of paragraph1. It consists of a quite a bit
more text than we will use in our example.
We are just using enough text to word wrap for a few lines. Please
note that we are also illustrating a good use of both the line break
"BR" and the paragraph "P" tags. I am repeating this paragraph over
and over again changing only the heading so that you can see how the
Intrapage Links work.<br>
<a href="#top">Jump to Top of Page</a>

<h2><a name="Par4">Paragraph 4</a></h2>
<p>This is the content of paragraph1. It consists of a quite a bit
more text than we will use in our example.
```

Figure 23.13: Example7.htm (part 1 of 2).

```
We are just using enough text to word wrap for a few lines. Please note
that we are also illustrating a good use of both the line break "BR" and
the paragraph "P" tags. I am repeating this paragraph over and over
again changing only the heading so that you can see how the Intrapage
Links work.<br>
<a href="#top">Jump to Top of Page</a>

<h2><a name="Par5">Paragraph 5</a></h2>
<p>This is the content of paragraph1. It consists of a quite a bit more
text than we will use in our example.
We are just using enough text to word wrap for a few lines. Please note
that we are also illustrating a good use of both the line break "BR" and
the paragraph "P" tags. I am repeating this paragraph over and over
again changing only the heading so that you can see how the Intrapage
Links work.<br>
<a href="#top">Jump to Top of Page</a>


</BODY>
</HTML>
```

Figure 23.13: Example7.htm (part 2 of 2).

In Figure 23.13, we created a mock-up of a document that has five paragraphs. Each paragraph has a heading, marked with a *<a name="Par1">* tag. The tag has descriptive text (Paragraph 1, Paragraph 2, etc.) that follows the name tag. At the end of each paragraph is a link tag to take you back to the top of the page. See the *<name="top">* tag right below the *<BODY>* tag.

We will provide three screen shots. Figure 23.14 shows the page as it would originally appear in the browser. When the user clicks on the underscored Paragraph 5, the screen shown in Figure 23.15 appears.

Finally, when the user clicks on the link at the bottom of the page, Jump to Top of Page, he is returned to the very top of the page. Notice that the none of the anchor points are marked as a link, only the text. When the browser pointer is placed over the text and clicked, it causes the browser to jump to the anchor point.

Now, let's look at a couple of other minor features to round out our discussion of links.

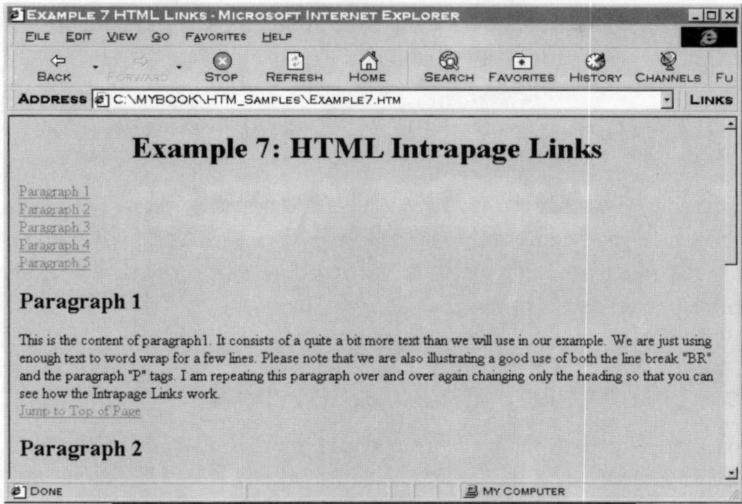

Figure 23.14: Example7.htm – before link to Paragraph 5.

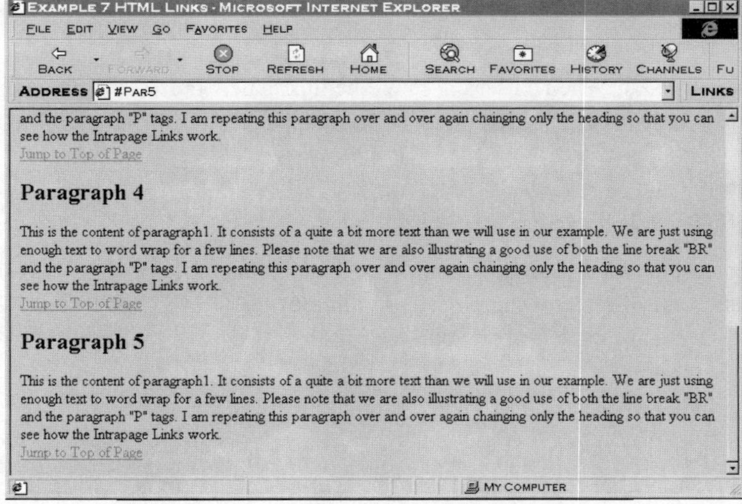

Figure 23.15: Example7.htm — after link to Paragraph 5.

MAIL-TO LINKS

The *mail-to link* is quite handy. There should be at least one mail-to link on a Web site that, when clicked, brings up the user's mail client software with a pre-addressed message that is ready to type and send. A link to the Webmaster's e-mail address is always a good idea to report technical problems or suggestions. A link to your marketing or sales department's e-mail address is almost a necessity if you plan to promote products on the Web. The tag is a simple variant of the standard hyperlink:

```
<a href="mailto://webmaster@ignite400.org">WEBMASTER</a>
```

You simply put the keyword *mailto* where you would normally put *HTTP*. In place of a URL, you enter an e-mail address (i.e. `webmaster@ignite400.org`). The rest of the tag works exactly like a normal hyperlink. The word *webmaster* will be blue and underscored when displayed on the browser.

OPENING A LINK IN A NEW BROWSER WINDOW

Complex? Tricky? Not at all! You use a standard hyperlink and add the keywords `target=body`:

```
<a href="http://www.ignite400.org
target=body">Link to IGNITe400</a>
```

That's all there is to it. When a user clicks on the link, a new browser window opens and IGNITe/400's home page is loaded in the new window.

RELATIVE ADDRESSES

Relative addresses are a technique to improve the maintainability of your Web site. If you make extensive use of relative addresses, you can move your Web site to a new server and not have to change each link on your Web site.

Consider the directory structure in Figure 23.16.

An absolute URL reference is a called a *fully qualified URL*, complete with the protocol HTTP:// and the full domain name:

`HTTP://www.ignite400.org` or
`HTTP://www.ignite400.org/member/index.htm`

If a Web site changes its domain name (oh yes, it really does happen) or if you change the directory structure and move a page to a different directory, each and every link within the site must be manually updated unless you use relative addressing.

```
/

      /wwwserv

              /webdocs  ß Server's root directory
                      index.htm
                      about_us.htm

                      /private
                              index.htm

                              /customer
                                      index.htm
                                      page1.htm
                                      page2.htm

                              /employee
                                      index.htm
                                      page1.htm
                                      page2.htm
```

Figure 23.16: A typical Web server directory structure.

Using the directory structure depicted above for our fictitious company, here are several relative addresses for Acme Quality Fruits' Web site:

The relative address `<a href="page1.htm">Page 1</a>` links to `page1.htm` as long as you are linking from the same directory. This would work if you wanted to link from `/private/employee/index.htm`.

You also may simply refer to the page if you are linking to pages in the same directory: `<a href="/private/index.htm">`. This is probably the most common form of relative link. It locates a page in the subdirectory /private, which is one level below the document root.

The relative address link `<a href="/private/customer/page2.htm">` links to a page in the /customer subdirectory.

The relative address link `<a href="../index.htm">` uses the "../", which is a universal symbol on almost all computer systems (Windows, UNIX, OS/400, S390) that tells the server to look in the document root directory.

The reference `<a href="./index.htm">` tells the server to look for a file called `index.htm` one directory level above the current directory. If this link were found in the page `/private/employee/page1.htm`, it would instruct the browser and server to look for a page in the /private directory. The "./" is a universal symbol that means parent directory.

WEB PAGE TEXT

Although most modern Web pages contain images and multimedia effects like full motion video and audio clips, the bulk of your Web site will consist of text. In the following pages, we start with the basic text manipulation tags and gradually take you through advanced layout and design techniques.

TEXT FORMATTING AND ALIGNMENT

Text formatting and alignment tags can be used anywhere text is typed on a Web page. This handful of very simple tags can help you greatly enhance your Web pages.

BOLDFACE, ITALICS, UNDERSCORE

The boldface, italic, and underscore are the most basic text manipulation tags. A word of caution, don't over use these tags. Reserve boldface for headings and emphasis. Overuse will confuse your reader. Use the tags to draw the user into your text and make them want to read it.

- `<b>BOLD</b>` makes the text appear bold.
- `<I>Italic</I>` displays the text between the tags in italics.
- `<U>underscore</U>` underlines your text. Be careful with this one. Don't confuse your users with unnecessary underlining, which is also used to designate hypertext links.

You may combine these tags for composite effects.

- `<b><I><u>BOLD, ITALIC, UNDERSCORED</b></I></u>`

You may intersperse tags with the text of a word, phrase, or sentence. For example, `<b>B</b>old` would display on the browser as "**B**old"

Character Formatting

HTML includes a series of tags that control the point size of text and provide special formatting for all text enclosed by the tags.

<small></small> pair reduces the size of the text within the tag pair by one font size. (Font size is not synonymous with point size.) You may use up to three consecutive <small> tags to decrease the size of the font. For example, <small><small>text</small></small> reduces the size of the font by two sizes.

<big></big> is exactly the opposite of *<small>*. It increases the size of the font by one size. You may use four consecutive *<big>* tags to increase the font up to four times normal size.

* or <super></super>* creates *superscripted* text, or text that appears above the normal line of print. This is extremely useful when you want to use the TM (trademark) or SM (service mark) symbols. It is often advisable to use *<small>* in conjunction with superscripting. IGNITe400sm is an example of a service mark created with <sup> and <small>. It would be written in HTML as:

```
IGNITe400<sup><small>sm</small></sup>
```

** is the tag to use for *subscripting*. It works like superscripting, but places the text below the normal line of print instead of above it.

<STRIKE></STRIKE> is useful in legal or technical documents where you wish to show text that has been deleted from the document without physically removing it. You will often see the *<strike>* tag used when looking at RFCs that are under development. For example, *<STRIKE>This is obsolete text</STRIKE>* produces: ~~This is obsolete text.~~

<TT></TT> or *teletypewriter* produces Monospaced (typewriter Courier) font text.

<tt>This is teletypewriter text</tt> would look like: `This is teletypewriter text.`

<PRE></PRE> is used to display text in a monospaced font and to preserve spaces typed by the user as well as carriage return line feeds typed by the user.

Important note: The browser strips out carriage return/line feed (new line) characters and extra spaces between or following words (it leaves one and only one space between words). The only way you can get the browser to display text exactly as you typed it is to use the *<pre>* tag.

Figure 23.17 illustrates all of the text formatting tags we have discussed so far.

```
<html>
<head>
<title>Example 8.htm Text and Character Formatting</title>
</head>
<body>

<h1 align="center">Example 8.htm - Text and Character Formatting</h1>

<p><big><big><b>T</b></big></big>his <i>text</i> illustrates the use
of the of the &lt;big&gt;, &lt;B&gt;<b>bold</b>, and the &lt;I&gt;
<i>italic</i> tags.</p>

<p><big><big><big><b><i><u>THIS TEXT IS 3 TIMES NORMAL SIZE, Bold,
Italic, and
Underlined.<br>
</big></u>This text is 2 times normal, bold, and italic.<br>
</big></i>This text is 1 times normal and bold</big></b><br>
This line should be normal for reference.</p>

<p><tt>This is teletype text using the &lt;tt&gt; tag.          No-
tice the spacing in the HTML source text and

then      notice       the    spacing when displayed by the
browser.</tt></p>

<p><PRE>This text uses the &lt;PRE&gt; tag.        Notice     the
spacing    in
the    HTML         and
in     the  output     text.</pre><p>

<p>This example<sup>demonstrates</sup> the superscript &lt;sup&gt;
tag.</p>
<p>This is an example<sub>of the</sub> subscript &lt;sub&gt; tag.</p>
<strike>This text illustrates the &lt;STRIKE&gt;</strike> tag.</p>
<p>NORMAL <small>SMALL <small>SMALL </SMALL></SMALL></SMALL>
Illustrates the use of the &lt;SMALL&gt; tag.</p>
<p>NORMAL <big>BIGGER <big>BIGGER <big>BIGGER <big>BIGGER
</big></big></big></big>
Illustrates the use of the &lt;BIG&gt; Tag.</p>
</body>
</html>
```

Figure 23.17: Example8.htm.

The code in Figure 23.17 illustrates all of the tags that have been used so far, and also demonstrates how tags can be combined to format a single letter, a word, or a sentence. It also illustrates how tags remain in effect until terminated with a termination tag.

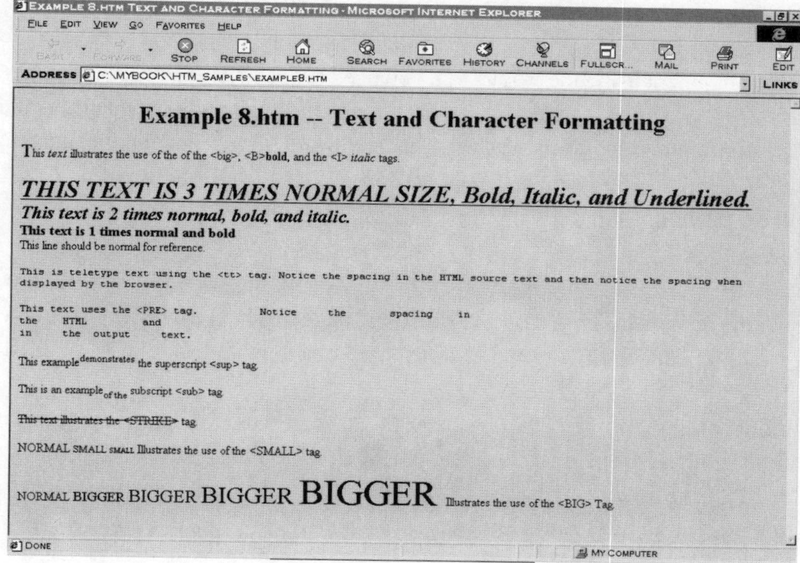

Figure 23.18: Example8.htm.

Figure 23.18 illustrates the result of tags presented in HTML example8.htm in Figure 23.17.

Text Alignment

Text aligns to the left by default. Text wrapping is enabled by default with ragged right margins. You can control text alignment by using the `align= parameter` of the *<p>* paragraph and the *<DIV>* division tags.

Until HTML 3.2, the tag didn't do anything. As of HTML 3.2, the tag sets the default alignment of a section defined with the *</DIV>* tag set. You may use *left, right, center*, and *justify* with the tag. The format of the division tag is `<DIV align="justify">` The text you want to format is followed by a *</DIV>* tag. Be sure to enclose the `align= "keyword"` in double quotes.

- *Left* causes all text to be left aligned with a ragged right margin.
- *Right* causes all text to be right aligned with a ragged left margin.

- *Center* causes all text to be centered.
- *Justify* results in text with an even left and right margin. Spacing is adjusted between words and letters to achieve the effect. This only works with HTML 3.2-compliant browsers such as Explorer 4.02 and Netscape Communicator 4.01 and above.

If you set the alignment using the `<DIV>` tag, you need not set it in each `<P>` tag within the division (to `</DIV>`). The paragraphs inherit the alignment from the division tags. You may override the division tags by placing an alignment keyword `align=` within the paragraph tag.

Paragraphs support the same parameters (left, right, center, or justify) that the division tag supports.

You may come across the `<center></center>` tag set. This centers any text that falls between the tags. The `<center>` tag is considered obsolete and should be avoided.

One additional alignment tag is the `<BLOCKQUOTE>` tag, which indents text approximately one-half inch from the left and one-half inch from the right for each `<BLOCKQUOTE>` tag used. You may nest multiple `<BLOCKQUOTE>` tags inside each other. Be sure to match up their termination tags.

Figure 23.19 shows the HTML code used to implement various text alignments.

```
<html>
<head>
<title>example9.htm - Text Alignment</title>
</head>
<body>

<h1 align="center">Example9.htm — Text Alignment</h1>


<p align="left">The text in this paragraph is aligned to the left. When
the text wraps you will see that it creates a ragged right margin.
Ragged right margins are currently in vogue. It is very popular in many
magazines and books. Personally, I prefer a
justified right hand margin, or a partially justified right margin (not
supported by HTML). We need a few more words to force the text to wrap
at least twice so we can
demonstrate the effect we are trying to illustrate.</p>
```

Figure 23.19: Example9.htm (part 1 of 2).

```
<p align="center">This text is centered.<br>You can clearly see what
happens to centered text.</p>

<p align="right">This text is aligned<br>to the right<br>as you can
see.</p>

<p align="justify">Justified text is adjusted by the browser to create
an even left and right margin. The effect looks more formalized and is
(in my opinion) easier to read. It simply looks better. Justified text
is frequently used in formal publications, magazines, and virtually
all newspapers. It works very well when using a multi-column format.
We need a few more words to force the text to wrap at least twice so
we can demonstrate the effect we are trying to illustrate.</p>

</DIV>

<DIV align="justify">

<p>This text assumes the justification specified by the division
&lt;DIV&gt; tag.
As you can see we specified justified text in the division tag and
that is inherited by this paragraph and any subsequent paragraph that
does not specify its own alignment.</P>

<blockquote>
This text falls within a &lt;BLOCKQUOTE&gt; tag. As you can see both
the left and right hand margins are indented approximately one half
inch. The amount will vary depending upon your browser, but it is in-
dented.

<blockquote>

This text falls within a second blockquote and will be indented even
further than the previous paragraph of text. You can nest blockquote
tags as many times as makes sense and looks good for your document.

</blockquote>

We have now terminated the first blockquote and you can see the effect
on this paragraph. The paragraph now conforms to the remaining
unterminated blockquote tag.

</blockquote>

Now we have terminated both blockquotes that we used so this paragraph
should revert to the left margin.

</DIV>

</body>
</html>
```

Figure 23.19: Example9.htm (part 2 of 2).

Figure 23.20 illustrates the results of each of the alignment tags. Look carefully at the left and right alignment of each block of text on the page.

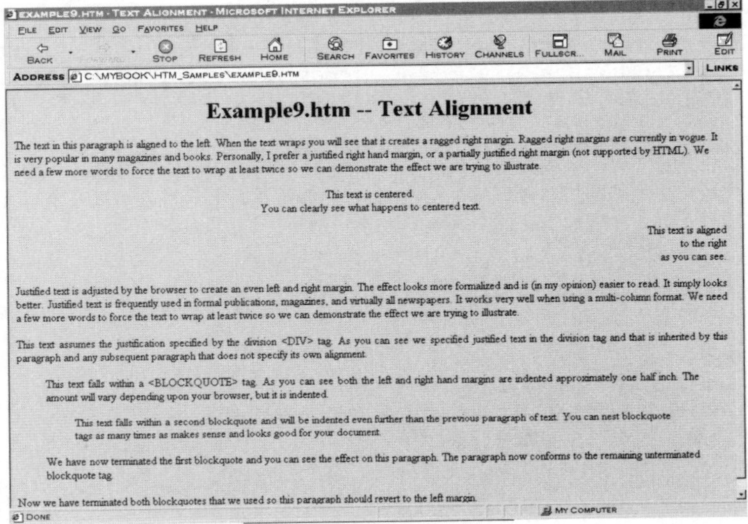

Figure 23.20: Example9.htm.

FONT SIZE, COLOR, AND TYPEFACE

You can control the size, color, and typeface by implementing parameters within the <FONT> tag set. Each parameter is explained separately below. The settings embedded in a <FONT> tag remain in effect until terminated by a </FONT> tag.

Font Size

Text size can be increased by using the <BIG> tag or reduced using the <SMALL> tag. A more direct method of setting the font size is to use the size parameter of the <FONT> tag.

Browsers recognize seven font sizes (1, 2, 3, 4, 5, 6, and 7). Font size 1 is the smallest font and is barely readable on a browser with normal font settings. Font size 7 is the largest. Normally, the default font size for a browser is 3. Each size increases the font by a fixed size. There is no concept of measurement other than the relative 1-to-7 scale. This is due to the fact that each browser may implement fonts as they choose. Most browsers also allow the user the ability to increase or decrease the size of the font displayed on the screen. To further complicate matters, a size 3 font on a 640 *x* 480 dpi screen is much larger than the same font when the screen is set to 800 i 600 or 1024 i 780 dpi resolution.

<FONT> tags, as implemented by the browser, are designed to control the size of fonts displayed on a screen, not on a printed page. For this reason, it is important to view your output at the lowest possible resolution that any user might use to view your Web site. Remember, many people use and prefer 640 *x* 480. You really need to consider these people when designing your Web site.

The format for *<FONT>* tags is:

> Example 1: `<font size="4">`
> Example 2: `<font size="+2">`

In Example 1: `<font size="4">`, the font size is explicitly set to font size 4. This is one size larger than normal.

Example 2, `<font size="+2">`, sets the font size to two sizes larger than the current or default font size. If the default font size is 3 and the last font tag set the font to `<font size="-1">` without a terminating tag, then `<font size="+2">` would set the current font size to 4, or 3 – 1 + 2 = 4.

If the default font size is 3, then `<font size="+2">` would set the font to 5.

You can change the default font size by using the `<basefont size="n">` tag. This tag changes the base or default font size for the page from the tag until it is terminated with a `</basefont>` tag or until another `<font size="n">` tag is encountered.

Color

The color of a font is changed with the `color=` parameter of the `<font>` tag. The format is `<font color="red">` or `<font color="#008000">`. Colors may be specified in two ways with HTML, either by name ("red") or by specifying a hexadecimal value for each of the three primary colors (red, green, and blue).

There are several excellent free tools to help you with color selection available for download from the Internet. Search on Web Color Picker or check out `www.tucows.com` and search on Color Picker. Products like Netscape Communicator's Composer, Microsoft FrontPage 98, Net Objects, or any of the many WSYWIG tools also include color selection aids.

Be careful with color. Many colors, especially subtle shades, must be constructed on a browser by introducing patterns with secondary colors to create the illusion of shades. If you examine colors carefully, you will see the *hashing patterns* in the background. Be sure to test your color combinations on several different monitors and PCs, because what looks good on your monitor may look terrible on someone else's. Be sure to check the relationship between text colors and backgrounds. Sometimes a great looking background will make it virtually impossible to select text colors.

Also, remember that backgrounds do not generally print. If you use white as a text color, it may disappear when printed.

Typefaces

Personal computers use fonts that are installed on the machine. Be especially careful if you have desktop publishing, graphics presentation, or word processing products installed on the machine you are using to develop your Web sites. Most of these products install additional typefaces that augment the basic typefaces provided by the vendor of your operating system (Windows 95/98, Window NT, UNIX, Mac OS, OS/2).

Typefaces may be implemented via the `<FONT FACE="FACE1,FACE2, FACEn">` tag with the FACE= parameter. The default typeface is whatever the user's computer is set to. On most Windows PCs, the default font is Times Roman.

Consider the tag `<font face="Arial,Helvetica">`.

The first typeface listed is the typeface that you as developer would prefer the user to see on his browser. The second and subsequent is your second choice, third choice, etc. If the primary typeface is not found, the browser will look for the secondary, etc. If it cannot find any of the fonts specified, it will default to the user's default font.

Special Characters

There are two types of special characters supported by HTML. The first type is usually called "symbols" by most word processors, desktop publishing, or presentation software. These include copyright symbols and currency marks like yen, pound sterling, etc.

A list of special characters can be found at the following Rice University site:

http://www.owlnet.rice.edu/~jwmitch/iso8859-1.html

The characters are documented in the ISO8859-1 specification.

One of the most common special characters is the hard space * * tag. This tag is required because the browser strips all extra spaces from the data stream as it formats and displays text. The exception is text encapsulated between a *<PRE>* and a *</PRE>* tag set. If you want an extra space or two, you must use one occurrence of the ` ` tag for each space character other than the first.

In CGI programming, any special characters like the < or > characters, single and double quotes, etc., are translated to the ASCII text decimal number for the character and preceded by a % sign.

TEXT LISTS

Lists are a useful feature of HTML and are the last text-formatting construct we will discuss. There are three types of list:

Ordered Lists

An ordered list automatically numbers the items in a list. You may choose to number with standard numbers, roman numerals (upper- and lowercase), or alphabetically (upper- and lowercase). Figure 23.21 is an example of an ordered list:

```
<OL>
   This is the first item in the list</LI>
   This is the second item in the list</LI>
   This is the third item in the list</LI>
</OL>
```

Figure 23.21: HTML tags to code ordered list.

The ordered list in Figure 23.21 defaults to standard numbers. You may add the *TYPE=* parameter to the ordered list to control the type of numbering. Valid types are A, a, I, I, or 1.

You may also control the starting number in the list and may continue list numbering after having other types of text or graphics inserted between the lists.

Note that the *</OL>* tag defines the list. This is a list item tag. You may specify if word wrapping is allowed or not. Wrap is the default. When word wrapping occurs, the browser aligns text under the first word to create the look of an indented list.

Unordered Lists

An unordered list is very similar to the ordered list except that it uses your choice of a filled circle, open circle, or filled square as a bullet tag. It uses the tag for the list items and is designated with the *</UL>* unordered list tag. It has a *TYPE=* parameter where you may specify *circle, disc,* or *square*.

Definition Lists

A definition list is quite a bit different from the ordered and unordered lists. It was originally intended to support the creation of a glossary. It uses three tags instead of the two used by the other lists.

- *<DL></DL>* defines the list.
- *<DT></DT>* is a definition list title. Enclose the text you are defining within these tags, and the text appears left aligned in the list
- *<DD></DD>* is the definition detail tag that defines the item listed in the *<DT>* tag. The text surrounded by this tag is indented. Indentation is preserved when word wrap occurs.

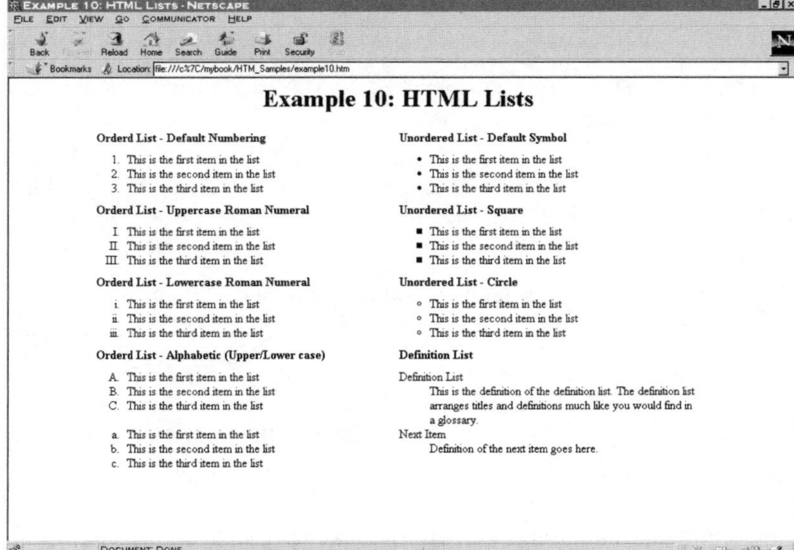

Figure 23.22: HTML lists.

Figure 23.22 illustrates all list types. Lists can be used as a creative form of text layout. You may nest lists within lists to create outlines or other graphic design effects. You may also embed images within a list.

WEB PAGE GRAPHICS

Web page graphics are what make the Web what it is today. In 1997, you could still find many Web sites that were text only and contained technical content, as was the intent of the Web's original inventors.

Today you will be hard pressed to find a Web site that does not make use of Web site graphics to sell its products or market its company.

Web site graphics are *bit-mapped graphic files*. There are two formats common use and supported by virtually all modern browsers: GIF and JPEG (.jpg). (There is an additional format called .png that has limited use.) Bit mapped graphics consist of a bunch of dots with a color bit. It is an easy task for the graphics software contained in your browser to map the bits and colors to your screen.

Adobe and Macromedia Inc. are competing to set a standard for *vector graphics*. Vector graphics send instructions to your browser to draw primitive graphic objects like circles, arcs, rectangles, polygons, etc., at specified locations on your screen. Vector graphics look better. Vector graphic files are also very small because the file only contains instructions and not the entire image.

GIF FILES

Originally developed by CompuServe, GIF is the standard for drawings and artwork. GIF files use the browser's color palette and are therefore limited in the number of colors they can display. GIF files may be compressed without much loss of resolution, which makse them very attractive for sending graphics across the Internet. GIFs are well suited to drawings and artwork or even black-and-white photographs. They cannot reproduce a colorful photograph due to the limitations of the color palette.

ANIMATED GIF FILES

You have no doubt seen animated figures on Web sites, or seen banners that change constantly. The GIF89A specification was created to support crude animation. It is accomplished by storing many images in one file and then displaying each image automatically for a predetermined length of time. The effect is like drawing a figure on each page of a note pad and then fanning the note pad to see animation.

GIF89A also introduced the concept of *transparent backgrounds.* A transparent background (a colored logo against a white background) makes the image look like it is part of the Web page.

JPEG

JPEG (usually stored as .jpg) files tend to be larger than GIF files, resulting in greater transmission times. They have the advantage of storing their own color palettes within the file and can faithfully reproduce photographs without quality or color loss.

TOOLS

There are literally dozens of high-quality graphics packages capable of creating GIF and JPEG images. If you buy a scanner for your computer, you will undoubtedly find that some graphics software is packaged with the scanner.

Most word processing software includes at least a rudimentary drawing package. Windows 95 includes the Windows Draw program, which is a very nice bitmap drawing package capable of creating GIF or JPEG images.

Microsoft FrontPage includes a free copy of Microsoft Image Composer that, in my opinion, is one of the best image manipulation packages on the market. Microsoft Office includes Microsoft PowerPoint, a very powerful graphics-based presentation tool. Microsoft Publisher, Adobe Illustrator, PhotoShop, Adobe PageMaker, and Lotus Freelance are but a few of the many graphics packages available.

Graphics animation is a little more difficult. There are many high-function, 3D animation packages available. These products are designed for professional animators who develop television commercials and even full feature animation for film. The products tend to be somewhat pricey ($1,000 to $3,000) and are designed for animation professionals who understand the language of animation. There are some low-cost products designed and built for Web site developers; try to get some references or recommendations before you buy. Those I tried were buggy and produced poor results.

Your best bet is to go to a professional animator for your animations. Costs start at about $200 per image. You can find many talented professional artists on the Web who show their skills on their Web site. Many give away hundreds of free samples of their work.

FREE GRAPHICS

Free graphic images, including animation, can be found on a search of the Web on Web Graphics. There are literally thousands of free images provided by software vendors like Microsoft, Netscape, and others who want you to develop attractive Web sites and be successful. Others are provided by commercial artists who want your custom work.

THE IMAGE TAG

Images are inserted into an HTML document via the `<IMG... >` tag. This tag has over 23 parameters in the HTML 3.2 specification. I am going to deal with a handful that are supported by both Netscape and Microsoft browsers and are needed on a regular basis.

The `ALT=` parameter was originally designed for use by browsers that cannot support images. It causes a block of text to be displayed where the graphic would normally be displayed. Version 4.x browsers (Microsoft and Netscape) now always display this as a little pop-up block of text in a browser-generated text box when you pass the mouse over the image.

The `<IMG SRC="myimage.GIF" ALT= "Alternate text">` parameter provides for alternate text that will be displayed by your browser when you pass the mouse over the image.

The `BORDER=` parameter causes a border to be drawn around the image. This parameter is expressed in pixels, which controls the thickness of the border. The default is 0 (zero) or no border. As a design note, professional graphic designers recommend that photographs of people always have a border and even a drop shadow (see your image tools) around them. It is almost a graphic art standard. The format is `<IMG SRC="mybosspic.jpg" BORDER="1" ALT="Mr. John Smith, President and CEO">`.

The `HEIGHT=` and `WIDTH=` parameters control the size of the image. Most graphics packages give you the height and width of your image in pixels. Specifying the height and width parameters greatly improves the speed at which your browser can render and display your Web page. It is not an error, but a serious mistake not to code the height and width on every image you use in your Web site. The format is `<IMG SRC="myimage.GIF" HEIGHT="50" WIDTH="30" ALT="My first image">`.

The `SRC=` parameter is identical in every respect to the `<A HREF= ...>` tag. You may use a fully qualified URL to refer to an image source: `<IMG RC=http://www.software.ibm.com/i/mast/v2/short.GIF>`

You may also use relative referencing described previously in the section describing the `<A HREF...>` tag.

Image placement dramatically affects performance. Careful placement of your images on your server can greatly improve the performance of your Web site by making sure that you client's browsers cache is fully used.

If an image is loaded from exactly the same location on your server, it is only needed by your browser once. If every page on your server uses the same logo, you may store your logo in a single directory and always refer to the exact same directory in your `<IMG SRC=...>` tag. The browser will load the image once and will use the cached copy on subsequent requests for the image. If you put a copy of the image in a different directory, the browser assumes that it is a different image and will load each unique reference to it. It cannot detect that the image is the same although the file name may be the same.

The ALIGN= parameter controls the placement of the image in relation to a paragraph of text. The valid keywords for ALIGN= are *absbottom, absmiddle, baseline, bottom, left, middle, right*, and *textop* or *top*.

This is definitely a case where a picture is worth a thousand words.

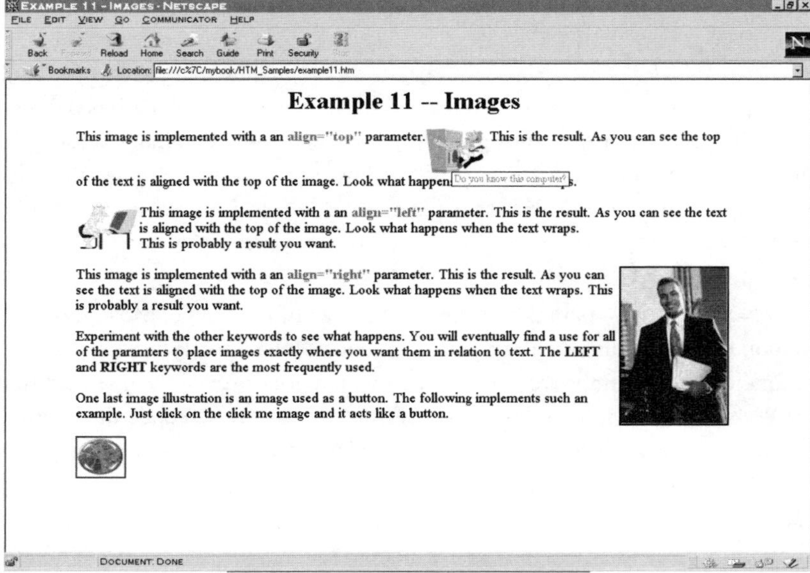

Figure 23.23: Example11.htm—images.

In Figure 23.23, the first image is aligned with the "TOP" keyword. Notice also the text in the box, which is alternate text because the cursor was passed over the image. The second image was created with an `align="LEFT"`, which causes the text to wrap to the left of the image. The third image was created with `align="RIGHT"`, which places the image to the right-hand side of the page.

The final image illustrates the use of an image as a link button. The format of this link is:

```
<A HREF=HTTP://www.ignite400.org>
    <IMG SRC="clickme.GIF"></A>
```

As you can see, the image source tag replaces the text that would normally be used for a standard link. The blue line around the button can be turned off.

One last trick is to use the link example shown above in catalogs or in photo or art gallery Web sites. You display a small low-resolution image that shows the user what the high-resolution image looks like. The low-resolution image is only 3k to 12k in size and loads quickly. When the small image is clicked, a high-resolution image, which can take up to a minute to load, is displayed.

BACKGROUNDS

The background of your Web site sets the tone and mood. Backgrounds and background colors are defined in the *<BODY>* tag.

```
<body bgcolor="red"> or <body background="back1.GIF">
```

The first example sets the color of the background to the color red. The second example uses a background image called back1.GIF. The background= parameter may use absolute or relative URL referencing as described under the *<A HREF=...>* tag.

Background images (usually GIF or JPG) are tiled horizontally and vertically by the browser. This allows you to define a very small image (often 1k to 3k or 50 *x* 50 pixels square) in size. The browser then repeats the pattern to the left and down the page to fill the page with the illusion of a solid pattern. It is actually a composite of many 50 *x* 50 pixel images.

You can also use a bar that is wide enough that the browser cannot tile it horizontally. The example in Figure 23.25 uses a two-color bar that is 8 pixels high and 1,024 pixels wide. It is tiled vertically to form the background.

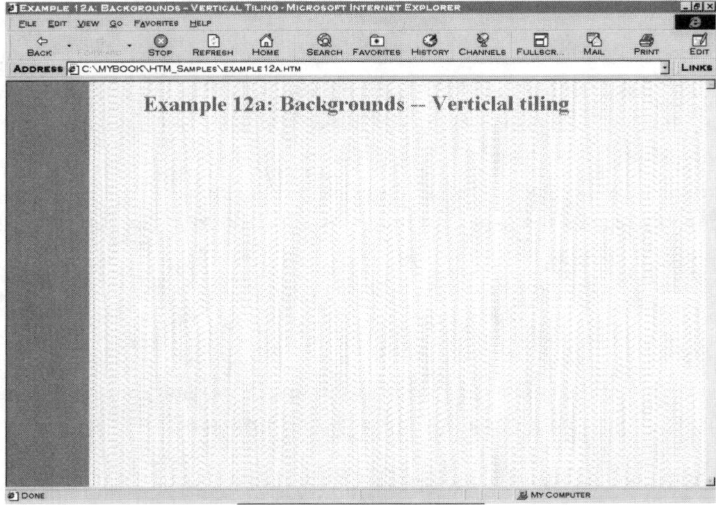

Figure 23.25: Vertical tiling.

Figure 23.25 illustrates how an image that is too wide for vertical tiling can be used to create the scholar's margin on the left. This background can be used with tables to place text in both color areas. Usually, links or bullets are placed in the dark area and the bulk of the page's content in the light area.

Figure 23.26: Full-page image.

The JPEG image used as the background of Figure 23.26 was manipulated in Microsoft Image Composer. The field of stars to the right was created by copying the background from a small square of the original image. It was then replicated until the entire image covered an area 1,100 *x* 1,100 pixels. Care must be taken to keep the text well within the boundaries of a single page using the lowest resolution monitor on which the page will be viewed. This is an extremely difficult effect to create, but very stunning. It also represents a significant performance problem, as the image is extremely large and will take a considerable amount of time to load.

The background has a dramatic effect upon the appearance of the font colors and the apparent clarity of the font. Due to the way in which fonts and images are rendered by the browser, some fonts will blur badly. Colors that may appear vivid and vibrant on a white or black background appear muddy and dull when displayed over many backgrounds. The best advice is to keep the backgrounds simple and use graphic art, images, fonts, and headlines as your major design tools.

HORIZONTAL RULES

HTML includes a horizontal line tag `<HR>` to draw a horizontal line across your page. You may specify the width of the line and the size or height of the line in pixels. The width is specified as `<HR width="400">` or `<HR width="60%">`. I generally recommend the use of percentages. `<HR size="10">` produces an extremely thick and bold line.

You may also specify the alignment of a line that is less than its default of 100 percent width. Alignment uses the standard `ALIGN=` parameter with left, right, center, or justify. Be careful with horizontal rules. They tell the eye to *stop*, and this may cause the reader to stop reading and not see very important parts of your page.

LAYOUT AND DESIGN WITH TABLES

Almost all sophisticated page layout designs are built with tables. You may nest tables inside of tables to build complex structures.

We present the basic table tags and parameters here. I urge you to buy a good HTML text and study and experiment with tables until you thoroughly understand their manipulation and use. The tags and parameters I am presenting here have served me well and it is rare that I need others.

Tables consist of:

- A table tag `<TABLE ...></TABLE>`, which defines the general characteristics of the table. Its parameters include the alignment of the table on the page, background color or image, spacing between cells, spacing inside a cell between the content and the edge of the cell, and borders.
- A row tag `<TR ..></TR>`, which defines the beginning and ending of a table row. The only parameter is the vertical alignment of the text in the rows cells.
- A table cell detail tag `<TD ...></TD>`, which is required for each and every cell in the table. Each cell may contain vertical and horizontal parameters, color, background, etc.
- A table heading cell tag `<TH ...></TH>`, which is almost identical to the table cell detail tag. The only significance is that a `<TH>` tag defaults text to BOLD.
- The `<TABLE><END TABLE>` tags are mandatory and must surround the table. Failure to code any required end tag in the table will result in the table not displaying on the browser.

SIMPLE TABLE

Figure 23.27 shows a basic table; Figure 23.28 illustrates the HTML code needed to create and format the table.

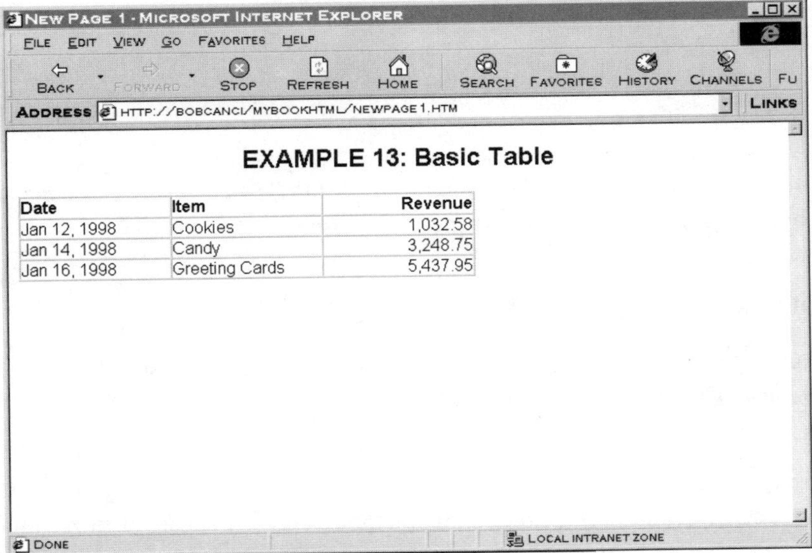

Figure 23.27: Example 13 — basic table.

```
<title>Example 13 – Basic Table</title>
</head>

<body bgcolor="#FFFFFF">

<p align="center"><font face="Arial"><b><big><big>EXAMPLE 13: Basic
 Table</big></big></b></font></p>

<table border="1" cellpadding="0" cellspacing="0" width="60%">
  <tr>
    <th width="25%" align="left"><font face="Arial">Date</font></th>
    <th width="25%"><font face="Arial">Item</font></th>
    <th width="25%" align="right"><font face="Arial">Reve-
nue</font></th>
  </tr>
  <tr>
    <td width="25%" align="left"><font face="Arial">Jan 12,
1998</font></td>
    <td width="25%"><font face="Arial">Cookies</font></td>
    <td width="25%" align="right"><font
face="Arial">1,032.58</font></td>
  </tr>
  <tr>
    <td width="25%" align="left"><font face="Arial">Jan 14,
1998</font></td>
    <td width="25%"><font face="Arial">Candy</font></td>
    <td width="25%" align="right"><font
face="Arial">3,248.75</font></td>
  </tr>
  <tr>
    <td width="25%" align="left"><font face="Arial">Jan 16,
1998</font></td>
    <td width="25%"><font face="Arial">Greeting Cards</font></td>
    <td width="25%" align="right"><font
face="Arial">5,437.95</font></td>
  </tr>
</table>

</body>
</html>
```

Figure 23.28: Example13.htm.

The table is defined with `<table border="1" cellpadding="0" cellspacing="0" width="60%">`, where `border="1"` sets the border to a one pixel width; `Cellpadding="0"` sets the space around the contents of the cell to zero or no spacing; `Cellspacing="0"` sets the spacing between table cells to zero or no spacing; `Width="60%"` parameter tells the browser to scale the table to 60 percent of the available page space (it is generally a good idea to set the width to some percentage less than the total width of the page to provide a nice visual border around the table);

<tr></tr> row tags default to their default settings; and <th></th> tags define the headings that appear in the top row of the table. Notice that they appear in boldface text.

The <th> tag introduces two new parameters that may be used within the <th> or <td> tags. The width parameter controls the width of the cell in relation to the table. So if the table is set to 60 percent of the total browser page width, then a 25 percent width for the cell is 25 percent of 60 percent.

The align tag in this example is set to left or right. The valid choices are left, right, center, and justify.

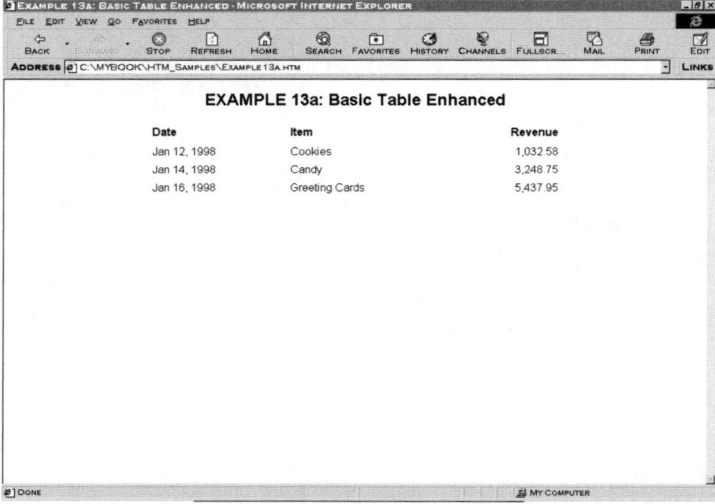

Figure 23.29: Basic table enhanced.

Figure 23.29 builds on the previous example. It centers the table on the page and suppresses the borders. Figure 23.30 shows the code

```
<html>

<head>
<title>Example 13a: Basic Table Enhanced</title>
</head>

<body bgcolor="#FFFFFF">

<p align="center"><font face="Arial"><strong><big><big>EXAMPLE 13a: Ba-
sic Table
Enhanced</big></big></strong></font></p>

<table border="0" cellpadding="5" cellspacing="0" width="60%"
align="center">
  <tr>
    <td width="25%" align="left"><font
face="Arial"><strong>Date</strong></font></td>
    <td width="25%"><font face="Arial"><strong>Item</strong></font></td>
    <td width="25%" align="right"><font face="Arial"><strong>Reve-
nue</strong></font></td>
  </tr>
  <tr>
    <td width="25%" align="left"><font face="Arial">Jan 12,
1998</font></td>
    <td width="25%"><font face="Arial">Cookies</font></td>
    <td width="25%" align="right"><font
face="Arial">1,032.58</font></td>
  </tr>
  <tr>
    <td width="25%" align="left"><font face="Arial">Jan 14,
1998</font></td>
    <td width="25%"><font face="Arial">Candy</font></td>
    <td width="25%" align="right"><font
face="Arial">3,248.75</font></td>
  </tr>
  <tr>
    <td width="25%" align="left"><font face="Arial">Jan 16,
1998</font></td>
    <td width="25%"><font face="Arial">Greeting Cards</font></td>
    <td width="25%" align="right"><font
face="Arial">5,437.95</font></td>
  </tr>
</table>

</body>
</html>
```

Figure 23.30: Example 13a—basic table enhanced.

The table in Figure 23.31 builds on the previous example by adding an `align="center"` parameter to the table tag. It also changes the `border="1"` to `border="0"`, which suppresses the borders around the table and its cells.

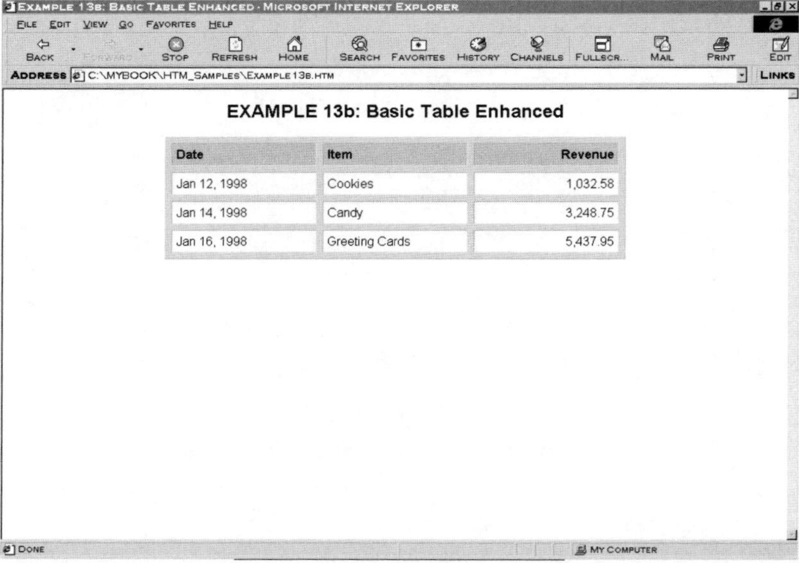

Date	Item	Revenue
Jan 12, 1998	Cookies	1,032.58
Jan 14, 1998	Candy	3,248.75
Jan 16, 1998	Greeting Cards	5,437.95

Figure 23.31: Basic table enhanced.

The table coded in Figure 23.32 is the same table depicted Figure 23.31, but it has a background color for the table, uses cellspacing, cellpadding, and inserts a color in each cell.

```
<html>

<head>
<title>Example 13b: Basic Table Enhanced</title>
</head>

<body bgcolor="#FFFFFF">

<p align="center"><font face="Arial"><strong><big><big>EXAMPLE 13b:
Basic Table Enhanced</big></big></strong></font></p>
<div align="center"><center>
```

Figure 23.32: Example13b.htm (part 1 of 2).

```
<table border="1" cellpadding="5" cellspacing="8" width="60%"
bgcolor="#C0C0C0" align="center">
  <tr>
    <td width="25%" align="left" bgcolor="#E1A253"><font
face="Arial"><strong>Date</strong></font></td>
    <td width="25%" bgcolor="#E1A253"><font
face="Arial"><strong>Item</strong></font></td>
    <td width="25%" align="right" bgcolor="#E1A253"><font
face="Arial"><strong> Revenue</strong></font></td>
  </tr>
  <tr>
    <td width="25%" align="left" bgcolor="#FFFACE"><font
face="Arial">Jan 12, 1998</font></td>
    <td width="25%" bgcolor="#FFFACE"><font
face="Arial">Cookies</font></td>
    <td width="25%" align="right" bgcolor="#FFFACE"><font
face="Arial">1,032.58</font></td>
  </tr>
  <tr>
    <td width="25%" align="left" bgcolor="#FFFACE"><font
face="Arial">Jan 14, 1998</font></td>
    <td width="25%" bgcolor="#FFFACE"><font
face="Arial">Candy</font></td>
    <td width="25%" align="right" bgcolor="#FFFACE"><font
face="Arial">3,248.75</font></td>
  </tr>
  <tr>
    <td width="25%" align="left" bgcolor="#FFFACE"><font
face="Arial">Jan 16, 1998</font></td>
    <td width="25%" bgcolor="#FFFACE"><font face="Arial">Greeting
Cards</font></td>
    <td width="25%" align="right" bgcolor="#FFFACE"><font
face="Arial">5,437.95</font></td>
  </tr>
</table>
</body>
</html>
```

Figure 23.32: Example13b.htm (part 2 of 2).

Notice in this example the settings for cellpadding, cellspacing, and border in the table tag. Notice also that `bgcolor=` is specified in the *<TABLE>* tag. This sets the gray background for the entire table.

Notice also that each *<TH>* and *<TD>* tag now includes a `bgcolor=` parameter to set the background color of each cell in the table.

With a very few tags, we have built some interesting and nice looking tables. Figure 23.30 is the form I use most often when displaying output retrieved from a database.

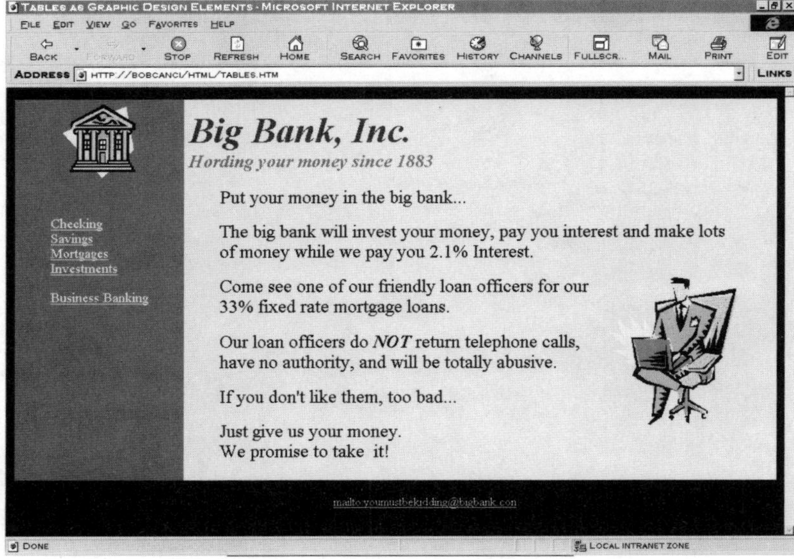

Figure 23.33: Tables to control layout.

In Figure 23.33 tables are used to lay out the page. The dark area is one column and the light area another column.

```
<html>

<head>
<title>Tables as Graphic Design Elements</title>
</head>

<body bgcolor="black" link="#FFFF00">
<div align="center"><center>

<table border="0" cellpadding="6" cellspacing="0" width="100%">
  <tr>
    <td width="15%" bgcolor="#008000" valign="middle" align="cen-
ter"><img src=
"facade.GIF"
    width="95" height="100" alt="Big Bank Logo"></td>
    <td width="96%" bgcolor="#FFFF00"><font
color="#0000FF"><em><strong><big><big><big><big>Big
    Bank, Inc.</big></big></big></big></strong></em></font><br>
    <font color="#FF0000"><em><strong><big><big>Hording your money
since 1883</big></big></strong></em></font></td>
```

Figure 23.34: BigBank.htm (part 1 of 2).

```
   </tr>
   <tr>
     <td width="17%" bgcolor="#008000" valign="top" align="left"
nowrap> <blockquote>
       <p><big><a href="business.htm">Checking<br>
       </a><a href="savings.htm">Savings<br>
       </a><a href="mort.htm">Mortgages<br>
       </a><a href="invest.htm">Investments</a></big></p>
       <p><big><a href="business.htm">Business Banking</a></big></p>
       <p><br>
       </p>
     </blockquote>
     </td>
     <td width="96%" bgcolor="#FFFF00"><blockquote>
       <big><big><em><strong><font
color="#FF0000"><p></font></strong></em><font color="#000000">Put
       your money in the big bank...</font><em><strong><font
color="#FF0000"></p>
       </font></strong></em></big></big><p><big><big><font
color="#000000">The big bank will
       invest your money, pay you interest and make lots of money while
we pay you 2.1% Interest.</font></big></big></p>
       <p><img src="bizman.GIF" width="168" height="200" alt="Your
banker"
       align="right"><font color="#000000"><big><big>Come see one of our
friendly loan officers
       for our 33% fixed rate mortgage loans. 
</big></big></font></p>
       <p><big><big><font color="#000000">Our loan officers do
<em><strong>NOT</strong></em>
       return telephone calls, have no authority, and will be totally
abusive.</font></big></big></p>
       <p><big><big><font color="#000000">If you don't like them, too
bad...</font></big></big></p>
       <p><font color="#000000"><big><big>Just give us your money. 
</big></big><br>
       <big><big>We promise to take  it!</big></big></font></p>
     </blockquote>
     </td>
   </tr>
</table>
</center></div>

<p align="center">Contact us:<font color="#8000FF">  <a

href="mailto:youmustbekidding@bigbank.con">mailto:youmustbekidding@
bigbank.con</a></font></p>
</body>
</html>
```

Figure 23.34: BigBank.htm (part 2 of 2).

Study the coding in Figure 23.34. You will see how we control the width and spacing of the page layout using tables. Notice that this example uses the center tag to center the table on the page instead of using the `align="center"` tag. Old browsers Version 3 and prior did not support the `align="center"` tag. If you have problems, use `<DIV align="center">` or just an old-fashioned `<CENTER>` tag to center your table on the page.

A few last notes on tables. You may embed an entire table within a single cell of a table. You may continue doing this as long as it makes visual sense to do so.

You may use the `colspan=` parameter to start text in one cell and skip over the top of one or more additional cells. This is useful for labeling sections of a table or producing a table row.

In Table 23.1, you use `colspan=3` to create a single row for the table's title and center the title in the row. The TOTALS cell uses a `colspan=2` to span the first two columns of the table. You can see that tables can be very flexible. Using COLSPAN and ROWSPAN, which does the same thing as COLSPAN but for rows, you have a great deal of control over tables.

Table 23.1: COLSPAN Example

Region	Percentage of Total Sales	Sales
West	70.00%	70,000,000
North	20.00%	20,000,000
East	10.00%	10,000,000
Totals		*100,000,000*

ADVANCED LAYOUT WITH FRAMES

In 1996, frames were a new feature on the Web. Thousands of technically oriented Web designers felt that because this new feature was introduced by Netscape, they were obliged to try them out on their Web sites.

Most frame-based Web sites were built to illustrate their designer's technical expertise with HTML. A typical design of a frame-based site featured a frame across the top of the page containing the heading and a logo. A narrow frame down the left side would contain links to other pages on the site. That left the lower right corner for the Web site's content. When you clicked a link in the frame on the left, new content appeared in the lower right frame space.

IBM's AS/400 Web site is built in this manner. Because it was going to be an extremely high volume Web site, with more than 1,000 hits per second on peak occasions, it had to be an artistically attractive Web site, but also had to handle the volume without shutting down under the load. Frames are an excellent choice to handle volume and still deliver artwork and images.

When you use frames, you reduce the amount of data that must be transferred between the Web site and the user. This is especially true when a user views many pages on the Web site. Only the lower right-hand portion of the IBM Web site needs to be transmitted to build each different page.

Another valid use for frames is when dealing with the execution of a CGI program provided by a vendor. This program puts out its own HTML page because of calling the program. You don't have source and can't modify the program; it simply does what it needs to do.

If you implement this program as a standard, full-screen, called CGI program, your user sees the program's output and is effectively out of your Web site. Will the user back up several steps and revisit your site? Better not take the chance. A simple way to avoid this is to create a frame set consisting of a top border frame and a bottom frame.

A specific example of this technique is the `http://www.ignite400.org` file upload function that allows users to upload and share files with other members.

Frames also can be used, to a limited degree, to hide page names from the user. The name of the frameset is displayed in the browser address field. This name remains in view of the user although the contents of the page frames change. Don't be too secure with this trick, because the user can still view the source of your frame and find the real name of each frame.

Another excellent use of frames is interactive applications using CGI programs or Net.Data macros. You can link to a frameset which calls programs or invokes macros that build the content of your pages.

Assume you have an insurance company claims processing application. You could put a title and some control buttons in a frame across the top of the page, list claims in one frame, reserve space for an image of the accident, and put another frame on the page that provides the claims adjuster with a form to update information about the claim. If you clicked a new claim in the list, the image and form would be updated to reflect the new data.

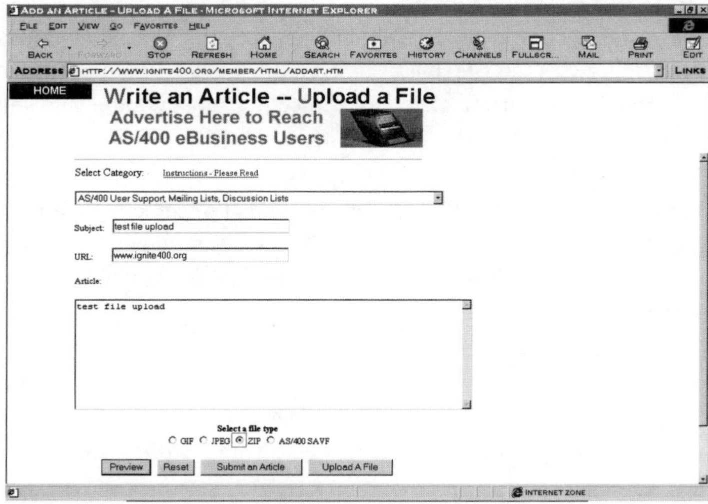

Figure 23.35: A simple two-frame page – Frame 1.

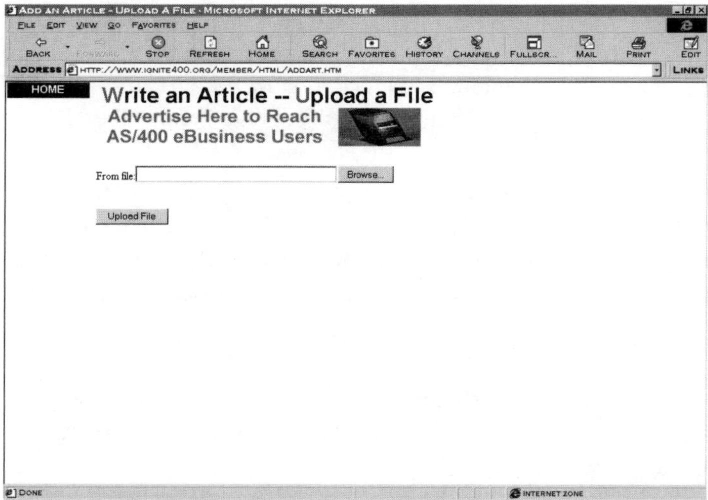

Figure 23.36: Another frame – Frame 2.

In Figure 23.36, we use two frames. The top or header frame is constant while the bottom part of the page changes as the user interacts with the form.

The top frame always features a navigation button that returns the user to a selected base point in the Web site. Trying to do this application without frames would leave the user at a point of no return because the next program to execute when Upload File is clicked, produces output that you have no control over. You cannot add a link or do anything with the output of the program.

There is one special HTML file called the FRAMESET that must be used to implement frames. All other frames are standard HTML pages. You target the page into a frame with the *TARGET=* parameter of the *<A ...>* anchor block.

FRAMESET

The *<FRAMESET>* tag contains no visible data. It defines the structure of the browser page that you are building and causes the browser to load the HTML pages specified into each frame that you have defined.

```
<html>

<head>
<title>Bob Cancilla's Laboratory</title>
<meta name="GENERATOR" content="Microsoft FrontPage 3.0">
</head>

<frameset framespacing="1" border="false" frameborder="0" rows="119,*">
  <frame name="header" scrolling="no" target="main"
src="bobcheader.htm">  ß first frame
  <frame name="main" src="about.htm" scrolling="auto">  ß second frame
  <noframes>
  <body>
  <p>This page uses frames, but your browser doesn't support them.</p>
  </body>
  </noframes>
</frameset>
</html>
```

Figure 23.37: Frames1.htm.

Figure 23.37 shows the FRAMESET HTML page that defines the two examples illustrated above. The FRAMESET HTML page does actually display. It defines the attributes of each of the two frames that will be displayed (height, location, borders, scrollbars, etc.). It then names the two HTML pages that will be displayed.

Notice that the *<FRAMESET>* tag is inside the *<HEAD></HEAD>*. Notice also that there is no *<BODY>* tag on this page. A very common and fatal error in working with frames is to put the *<FRAMESET>* tag inside the *<BODY>* tag. This will fail and cause unpredictable results.

Let's examine the parameters of the *<FRAMESET>* tag:

- *BORDER=0* defines a frame without borders. By default, frames are drawn with a border much like the border that outlines a table. This parameter sets the width of the border in pixels.

- *FRAMEBORDER=0* indicates that no frame is desired around each frame. Both FRAMEBORDER and BORDER are required to ensure compatibility between Microsoft and Netscape browsers.

- *FRAMESPACING=0* determines the space in pixels between frame content and the frame border.

- *ROWS="105,*"* indicates that we split the page into two frames vertically. There will be a top frame that is 105 pixels in height and the "*" indicates that the bottom frame fills the remainder of the page. You could define three frames with *ROWS="20%,*,20%"*. I normally recommend using percentages, because the browsers will adjust better. Sometimes it is necessary to specify pixels.

- *COLS=* splits the frame into columns; the syntax is identical to ROWS. You can combine both ROWS and COLS to split the page into many little windows.

FRAME TAG

The *<FRAME>* tag is required for each frame defined in the *<FRAMESET>* via *ROWS=* and *COLS=*.

```
<FRAME NAME="header" SRC="/member/html/addart_header.htm"
SCROLLING="auto" MARGINWIDTH="2" MARGINHEIGHT="1" FRAMEBORDER="no"
BORDER="0" NORESIZE>
```

Figure 23.38: Code to define frame type, size, position.

Figure 23.38 defines the top frame for the IGNITe/400 Web page. It must have a *NAME=* parameter if you are going to refer to the frame.

The *SRC=* defines the content of the frame. In this case it is a standard HTML page called *addart_header.htm* It is defined in this case using a relative address.

SCROLLING="auto" lets the browser manage scrolling. If the content of the frame will not fit within the 105 pixels that were allocated on the FRAMESET, then the browser displays a scroll bar and lets the user scroll the page within the frame. Other valid values for *SCROLLING=* are YES (always display scroll bars) and NO (never display scroll bars).

MARGINWIDTH="2" MARGINHEIGHT="1" control the width of a white space border around the frame content.

FRAMEBORDER="no" indicates that no border around the frame is desired.

BORDER=0 specifies the size of the frame border. Both FRAMEBORDER and BORDER are required to ensure compatibility between Microsoft and Netscape browsers.

NORESIZE="yes" prevents the user from resizing the frame. If you specified *"NO"* or left the parameter out, then the user could drag borders of the frame up, down, left, or right to increase or decrease the size of the frame on the page.

LINKING BETWEEN FRAMES

As mentioned before, the *<A HREF=...>* tag is used to target a frame.

When FRAMESET loads the pages specified within its page, it assumes that a user will click the SUBMIT button in the first IGNITe/400 example. It executes a Net.Data macro because of the *ACTION=* parameter specified in the HTML form.

ACTION="/member/cgi-dta/upload.mac/main"No target= is specified so the page will replace the current frame.

We could also put a link on the page that might look like:

<A HREF="/member/html/new_top.htm" target="header">

This link causes the page to replace the current content of the top frame, which is named *header*.

To have a link in the header that replaces the main part of the screen, use the link: *<A HREF="/member/html/new_main.htm" target="main">*. This time, the main page is replaced because the frame was named *main*.

There are four frame names with special meaning and actions:

- `_blank` loads the page referenced in the link into a new unnamed browser window.
- `_self` loads the page into the frame where the link is replacing the content of the frame.
- `_Top` causes the page to load as a full-screen page and escape from frames completely. I always use this tag when linking to another Web site; it is extremely rude to keep a user locked into your frameset!
- `_paren` loads over the parent frame of the frame containing this link. Used when multiple nested framesets are used.

A last word about frames. Framesets can be nested within each other. The first frameset can link to another frameset that in turn could link to another frameset. I've not done this and hope I don't have to, but it is nice to know I could!

FORMS AND INTERACTIVE HTML

Forms are the means by which you and your user communicate. There are two ways to send the content of a form back to your computer: You can e-mail it using the MAILTO: protocol tag described earlier, or you can send the data to a CGI program for processing.

We will use CGI from this point forward. Just be aware that if you do mail a form to yourself, you will get a funny looking message that contains `Name=value`, where name is the name you assigned to the field when you created it, and value is the value that the user typed in to the field. It may be the poor man's way of developing interactive Web-based systems, but it works. Once you get the e-mail message, you could parse it down with a PC program or editor. Most people who use this technique print the messages and hand them to data entry operators for re-keying into an application program.

You could even create a file for upload to an AS/400, but the method we are going to describe is a bit more direct and easier to use.

THE <FORM> TAG

A form is a container with one or more fields and a method of interacting with your server. You may define many forms on the same HTML page. The tag has two parameters:

The *ACTION=* parameter is the URL where the data collected from the user is to be directed. It is normally a CGI script (program). The code *ACTION="/cgi-bin/myprog.pgm"* sends output to the CGI program *myprog.pgm*, which would be executed by the server and passed the input from the form.

The *METHOD=* parameter instructs the browser how to send the data to the server. There are two methods in common use.

- The POST method is by far the best choice It allows you to send virtually unlimited amounts of input to the server. The server writes the data to a special STDIN file that is then made available to your program.
- The GET method is commonly used by many novice Webmasters. It sends data to the server in the QUERY_STRING as name value pairs. However, there is a 4096-byte limit on the query string on the AS/400. The other negative aspect of this method is the fact that the data is visible to the user via the URL.

I recommend using the POST method. A sample form tag would look like:

```
<FORM METHOD="POST" ACTION="/CGI-BIN/myprog.pgm">
```

After you define the form, its ACTION, and METHOD, you define the form's input fields, selection boxes, and buttons. Figure 23.39 illustrates all currently supported type of fields.

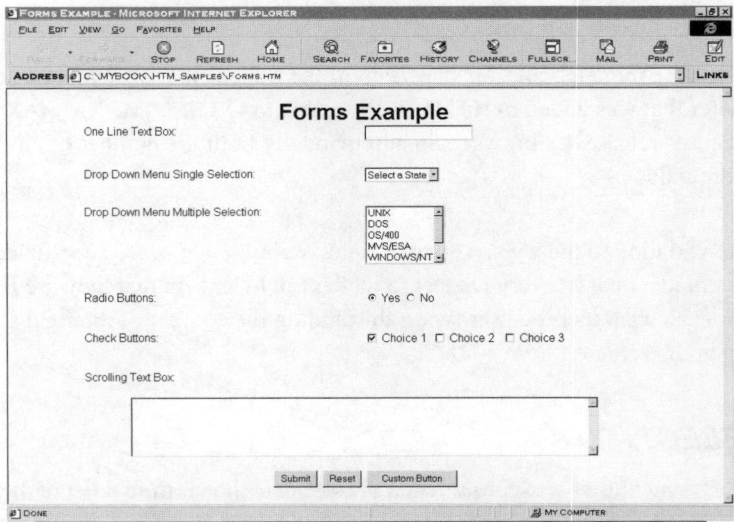

Figure 23.39: Forms.htm—the currently available form elements in HTML.

TEXT BOX

The one-line text box is the most commonly used forms element in HTML. It allows a user to type characters, numbers, or mixed characters and numbers into the field. The content typed by the user is returned to the server in a name value pair identified by the name of the field.

```
<input type="text" name="textbox" size="20">
```

The preceding `<INPUT>` tag defines the text box. It is identified as a text box through the `type="text"` parameter. If the user typed the value *08/01/1998* into the field, the browser returns *textbox=08%2F01%2F1998* to the server. If the user typed *Bob Cancilla* in the field then *textbox=Bob%20Cancilla* is returned to the server. If the user typed *1234.00* in the field, then *textbox=1234.00* would be returned to the server.

This example illustrates three points:

- Fields are returned to the server as a name value pair, with the name being that which is defined in the input tag. The value is the value typed by the user.
- If spaces or special characters are typed by the user, they are URL encoded using HTML's ASCII hexadecimal encoding scheme. If you use a native language CGI program, you must decode these characters.
- There is no concept of data typing in HTML. All data is returned as a character string to the server.

The `size="20"` parameter controls the width of the field as it appears on the screen. A new parameter that was added to HTML 3.2 is called MAXLENGTH. The MAXLENGTH parameter causes release 4.x browsers to automatically limit the number of characters typed into the field.

There is one variation to the `type="text"` field, the `type="password"` field. Password fields are identical in every respect to the text field, except that they are filled with asterisks for each character the user types, thus hiding the content of the field from anyone looking at the screen.

THE <SELECT> TAG

The `<SELECT>` tag allows a user to select a pre-defined choice from a list of valid choices. This is an easy-to-implement feature and is a great tool for assisting your user in filling out a form and insuring valid content.

There are two variations of the *<SELECT>* tag. The first is the drop-down selection list illustrated in Figure 23.39 as the field containing the words Select a State. The code appears in Figure 23.40.

```
<select name="state" size="1">
    <option selected>Select a State</option>
    <option value="AK">Alaska</option>
    <option value="AZ">Arizona</option>
    <option value="CA">California</option>
 </select>
```

Figure 23.40: Coding a <select> tag.

The *<select ...>* tag identifies this form element as a selection list type element. The *name="state"* parameter identifies the name of the field that will be returned to the server. The *parameter size="1"* defines the number of rows visible to the user. A select tag with a size of one row tells the browser to display the drop-down selection list form of the element.

Choices are defined via the *<option ...>* tag. The keyword *selected* indicates that if the user does not choose another option, the value of this option will be returned to the server.

Notice that the *selected* option does not have a *value=* parameter. This causes HTML 3.2-capable browsers to generate an error and instruct the user to make a selection.

The value between the *<option ...>* and *</option>* tags is the prompt that displays in the list. The *value="AK"* parameter specified within the *<option >* tag is the value that will be returned to the server. This select statement returns *state=AK* to the server if the user clicked on the option for Alaska.

This implementation of the *<select>* tag allows the user to select one and only one item from the list.

The second form of the select list is illustrated as the box with the five operating system choices displayed in Figure 23.39. This form of the select allows a user to choose one or more items from the list.

Clicking a single item causes it to display in reverse video on the browser and marks it as selected. The browser uses standard Microsoft Windows and UNIX XWINDOWS conventions (press CTRL while left clicking additional items to select multiple choices). This technique is fine if a user is experienced with the keystrokes necessary to make multiple selections. It can be problematic for less experienced computer users. The code is shown in Figure 23.41.

```
<select name="computer_os" size="5" multiple>
   <option value="1">UNIX</option>
   <option value="2">DOS</option>
   <option value="3">OS/400</option>
   <option value="4">MVS/ESA</option>
   <option value="5">WINDOWS NT</option>
   <option value="6">OS/2</option>
   <option value="7">VSE</option>
</select>
```

Figure 23.41: Coding a multiple-choice <select> tag.

This form of the `<select ...>` tag is very similar to the single-selection form described above. The major difference is that a `size="5"` (rows) and the special parameter "*multiple*" has been specified.

The `<option ...>` tags also are identical to those described for the single-selection form, with the exception that the size and multiple keyword parameters are defined.

The `size="5"` indicates that five rows will be displayed. Notice that we have defined seven `<options>`. Because there are more options than the number of rows that we want to display, the browser automatically displays the list with a scroll bar.

The multiple parameter instructs the browser to allow the user to select more than one entry from the list.

The data is returned to the browser in the variable named COMPUTER_OS. Assume that the user selected UNIX, DOS, MVS/ESA, and OS/2 from the list. The data returned to the server would be returned in the form `computer_os=1,2,4,6`.

RADIO BUTTONS

The radio button metaphor was developed based on the example of the buttons on a car radio. When you press one button, it becomes the selected choice. One and only one radio button can be selected at a time. In Figure 23.39, a simple yes or no example is used to illustrate the use of radio buttons. The code is shown in Figure 23.42. Any number of buttons can be specified.

```
<input type="radio" value="Y" checked name="radio"> Yes
<input type="radio" name="radio" value="N"> No
```

Figure 23.42: Coding a radio button.

This tag is very straightforward. It uses one `<input type="radio" ...>` tag for each button on the form. The `name= parameter` ties them together and makes them work as a single unit. All radio buttons that are part of the same form element must have the same name.

In this example, the named variable radio contains the value "Y" or "N." If the user clicks the "NO" button, then `radio=N` is returned to the server. The "Y" value has the keyword *checked* coded within its `<input ..>` tag. This makes it the default choice. The value "Y" is returned to the server if the user does nothing.

CHECK BOXES

The check box is a simple form element that allows the user to click one or many of the boxes. It is implemented with the code in Figure 23.43.

```
<input type="checkbox" name="check" value="1" checked> Choice 1 
<input type="checkbox" name="check" value="2"> Choice 2  
<input type="checkbox" name="check" value="3"> Choice 3
```

Figure 23.43: Coding a check box.

In this example, `type="checkbox"` identifies the element as a checkbox. As with radio buttons, all boxes with the same `name=` parameter are part of the same set of check boxes. In this example `name="check"` ties all three of the boxes together.

The item labeled "Choice 1" contains the keyword *checked*. If no other options are selected (clicked) by the user, then a value of "1" is returned to the server. The user may select one or many. If the user clicks Choice 1 and Choice 3, then `check=1,3` is returned to the server.

THE <TEXTAREA> TAG

The `<TEXTAREA>` tag creates a scrolling text box that allows the user to type freeform text into the field. This field is appropriate for recording large blocks of descriptive text. The code is shown in Figure 23.44.

```
<textarea rows="5" name="scroll_text" cols="80"></textarea>
```

Figure 23.44: Coding a <textarea> tag for freeform text entry.

The *<TEXTAREA>* tag is identified by name. The `rows="5"` defines the number of rows that text area box will occupy on the screen. If the user types more than five rows in our example, the browser displays a scroll bar. The tag does not limit the amount of text a user may type.

The `cols="80"` parameter controls the visible width of the form on the browser page. It does not restrict the width of the line. In fact, a user must hit the Return key on the keyboard to start a new line of text. If he does not, the box automatically scrolls to the right until the user hits Enter to place all text on a single line.

As of HTML 3.2, a new parameter, `wrap=` (left, center, right, or justify), was added to the *<TEXTAREA>* tag. When you specify `wrap="left"` or `wrap= "justify"`, text wrapping is enabled and text is wrapped to the next line at the `cols=limit`.

A word of caution: The `wrap=` parameter has no effect on how the data is stored. In fact, unless you output the stored text to an area defined by *<PRE>* and terminated by *</PRE>*, the user's carriage returns are ignored by the browser.

BUTTONS

Form buttons cause the browser to transmit the completed form data to the server for processing. The browser and client computer are in complete control while a user is entering data in a form. The browser knows what the form elements look like. It knows the properties of each form element and how to process each element. There is no interaction with the server until the user clicks a button of `type="submit"`.

There are two types of button:

- The Submit button causes data to be transmitted back to the server. It causes the server to output the field names and values to either the QUERY_STRING or write them to the STDIN file and invoke the URL listed in the form's *ACTION=* parameter.
- A Reset button (`type="reset"`) is processed by the browser to restore the form to the condition it was in when it was first displayed on the browser. It clears all

data entry fields and resets all conditions. There is no interaction with the server. Figure 23.47 shows the coding for both types of buttons.

You sometimes see forms that display data in a form and then give the user an Update and a Delete button. If you click Update, the data in the database is updated with the values typed by the user on the form. If the user clicks Delete, then the record is deleted.

```
<input type="submit" value="Submit" name="button_1"> 
<input type="reset" value="Reset" name="B2"> 
<input type="submit" value="Custom Button" name="button_1">
```

Figure 23.45: Coding the Submit and Reset buttons.

Figure 23.39 illustrates the three buttons defined in Figure 23.45. This example implements two Submit buttons and a Reset button. When the Submit button is clicked, the server script processes code that deals with a standard Submit action. If the user clicks on the Custom button, the server script may choose to perform different processing.

- The `type=` parameter determines if this is a Submit or a Reset button.
- The `name=` gives the name of the name value pair returned by the browser to the server when the user clicks a `type="submit"` button.
- The `value=` parameter shows the name displayed on the button in the browser and is the value that is transmitted to the server.

If the user clicks on the Submit button in our example, `"button_1=Submit"` is transmitted to the server.

If the user clicks the Custom button in our example, `"button_1=Custom Button"` is transmitted to the server.

HIDDEN FIELDS

Hidden fields are a primary tool of the Web site developer. They are essential to facilitating navigation between HTML forms and CGI scripts. Because Web servers are stateless, the server and CGI program have no way of knowing what was just sent to the browser. The server does not even know that the user ever visited the site. Hidden fields give the user the illusion of an ongoing "conversation" between the server and browser.

Suppose that you create a simple query form that contains one text field where the user enters a customer number and clicks a Submit key. The CGI program retrieves information about the customer and displays the output in a form that allows the user to update the customer information.

Without asking the user to type the customer number again, how is the customer number sent back to the browser? The answer is a hidden field. You store the value of the customer number in a hidden field along with a name. An example is shown in Figure 23.46.

```
<input type="hidden" name="custno" value="1234">
<input type="hidden" name="terr" value="LA">
```

Figure 23.46:Coding a hidden field.

The hidden field tag is extremely simple. It uses a `type="hidden"` parameter to identify it as a hidden tag, a `name=` parameter to assign a name to the tag, and `value=` tag to assign a value to the field. Hidden fields are not hidden from users if they display the HTML source, but are "hidden" from view on the screen. The value returned to the server in the first example would be `custno=1234` and `terr=LA` in the second example.

MULTIMEDIA

Today everyone wants to put the latest and greatest technology on his Web site. We want to play music or speeches, we want to display full motion video with an audio channel, streaming audio and streaming video. Can the AS/400 do this?

Of course, it can! The AS/400 can serve any type of file; it is up to your browser to process it. The only limit is that, until the manufacturers of live audio and video software port their capture software to the AS/400, AS/400 Webmasters can't serve live audio or video.

VIDEO

There are three ways to embed audio and video into your Web pages and/or play background audio automatically when the page is loaded.

A standard method that uses an HTML link is shown in Figure 23.47.

```
<A HREF=”mymovie.avi”>View My movie</A>
```

Figure 23.47: Code to play a movie in a Web page.

This method downloads an AVI file to the PC and uses the PC's movie player to play the movie when the user clicks on the link.

Microsoft Internet Explorer supports a new parameter for the *<IMG>* keyword called DYNSRC. If you enter the code shown in Figure 23.48, Explorer seamlessly downloads the video and plays it as soon as it is loaded within the Web page. You can still code an SRC parameter so that browsers that don't support the DYNSRC parameter display a static image.

```
<IMG DYNSRC="mymovie.avi"  width="160" height="120" SRC="staticpic.GIF">
```

Figure 23.48: Using the DYNSRC parameter to seamlessly load and play a movie.

You could put the whole thing inside a link so if a Netscape user clicked the image, the video file would play. There is a great deal happening in this area. Check you browser documentation and visit Microsoft (*www.microsoft.com*), Netscape (*home.netscape.com*), and the W3 Consortium (*www.w3.org*) to check out the latest in video technology.

Netscape uses the *<EMBED>* tag to play audio and video. It looks like the code in Figure 23.49.

```
<EMBED SRC="mymovie.avi" WIDTH="160" HEIGHT="120" ALIGN="left"
   AUTOPLAY="true" LOOP="true" ONCURSOR="play">
```

Figure 23.49: Netscape's <EMBED> tag for audio and video.

The Netscape tag gives you greater control over your video or audio. If you want it to play once and stop, code *LOOP="false"*. If you do not want it to play automatically, code *AUTOPLAY="false"*.

Be cautious and conservative in putting video on your Web site. I personally don't use the Microsoft tag due to the tremendous size of video files and the amount of time required to download them. A relatively short video ranges between 1MB and 3MB in size and, at 28.8kbs, can take more than 20 minutes to download.

Advances are constantly being made in terms of higher bandwidth for users and for video image compression to reduce file size. Video will soon be feasible, but it is highly questionable today with slow dial-up bandwidth.

AUDIO

Audio is a very popular addition to some Web sites. There are two forms in common use: background music that plays when the Web page loads and files that are played when clicked on by the user.

To let a user click a link and play an audio file, just code a standard link as shown in Figure 23.50.

```
<A HREF="mysoundfile.wav">Click here to play sounds</A>
```

Figure 23.50: A link to play an audio file.

Microsoft and Netscape each have their own way of playing sounds dynamically when the page loads. The W3 Consortium is working on a compromise that both can agree on, but for now, know that you must code separately for both.

Microsoft uses the tag *<BGSOUND="mysound.wav">*. Just stick it in your Web page somewhere after the *<BODY>* tag. The file loads and plays. Netscape ignores it as if it does not exist. Netscape uses the *<EMBED>* tag to play audio files as well as video files.

To handle both Microsoft and Netscape in the same page, code something like the snippet shown in Figure 23.51.

```
<BGSOUND="mysound.wav">
<EMBED SRC="mysound.wav" AUTOPLAY="true" LOOP="true"
ONCURSOR="play">
<NOEMBED>
<A HREF="mysound.wav">Click here to play audio</A>
</NOEMBED>
```

Figure 23.51: Coding audio for both Microsoft and Netscape browsers.

In this scenario, a Microsoft browser plays the sound because of the *<BGSOUND>* tag, while ignoring the *<EMBED>* and *<NOEMBED>* tags. A Netscape browser ignores the *<BGSOUND>* tag and uses the *<NOEMBED>* *</NOEMBED>* block to play audio files in the *<EMBED>* tag. Another browser would use the *<A HREF=...>* tag in the NOEMBED section.

Do you want streaming audio or video that plays as the file is being transferred from the server to the browser? Checkout RealAudio at *www.realaudio.com*. RealAudio provides add-ins for browsers to process and play audio and video as it is received from the server.

JAVA APPLETS

To date, Java applets have provided some degree of animation and special-purpose applications to enhance Web pages that cannot be done in other languages or via HTML. One very good use of Java applets is to display and format business data into business graphics.

Figure 23.52 is a sample from the demo section of the *www.netcharts.com* Web page, where they are demonstrating their NetCharts Java applet-based product is downloaded. You can easily install and run this product on an AS/400 and populate the parameters via IBM's Net.Data macro language.

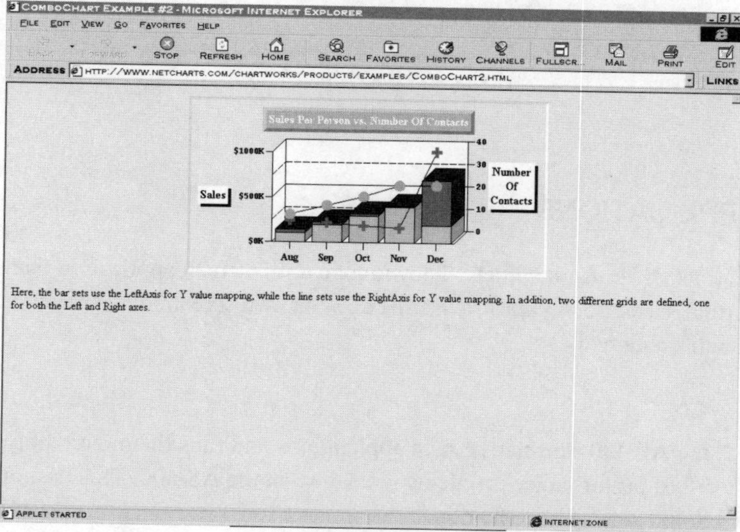

Figure 23.52: JavaApplet.htm.

This applet is implemented in HTML, as shown in Figure 23.53.

The *<APPLET>* tag allows you to embed an applet in your Web page. The *<APPLET>* tag defines the location of the applet on the server. The *<PARAM>* tag defines the parameters coded in the macro for expected input. Please read up on this tag and its parameters in an appropriate Java manual or Web page.

Note that the *<IMG SRC=...>* tag is coded immediately prior to the *</APPLET>* tag. If your browser does not support Java, it will process this statement and display the GIF image file referenced in the tag.

```
<center>
<applet name="combochart"
       codebase="../classes2.01"
       code="NFComboChartApp.class" width="500" height="250">
 <param name="NFParamScript" value='Background= (antiquewhite, RECESS,
4);
Header=("Sales Per Person vs. Number Of Contacts");
HeaderBox=(lightGray, RAISED, 5);
...
Grid=(black, white, black), (black, null, null);
GridLine=(HORIZONTAL, SOLID),   (HORIZONTAL, DASHED);
GridAxis=(BOTTOM, LEFT),(BOTTOM, RIGHT);'>
<IMG SRC="NOJava.GIF">
</applet>
</center>
```

Figure 23.53: Java applet to display business data in chart form.

JAVA APPLICATIONS

Java applications differ from applets. They invoke a full screen application that runs in the Java Virtual Machine in your browser. It does its own screen management and is completely self-contained.

As of V4R2, the AS/400 runs native Java applications and runs them incredibly fast. You may have heard of performance problems with Java on the AS/400. This is simply not true on the AS/400 side of the equation.

The problem with Java is that you must download the client piece to the client PC or browser before it will run. When processing for that piece of data is completed, the Java application is discarded. Although this represents one of the purported benefits of Java, it is also its downfall. Dial-up lines are just too slow to support Java. When we have high-speed remote access to the Internet for remote users, Java will become truly viable to Web site designers. (It may, however, be perfectly suitable for intranet applications running 100MB Ethernet internally.)

JAVASCRIPT

JavaScript has absolutely nothing to do with Java. It is a browser-based scripting language developed by Netscape. Microsoft calls its version J-Script.

JavaScript programming is way beyond the scope of this book. I recommend that you read *JavaScript Unleashed* by Richard Wagner, published by Sams Net (ISBN 1-57521-306-0).

See also `http://www.yahoo.com`. Look in the WWW section and then in JavaScript. There are over 30 Web sites that provide education and sample code (some applications are quite robust).

REFERENCES

First and foremost, visit `http://www.yahoo.com` and look in the WWW category and in the HTML, HTTP, and CGI programming areas. There are hundreds of references to tutorials, specifications, and reference pages.

My personal favorite for learning HTML is *snowwhite.it.brighton.ac.uk/~mas/mas/courses/html/html.html*. It is loaded with examples and simple, easy-to-understand explanations.

An excellent reference site for tips and techniques and some HTML sample code is *www.htmlgoodies.com/html_ref.html*.

Another very comprehensive site is *www.geocities.com/SunsetStrip/Alley/5616/index.html*.

And, of course we mustn't forget the ultimate authority for HTML, HTTP, and emerging technology for the Web: *www.w3.org/MarkUp/*.

home.netscape.com/eng/mozilla/3.0/handbook/javascript/ is the ultimate authority for JavaScript on the Web. This is Netscape's official JavaScript Web site.

www.webcoder.com/index_real.html provides tutorials and sample JavaScript code that you can simply borrow for use in your Web site. Dozens of samples and numerous references to other JavaScript Web sites are included.

publib.boulder.ibm.com/pubs/html/as400/java/java.htm is perhaps IBM's most comprehensive site for Java information on the Web.

CGI Programming with AS/400 Languages

24

This chapter outlines the basics of CGI programming in native AS/400 languages. While this topic is largely outside the scope of this book, I have provided this high-level overview so that you can be aware of the technique. Some "real" programmers may want to write native language programs.

There is a slight performance advantage with native language CGI programming, but this advantage is easily overcome with the current generation of AS/400 hardware. If you have a D40, you might need this approach, but as a matter of personal preference, I choose alternatives that are easier and faster.

In Chapter 22, we described the basic overview of the CGI environment. In Chapter 23, we described how a browser user displays an HTML form, types input on the form, and clicks an HTML button on the page. Clicking the button passes the data entered on the form to the Web server and requests that the program identified on the form (`ACTION =` ...) be invoked.

Now let's look at what happens on the server and what the server and program must do. Messages to the server always contain a request header and may contain a request body. All of the special characters and spaces in the data transmitted to the server are escaped or URL encoded as *%nn*, where *nn* is an ASCII hexadecimal representation of the character.

There are several methods of passing data to the CGI program. We will deal with the GET and the POST method. The other method is the PUT method, which is used only in very special cases.

To summarize the steps that occur during the CGI program's life cycle, consider the following:

- The browser displays the initial HTML form
- The user fills in the form and submits the request
- The browser requests the script's URL and transmits the data entered by the user to the server
- The server receives the request and prepares the script input data
- The server calls the script program
- The script receives input from the Web server by calling server-provided APIs
- The script parses the input and removes URL encoding
- The script performs any required processing
- The script prepares any output
- The script returns its output to the server by calling the server-provided APIs
- The script program ends
- The server sends output to the browser
- The browser displays the output

GET METHOD

As we described in Chapter 22, the GET method passes data to the server in the QUERY_STRING, which is attached to the end of the URL. The QUERY_STRING in total is parsed and stored in an environment variable by all Web servers. A typical QUERY_STRING might look something like this:

```
?custno=1234578A12&fone=%28512%29+894-0704&itemno=AEX1234&qty=10
```

This QUERY_STRING passes the variables `custno`, `fone`, `itemno`, and `qty` to the CGI program that will process the data. As you can see, the data is stored in `name` = value pairs.

In the `fone` variable's value, note the character string %28, the URL encoding for a left parenthesis , %29 the URL encoding for a right parenthesis, and the plus sign, the URL encoding for a space.

Table 24.1: Query_String Name/Value Pairs

Name	Value
custno	12345678A12
fone	%28512%29+894-0704
itemno	AEX1234
qty	10

There is a 4,096-byte limit to the size of a QUERY_STRING. This space can be quickly exhausted. When the space is exhausted, no errors occur, you simply don't get all of your input.

POST METHOD

The POST method uses a special AS/400 file called STDIN to receive the data. All form input data (unlimited size) is placed in the HTTP message body and written to the STDIN file.

At present, only a C, C++, or Java program running on the AS/400 can read and write IFS stream files directly. All other programs must call APIs to access this data. IBM provides server-specific APIs to retrieve data from the STDIN file.

As is the case with the GET method and the QUERY_STRING, data written to STDIN is stored in `name` = value pairs. It is also escaped or URL encoded.

CGI was first developed on UNIX systems and written in the C programming language. The CGI interface was simple, but the burden of work was placed on the programmer.

CGI OVERVIEW

Data exists in two places in all computer systems: the environment and STDIN. As described in Chapter 22, the environment is a large but fixed area of memory that is shared among all programs running in the same process (or *job* on the AS/400). The other area that is shared by programs running in the same job is the STDIN file.

When a CGI program is called, the first thing it must do is retrieve input from the Web server. This process varies slightly depending on which Web server is used and what method is used to invoke the program.

The program must parse its input fields and remove the URL encoding. In most cases (standard HTML and standard text), the servers convert the ASCII text received into EBCIDIC that you can process. There are, however, some types of data that are not automatically translated from ASCII to EBCIDIC by the server. You will not generally encounter these types, but they do exist.

Once you parse out the variables, their names and values, and decode the data, you may then perform any required processing. At this point, your program is like any other program running on the AS/400 and may do anything that any other program can do.

When the processing is done, your program must begin formatting output and writing output back to a special file called STDOUT. Like STDIN, STDOUT is a special stream file that is shared by all programs running in the job (or process, on other systems).

HTTP HEADERS

The first thing you must write out is an HTTP header[1]. A header contains HTTP instructions to the browser that tell it how to process the data it receives from the server. A typical header like:

```
Content-type: text/html
```

This is the minimum data required. Please note that the HTTP header must be terminated with two carriage return line feed characters. Your program will fail if they are not there.

After you have formatted and written your header (with its two CRLFs), you may begin preparing your output.

You must write all HTML tags and variable data created by your program. When using RPG, COBOL, or even C, C++, or Java, there is no nice or easy way to format your HTML and merge your variable data. Every tag and every variable must be handcrafted.

You must also URL encode every character that requires encoding. Finally, you write your output to STDOUT—limit output to about 80 characters per line so you can read it when you do a View Source on your browser. If you don't limit the line length, it will appear as one

1 There are many additional headers and parameters you may need to build. See I/Net's WebServer/400 manual at www.inetmi.com or IBM's *Web Programming Guide Version 4.2 for AS/400* GC41-5435-01, which is available at: as400bks.rochester.ibm.com.

long string at the top of your browser. You need not limit the overall length, but limiting the per-line length certainly makes it easier to read when you use View Source.

You then return back to the server that called you.

The server then sends the data to the browser, and you can see how many changes you must make to get the output to look like you had originally intended. It will be a true miracle if your first try produces a usable HTML page! I hope you have a fast development machine because you will be recompiling your program every time you want to make a minor cosmetic change to the appearance of the page.

This process is complex and can be frustrating if you don't get all the details just right. Vendor-provided APIs can make your life a little easier, but CGI programming is not for the faint of heart! As I said, it takes a *real programmer* to do this stuff. IBM, however, offers a set of APIs that can make life easier for the CGI programmer.

IBM ICS/ICSS APIs

IBM supports only the ILE program model. There are some code samples and a great deal of useful information to assist you at the IBM Technical Studio: `http://www.as400.ibm.com/tstudio/index.htm`. When writing CGI programs, you also will want to refer to the document *Web Programming Guide for IBM HTTP Server for AS/400,*" which may be found at: `www.as400.ibm.com/tstudio/http/docs/docs.htm`.

QTMHGETENV

This is IBM's version of Get Environment Variable. It retrieves a named variable from the server job's environment.

QTMHPUTENV

This API allows you to create or modify an environment variable. It is useful for communication between programs in the same job. It is rare that you would ever modify a server-provided environment variable.

QTMHRDSTIN

This is the Read From STDIN API. It allows languages other than C, C++, or Java to read from STDIN. The API translates ASCII to EBCIDIC, but does not remove URL encoding. You must define maximum length for the data, and you will receive a single field containing a string of data. It is up to you to parse it and extract variable names and values.

QTMHWRSTOUT

This is the Write To STDOUT API. It allows languages other than C, C++, or Java to write to STDOUT. The API translates EBCIDIC to ASCII, but does not URL encode any data. You must define the maximum length to be written to STDOUT and provide the properly prepared text.

QTMHCVTDB

The Convert To DB API is a sophisticated tool that extracts name value pairs from an input buffer and maps them to a DDS-like data structure where fields can be referenced by name.

NATIVE LANGUAGE PROGRAMMING SUMMARY

If the preceding discussion discourages you from writing native language programs in languages such as RPG, COBOL, or even C on the AS/400, I will feel like I've done a good job.

One of the objectives of e-business Web site development is to quickly deliver systems that are flexible and easily enhanced. Native languages are not my choice to meet these objectives. A competent RPG programmer can write CGI programs, but the learning curve is significant. IBM manuals contain a number of important terms unfamiliar to most RPG programmers.

But don't despair! If there weren't a solution to the programming problem, I wouldn't be writing this book. Chapter 25 describes Net.Data, IBM's no charge Internet development tool. But before we leave CGI programming, however, let's look at a few more solutions.

A SPECIAL USE FOR MESSAGE FILES

One developer I know has solved the problem of developing CGI programs in RPG and constantly recompiling to make minor cosmetic changes in the presentation. She has developed a technique where HTML tags are stored in message files and variable data are stored as message variables. The programs need only set the message variables and send the message. An override from the message file to STDOUT does the dirty work. This is a rather incredible and creative trick that saves countless hours of development.

PERL

Perl is an interpreted language specifically designed for the development of CGI programs or scripts. It is written as plain text and interpreted by the Perl interpreter. IBM has been instrumental in porting Perl to the AS/400, but it is a public-domain product and is not supported by IBM. Perl freeware is available at the AS/400 Technical Studio site (`www.as400.ibm.com/techstudio`). Click on "AS/400 Web Tools."

As of V4R2, a new version of Perl 5.003 (available at the Tech Studio site) was ported to the AS/400 that makes full use of STDIN, STDOUT, and named pipes. In July1999, IBM refreshed the Perl interpreter to 5.005 for V4R3 and above. Although Perl is still a programming language, it is easy to learn, there are many good books about it available, and it now runs on just about every platform that supports a Web server. An essential addition to your Internet library is *Teach yourself CGI Programming with PERL 5 in a Week*, by Eric Herrman, Sam's Net (ISBN 1-57521-196-3).

A LITTLE JAVA?

With the introduction of *servlets*, which are tiny applet-like programs embedded in an HTML page that call and run Java programs that reside on the AS/400, Java and IBM's VisualAge for Java may be a viable choice for writing Web applications.

The new servlets may reduce the time required to download applications from a server to the client. I have tested some server-side Java applications that run native on the AS/400 at V4R2. The performance is nothing short of amazing. If servlets solve the delivery problem, this is an excellent choice.

NET.DATA, IBM'S HIDDEN TREASURE

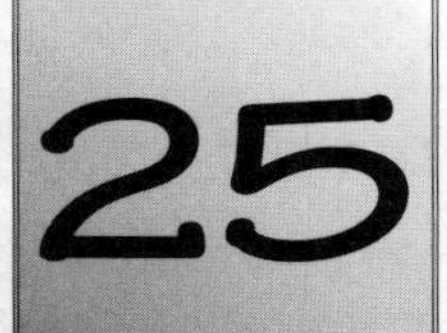

This chapter is devoted to what I consider one of the best software products that IBM has written for the AS/400. Net.Data for the AS/400 is *free*. It is bundled into TCP/IP as a utility. Net.Data is a cross-platform product that runs almost identical code on UNIX, Windows NT, S/390, and OS/2 platforms, as well as the AS/400. If you have concerns about cross-platform issues, Net.Data is the correct product for you.

Perhaps the most important feature of Net.Data is that it is easy to learn. People with minimal technical skills can learn Net.Data, experienced programmers can become proficient in developing interactive Web based applications within 10 days with a minimum amount of training.

Many of the issues and tasks that a native language CGI programmer must address when writing CGI programs are identified inChapter 24. These issues included URL encoding and decoding, API-based interfaces between the environment and your program, and API-based programming to exchange variables between your program and HTML. The difficulties and development time required to make cosmetic changes to the CGI-generated Web pages are also addressed.

Net.Data solves all of these problems. Regardless of your programming background, you can develop Net.Data macros in a few days. Net.Data is the glue that ties HTML, CL, SQL, and native language programming together via a quick and easy-to-use macro language.

Let's examine the basic concepts and facilities of Net.Data macro language programming and look at some examples that should be useful in developing a Web site.

GETTING STARTED with NET.DATA

First, set up and install your Web server. Then visit IBM's AS/400 Net.Data home page, which contains ample documentation (see `www.as400.ibm.com/netdata` for the link). If you need further assitance, post a message at `http://www.ignite400.org`.

DEVELOPMENT TOOLS

I write all of my macros on a Windows/95 PC using a free programmer's text-editor product called EditPad.exe. It can be downloaded from the HTML editors section at `www.tucows.com`. It has many features that make editing programs very easy.

Perhaps the Rolls-Royce of PC program text editors is a product called Ultra_Edit32, also available from `www.tucows.com`. This one has a 30-day trial and costs about $50. It is a real programmer's power tool. Utra_Edit32 has many great features, and is the only product that I have seen that includes hex-to-character translation, as well as ASCII-to-EBCDIC translations.

There are other text-editing options, including your word processor or Notepad.exe. If you use a word processor like WordPro, Word, or WordPerfect be sure you save your files as ASCII text.

Site Boss/400 from Better Online Solutions, another text-editing option, is a dedicated Net.Data editor. It was written specifically to simplify the Net.Data programming experience. It uses a structured modular approach where each function, HTML section, and Net.Data include file is represented as a collapsed section. You can load macros from your Web site and work on them within the product's dedicated editor.

This product is designed for Net.Data's syntax and prompts for the correct parameters. It also incorporates an SQL builder to help write SQL functions. You can download it for a 30-day trial from `www.siteboss.com/`.

STORING MACROS ON THE AS/400

Once Net.Data is installed and configured, you must decide where the macros and include files will be stored. Macros and include files can be stored in source-file text members, but I recommend storing them as text files in IFS directories. The macros load faster and are much easier to manage and maintain.

Using IBM's Client Access/400 (CA/400) as your communications and emulation client makes it easier to store macros and include file in an IFS directory. When CA/400 is installed, it automatically sets up a file and directory interface to your AS/400 in the Network Neighborhood. When you double click the Network Neighborhood, you will see an icon representing your AS/400. When you double click the AS/400 icon, CA/400 connects to your AS/400 and, if you are authorized, displays all of the files and file systems on your AS/400. You can double-click any directory name and the AS/400 behaves like any directory or file on your PC. CA/400 supports all of the features of Windows Explorer, including drag and drop. You can now edit files in your favorite PC editor and simply save them to the AS/400 in the directory of your choice. Client Access/400 automatically handles the conversion between ASCII and EBCDIC.

Another approach is to save the files on your PC. You may then use FTP to transfer them to the AS/400. While I don't recommend this approach, you can create a Source Physical File and maintain the macros as members of this file with SEU. There are many problems with this approach, including a record-length limitation of 240 characters. You will not be able to download my sample macros from `www.ignite400.org` or the AS/400 Web site. If you use QSYS libraries, you will pay a performance penalty. You will also be stuck with SEU, which may be great for RPG, but is horrible for Net.Data.

NET.DATA FEATURES AND FUNCTIONS

Let's look at Net.Data more closely. Figure 25.1 illustrates the flow of data necessary to satisfy a request through an AS/400 configured with a Web server and Net.Data. A user may type a URL or (more likely)

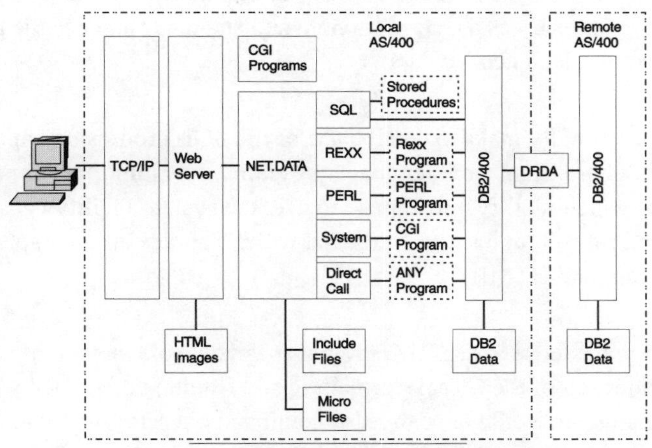

Figure 25.1 Net.Data facilities.

click a link on an HTML page that will invoke a Net.Data macro. Net.Data is a CGI program called DB2WWW that is always called to process Net.Data macros. This URL will call a Net.Data Macro: *http://www.mycompany.com/db2www/mymacro.mac/main*

In this URL, DB2WWW is the name of an alias that points to a CGI library on your AS/400 containing the program DB2WWW. This is the main Net.Data program. */MYMACRO.MAC* is passed to the program and tells DB2WWW the name of the macro to load from the macro directory or file. *MAIN* is a section name within the macro that tells Net.Data to start executing the macro at that point.

A Net.Data macro can call external functions that consist of:

- SQL statements processed directly by Net.Data
- SQL stored procedures
- REXX statements or external programs
- PERL5 statements or programs
- Other programs written in RPG, COBOL, C, C++, Java, or CL; it can also call AS/400 commands directly via this facility

The SQL, REXX, Perl, and native language programs and commands can perform any function that they might perform when called from any other AS/400 job. Programs are passed parameters. They perform their required processing and return parameters back to Net.Data.

There is a big difference between calling an external function via Net.Data and calling them directly as a CGI program. Net.Data maps name value pairs into variables, and decodes URL encoded data.

I personally make extensive use of the SQL processing capabilities. Other users call RPG programs or C language programs. The important concept here is that regardless of which facility you choose to use, the system facility is passed input parameters and returns output back to Net.Data, which handles all communications between your program and HTML.

If you choose to use RPG programs as your sole method of accessing data on your machine, all of the HTML formatting and handling are done by Net.Data. Your RPG programmers would have to learn nothing about servers or HTML. You can distribute the development process between different people with different skill sets.

Notice Figure 25.1 illustrates access to both local databases on the same machine where Net.Data and the Web server reside or a remote machine connected via DRDA. At V4R2, DRDA connections may be established with SNA or TCP/IP. TCP/IP connections eliminate all of the SNA LU 6.2 overhead and outperform SNA by a factor of about 3:1! You can also connect to a machine across the room or around the world. I ran a test between Los Angeles and London retrieving data from both machines. The performance via DRDA over TCP/IP was better than using my local SNA connection to a very large machine in the same room.

Net.Data handles all of the variable manipulation and HTML formatting. Your programs can be written in a language that is most suitable to your organization. Programmers can focus on the specific processing required by the application.

THE NET.DATA LANGUAGE

Net.Data, like any other programming language, lets you define variables and functions and process control logic. It is a freeform language that allows you to format your Net.Data statements in a orderly and legible fashion.

Net.Data is case-sensitive. If you refer to USERID, it is not the same field as UserId or userid. Be careful, because this is a frequent cause of errors in Net.Data macros. Names can be up to 256 characters long. Avoid embedded blanks in any type of name you use in Net.Data. If you would like to separate words in a long name, consider using the underscore character where you would normally type a space (My_Variable). Avoid using the hyphen as a word separator.

If you are familiar with the C programming language, you will see many familiar constructs used within Net.Data. Net.Data is written in C and many of the C language constructs find their way into the macro language.

VARIABLES

Net.Data supports global and local user-defined variables. You define a variable via the *%DEFINE* macro keyword, shown in Figure 25.2.

```
%DEFINE mystring = "ABC"
%DEFINE mynumber = "-123.15"
%DEFINE mynullvar = ""
```

Figure 25.2: Defining user-defined variables with %DEFINE.

Net.Data does not support the concept of data types. All data is considered to be character or string data. Net.Data does recognize string data that contains numeric values. The variable "mynumber" illustrated in Figure 25.2 can be used in Net.Data's math functions and would be considered a valid number. So would numbers such as "123" or "123.15." A string that contains formatting like "123,456.00CR" would be considered a character text string due to the commas. Any attempts to perform math on it would result in an error.

The variable "mynullvar" contains a null value. When you need to refer to a global variable that will be set somewhere within the macro, it is necessary to declare the variable before it is referenced.

Variables declared outside of a function are considered *global variables* to Net.Data. A global variable can be referenced anywhere within the macro.

In Figure 25.2, you see the simple form of the *%DEFINE* keyword. *%DEFINE* may also be used to declare a number of variables within a *%DEFINE block,* as shown in Figure 25.3.

```
%DEFINE {

    var1 = ""
    var2 = "123"
    var3 = "ABC"
%}
```

Figure 25.3: A %DEFINE block for defining several variables.

The { ... %} denotes a block of Net.Data statements that are treated as a unit.

The *%DEFINE* block is a shortcut that reduces the amount of typing you have to do. Using the block construct over a series of discrete *%DEFINE* varname = "value" statements may result in a small performance gain.

The left and right curly braces are borrowed from the C programming language. A frequent Net.Data programming error is to forget the %} when terminating a block.

Net.Data also provides access to the server environment. The environment is a list of predefined variables that are set by the server and browser. Environment variables provide information about the environment in which you are running. These variables include things such as the type of browser your user has on his desktop to the name and version of the Web server running on your machine.

Net.Data also provides a series of predefined variables that it obtains and sets for you from the AS/400 system environment. These variables include information like the current date and time, file modification dates, etc.

Named fields on an HTML form and fields defined via the QUERY_STRING on a URL are parsed and decoded by Net.Data and made available to you as global variables within the macro. This is a huge benefit and time saver when compared to writing native language CGI programs.

Consider the URL:

```
http://www.myco.com/cgi-bin/mymac.mac/main?
    comp=123456&dept=sales&rep=Fred+Jones
```

Three name value pairs are passed into the macro MYMAC.MAC. They are *comp=123456*, *dept=sales*, and *rep=Fred Jones*.

Net.Data automatically declares global variables for you named COMP, DEPT, and REP. These variables contain the values passed into the macro and the values will be decoded. In the case of "Fred+Jones," the plus sign is decoded into a space.

Net.Data also processes variables defined in an HTML form and processed via the POST method. Net.Data creates variables for you with the name of the variable picked up from the *name=* parameter of the *<INPUT...*, *<SELECT...*, and other form fields. You do not have to parse the QUERY_STRING or deal with STDIN.

TABLES

One special type of variable is the Net.Data table. You can define a table with the following *%DEFINE* keyword: *%DEFINE mytable = %TABLE*

A table can hold the output of an SQL statement that returns multiple rows and columns of data, or the output of an array returned from a programming language call. Net.Data provides the ability to manipulate the table and format output for presentation to the Web page.

Variables are referred to by name within functions and with the following syntax anywhere within the macro: $(VAR).

This construct tells Net.Data to replace the variable $(VAR) with the value assigned to the variable "VAR."

FUNCTIONS

A Net.Data function is the construct that allows you to interface with the rest of the AS/400. A function is similar to a procedure or subroutine in other programming languages. It is very much like a procedure in the C or BASIC languages.

You must declare a function before it can be called. You then call a function. The function performs some meaningful work and may return the result or perhaps just a return code to the macro that called it. Functions may be declared with input, output, or I/O parameters.

An input parameter allows the function call to pass a parameter in from the macro to the function. Input variables are not modified by the function.

An output parameter allows the function to return data to the macro. An output variable might result from a calculation performed by the function. It may also contain data returned from an I/O operation performed by the function.

Input/output parameters allow the function to modify an input variable. Suppose your function adds 1 to a variable passed into it as an INOUT variable. You call the function passing in a value of 8. The Input/Output parameter would contain 9 when the function completed its processing. A function is declared using the syntax shown in Figure 25.4.

```
%FUNCTION(DTW_xxx) function_name(IN invar1, invar2, OUT outvar1,
outvar2, INOUT inoutvar1) RETURN(outvar3) {
   function statements…
%}
```

Figure 25.4: Declaring a function.

The keyword *%FUNCTION* identifies the macro code that follows as a function declaration. The (*DTW_xxx*) tells Net.Data what type of function you wish to declare. At present, there are three types[1] of Net.Data functions. They are:

- *DTW_SQL*, a standard SQL statement conforming to the rules for interactive SQL

1 Types of Net.Data functions are most correctly called Net.Data Language Environments. For details, consult the manual, *Net.Data Language Environment Reference.*

- *DTW_REXX*, the REXX programming environment; you can code REXX statements in the body of the function or refer to an external REXX function (stored in a Source Physical File Member)

- *DTW_SYSTEM*, which calls any CL, RPG, COBOL, Java, C, Perl, or C++ program or AS/400 command

Functions are called by placing an @ symbol in front of the function name, as illustrated in Figure 25.5:

```
@Function_name(parm, parm, parm, parm)
OR
@Function()
```

Figure 25.5: Calling a function.

The first form of the call passes input, output, or INOUT parameters to the function and executes the function. You must pass in the exact number of parameters defined in the *%FUNCTION* definition.

The second example is a call to a function that does not require input, output, or INOUT parameters. If you are familiar with the C language, you will be comfortable with this construct.

Functions can be called from virtually anywhere in the macro as long as the function is defined physically before you call it.

Net.Data also provides a rich library of built-in functions to perform mathematics, string manipulation, and many other programming or Internet functions for you. These are described later in this chapter.

FLOW CONTROL AND LOGIC

Net.Data supports multiple entry points called *HTML sections*. The term HTML section is a throwback to Net.Data's ancestor: DB2WWW. DB2WWW was a simplistic facility that allowed you to query the database and format the output as HTML. Net.Data has come a long way since DB2WWW was introduced.

The HTML section is really nothing more than the point where your macro begins to execute. It is extremely useful because you can have many entry points in a Net.Data macro.

You can define one section that displays a form that might ask the user for selection criteria for a query, and another section that retrieves and displays the data.

I frequently define sections that handle database updates, deletes, inserts, and other actions that display forms or data. By defining multiple sections, I can share common routines within the macro and save a lot of coding and time.

The HTML section is defined as shown in Figure 25.6.

```
%HTML(section_name) {
Net.Data statements …
%}
```

Figure 25.6: HTML section.

Despite its name, the HTML section need not include any HTML. I often embed all of my HTML within a `%FUNCTION` definition. Net.Data also provides flow control logic in the form of an `IF THEN ELSE` and a `WHILE` construct.

A SIMPLE MACRO

The following sample macro could be written entirely in HTML. It performs no significant processing, but is designed to illustrate the basic concepts that we have just discussed and put the concepts into a meaningful context.

The macro is executed from the following URL[2]:

http://www.ignite400.org/member/cgi-dat/bcbk_hello.mac/main

It outputs a simple message displayed in blue. There is a link that when clicked outputs the message in red.

The page depicted in Figure 25.7 is generated when the macro is executed beginning at the `%HTML(main)` section. Notice that the section name (MIN) is part of the `QUERY_STRING` passed into the macro. When a user clicks on the link labeled "RED," the macro displays the screen in Figure 25.8.

2 The macro samples used in this chapter may be viewed at www.ignite400.org . Look for the section called "BobC's Book."

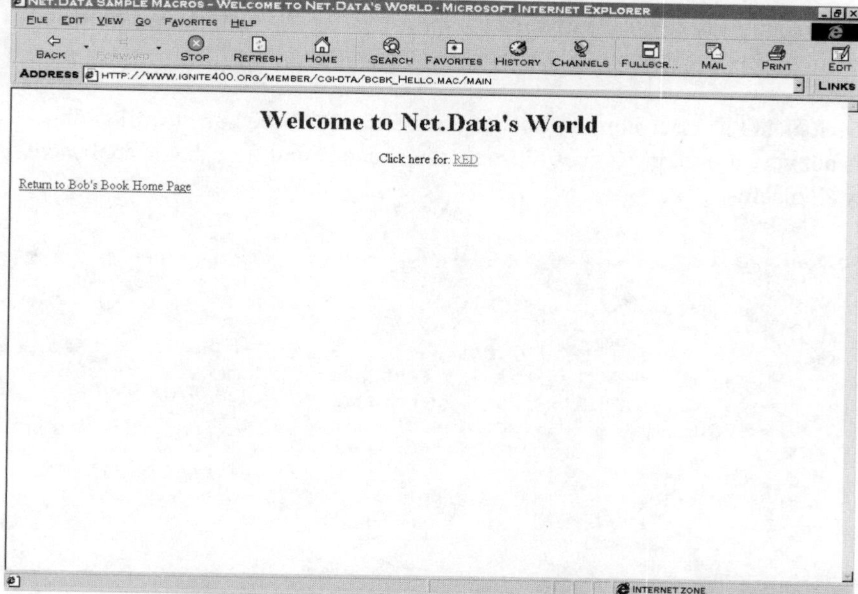

Figure 25.7: Bcbk_hello.mac/main.

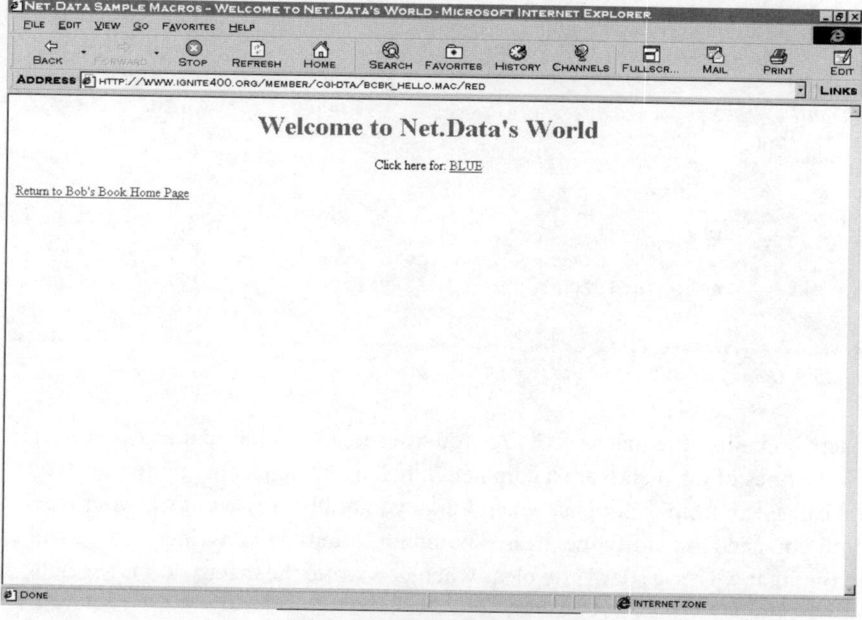

Figure 25.8: Bcbk_hello.mac/red.

This is the macro's display when executed at the `%HTML(red)` section. Notice the URL displayed in the browser address field ends with the section name "red."

Now, lets look at this macro line by line (in Figure 25.9) and see how it works. This macro is not very useful, but it does illustrate the structure and flow that is applicable to virtually all macros.

```
%{ Macro: bcbk_hello.mac - A simple hello world macro

This macro introduces a new Net.Data developer to the basics of Net.Data
macro development. It introduces the concepts of comments, variables,
and the general organization and flow of a macro. It doesn't do much. It
just displays the phrase "Welcome to Net.Data's World" in Blue or Red.
Please note that this is comment block.
As you can see comments are started with a percent sign and left curly
brace and may continue until they are terminated by a percent sign and
right curly brace. They can go anywhere in a macro.
%}

%DEFINE {   %{ This is an inline comment %}
   ND = "Net.Data"
   world = "World"
%}

%HTML(main) {   %{ Initial Entry point Displays the text in Blue %}

<html>
<head>
<title>Net.Data Sample Macros – Welcome to Net.Data's World</title>
</head> <body bgcolor="white">
<H1 align="center"><font color="BLUE">Welcome to $(ND)'s
$(world)</font></H1>
<p align="center">Click here for: <a HREF="/mem-
ber/cgi-dta/bcbk_hello.mac/red">
   <font color="red">RED</font></a></p>
<p><a HREF="/member/html/bobsbook.htm">Return to Bob's Book Home
Page</a></p>
```

Figure 25.9: Bcbk_hello.mac – macro source.

This macro contains little macro code. As you can see, the bulk of the text is pure HTML. The first 12 lines of the macro are a comment block. Comments are ignored by the macro. I can speak from experience when I urge you to liberally comment your macro. Wait until you need to modify the macro six months after you've written it; you will quickly find that what was perfectly clear when you wrote the macro doesn't seem to make sense now.

There are no formal constructs to document the name, author, date-written, or date-modified as there are with other AS/400 objects. It is a good idea to code the name, description, and a brief narrative summarizing the function of the macro.

The statement `%{ Initial Entry point Displays the text in Blue %}` is an example of an embedded comment. Comments can be placed anywhere in the macro as long as they are delimited by a %{ and terminated with a }%.

In the block of code in Figure 25.10, we will define two variables to illustrate how variables are defined and how they work.

```
%DEFINE {
   ND = "Net.Data"
   world = "World"
%}
```

Figure 25.10: Defining two variables.

In this example both the variables "ND" and "world" are assigned character strings within a *%DEFINE* block. The code in Figure 25.11 is the complete *%HTML (main)* section of the macro.

```
%HTML(main) {
     %{Initial Entry point Displays the text in Blue %}

<html>
<head>
<title>Net.Data Sample Macros - Welcome to Net.Data's World</title>
</head>

<body bgcolor="white">
<H1 align="center"><font color="BLUE">Welcome to $(ND)'s
$(world)</font></H1>
<p align="center">Click here for: <a HREF="/mem-
ber/cgi-dta/bcbk_hello.mac/red">
   <font color="red">RED</font></a></p>
<p><a HREF="/member/html/bobsbook.htm">Return to Bob's Book Home
Page</a></p>

</body>
</html>
%}
```

Figure 25.11: HTML (main) section code.

%HTML(main) { is the point where the macro begins executing. Net.Data finds the point in the macro identified in the URL that invoked the macro.

It reads and ignores the comment. It then sees a series of pure HTML tags. It reads and writes the HTML to the STDOUT file.

When Net.Data encounters the variable $(ND), it substitutes the value assigned to the variable ND (Net.Data) and writes out the value "Net.Data" to STDOUT. When it encounters the variable $(WORLD), it substitutes the previously assigned value "world" and writes it out.

Net.Data continues writing to STDOUT until it encounters the %} end-of-block tag, which indicates the end of the %HTML section. Net.Data then returns control to the Web server. The Web server sends the contents of STDOUT to the user's browser.

The HTML *<a HREF="/member/cgi-dta/bcbk_hello.mac/red">* is a standard HTML link definition. It instructs the server to execute this macro and instructs Net.Data to begin execution at the *%HTML(red)* section instead of "main."

%HTML(red) { contains virtually the same code as the previously described "main" section only this time the color is set to red instead of blue.

This code can be written far more elegantly than the code in my example. A good programmer can be quite creative with Net.Data. In Figure 25.11, I could have put the contents of both the "main" and the "red" sections into a Macro_Function, or even an include file. I could have defined the *color="blue"* and *color="red"* as *color="$(clr)"*. Then I could have coded something like the fragment in Figure 25.12.

```
%HTML(main) {

@DTW_ASSIGN(clr,"blue")
%INCLUDE "hello.hti"
%}

%HTML(red) {
@DTW_ASSIGN(clr,"red")
%INCLUDE "hello.hti"
%}
```

Figure 25.12: Storing HTML in an include file.

In this modified example the HTML that was previously coded in the body of each of the `%HTML` sections is now stored in a single include file. An include file can store any HTML or macro source.

The macro instruction `%INCLUDE "name"` instructs Net.Data to read the content of the file name following the keyword `%INCLUDE` and process it as if it were part of the macro beginning at the line where the `%INCLUDE` was found. It is a very handy method of keeping long redundant macros short and readable. You will find that some HTML constructs, like forms and reports, can get quite lengthy.

I often store the HTML in an include file just to keep my macro readable. There is no noticeable performance degradation when using an include file. I have used as many as 10 includes with no discernible performance degradation.

In the previous code fragment, I introduced a Net.Data *built-in function* `@DTW_ASSIGN`. If you remember, prefixing a function name with an @ sign is the same as writing `CALL DTW_ASSIGN` in a language that recognizes the CALL statement.

The statement `@DTW_ASSIGN(clr,"blue")` instructs Net.Data to assign the literal text string "blue" to a variable named "CLR." Because "CLR" has not been previously defined, Net.Data creates it as a local variable (local to the %HTML block where it was first declared).

The `@DTW_ASSIGN` built-in function is one of the most used functions available within the Net.Data language. You may assign literals to variables or variables to variables. Most languages use an = sign to perform an assignment. The equal sign would be ambiguous within Net.Data.

The variable ceases to exist when Net.Data completes its processing of the `%HTML(xxx)` section where the variable was defined. Be careful with local variables. If you use local variables and do not get the result you expect, try adding the variable to a `%DEFINE` block at the beginning of the macro, as shown in Figure 25.13.

```
%DEFINE {
   ND = "Net.Data"
   World = "World"
   clr = ""
%}
```

Figure 25.13: Local variable in a %DEFINE block.

In this code fragment, we are declaring "CLR" as a global variable (available anywhere in the macro) and initializing it to a null value signified by the pair of double quotes.

NET.DATA SYNTAX

By now, you may wonder why Net.Data uses such a strange syntax. You must remember that Net.Data is handling dozens of minor chores for you that you would have to deal yourself if you wrote a CGI program in a native language. Net.Data is a very intelligent text parser. It must read and interpret every character that you type in a macro definition.

Net.Data must know the difference between a comment, a Net.Data operation keyword, a function call, HTML, and plain text. It is necessary for the developers to use some unique syntactical constructs to avoid ambiguity in a macro.

It is as important for Net.Data to know when to do nothing but read and write text to the STDOUT file as it is to know that it must perform some processing.

MORE ABOUT VARIABLES

When I first started writing Net.Data macros, understanding Net.Data variables was one of the most difficult concepts to learn. The following macro illustrates some basic variable handling and introduces the Net.Data built-in function *@DTW_ASSIGN*.

Unlike other languages where the equal sign is used to assign values to a variable, there are four ways that values are assigned to variables in Net.Data: the *%DEFINE* statement, the *@DTW_ASSIGN* built-in function, the *@DTW_SUBSTR* built-in function, and the *QUERY_STRING* function.

The *%DEFINE var_name = "value"* or the *%DEFINE* block allows you to declare a variable and assign it a value. We have illustrated this concept in the previous pages and examples. Remember, variables declared with the *%DEFINE* statement are global variables and may be referenced anywhere in the macro.

The *@DTW_ASSIGN(var,"value")* built-in function allows you to assign a value to a previously declared variable. You may use the *%DEFINE myvar = ""* at the beginning of the macro to declare a value named MYVAR and initialize it to a null value.

This process declares the variable MYVAR to Net.Data and reserves space for it when it is assigned a value later. The *@DTW_ASSIGN* function, when invoked from anywhere in the macro, assigns a value to the variable upon execution.

If you use the *@DTW_ASSIGN* within a function to assign a value to a variable that was not previously declared, the variable is considered a local variable (local to the function) and ceases to exist when the function completes its processing.

Other Net.Data built-in functions such as the string function *@DTW_SUBSTR (datestring,"5,""2,"month)* extracts the two characters beginning at position five in the variable datestring and places the results in the variable month. Most of the Net.Data built-in functions provides an option of placing the result of the function into a variable of your choosing.

As is the case with @DTW_ASSIGN, if the result variable was previously declared, the result is global. If the result variable was not previously declared, the result is local to the current function.

The fourth method of declaring and using variables has to do with variables passed into your macro via the QUERY_STRING or from an HTML form that uses the *METHOD="POST" HTTP* method (writes to the STDIN file).

Consider the URL *www.mycom.com/cgi-dta/mymac.mac/main?custno=123456.* Net.Data implicitly declares a global variable named "CUSTNO" and assigns it the value "123456." This variable and its value are available throughout the macro.

Consider the following HTML form text field definition *<INPUT TYPE="TEXT" NAME="actno">.*

When the user clicks the Submit button on the HTML form and transmits data to the server, Net.Data implicitly declares a variable named "ACTNO" and assigns the value that the user typed in the field to it. Figure 25.14 shows a very simple macro that deals with very simple variable assignments and manipulation. It uses the *@DTW_ASSIGN* built-in function.

```
%{ macro bcbk_basic_var.mac - basic variable handling %}

%DEFINE {
   XXX = "123"  %{assign the value 123 to the variable XXX %}
   YYY = "789"  %{assign the value 789 to the variable YYY %}
%}

%HTML(main) {
```

Figure 25.14: Basic variable handling (part 1 of 2).

```
<html>
<head>
<title>Net.Data basic variable handling</title>
</head>
<body bgcolor="white">
<h1 align="center">Basic Net.Data Variable handling</h1>

<p>The value of XXX is $(XXX)<br>      %{display the variable XXX %}
   @DTW_ASSIGN(XXX,"456")              %{assign the value 456 to the
variable XXX %}
   The value of XXX is $(XXX)<br>      %{display the variable XXX %}
   @DTW_ASSIGN(XXX,YYY)                %{assign the value of variable
YYY to XXX %}
   The value of XXX is $(XXX)</p>      %{display the variable YYY %}

<p><a HREF="/member/html/bobsbook.htm">Return to Bob's Book Home
Page</a></p>

</body>
</hmtl>
%}
```

Figure 25.14: Basic variable handling (part 2 of 2).

In this example, two variables "XXX" and "YYY" are declared. "XXX" is assigned the value "123" and "YYY" is assigned the value "789." In the `%HTML(main)` section of the macro, the $() construct is first used to display the value of XXX on the HTML page produced by the macro:

```
<p>The value of XXX is $(XXX)<br>
```

This will result in the browser displaying: `The value of XXX is 123`

The next line of macro code is `@DTW_ASSIGN(XXX,"456")`. This function replaces the current value of XXX (123) with the new value (456). It illustrates how literals are assigned to variables via the `@DTW_ASSIGN` function.

The next line of HTML displays the value of XXX, which now contains "456." The next Net.Data `@DTW_ASSIGN` function assigns the value contained in the variable YYY to the variable XXX: `@DTW_ASSIGN(XXX,YYY)`.

It is important to point out that, when dealing with variables within a function you simply type the variable's name (XXX and YYY in the example). When you want to display the value of the variable, you use the $(XXX) form.

After assigning the value of YYY to XXX, the final HTML statement reads: *The value of XXX is $(XXX)</p>*, which displays on the browser as: *The value of XXX is 789*. This macro produces the display shown in Figure 25.15.

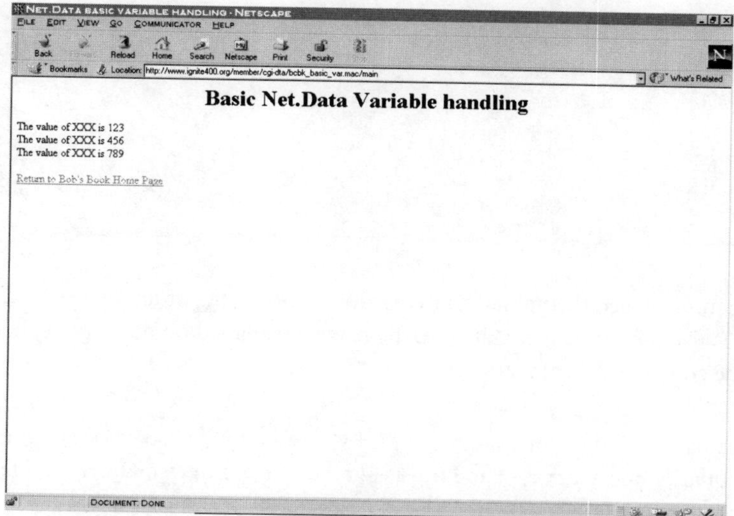

Figure 25.15: Basic variable handling.

CONDITIONAL PROCESSING CONSTRUCTS

Net.Data provides two conditional processing constructs, the IF THEN ELSE construct and the WHILE construct.

The %IF block is similar to most other languages with the exception of the syntax for the logical operator:

```
%IF (value logical_operator value)
     statements…
%ELIF(value logical_operator value)  ß optional
     statements…
%ELSE  ß optional
     statements …
%ENDIF
```

%IF blocks can be placed anywhere in a macro to process just about anything conditionally. I first used them to suppress menu-type options unless a user met certain criteria.

This statement might be written as:

```
%IF(user_type == "manager")
   <TR>
      <TD>
      ...
   </TR>
%ENDIF
```

This statement is placed in a table following the *<TABLE>* tag or another *<TR>...</TR>* row block. If the user_type is a manager, the row is displayed on the page. If it is not a manager, the row is not displayed.

Note the special = = logical operator. C- or C++-like syntax is used to distinguish between the equality operator (= =) and the assignment operator (=). Other double operators inlcude:

```
&& - AND
|| - OR
```

Other valid operators include:

```
>greater than
< less than
>= greater than or equal
<= less than or equal
!=  not equal
```

%WHILE is Net.Data's looping construct. A typical loop might look like:

```
%WHILE(loopcounter <= "100")
  statements...
  @DTW_ADD(loopcounter,"1",loopcounter)
%}
```

You can perform any valid statement within a loop. I recently wrote a macro that built a series of rows in a table containing HTML input form fields depending on a value provided by the user on a previous form. I loop until the user-provided value is reached and write out the row for each iteration of the loop.

FUNCTIONS

Functions are the heart of Net.Data. User-defined functions retrieve data from the DB2/400 database and call native language programs like RPG, COBOL, C/C++, PL1, CL, REXX, or PERL5.

Net.Data classifies external functions into three classes or language environments. These are SQL, SYSTEM, and REXX.

Functions can be placed in many places within a Net.Data macro. I generally start my macros out by creating a `%DEFINE` block with any variables I need to declare and then follow that with any `%FUNCTION` blocks that I need to declare.

A very important point is that a `%FUNCTION` must be physically declared before it may be called. That means it must physically exist in the macro above any calls to the function. The following paragraphs provide simple illustrations of each type of language environment when used in a function.

DTW_SQL: SQL LANGUAGE ENVIRONMENT

The SQL language environment allows you to embed a modified form of interactive SQL in a macro function. You may use `SELECT`, `INSERT`, `UPDATE`, and `DELETE`. You may also invoke SQL stored procedures written in the new SQL Stored Procedure Language, or call a native language program.

```
%{ Macro: bcbk_basic_sql.mac – a very simple macro that demonstrates elementary SQL %}

%DEFINE {
   DATABASE = "*LOCAL"     %{<- Tells Net.Data where the database is located %}
   SHOWSQL  = "YES"        %{<- Yes turns SQL debugging on. No - turns it off. %}
%}

%FUNCTION(DTW_SQL) getinv() {
   SELECT cat, subcat, prdnam
```

Figure 25.16: Basic SQL macro sample (part 1 of 2).

```
    FROM ignsql.bcbkinv2
    order by cat, subcat, prdnam
    for fetch only
%}

%HTML(main) {

    <head>
    <title>Bob's Samples - Basic SQL Example</title>
    </head>

    <body bgcolor="white">
    <H1 align="center">Basic SQL Example</h1>
    <p align="center"><a HREF="/member/html/bobsbook.htm">Return to Bob's Book Home
Page</a></p>

    @getinv()

    </body>
    </head>
%}
```

Figure 25.16: Basic SQL macro sample (part 2 of 2).

The macro in Figure 25.16 selects all records from the BCBKINV2 file in the IGNSQL library. It displays the fields "CAT," "SUBCAT," and "PRDNAM."

A SIMPLE SQL MACRO

The first thing you must do when using SQL in a Net.Data macro is define on which the database is located. This is done in the *%DEFINE* block by setting the Net.Data special variable *DATABASE*. In our example, the database is located on the same machine where Net.Data and the Web server are running, so we set *DATABASE="*LOCAL."* **LOCAL* is a special variable that tells Net.Data to use the local database.

If the database is located on a remote AS/400 or other supported machine (Oracle, DB2/Universal, Sybase running on OS/390, UNIX, or Windows NT), then you must specify the name of the remote machine.

DATABASE = "IGN04" instructs Net.Data to issue an SQL CONNECT statement to the machine or database named "IGN04." IGN04 must be defined to your local machine via the relational database (RDB) command GO CMDRDB. You must define an SNA or TCP/IP connection to the remote machine.

If you use a remote connection, you must also specify a user profile and password to access the remote database. In your define block code, *LOGIN = "user_profile"* and *PASSWORD = "password"*.

I strongly recommend using a single user profile and password for all Net.Data macros. I also suggest storing all of the database information in an *%INCLUDE* file. This user profile must be created as a valid profile on the remote machine. You should set the initial program for the profile to SIGNOFF so that it cannot log on to a 5250 session or any other AS/400 function. Its authority should be restricted to the data required by Net.Data.

You certainly can create multiple user profiles and passwords with specific authorities, depending upon your specific needs. I suggest avoiding the temptation to set up a distinct user profile and password for each Web user accessing your system.

The next variable in the *%DEFINE* block is another SQL system variable, SHOWSQL, which is a debug feature provided by Net.Data. I personally use it in about 98 percent of the SQL macros I write to assist me in identifying and correcting errors. SHOWSQL causes each SQL statement that your macro executes to be displayed on the browser with all variable substitutions performed so you can see exactly what is being passed to SQL for processing.

The most common error is to forget to put single quotes around a $(VAR) when it is used as an argument in an SQL statement for a character field. If you recall, Net.Data is case sensitive. This often shows up in SQL, where clauses referencing $(VAR) variables are typed in the wrong case. When you run the SQL statement, the mistyped variable contains a null value.

Figure 25.17 shows the actual function definition from the sample macro.

```
%FUNCTION(DTW_SQL) getinv() {
   SELECT cat, subcat, prdnam
   FROM ignsql.bcbkinv2
   ORDER BY cat, subcat, prdnam
   FOR FETCH ONLY
%}
```

Figure 25.17: DTW_SQL function definition.

%FUNCTION informs Net.Data that a user-defined function is being declared. *DTW_SQL* indicates that it is an SQL function and instructs Net.Data to use the SQL Language Environment. (For more information, read the *Language Environment Manual* at www.software.ibm.com/data/net.data/docs/dtwl1mst.htm.

GETINV() is an arbitrary name that I gave to the function. This name will be used when the function is called. The () indicates that no input or output parameters will be passed to or returned from the function. The { indicates the start of the function content. Function content continues until the %} is encountered, which terminates the function.

The text beginning with *SELECT* and continuing through *FOR FETCH ONLY* is a standard interactive SQL statement.

The *FOR FETCH ONLY* clause works in conjunction with Net.Data's *ISOLATION_LEVEL* parameter in the Net.Data INI file. I personally set my *ISOLATION_LEVEL* to *READ_UNCOMMITTED*, which instructs SQL to read without locking rows in the target tables. *FOR FETCH ONLY* instructs SQL to optimize the query for retrieval.

I strongly recommend using *READ_UNCOMMITTED* if you are going to be updating, deleting, or inserting records into your database via Net.Data. This places all records inserted, changed, or deleted under commitment control. Net.Data automatically issues commit and rollback commands as required.

Figure 25.18 shows this simple query, which lists the entire file and uses Net.Data's default output formatting to display the results.

The text below the title appears because we set the Net.Data special variable SHOWSQL equal to "YES." Notice that Net.Data formats the output and displays it. This is not a very useful display to users, but it is very useful to test your SQL statements and to be sure that they are working correctly.

I build my Net.Data macros incrementally, adding a bit of code and testing it as I write the macro. I find that this technique greatly simplifies macro development by eliminating error conditions as you develop the macro.

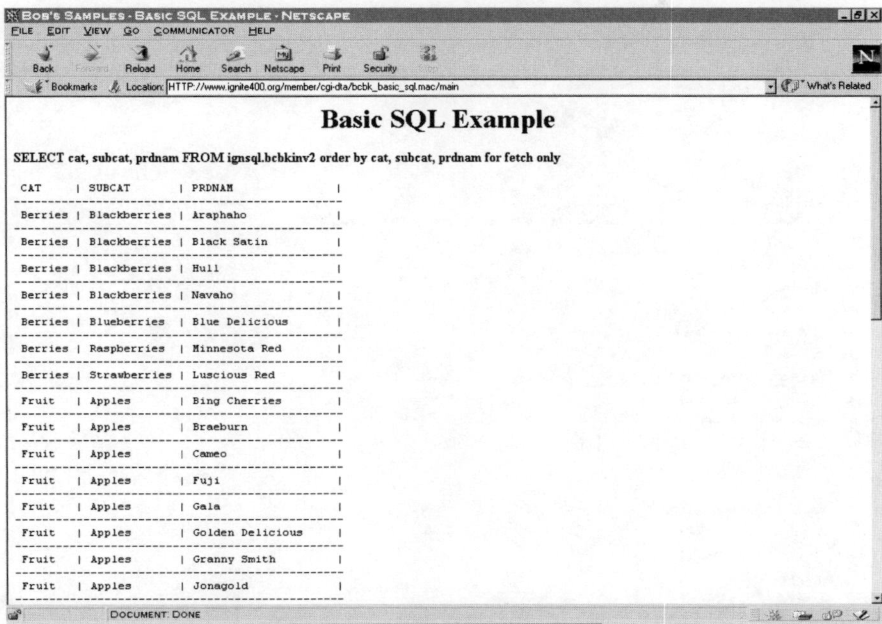

Figure 25.18: Basic SQL example.

A couple of notes about this simple SQL function block that uses no `%REPORT` or `%ROW` section:

- You may code `%DEFINE DTW_DEFAULT_REPORT = "NO"` prior to declaring the function. Net.Data will retrieve the data from the query when the function is called. The data will be stored in its default table. You can then refer to the table in other functions within the macro. `DTW_DEFAULT_REPORT = "NO"` prevents Net.Data from displaying the results of the query.

- `DTW_HTML_TABLE = "YES"` (Figure 25.19) causes Net.Data to format the output of a default query using HTML table tags to produce a somewhat more attractive presentation.

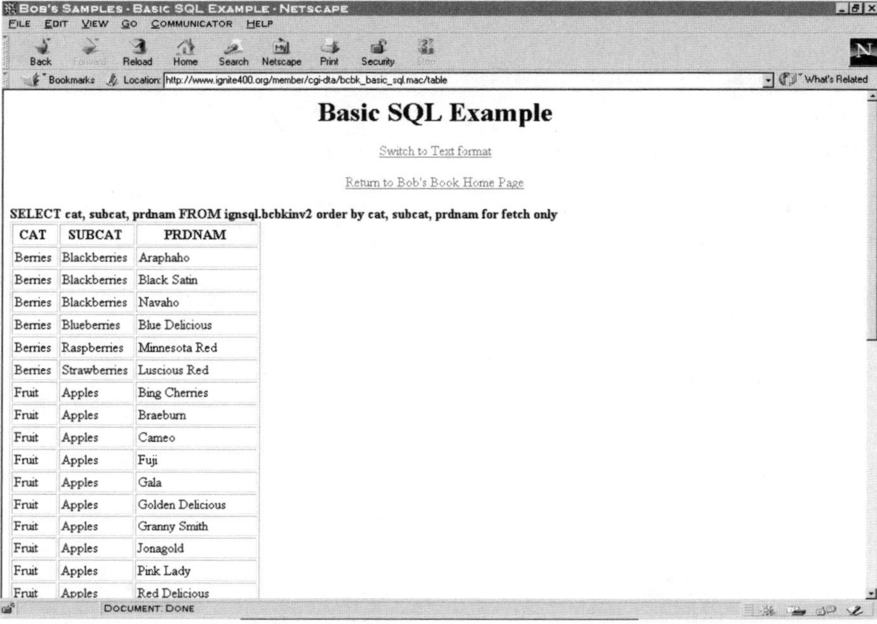

CAT	SUBCAT	PRDNAM
Berries	Blackberries	Araphaho
Berries	Blackberries	Black Satin
Berries	Blackberries	Navaho
Berries	Blueberries	Blue Delicious
Berries	Raspberries	Minnesota Red
Berries	Strawberries	Luscious Red
Fruit	Apples	Bing Cherries
Fruit	Apples	Braeburn
Fruit	Apples	Cameo
Fruit	Apples	Fuji
Fruit	Apples	Gala
Fruit	Apples	Golden Delicious
Fruit	Apples	Granny Smith
Fruit	Apples	Jonagold
Fruit	Apples	Pink Lady
Fruit	Apples	Red Delicious

Figure 25.19: DTW_HTML_TABLE = "YES."

As you can see, Net.Data can format the output of the SQL SELECT statement into a quick table format, but does not produce an attractive Web page.

FORMATTING SQL OUTPUT WITH %REPORT AND %ROW

So far, I have illustrated a very basic SQL function that retrieves data from your database and literally dumps the results on a browser. Net.Data includes some very powerful output formatting tools to produce virtually unlimited creativity in formatting and presenting output.

Figure 25.20 illustrates a page produced using the `%REPORT` and `%ROW` blocks within an SQL function.

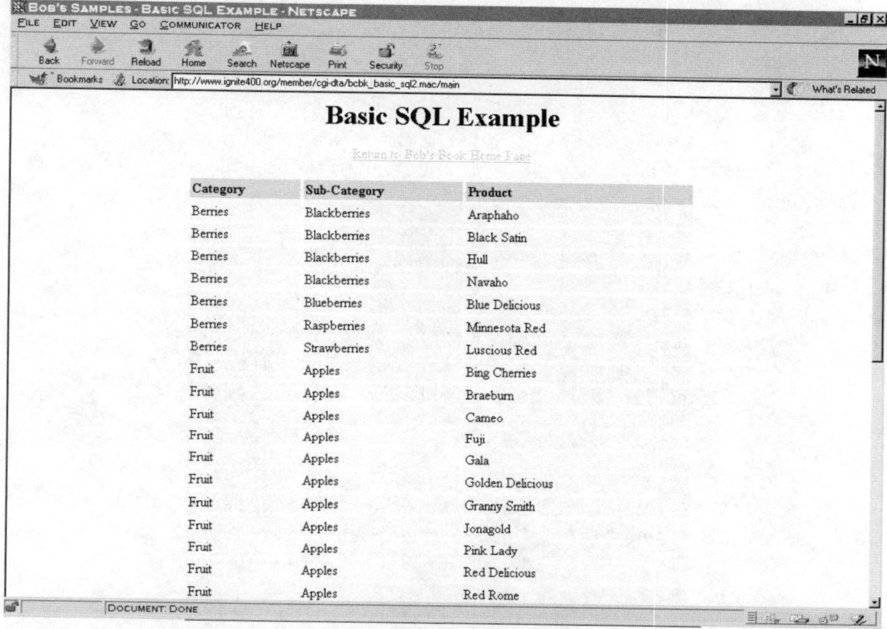

Figure 25.20: Basic SQL example with formatted output.

It uses an HTML table that I created and formatted by hand using the *%REPORT* and *%ROW* blocks of the *%FUNCTION* feature of Net.Data. The coding appears in Figure 25.21.

```
%{ Macro: bcbk_basic_sql2.mac — a simple macro that demonstrates
elementary SQL with formatting  %}

%DEFINE {
   DATABASE = "*LOCAL"
   SHOWSQL  = "NO"
%}

%FUNCTION(DTW_SQL) getinv() {
   SELECT cat, subcat, prdnam
   FROM ignsql.bcbkinv2
   order by cat, subcat, prdnam
   for fetch only
   %REPORT {
      <head>
      <title>Bob's Samples - Basic SQL Example</title>
```

Figure 25.21: Basic SQL sample with formatting (part 1 of 2).

```
    </head>

    <body bgcolor="white">
    <H1 align="center">Basic SQL Example</h1>
    <p align="center"><a HREF="/member/html/bobsbook.htm">Return to
 Bob's Book Home Page</a></p>

    <table border="0" cellpadding="2" cellspacing="4" width="60%"
 align="center">
    <tr valign="top">
       <th align="left" bgcolor="#FFC23B">Category</th>
       <th align="left" bgcolor="#FFC23B">Sub-Category</th>
       <th align="left" bgcolor="#FFC23B">Product</th>
    </tr>
    %ROW {
       <tr valign="top">
          <td align="left" bgcolor="#FFFFCA">$(V_cat)</td>
          <td align="left" bgcolor="#FFFFCA">$(V_subcat)</td>
          <td align="left" bgcolor="#FFFFCA">$(V_prdnam)</td>
       </tr>
    %}
    </table>
  %}
  %MESSAGE {
   100 : { <p align="center"><font color="red"><b>No Inventory Items
Found</font></p>
         %} : continue
  %}
%}

%HTML(main) {

  @getinv()

  </body>
  </head>
%}
```

Figure 25.21: Basic SQL sample with formatting (part 2 of 2).

Before we begin to examine the changes to the `%FUNCTION` block of this macro, take a look at the `%HTML` section. I mentioned previously that the `%HTML` section does not have to have any HTML within the section. The macro in Figure 25.22 illustrates this point.

```
%HTML(main) {

   @getinv()

   </body>
   </head>
%}
```

Figure 25.22: HTML section without HTML code.

Notice that the only HTML in the section is the *</BODY>* and *</HTML>* tags. The code `@getinv()` is the real meat of the section. It is a call to the function `getinv` that contains all of the HTML and data.

Before we dissect this function, let's look at a diagram of the structure of the function, which is shown in Figure 25.23.

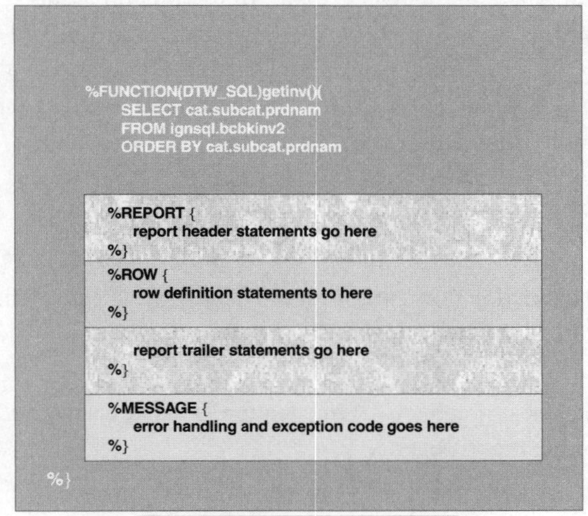

Figure 25.23: SQL function block.

This diagram is color coded to illustrate the structure of an SQL function. Notice that the function definition begins with the *%FUNCTION* statement and terminates at the bottom with a %}. Notice also that the function definition includes the actual SQL statements.

The *%REPORT* block has a header, detail (*%ROW*), and a trailer section. This construct is similar to any major programming language's representation of a report. You may put any header type information, including titles, column headings, etc., immediately after the *%REPORT {* statement.

You then insert a *%ROW* block after you have defined any report header text. The *%REPORT* section is executed once per call to the function.

The `%ROW` block defines one row of output. It is executed one time for each row retrieved by your SQL statement. You can get fancy and use Net.Data conditional statements to format rows containing different data differently. I am not going to illustrate that type of processing because it is fairly rare and unusual.

Net.Data processes each row returned from your SQL statement. It stops processing the `%ROW` block and processes any trailer statements that you may have coded following the %}, which terminates the `%ROW` block, but prior to the %}, which terminates the `%REPORT` block. I have used this construct along with Net.Data built-in math functions in the `%ROW` block to accumulate totals and display the totals in the trailer section.

The final optional section is the `%MESSAGE` block. This section is provided to handle errors that may be detected while processing the SQL statement. We will look at `%MESSAGE` in detail later.

Finally, the function must be terminated with a %}. Watch your use of the %} and be sure that you match each part of the function with a %}. Leaving one or more out is a very common source of Net.Data macro errors. The errors may also produce some rather confusing results, because Net.Data expects all sections to be properly terminated. If you leave off the %} terminator, Net.Data assumes that subsequent text is part of the function block.

Now let's look at the sample macro in Figure 25.24.

The section that starts with `%FUNCTION` and ends with `for fetch only` in the sample code displayed above is the function declaration, which includes your SQL statement.

The next notable language feature is the keyword `%REPORT` {, which begins the definition of the report section.

The text between `%REPORT` { and `%ROW` { is the report header. In this case, the report header section includes all of the HTML used to define the page we are going to produce. Beginning with the HTML statement `<table border=`... through the `</tr>` tag preceding the `%ROW` { statement is a table that defines the column headings for the report that we are going to produce.

Notice the table heading lines `<th>` that assign a more user-friendly column heading to each of the three columns.

```
%FUNCTION(DTW_SQL) getinv() {
   SELECT cat, subcat, prdnam
   FROM ignsql.bcbkinv2
   order by cat, subcat, prdnam
   for fetch only
   %REPORT {
      <head>
      <title>Bob's Samples - Basic SQL Example</title>
      </head>

      <body bgcolor="white">
      <H1 align="center">Basic SQL Example</h1>
      <p align="center"><a HREF="/member/html/bobsbook.htm">Return to
  Bob's Book Home Page</a></p>

      <table border="0" cellpadding="2" cellspacing="4" width="60%"
  align="center">
      <tr valign="top">
         <th align="left" bgcolor="#FFC23B">Category</th>
         <th align="left" bgcolor="#FFC23B">Sub-Category</th>
         <th align="left" bgcolor="#FFC23B">Product</th>
      </tr>
      %ROW {
```

Figure 25.24: Sample macro using %REPORT and %ROW functions.

The code segment in Figure 25.25 is the `%ROW` block, which defines how the data retrieved by the SQL statement will be formatted and presented. The `%ROW` block is executed once for each row retrieved by the SQL statement.

```
%ROW {
         <tr valign="top">
            <td align="left" bgcolor="#FFFFCA">$(V_cat)</td>
            <td align="left" bgcolor="#FFFFCA">$(V_subcat)</td>
            <td align="left" bgcolor="#FFFFCA">$(V_prdnam)</td>
         </tr>
     %}
```

Figure 25.25: The %ROW block.

A special variable usage is illustrated in this example also. In the SQL statement, we specified that SQL should retrieve three fields from the table: cat, subcat, and prdnam. Notice that Net.Data automatically assigns a special variable name to each of these fields. Net.Data prefixes each SQL field name with "V_." These are local variables (they only exist within the function definition).

If you wish to use the data retrieved outside the scope of the function, you must assign the value of the report variable (i.e. V_CAT) to a previously declared variable via the DTW_ASSIGN function.

```
</Table>
   %}
```

Figure 25.26: Table terminator tag placement.

Figure 25.26 shows the table terminator tag *</table>* placed in the report trailer section, after the %} tag that terminates the %ROW block, but prior to the %} tag that terminates the %REPORT block. The %} that follows the *</table>* tag terminates the %REPORT block.

```
%MESSAGE {
     100 : { <p align="center"><font color="red"><b>No Inventory Items
Found</font></p>
          %} : continue
   %}
%}
```

Figure 25.27: The %MESSAGE code segment to trap SQL return codes.

The %MESSAGE code segment illustrated in Figure 25.27 allows you to trap SQL return codes and process them as you choose. Many codes such as 100 (Record Not Found) or Duplicate Record on an INSERT are valid normal return codes that you may wish to trap and process. The example illustrated is one I commonly use. It traps for a Not Found condition, which is a normal condition in many of my Net.Data macros. Notice that the %MESSAGE block terminates with its own %} terminator tag. The %} following the end of the message block terminates the function.

As you can see, I put out a message informing the user of the condition No Inventory Items Found and continue processing.

Net.Data does a very good job of displaying SQL error messages and showing you the problem and reason. Unfortunately, the default action is to terminate execution of the macro. Additionally, the messages are very typical of IBM messages (not something I want my users to see).

In the example shown in Figure 25.27, I use the message block to trap a specific condition, display a message on the HTML page, and let the macro continue processing. To learn more about this technique, read and try out the %MESSAGE block variations as documented in the Net.Data reference manual.

SQL FUNCTION TIPS

Native SQL coded in Net.Data macros can be extremely powerful. My Republic Indemnity Companies Web site has several hundred macros that use SQL for retrieval of data as well as for inserting, deleting, and updating data.

The developers of Net.Data have worked very hard to ensure excellent performance of SQL embedded in Net.Data macros. The IBM database developers have also worked very hard to ensure that SQL performs extremely well.

I personally do not store any data on the machine where I run my Web servers and Net.Data with the exception of `www.ignite400.org`, where I have created test databases to store the data for the macros in this book. I use DRDA to connect to a remote machine containing my production data. I strongly recommend this approach as a good security precaution.

Many programmers are more comfortable with the old RPG read and chain logic and are uncomfortable with joining tables in a single SQL statement. Personally, I make extensive use of SQL joins. I must caution that it takes some work and careful analysis of a SQL statement to ensure good performance when using joins.

I start a service job (STRSRVJOB) on the remote system where my data resides. Once the service job is started, I issue a simple STRDBG (Start Debug) command. I then execute the Net.Data macros that access the database. I then look at the job log of the remote request processor job for database performance messages. If you see something like Data Mapping Error, Temporary Index, or Access Path Created in the job log, place your cursor on the message and press the F1 Help key. Detailed specific messages are displayed that explain why the database is doing what it is and recommendations are offered on how to improve the query's performance.

If for some reason you choose not to use database joins, or on those rare occasions where it may be difficult or impossible to use a join, you may call another *%FUNCTION* from within a function.

Consider the following code snippet:

```
<td align="left" bgcolor="#FFFFCA">@getcatnam(V_cat)</td>
```

In this example, a call to the function named getcatnam is embedded in a table row, which is inside the *%ROW* block of the previous macro. Notice that the variable V_CAT is passed to the getcatnam function. This function executes a function to return the name of the category based on the value of V_CAT.

This illustrates that you can call functions from just about anywhere in a macro. You can also call another function from within an SQL statement that retrieves data.

DTW_SYSTEM: SYSTEM LANGUAGE ENVIRONMENT

The major differences between the DTW_SYSTEM and the DTW_SQL environment is the fact that the SYSTEM environment uses the C language SYSTEM call function to call programs external to the Net.Data macro.

Here we describe calling native-language and CL programs via the DTW_SYSTEM (System Language Environment). The basic syntax of a call to a system function is similar to that of the DTW_SQL language environment. The DTW_SYSTEM environment may have an optional %REPORT, %ROW, and %MESSAGE block. The function may return individual variables, or it may format a table and return a table as output to Net.Data.

Calling an RPG/ILE Program

Figure 25.28 calls an RPG/ILE program that calculates an inputted date and the number of days to add or subtract from the date.

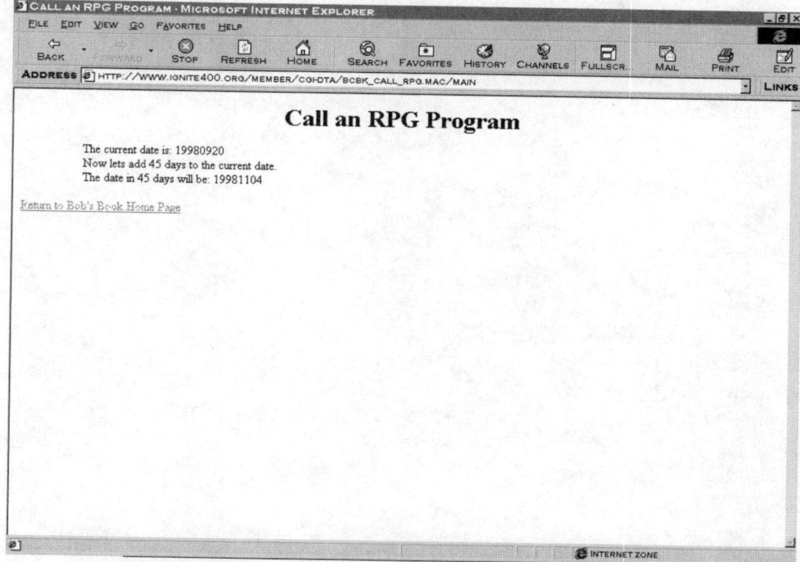

Figure 25.28: Simple RPG function call using DTW_SYSTEM.

We also introduce a new Net.Data built-in function @DTW_DATE. In Figure 25.29, we issue a call to @DTW_DATE("S,"DATE_IN) built-in function. This function returns the current system date to the macro. The "S" parameter returns the date in the system format or (YYYYMMDD). "DATE_IN" is a previously declared variable that will store the date returned from the macro.

```
%DEFINE {
   date_in = ""
   days_in = "045"
   date_out = ""
%}

@DTW_DATE("S,"date_in)

%FUNCTION(DTW_SYSTEM) DateCalc(IN P1, P2, OUT P3) {
   %EXEC {
      /QSYS.LIB/IGNITE.LIB/UPDRPG1.PGM
   %}
%}
```

Figure 25.29: Sample DTW_SYSTEM call function (part 1 of 2).

```
%HTML(main) {

<html>
<head>
<title>Call an RPG Program</title>
</head>
<body bgcolor="white">
<h1 align="center">Call an RPG Program</h1>
<blockquote><blockquote>
<p>The current date is: $(date_in)<br>
   Now lets add 45 days to the current date.<br>
   @DateCalc(date_in,days_in,date_out)
   The date in 45 days will be: $(date_out)</P>
</blockquote></blockquote>
<p><a HREF="/member/html/bobsbook.htm">Return to Bob's Book Home
Page</a></p>


</body>
</html>
%}
```

Figure 25.29: Sample DTW_SYSTEM call function.

The variable "DATE_IN" (today's date) and the variable "DAYS_IN" are input to the RPG program, which adds 45 days to today's date and returns the result into a variable called "DATE_OUT." Note that all three variables were declared and initialized in the %DEFINE block.

The code snippet in Figure 25.30 shows the entire function definition. As we saw in the SQL example, *%FUNCTION* informs Net.Data that a function declaration follows. *DTW_SYSTEM* instructs Net.Data to use the System Language Environment. DATECALC is the name assigned to the function.

```
%FUNCTION(DTW_SYSTEM) DateCalc(IN P1, P2, OUT P3) {
   %EXEC {
      /QSYS.LIB/IGNITE.LIB/UPDRPG1.PGM
   %}
%}
```

Figure 25.30: @DTW_DATE function definition.

In this example there are two input parameters (*IN P1, P2)* and one output parameter *(OUT P3*).

If you skip ahead to the `%HTML` section you will see the call to the function:

```
@DateCalc(date_in,days_in,date_out)
```

In the function declaration, the three variables P1, P2, and P3 are simply placeholders. They enable Net.Data to format the function declaration as a template. In the @DATECALC call, the value contained in the variable DATE_IN is mapped to P1. The value contained in the variable DAYS_IN is mapped to P2, and the program when called will return the result of its processing into the field P3, which maps back to DATE_OUT.

Within the function is a new Net.Data construct, the %EXEC block. The %EXEC block is actually quite simple. It says execute the program UPDRPG1.PGM stored in the library IGNITE.LIB that is defined in the QSYS.LIB (see Figure 25.31).

```
%EXEC {
        /QSYS.LIB/IGNITE.LIB/UPDRPG1.PGM
   %}
```

Figure 25.31: The %EXEC block.

This is the same as typing CALL IGNITE/UPDRPG1 on a command line. It uses ROOT file system naming conventions, which may be unfamiliar to many AS/400 developers.

It must receive the full path to the program that is to be executed. Using the ROOT IFS file system notation, QSYS.LIB (QSYS) is the root directory. IGNITE.LIB is a library (or in IFS terms, a subdirectory) of QSYS, and UPDRPG1.PGM resides in IGNITE.LIB. Notice that the object type is suffixed to the libraries and the program itself. IBM has created a list of object type suffixes that must be used when using IFS file paths to access objects stored in the QSYS library file system. LIB is library, PGM is program, FILE is a file, MBR is a member, etc.

THE ENVIRONMENT AND PARAMETERS

Well, that all looks pretty simple from the Net.Data macro's perspective. It is very simple, but RPG programmers must understand the system environment and how data is passed to and returned from the program.

The variables P1, P2, and P3 are placed in the job's environment as name value pairs. Assuming that today's date is September 27, 1998, then the following values would be placed by Net.Data into the job's environment:

```
P1="19980927"
P2="045"
P3=""
```

The RPG/ILE program must use the QTMHGETENV API to retrieve data from the environment. The program must use the QTMHPUTENV API to put its output back into the environment. Net.Data retrieves the variable P3 from the environment.

The Date Calculation Program shown in Figure 25.32 retrieves the variables P1 (today's date) and P2 (number of days) from the environment using the QTMHGETENV API. The API must be called once for each variable to be retrieved. This program calls it once for P1 and once for P2.

```
FMT H
HKeywords++++++++++++++++++++++++++++++++++++++++++++++++++++++++++++++++++
         *************** Beginning of data ******************************
H DATEDIT(*YMD)
 *
D GetEnv              PR                      ExtProc('QtmhGetEnv')
D                                32767
D                                   10I 0
D                                   10I 0
D                                   30
D                                   10I 0
D                                   16
 *
D PutEnv              PR                      ExtProc('QtmhPutEnv')
D                                32767
D                                   10I 0
D                                   16
 *
D envVal              S          32767
D envBufLn            S             10I 0
```

Figure 25.32: Date calculation program (part 1 of 2).

```
D envValLn        S                10I 0
D envNm           S                30
D envNmLn         S                10I 0
D errorCode       S                16
 *
D CYMD_Date       S                  D   DATFMT(*ISO)
 *
D Date_In         S                 8S 0 INZ
D Date_Out        S                 8S 0 INZ
 *
DDays             DS
D   Sign                            1    INZ
D   Nbr_Days                        2S 0 INZ
 *
 * Get P1 value
C                   EVAL      envNm    = 'P1'
C                   EVAL      envNmLn  = 2
C                   EVAL      envBufLn = 32767
C                   CALLp     getenv(envVal:envBufLn:envvalLn:
C                                    envNm:envNmLn:errorCode)
 *
C                   MOVEL     envVal        Date_IN
 * Get P2 value
C                   EVAL      envNm    = 'P2'
C                   EVAL      envNmLn  = 2
C                   EVAL      envBufLn = 32767
C                   CALLp     getenv(envVal:envBufLn:envvalLn:
C                                    envNm:envNmLn:errorCode)
 *
C                   MOVEL     envVal        Days
 * Calculate  Date_Out = (Date_In + Nbr_Days)
C                   MOVE      Date_In       CYMD_Date
 *
C                   IF        Sign = '-'
C                   SUBDUR    Nbr_Days:*D   CYMD_Date
C                   ELSE
C                   ADDDUR    Nbr_Days:*D   CYMD_Date
C                   ENDIF
 *
C                   MOVE      CYMD_Date     Date_Out
C                   MOVE      Date_Out      Wrk_Date           8
 * Set P3 to a new value
C     'P3='         CAT(P)    Wrk_Date      envVal
C                   EVAL      envValLn = 11
C                   CALLp     putenv(envVal:envValLn:errorCode)
 *
C                   RETURN
       ***************** End of data ********************************
```

Figure 25.32: Date calculation program (part 2 of 2).

It performs the required processing to compute the new date by adding the value of P2 to the date retrieved from P1. It then calls QTMHPUTENV to place the result into P3 in the environment. It then exits and returns to Net.Data.

Please be aware that QTMHGETENV and QTMHPUTENV are contained in a service program provided by IBM that must be bound to your RPG program when you compile it and create a program. See the system API manual and the Net.Data programming guide for a detailed explanation of the API's usage and parameters.

CL PROGRAMS AND COMMANDS

You may call programs written in any language, including CL. You may also directly invoke system or user-written commands. There are several examples of invoking commands on the Net.Data Web site.

A relatively new facility that may be called via the DTW_SYSTEM language environment is a utility called Qshell. Qshell is IBM's port of the UNIX Korn shell. This is a command-processing environment that includes a language and access to a subset of UNIX commands. It has certain advantages over CL programs, one of the biggest being that you can *redirect* output from the UNIX equivalents of OS/400 commands to files or back to the Net.Data macro. You can format the output returned to Net.Data for presentation via HTML. Qshell debuted on the AS/400 in V4R1 was greatly enhanced in V4R2. The AS/400 Partners in Development site (*www.as400.ibm.com/developer/qshell/index.html*) has details.

Java programs can be called via the DTW_SYSTEM interface by invoking the Java CL command.

DTW_DIRECT_CALL

In March 1999, IBM released a major enhancement to Net.Data. This enhancement introduced the DTW_DIRECT call built-in function. This powerful enhancement allows you to call *any* program on the AS/400 using conventional parameters. You can use it to call your own programs as well as IBM's rich library of APIs. This facility enables you to call programs without having to use the *environment*.

The code in Figure 25.33 illustrates the DTW_DIRECTCALL environment. In this example, a function of type DTW_DIRECTCALL named DCFUNCTION2 is defined. The next statements define the characteristics of the input and output parameters. %EXEC works exactly as it does in the DTW_SYSTEM environment.

```
%define ilepgm = "/QSYS.LIB/NETDATADEV.LIB/TDCRPGI01.PGM"

%FUNCTION(DTW_DIRECTCALL) dcFunction2(
    IN char(23) inp1, IN decimal(10,2) inp2,
    IN numeric(7,4) inp3, IN int inp4,
    OUT char(23) outp5, OUT decimal(10,2) outp6,
    OUT numeric(7,4) outp7, OUT int outp8)
    {
       %EXEC ilepgm %}
%}
```

Figure 25.33: DTW_DIRECTCALL environment.

Note that you specify the length and type of each input or output parameter that you will pass to the program to be called.

One word of caution concerning passing Net.Data parameters to a program. Net.Data null terminates its strings (like C) by placing a X'00' character in the character following the last valid character. If you passed 12345 into the char(23) field, it would contain 12345X'00' with hexadecimal 00 in the sixth byte of the field. This can cause you some problems. To avoid it, use the @DTW_CONCAT built-in function to concatenate a string of blanks to the left or right side of the field as required, forcing the X'00' to be truncated.

DTW_REXX: REXX LANGUAGE ENVIRONMENT

REXX is a text manipulation and parsing language that has existed on the AS/400 since at least V3R1. IBM developed the REXX language as an attempt to provide a common command processing language on all of its platforms. There is a version of REXX available for all platforms that IBM supports. REXX on the AS/400 has been extended to call CL programs and commands, and handle unique AS/400 facilities such as data queues.

REXX includes some very powerful and easy to use text manipulation capabilities. I use REXX to provide the functionality that Net.Data is missing in its built-in functions. Net.Data handles REXX in two different ways:

- It can execute a REXX program stored in a Source Physical File member on your machine. There are significant performance advantages to this approach. IBM pre-processes your REXX program when you save it via PDM.

- It allows you to code REXX source within your macro and invoke the REXX processor to execute the REXX code without having to store the REXX code in an external file. You pay a significant performance penalty for this convenience. The penalty is, however, a trade off for the ease with which you can write code.

One example is a simple REXX program that formats numbers with commas for presentation. Net.Data includes a function to format numeric fields, but once you use it, the number becomes a string that cannot be used in mathematical functions. I frequently use Net.Data math functions to total rows and display the totals at the bottom of a page or to perform calculations that I can't perform using SQL when I retrieve the data.

The actual REXX program (Figure 25.34) is a modified version of an example provided by IBM in the REXX programming guide.

```
%{ Macro: bcbk_call_rexx.mac - call an external REXX program
   This macro demonstrates calling an external REXX Language program.
The program
   formats a decimal number inserting commas for presentation. It re-
quires a real number
   with two decimal places as input. It uses a single INOUT parameter.
%}

%DEFINE {
   num_in = "21456.72"
   num_out = "0"
%}

%FUNCTION(DTW_REXX) editnum(IN number,OUT bucks) {
   %EXEC {
      /QSYS.LIB/IGNITE.LIB/IGNREXSRC.FILE/EDTNUM.MBR
   %}
%}

%HTML(main) {
<html>
<head>
<title>Call an External REXX Program</title>
</head>
<body bgcolor="white">
<h1 align="center">Call an External REXX Program</h1>
```

Figure 25.34: Macro to call an external REXX program (part 1 of 2).

```
<blockquote><blockquote>
   <p>This is what our number looks like before we format it:
$(num_in)<br>
   @editnum(num_in,num_out)
      This is what it looks like after REXX formats it: $(num_out)</p>
</blockquote></blockquote>
<p><a HREF="/member/html/bobsbook.htm">Return to Bob's Book Home
Page</a></p>

</body>
</hmtl>
%}
```

Figure 25.34: Macro to call an external REXX program (part 2 of 2).

The structure of a REXX function is identical to that of the DTW_SYSTEM functions. The language environment DTW_REXX in %FUNCTION(DTW_REXX) tells Net.Data to invoke the REXX interpreter. In the function "editnum," we pass in a number as an input parameter and receive a formatted text string out.

In the *%DEFINE* section of the macro, we define two variables: "NUM_IN" and "NUM_OUT." The variable "num_in" is assigned a default value of 21456.72 and "NUM_OUT" is initialized to zero (we could have initialized to nulls).

If we skip down to the %HTML section and locate the function call @EDITNUM (NUM_IN,NUM_OUT), we see that the function passes the two previously defined parameters to the function. The function performs its processing and stores the result in "NUM_OUT." The function call does not produce any HTML output. You must use $(NUM_OUT) to display the result of the function.

This function could have been written as an INOUT function. If it did use INOUT it would have been called as @EDITNUM(NUM). You would pass the number in and receive the formatted output in the variable "NUM."

Another way to write the macro and the function would have been to use the RETURN(FLD) option of the Net.Data macro language. Parameter types "IN," "OUT," and "INOUT" assign values to variables. If you want the function to output data directly to the HTML page where you place the function, then use RETURN(VALUE). RETURN instructs Net.Data to place the result of the function into the text stream being written to STDOUT at the point where you put the function call.

In the example, I have called the IN parameter "number" and the OUT parameter "bucks." The names are significant within the function. When you call this function, you can pass any two variables to it in the call. The function definition determines that you need two parameters and gives you an error if you pass more or less. The names passed in the call statement are not relevant. Any variable may be passed in.

The REXX program that is called by this function depends upon the names of the variables defined in the function's parameter definition. The REXX program looks for a variable named "NUMBER" to contain its input and places its output in a variable named "BUCKS." Figure 25.35 shows the REXX program source.

```
SEU==>
 FMT **  ...+... 1 ...+... 2 ...+... 3 ...+... 4 ...+... 5 ...+... 6 ...+... 7 ...+... 8
        *************** Beginning of data ***************************************************
/* Test format command */                                               971001
x = format(number,,2,0)                                                 971001
PARSE VALUE x WITH dollars ."" cents                                    971001
dollars = ABS(dollars)                                                  971001
backin = REVERSE(dollars)                                               971001
backout = ""                                                            971001
DO WHILE LENGTH(backin) > 3                                             971001
   PARSE VAR backin group 4 backin                                      971001
   backout = backout||group||,""                                        971001
END                                                                     971001
backout = backout||backin                                               971001
bucks = REVERSE(backout)||.""||cents                                    971001
                                                                        971001
IF number < 0 THEN                                                      971001
   bucks = bucks||"-"                                                   971001
ELSE                                                                    971001
   bucks = bucks||" "                                                   971001
        ****************** End of data*************************************************************
```

Figure 25.35: REXX program to format numbers.

You can see in the example that "NUMBER" is the input variable that is parsed by the REXX program. You can see at the bottom of the listing that "BUCKS" is the output variable.

Figure 25.36 shows a REXX function and Net.Data function call, extracted from a Net.Data function that I wrote to handle carriage return line feeds in text captured in a TEXTAREA. I will illustrate the macro later and describe the problem.

REXX comes to the aid of Net.Data by providing the TRANSLATE function. TRANSLATE translates all occurrences of a character or hexadecimal character in a text string to another. Net.Data does not have a comparable function.

```
%FUNCTION(DTW_REXX) TransCRLF(INOUT STRING) {
   STRING = TRANSLATE(STRING, X2C('E0'), X2C('OD'))
%}
...
@TransCRLF(S)
```

Figure 25.36: In-line REXX function.

As you can see from the example, the function definition is the same as the previous definition. We replace the %EXEC block, which causes Net.Data to load and execute an external program, with the actual REXX program code.

The variable "S" is passed into the function into an INOUT variable named "STRING." STRING is translated by the REXX TRANSLATE function and the result replaces the input value.

REXX is a very simple language. *The REXX Programming Guide* and *The REXX Language Reference,* two IBM manuals, are full of examples. The editnum macro is almost line for line from an example in the manual.

The decision to support REXX within Net.Data was a brilliant one by the Net.Data developers. It allows users to provide any additional functionality to Net.Data that the developers didn't build into the language. Often, the Net.Data developers provide functions that users tell them they are using REXX to perform.

%INCLUDE

The Net.Data %INCLUDE function allows you to store virtually any Net.Data construct in an external file that is loaded and processed as in-line macro code.

Because Net.Data integrates standard HTML and JavaScript code within a macro, macros can become extremely long and difficult to read. I have developed a habit of storing the bulk of my HTML code in external files that are then included in the macro via the %INCLUDE function.

%INCLUDE has the format of %INCLUDE "FILENAME.HTI"

When Net.Data encounters an %INCLUDE, it reads and processes the content of the %INCLUDE file as if it were a part of the macro being executed. I was initially concerned that the use of %INCLUDE files would add significant overhead to the processing of my macros. It seems that stream file processing (i.e. open and read) is remarkably efficient, and I cannot detect a noticeable degradation in performance by using %INCLUDE files.

NET.DATA MACRO_FUNCTION

The Net.Data MACRO_FUNCTION is a recent addition to the Net.Data macro language. It allows you to develop subroutines in Net.Data and reuse Net.Data macro language code. The MACRO_FUNCTION, coupled with the %INCLUDE file function, allows you to store reusable common routines externally.

MACRO_FUNCTIONS are similar to other types of functions supported by Net.Data except that MACRO_FUNCTIONS are built using the Net.Data macro language.

The little macro in Figure 25.37 is used to rearrange a date string in the format YYYYMMDD into the date format of MM/DD/YYYY. It uses a series of Net.Data built-in functions to accomplish the task.

```
%{Macro: bcbk_mac_func.mac – call a Macro Function
   This macro enhances the macro called bcbk_call_rpg.mac. It introduces
a Net.Data
   macro function that can be called as required to format a system date
for
   presentation to the user.
%}
%DEFINE {
   date_in = ""
   days_in = "045"
   date_out = ""
%}
%MACRO_FUNCTION FormatDate(IN D,OUT DF) {
   @DTW_SUBSTR(D,"1,""4,"yr)
   @DTW_ASSIGN(DF,@DTW_rCONCAT("/,"yr))
   @DTW_SUBSTR(D,"7,""2,"dy)
   @DTW_CONCAT(@DTW_rCONCAT("/,"dy),DF,DF)
   @DTW_SUBSTR(D,"5,""2,"mo)
   @DTW_CONCAT(mo,DF,DF)
```

Figure 25.37: A Net.Data macro using the %MACRO_FUNCTION (Part 1 of 2).

```
   @DTW_ASSIGN(D,DF)
%}
@DTW_DATE("S,"date_in)
%FUNCTION(DTW_SYSTEM) DateCalc(IN P1, P2, OUT P3) {
   %EXEC {
      /QSYS.LIB/IGNITE.LIB/UPDRPG1.PGM
   %}
%}
%HTML(main) {
<html>
<head>
<title>Using Macro_Functions</title>
</head>
<body bgcolor="white">
<h1 align="center">Using Macro_Functions</h1>
<blockquote><blockquote>
<p>The current date is: @FormatDate(date_in,fdate)$(fdate)<br>
   Now lets add 45 days to the current date.<br>
   @DateCalc(date_in,days_in,date_out)
   The date in 45 days will be: @FormatDate(date_out,fdate)$(fdate)</P>
</blockquote></blockquote>
<p><a HREF="/member/html/bobsbook.htm">Return to Bob's Book Home
Page</a></p>
</body>
</html>
%}
```

Figure 25.37: A Net.Data macro using the %MACRO_FUNCTION (Part 2 of 2).

First look at the call statements embedded in the HTML coded in the %HTML section of the macro. The *@FormatDate(date_in,fdate)* statement calls the function "FORMATDATE." The call passes the variable "DATE_IN" to the function that contains a date in the format YYYMMDD. It also instructs the function to return its output to the variable "FDATE."

The MACRO_FUNCTION contains the code shown in Figure 25.38:

```
%MACRO_FUNCTION FormatDate(IN D,OUT DF) {
   @DTW_SUBSTR(D,"1,""4,"yr)
   @DTW_ASSIGN(DF,@DTW_rCONCAT("/,"yr))
   @DTW_SUBSTR(D,"7,""2,"dy)
   @DTW_CONCAT(@DTW_rCONCAT("/,"dy),DF,DF)
   @DTW_SUBSTR(D,"5,""2,"mo)
   @DTW_CONCAT(mo,DF,DF)
   @DTW_ASSIGN(D,DF)
%}
```

Figure 25.38: MACRO_FUNCTION code.

Notice that the macro function is declared with the Net.Data keyword %MACRO_FUNCTION. Because macro functions use Net.Data's own language, no language environment is required. We then assign a name to the macro (FormatDate), and define the input and output variables (IN D, OUT DF).

The function then executes a series of Net.Data built-in functions. When the macro completes, it returns the value stored in "DF" to the variable "FDATE" passed into the function via the function call. This macro produces the output shown in Figure 25.39.

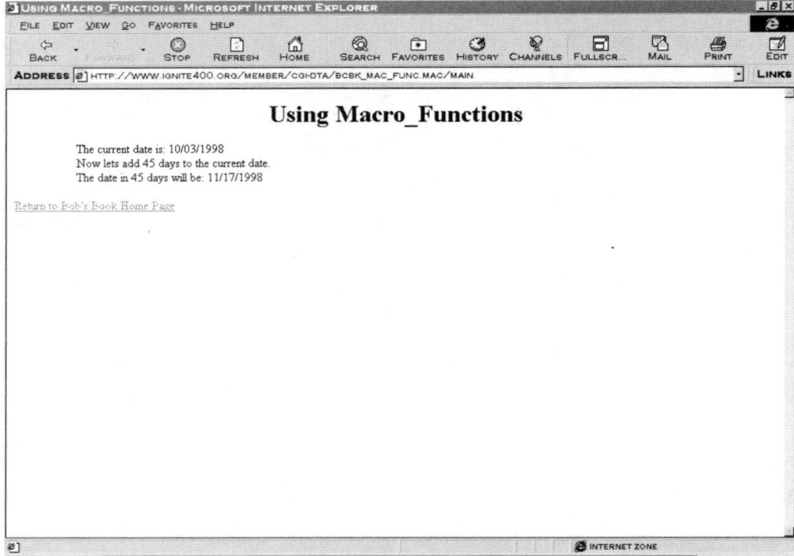

Figure 25.39: Output from a macro using a MACRO_FUNCTION.

NET.DATA BUILT-IN FUNCTIONS

I cannot describe all of the built-in functions included in the Net.Data language. I will, however, describe some that I frequently use. For a more complete list, check out the Net.Data reference manual. And look to the AS/400 Net.Data home page for PTFs. Most PTFs are backward compatible to V3R7 and V3R2.

TYPES OF BUILT-IN FUNCTIONS

Most built-in functions have more than one form. By form I am talking about the parameter structure of the function and where the function returns its output.

DTW_R..., DTWF_R..., or DTWR_R. . functions (notice the letter "R" following the underscore) replace the function call with the result.

If we were to call the date function @DTW_RDATE( ), you would see the value 19981003 displayed where the call statement is coded in the macro.

Another variant is the DTW_M...or multiple parameter variant. This variation performs the function on each of the parameters passed to the function. It treats the parameter as an INOUT parameter and stores the result in the input parameter. Consider the following:

Assume that *make* = "*buick*," *model* = "*park avenue*," and *color* = "*white*."

We then call the function: @DTW_MUPPERCASE(MAKE, MODEL, COLOR)

Now *make* contains BUICK, model contains PARK AVENUE, and *color* contains WHITE. The final variant stores the result in an output variable named in the function call.

Consider the function @DTW_UPPERCASE("ABCD,"OUTVAR).

In this example, we will store the uppercase translation of the literal "abcd" in a variable that we have created named outvar. If you were to display the value contained in outvar it would display ABCD.

GENERAL BUILT-IN FUNCTIONS

This collection of functions doesn't fit in other categories of function documented in the Net.Data Reference.

@DTW_ADDQUOTE

This function formats data correctly when dealing with names such as O'Brien or anywhere that single or double quotes may be part of the text string you are processing.

I use this function anytime I am inserting or updating data typed on a form and stored in the database via SQL. This ensures that the proper quote strings are placed into the text so that an SQL statement will not fail.

@DTW_DATE

This function returns the system date in one of several formats. Unfortunately, this function needs a good deal of enhancement and more output formats. It does what it is supposed to do, but you have to calculate the day of the week, or translate month and day numbers to words if you like to use long formal dates.

@DTW_EXIT

This function is new to the AS/400. It causes the macro to stop processing when the function is encountered and write all output generated before encountering the function to the browser.

@GET_ENVVAR

This is one of the single most valuable built-in functions. I have previously told you that CGI, the browser, and the Web server provide a great deal of information about the user and the environment via a shared area called the environment. This function retrieves variables from the environment and makes them available to your macro.

Would you like to know what browser your user is using?

Use @GET_ENVVAR("HTTP_USER_AGENT"); it will return Mozilla/4.0 (compatible; MSIE 4.01; Windows 95) if you are using Microsoft Internet Explorer 4.01. It will return Mozilla/4.06 [en] (Win95; U) if you are using Netscape Communicator 4.06.

See `http://www.ignite400.org/bobsbook.htm` to see the macro source and run the macro cgitest.mac. This macro displays all of the standard environment variables that I know.

@DTW_TIME

This function returns the system time.

@DTW_URLESCSEQ

This very important function is essential to condition variable values passed between URLs as part of a QUERY_STRING. Look carefully at the following link:

```
<A HREF="/CGI-DTA/mymacro.mac/main?custno=$(custno)
&custname=John Smith">
```

If you were to try and process the variable "CUSTNAME" expecting it to contain "John Smith," you would be very disappointed. The space causes the browser to ignore everything following the space between John and Smith. The variable "CUSTNAME" would contain simply the value "John."

To handle this situation you must instruct Net.Data to URL encode the text string contained in the variable for you. Look at following HTML link tag and see how it has been revised to accommodate URL encoding:

```
<A HREF="/CGI-DTA/mymacro.mac/main?custno=$(custno)
      &custname=@DTW_URLESCSEQ("John Smith")">
```

The built-in function @DTW_URLESCSEQ translates the offending space character to the URL encoded string "%20." Now the variable "CUSTNAME" will in fact contain "John Smith."

MATH FUNCTIONS

Net.Data includes a full complement of basic math functions, including addition, subtraction, multiplication, division, and exponentiation. The math functions are fairly basic; hopefully, more functions will be added over time.

STRING FUNCTIONS

These very powerful functions manipulate characters within text strings. They are the most useful of all of Net.Data's built-in functions. You will use these functions more frequently than any of the others.

If you work with other programming languages, or spreadsheets like Lotus 123 or Excel you will be readily familiar with these functions. Watch the syntax carefully when you read the manual.

WORD FUNCTIONS

Word functions are very similar to string functions except that they operate on words instead of individual characters.

Consider the following example:

```
class_code = "8234 1"
```

In Net.Data's terms, 8234 is a word and the following digit 1 is a second word. If you use the @DTW_RWORD(CLASS_CODE,"1"), it will return the value 8234 (the first word). @DTW_RWORD(CLASS_CODE,"2") will return 1 (the second word).

What you need to understand is that any string of characters separated from another string of characters is considered to be a word. Alphabetic and numeric characters are both considered to be characters.

CACHE FUNCTIONS

These functions are not yet supported on the AS/400. When looking at the reference manual, it is important to remember that Net.Data runs on all IBM platforms. There is a chart above each built-in function that tells you if it is available on the AS/400.

You will notice that more functions are available for the AS/400 than any other platform!

FLAT FILE FUNCTIONS

These are a built-in set of macro functions that allow you to manipulate files stored in the IFS directory. The functions are fairly straightforward, including OPEN, CLOSE, READ, WRITE, APPEND, UPDATE, DELETE, REMOVE, and SEARCH.

You must open a file before you can read, write, update, or append data to it. You should close a file when you are done with it.

Flat files are defined as *stream files*. These are unstructured text files containing a long stream of data. They are roughly equivalent to PC files.

Care must be taken in selecting the appropriate data storage format. By default, data is stored in the AS/400's native EBCIDIC. This will not look very nice when you try to display the contents of the file on a Web page. There is an option that will allow you to store ASCII text, which is what the browser is expecting to see. Look at the WRITE, UPDATE, and APPEND functions.

WEB REGISTRY FUNCTIONS

No one has given me an adequate explanation of the Web Registry, yet I've been able to develop a very large number of Net.Data macros without it. If you figure out a use for it, send me an e-mail message and let me know how you used it.

TABLE FUNCTIONS

Tables and table functions are very powerful features of Net.Data. They also may be somewhat confusing when first encountered when you use the DTW_SQL function. Net.Data stores the output of each query in a storage area called the *default table*. Tables in Net.Data are arrays of rows and columns.

If you have several SQL functions in your macro, the first one executed stores its output in the default table. Net.Data assumes that you will process all of the rows and columns of the table formatting the output or assigning the data to variables via the DTW_ASSIGN function.

When you execute the next function, the previous contents of the default table are overlaid and destroyed by the result of the next query.

This means if you wanted to retrieve data from the first result table, you would not be able to. Net.Data provides functions and special variables to allow you to deal with this situation.

The special variable %TABLE used in a %DEFINE statement allows you to declare your own tables and then map the output of functions to the table you have declared. Consider the example in Figure 25.40.

```
%DEFINE
   table1 = %TABLE
   table2 = %TABLE
%}
```

Figure 25.40: Declare two tables for use in a macro.

In this example, we are declaring two tables for subsequent use within the macro. You would then define an output parameter in your function definitions, and finally specify the name of the table variable that you have declared when you call the function.

In Figure 25.41, you instruct Net.Data to store the output of "FUNC01" in "TABLE1" and the output of "FUNC02" in "TABLE2." Using this method of allocating your own tables and calling the functions and specifying output parameters leaves TABLE1 and TABLE2 available for your use through the life of the macro. This is particularly useful with the introduction of a new series of table functions that allow you to create tables or retrieve specific rows and columns from the tables.

```
%FUNCTION(DTW_SQL) func01 (OUT t1) {
   SELECT ...
   ...
%}

%FUNCTION(DTW_SQL) func02 (OUT t2) {
   SELECT ...
   ...
%}

@func01(table1)
@func02(table2)
```

Figure 25.41: Allocating tables to store output.

Please note that all of Net.Data's function types can create tables as output, but be sure to consult the documentation for details when using functions other than SQL.

It is advisable to use the tables' built-in functions wherever possible as Net.Data is optimized to process and format entire tables at significantly reduced processing costs (i.e. better performance).

SQL STORED PROCEDURES

Another recent feature added to Net.Data is full support for SQL stored procedures. Net.Data can declare and pass any number of parameters to an SQL stored procedure. A stored procedure can be written in any language supported by the AS/400 or SQL's new procedure language.

A stored procedure can return specific variables or one or more tables to the macro. If you use separate AS/400s for your Web server and database server, stored procedures provide a very efficient means of accessing remote data.

Stored procedures allow you to use static SQL in programs stored on your remote database machine and exchange all of the data in one request and response between the two machines.

PERSISTENT STATE CGI

Under V4R3 of OS/400 with IBM's HTTPd Server, you may choose to use *persistent state CGI*. Persistent state CGI keeps the job where your Net.Data macro runs active for a specific period of time or until the user responds.

This means that tables and variables are kept in memory while the job is active. This approach is a trade-off, because you tie up a job for a specific user for some extended period of time. There are some error-handling conditions if the job times out and the user responds after the job has terminated.

You must balance the cost of creating and maintaining jobs on the system to gain the performance advantages of this methodology with the resource cost of idle jobs.

I have found that Net.Data's persistent-state support provides incredibly fast response times during a prolonged dialog with a user (i.e. multiple HTML input forms with server-side validation and responses). Care should be taken to use this facility judiciously as it does have a major cost in terms of AS/400 resources. A large amount of physical memory on the machine greatly facilitates the use of this option.

As with many facilities, there are pros and cons to the use of persistent-state CGIs. It might be great for an electronic store, where you have a fairly high degree of certainty that a user will respond within a short time limit and you can predict his path through your system.

NEW IN V4R3 AND V4R4

The developers of Net.Data constantly enhance this product and release enhancements via PTF's. Since this chapter was first written, we have seen dramatic improvements and new features added to Net.Data.

V4R3 brought us a new facility called DirectCall. DTW_DIRECTCALL is a new functionality that allows you to call any program on an AS/400 with standard parameter passing techniques. You no longer have to use the ENVIRONMENT to pass parameters.

V4R4 brought us dynamic variables. I found this useful in creating a form very much like an order form that had a variable number of rows depending upon what the user selected on the previous form.

When you create an HTML input form you can easily create variable number of rows with dynamically named variable using a Net.Data %WHILE loop or the %ROW section of a %FUNCTION block.

If you have PRODUCT_NUMBER, QUANTITY, and AMOUNT as entry fields, you would create code as shown inFigure 25.42.

```
%ROW {
   <input type="text" name="PRODUCT_NUMER$(ROW_NUM)" value="$(V_prdno)">
   <input type="text" name="QUANTITY$(ROW_NUM)>

%}
```

Figure 25.42: Example of coding variable rows.

The issue that dynamic variables solved was how to process this form on input. You can now build a simple %WHILE loop concatenating a counter to the name of the variable and retrieve the data.

A FEW FINAL WORDS ABOUT NET.DATA

Net.Data is a very simple and easy-to-use macro language. Although it is simple, I have not found anything that I cannot do with Net.Data. As I mentioned in the beginning of the chapter, the IBM developers for this product are some of the best I have ever met, and certainly the most user friendly. This product is maturing at a very rapid rate of development, spurred on by the fact that IBM's Net.Commerce product is built using a substantial amount of Net.Data macro code.

REFERENCES

For more information, the following Web pages have copies of the most current documentation and information about Net.Data.

www.as400.ibm.com/netdata. The resource for AS/400 specific Net.Data issues.

www.software.ibm.com/data/net.data/. This is the Net.Data home page for all versions of Net.Data on all supported platforms.

`www.software.ibm.com/data/net.data/docs/v2.htm` Manuals are provided on-line, in HTML, Adobe Acrobat PDF form, and in Postscript. You may view or download them as you choose. Be sure and read the *Net.Data Administration and Programming Guide* and the must-have *Net.Data Reference.* You will need this manual every time you work with Net.Data.

The development team for Net.Data maintains and operates a Web-based forum at: `testcase.boulder.ibm.com:8081/cgi-bin/db2www/forum.tc/main` This forum is frequented by IBM developers, who answer most questions, as well as new and experienced users who help each other solve application development challenges.

Net.Data questions and answers can also be directed to newsgroups hosted by IGNITe/400 (`www.ignite400.org`, a Web-based forum (developed in Net.Data) for those who do not have a NNTP news account and a mailing list.

Visit IBM's Net.Data forum and IGNITe/400's Web site for the very latest breaking news on NEW Net.Data features and facilities. IGNITe/400 also has working copies of every macro in this book as well as many others that are not included here.

INDEX

A

Note: Boldface numbers indicate illustrations.

D

E

F

G

I

J

R

S

 Note: Boldface numbers indicate illustrations.

Note: Boldface numbers indicate illustrations.

U

V

W

X

Y

Z

Other Best-sellers of Related Interest

AS/400 TCP/IP Handbook

TCP/IP Networking Concepts, Configurations, Services, and Programming for the AS/400 Server Environment

by Chris Peters

Understand the protocol that is the heart of Internet and intranet communications, and position yourself to take full advantage of the AS/400's potential with *AS/400 TCP/IP Handbook*, the new book from Chris Peters.

This handbook is the most complete TCP/IP book on the market. It has the concepts and background material that traditional AS/400 professionals need as they start their Internet development journey. Gain an understanding of the significant TCP/IP utilities available on the AS/400. Plus, explore sockets technology in detail through the use of a full-featured, production-quality TCP/IP sockets server program with ILE RPG. This book is truly the single source for AS/400 TCP/IP programming information.

400 pages. Level: Novice, Intermediate, and Advanced.

BOOK 5008 ....$99

ISBN 1-58347-005-0

Re-engineering AS/400 Legacy Applications

by Paul Tuohy

Now you can use IBM's recent enhancements to the AS/400, OS/400, and RPG to immediately increase the reliability of your legacy applications, improve programmer productivity, and build a firm basis for the future of your business. This book and companion CD-ROM provide a tutorial aimed at showing you how to modernize your applications by taking you through a re-engineering of a sample application step by step. Author Paul Tuohy covers conversion of RPG IV programs as well as re-engineering them to take full advantage of RPG IV and ILE. He also covers triggers, referential integrity, and APIs so that your applications can take advantage of all the new technology that is available today. This book will be a valuable aid as you evaluate your legacy applications and then move into re-engineering.

Putting your company's IT resources in a condition of stasis while technology moves on may be a costly business mistake. It is possible, and profitable, to derive some of the benefits of new technology from within a legacy application. Best of all, re-engineering gives you the opportunity to learn new programming concepts and acquire new skills. 432 pages. Level: Intermediate to Advanced.

BOOK 5009 ....$99

ISBN 1-58347-006-9

CL Programming for the AS/400—Second Edition

by Greg Veal

Learning CL programming has never been easier, thanks to *CL Programming for the AS/400—Second Edition*, the enhanced version of Greg Veal's 1992 best-seller.

Completely updated for V4R4, this book has new, comprehensive information on CL in the ILE, and each of its 14 chapters has been refined to include comparisons of important concepts from the ILE and Original Program Model (OPM) perspectives. Learning the material will be easy as you progress through the more advanced concepts using examples of real-world programs just like those that support user applications and system operations in many companies. In addition, review questions at the end of each chapter will allow you to self-test your knowledge. An optional instructor's guide with progressive lab assignments, exercise hints, and sample solutions is also available. Whether for self-study or formal classroom education, *CL Programming for the AS/400—Second Edition* is the perfect resource for learning CL programming. 368 pages. Level: Novice, Intermediate, and Advanced.

❑ BOOK 5007 ....$69

ISBN 1-58347-004-2

Java® Applications Strategies for the AS/400

An Introduction to AS/400 Java Development Strategies for RPG Programmers

by Don Denoncourt

Gain real-world strategies for the development of AS/400 Java applications with this new book from Don Denoncourt. Written specifically for AS/400 RPG programmers, *Java Application Strategies for the AS/400* will help you understand the structure and intent of the Java programming language and why Java applications developed with the same structure techniques employed in RPG will fail. A companion CD-ROM contains all the source code presented in the book, the complete source for Midrange Computing's object-to-relational framework classes, a Sun Java Development Kit and much more! 448 pages. Level: Intermediate to Advanced.

BOOK 591 ....$79

ISBN 1-883884 -61-6

For a complete list of titles, call 1-800-477-5665 or visit our Web site at *www.midrangecomputing.com.*

ORDER FORM

BILL TO:

Name ______________________

Title ______________________

Company ______________________

Address ______________________

City ____________ State ________ ZIP ________

YTQBZ

SHIP TO (if different from above):

Name ______________________ Title ____________

Company ______________________

Address ______________________

City/State/ZIP ______________________

ITEMS ORDERED:

Item No.	Description	Price	Quantity	Total Price

ADDITIONAL INFORMATION:

Daytime Phone (required to process order):
( ) ________ - ______________

Fax ( ) ________ - ______________

Email ______________________

Subtotal

Add 7.75% sales tax (CA residents only), 6.25% sales tax (TX residents only), or 6% sales tax (NJ residents only). Residents of Canada add 7% GST.

Shipping/Handling—$6.25 per item (ground, continental United States only)

Total

* Note: All prices are U.S. only. Please call for orders and prices outside the United States. Prices subject to change.

BILLING INFORMATION:

☐ Payment Enclosed (Make check payable to Midrange Computing.)

CREDIT CARD: ☐ VISA ☐ MasterCard ☐ AmEx ☐ Discover

Card # ______________________ Exp. Date ________

BILL ME, P.O. # ______________________

Signature (required)______________________

Priority code: Y9CHBPAA

5 Easy Ways to Order!

FAX

this order form to 760-931-9935, 24 hours a day, 365 days a year.

MAIL

your order to 5650 El Camino Real, Suite 225, Carlsbad, CA 92008.

EMAIL

your order to *custsvc@ midrangecomputing.com.*

PHONE

toll-free 1-800-477-5665 (Mon. to Fri., 6 a.m. to 5 p.m. PST).

ONLINE

ordering is available at *www. mc-store.com.*